THE LOGIC OF HATRED

D1528805

The Logic of Hatred

FROM WITCH HUNTS TO THE TERROR

Jacob Rogozinski

TRANSLATED BY SEPHR RAZAVI
AFTERWORD BY CARLO GINZBURG

FORDHAM UNIVERSITY PRESS   NEW YORK   2024

Copyright © 2024 Fordham University Press

All rights reserved. No part of this publication may be reproduced, stored in
a retrieval system, or transmitted in any form or by any means — electronic,
mechanical, photocopy, recording, or any other — except for brief quotations
in printed reviews, without the prior permission of the publisher.

This book was first published in French as *Ils m'ont haï sans raison: De la
chasse aux sorcières à la Terreur*, by Jacob Rogozinski © Les Éditions du Cerf,
2015.

Fordham University Press has no responsibility for the persistence or accuracy
of URLs for external or third-party Internet websites referred to in this
publication and does not guarantee that any content on such websites is, or
will remain, accurate or appropriate.

Fordham University Press also publishes its books in a variety of electronic
formats. Some content that appears in print may not be available in electronic
books.

Visit us online at www.fordhampress.com.

Library of Congress Cataloging-in-Publication Data available online at
https://catalog.loc.gov.

Printed in the United States of America

26 25 24 5 4

Contents

THE LOGIC OF HATRED

Introduction

A Forgotten Massacre

We have to hear the words never uttered [. . .] we have to lend a voice
to these historical silences, at the horrible *fermata* where history stops
speaking.

JULES MICHELET

On August 31, 1601, in the village of Bazuel in Flanders, a peasant named Aldegonde de Rue, condemned for "witchcraft," died at the stake. She was seventy
years old. Because she had confessed her "crimes," her judges granted her
the privilege of being strangled by the executioner before the flames reached
her body. Some years prior, a soldier passing by had publicly identified her
as a witch. Upon seeing her, he exclaimed, "Now here's a woman who is a
witch! If I met you outside this town, I would put a sword through your body
and if I knew where your house was, I would burn you inside it!" "Would
you listen to that," huffed Aldegonde, "but what is there to do: all women
are said to be witches!" She was thus *identified*: Her *infamia*, that is, her bad
reputation, was established; henceforth they would never let go of her. During
the summer of 1601, one of her neighbors, a rich farmer with whom she had
quarreled, accused her before the bailiwick's court of being a witch and of
having, through the use of magic, caused the death of one of his horses. Several other villagers confirmed the accusation, adding those of the deaths of a
cow, two other horses, and the "strange illness" of a little girl. In order to prove
her innocence, Aldegonde decided to go to the neighboring town of Rocroi
and to be examined by their executioner, because it was claimed that he was
unerringly able to spot witches. Unwittingly, she had thrown herself into the
lion's den. After having completely shaved her and inspected her "through all

1

the spaces and places of her body, even in the inside spaces like in the mouth and in the shameful parts," the executioner discovered on her left shoulder a small mark similar, he insisted, to those he had found on the bodies of 274 women he had executed, "and that these executed women recognized their marks as authentic, and that the Enemy of the human beings marks them when he first copulates with the aforementioned witches." The trap closed in. Repeatedly tortured per the judges' orders, Aldegonde eventually admitted that she had participated in the Sabbath, rendered homage to Satan, and fornicated with a demon named Gauwe, and that he gave her a nocent powder that had allowed her to kill her neighbors' horses and cow. Condemned to death, she would soon be executed.[1] She would not be the first victim: Two years earlier, another resident of Bazuel, Reine Percheval, had also been sent to the stake as she had "bewitched" a cow that had given birth to a skinless calf . . . The executions of so-called witches would continue sporadically in the region for some years: The last French stakes also burned in Flanders, in Bouvignies, in 1679.

The life and death of an ordinary "witch," of a victim among so many of the Great Witch Hunt that broke out in the middle of the fifteenth and lasted well into the seventeenth century. As we learn from historians, its victims number in the tens of thousands — counting 80,000 deaths does not seem exaggerated, and some historians even speak of 200,000 victims — in great majority women. Appearing first in Switzerland, these witch hunts progressively stretched across most of Europe, in multiple successive yet very unequal waves: Whereas England would be almost entirely spared, and the persecution remained uncommon in Italy, Spain, and France (except in peripheral regions: the Loraine, Flanders, and the Basque Country), it reached its apogee in Germany, which a contemporary witness described as the "country of stakes." It is maintained that, in certain villages of Westphalia, there were hardly any women who escaped the stake . . . It would surge back, little by little, first stopping in the Netherlands, then in other countries — the practice of "witchcraft" remained a crime in France until 1682 — and it would be extinguished entirely during the eighteenth century. Under torture, the accused almost always admit that they belonged to a "satanic sect," that they renounced the Christian faith, poisoned men and livestock alike, and committed abominable crimes in the nocturnal meetings of the Sabbath: profaning hosts and crucifixes, practicing sodomy and incest, copulating with demons, sacrificing children to the devil while eating their flesh and drinking their blood . . . If voices were raised here and there to contest the judges' methods and condemn their persecutions — those of clerks, jurists, doctors, or of thinkers such as Montaigne and Cyrano de Bergerac — the immense majority of the population and the cultivated elites seemed to have adhered to these accusations.

Who still recalls this persecution? What trace have we kept of these thousands of victims, and how will we help them find justice? The term "witch hunt" has become synonymous with unjust violence and arbitrary exclusion, but how many who use it know that it refers to a specific historical phenomenon? There is no one who, in the name of the victims, could demand justice; and if that were to happen, there would be no one to answer for it. It is laudable of the Catholic Church to have recently apologized for the crimes committed in the past in its name. And yet, when feminists addressed the pope to have him officially condemn the extermination of witches, their request remained unanswered. No "tradition of the oppressed" was created, of which the witnesses could gainsay the official version of the murderers. Why is the memory of this persecution so elusive? We are told that the reason for this is that most of the accused were obscure and illiterate peasants who were of no interest to historians and could do nothing to pass down their stories. But are we certain of this? If we hear no resounding echo of their cries of pain, it is because their voices have been muzzled, because the traces of their massacre have been deliberately erased. Of course, the judges and the torturers made no effort to hide their crimes: The executions were public and drew large crowds. But the "crimes" of the so-called witches seemed so heinous that, to "purify" the city, they had to eliminate all reminders of their existence. It wasn't enough to burn their bodies and to spread their ashes; often, the archives of their trial were also thrown into the flames. But that was not enough: They were disfigured. At the moment they were assassinated, they were depicted as hideous old women, perched on their broomstick, roasting human flesh, or concocting evil potions in their cauldrons. Literature and now cinema have taken hold of these caricatures. From the wicked witch of *Snow White* to that of the *Wizard of Oz*, the vision that the persecutors had of their victims still captures our imagination and keeps us from understanding the truth behind the Great Witch Hunt. Thus, the victory of the murderers seems to have been total and has made the work of memory exceedingly difficult.

We are therefore grateful for the patient work of the historians who have exhumed from the archives traces of these annihilated lives and have, behind the starkness of statistics and transcripts, allowed us to hear singular voices. What do these voices have left to tell us? We who no longer believe in Satan, in the evil spells and orgies of the Sabbath, how could their story interest us? Why evoke an experience that, through centuries, has become truly foreign to us? It is to try to understand the *logic of hatred*. For it is truly hatred that motivates persecution. Fear, envy, anger, and desire to avenge real or imaginary wrongdoing also play a role, but the major affect that drives them all, the only affect that does not incite flight or repulsion of its object, or rather to inflict violence on it while nonetheless allowing it to live, the only affect that solely aims to annihilate, is hatred. It is said that occasionally envy plays a decisive role in persecutions. That is often the case, and we must therefore ask ourselves what precious possession a poor peasant like Aldegonde could have had to provoke a murderous impulse in her persecutors. And yet, Spinoza was aware of this, that "Envy is nothing but hatred itself":[2] The object after which the envious believes he is lusting is no more than a pretext for manifesting his hatred. It is not true, however, that hate is indifferent about its targets. This is what distinguishes it from aggressivity, from a simple and indeterminate "instinct of aggression." Like love, hate always attaches itself to a singular object (or to a certain part of this object), and its relation to this object is as intense and exclusive as that of lovers. He who is under the influence of hatred allows himself to be captivated by those whom or which he hates, to the point of obsession, to the point of delirium, as though he were not able to move past that which he is straining to destroy. This is why the victory of hatred — the murder of the hated object — signals all at once its failure. And yet, instead of fading away, hatred most often searches for another target, which shows that the object of hatred is nothing more than an opportunity for its expression. Hatred then appears all at once indifferent to its object *and* indissociable from it. We must shed light on this paradox by questioning the status of the object-of-hatred.

Philosophers have been grappling with the question of evil, its "radicality" or its "banality," for a long time. Their reflections risk falling short, however, so long as they do not take into account the affective matrix of evil, the banal feeling, shared universally (who dares to claim that they have never felt hatred?), that is at the root of the most radical evil. The thinkers who have confronted the topic are few in number. Spinoza gave it an eminent place among his "sad passions" that keep men in servitude and unhappiness. Indeed, he argues that feelings as diverse as envy, indignation, contempt, or anger are rooted in hatred; and he drew certain important connections, like its contagious character and the fact that we can be dominated "all at once by hate and by love" toward the same person. His analysis is not psychological, but ontological, for such affects express, according to him, the fundamental modalities of our power of being, that is, our *conatus*. However, he considers hatred as a passion, which is to say a passive affection provoked by an external cause; and a passion born out of sadness, which is where only the weakening of our power prevails, the decrease of the *conatus*. What eludes him, therefore, is an understanding of the immanent power of hatred, which surges without reason and intensifies by affecting only itself. Freud seems nearer to the truth when he assigns what he calls an "original sadism" to an unconscious drive, but he defines this as a "death-drive" that stands opposed to a life-drive. He is mistaken: All drives are life-drives, pulsations of our lives; but it could be that this life is blind to itself, that it could turn against itself and, in believing that it is protecting itself, make desperate attempts to destroy itself. It is this blindness of life that we must analyze.

Hatred is an affect; here is where we must start. This does not mean that it can be reduced to a fugitive "mood" that could be then "explained" through psychological causes. Like all our fundamental affects, like love, to which hatred is intimately knitted, like angst, like sorrow and joy, despair and hope, hatred is a primordial tonality of our lives, of a life that gives itself and reveals itself through self-affection; hatred defines the style in which our life finds expression but also our openness to the world. It defines a singular horizon, a way of being and of living that moves us from end to end and permeates all our relations with others. Common language has duly taken notice of this: One no longer says, "I have hatred *for*" (j'ai *de* la haine), but "I hate" (j'ai la haine), as though it had unitarily taken hold of us without leaving room for any other feeling. Our affects are too often considered as "irrational" and passing emotions that would be pointless to try and understand. Nothing could be further from the truth. A fundamental affect such as hatred possesses a determinate structure, and it must be possible to understand its logic. How to gain access to the phenomenon of hatred, this phenomenon that is all at once so ordinary and so difficult to grasp? First, by describing it in its most obvious expressions. Given that this affect is as present in individual existence as in human communities, it is possible to approach it from various angles. I have decided to approach it by calling on history, on the long and bloody history of persecutions. One specification is required: When I speak of "persecution," I am not referring to an implicit or simply verbal violence. In Latin, the word *persecutio* first designated ordeals, endured by early Christians on their path to martyrdom. Indeed, *persequi* means ceaselessly pursuing, pursuing until the end, up to the endpoint that is murder. If exclusionary and stigmatizing violence most often precedes persecutorial violence, the latter intensifies it, radicalizes it by recurring to the threat of murder. It is not a matter of numbers: There are cases of systematic harassment, of microterrors concentrated on just a few individuals, which endeavor to push them to suicide or end with their lynching. When hatred takes on a greater number, at the horizon of persecution, mass terror and extermination appear. This entails sending to their death men and women who are considered unworthy of living, but it also entails erasing every trace of their existence, annihilating their bodies — most often reducing them to ashes — and also their names and memory in the mind of others (the archives of the witch trials were also frequently thrown into the flames). It is this *passage from exclusion to persecution* and to terror that I am attempting to understand in this book.

I hope that this will offer a new perspective on the dark enigma of our time. In its own way, Aldegonde's story also speaks of us: Must it be recalled that the most large-scale exterminations occurred during the twentieth century? Is there a radical caesura between the witch hunts and the genocides of our times? Is this "genocidal logic" that presided over the extermination of Armenians, Jews, or Tutsis absolutely without precedent in history, or does it simply repeat and amplify past phenomena? Can we miss, regardless of the distance that separates them, the strange similitudes between these different persecutions? Could it be that they obey the same logic? This is, in any case, the opinion held by one of the men who organized the Final Solution. Before being executed in 1945, one of Eichmann's close collaborators, the SS officer Wisliceny, revealed to his judges what he believed to be the basis for the Nazi extermination policy. According to him, it was an error to consider Hitler and Himmler as "political cynics": They were "mystics" who pictured history as a fight to the death between the Aryan race and the "principle of Evil personified by the Jew." At stake, he said, was a "religious mentality" that "could only be compared with similar phenomena of the Middle Ages, such as the witch hunt."[3] No doubt he was mistaken on several points: Hitler was in no way a mystic (perhaps "Gnostic" would serve as a better label here), and the witch hunts were not medieval phenomena, nor were they, as we will see, a uniquely "religious" phenomenon. In the minds of the witch-hunters, there was no place for a racist ideology in the modern sense of the term, a theory with scientific pretensions affirming the inequality of races. Moreover, the persecution had adopted from the outset a judicial form that had nothing to do with exterminations as they would be carried out by the Nazis. It was judges who condemned tens of thousands of women to the stake, through trials where torture and confession had played a vital role; but no Jew, no Roma was ever tried at Auschwitz. If we must absolutely find an equivalent, it should rather be compared with Stalin's terror. And yet . . . they were designated as "races of witches" or "races of smoke," which is to say a damned lineage destined for the stake. Many judges indeed believed that sorcery was hereditary, and they sent entire families to their deaths, including the children and the grandchildren of the so-called witches. Common to the Nazis and the witch hunts is not only this wish to annihilate evil kin; there is a similar demonization of their victims, the same dread of a hidden Enemy, of a "conspiracy" working in secret to corrupt society so as to take hold of power. Wisliceny was not wrong: We can see an air of resemblance between Jean Bodin's *Demon-Mania* and the *Protocols of the Elders of Zion*.

Would we, in affirming this, succumb to the cardinal sin denounced by historians, that is, anachronism? Yet a history of persecutions can only be *anachronistic*, as understood by Rancière: It takes temporal flow "against the grain," subtracting an event from "its" time to reveal unexpected connections between one phenomenon and another.[4] From this angle, witch hunts aren't only an occurrence from a foregone era. From this forgotten persecution to the ones of the twentieth century, the same horror persists; similar accusations are repeated and produce the same effects. It may thus be possible to reintegrate the extermination of witches within a *long duration*, within these slow-rhythmed processes of which Fernand Braudel spoke, these "great underlying currents, often silent, and whose meaning becomes apparent only if we take into account large periods of time."[5] What do these "nappes of slow history" consist of here? What prevails in the long history of persecutions? What allows persecutory hatred to give itself a target is not reducible to a "mentality" or an institution but mobilizes certain schemes by inserting them into power apparatuses. It is their history that must be deciphered. To this end, it will not be enough to turn toward witch hunts: We must also put these in dialogue with analogous events that have occurred prior or afterward—from the lepers' massacre to the Jacobine Terror—which seem to foreshadow or restart it under very different conditions. Of course, this is not to say that such phenomena would inevitably reproduce themselves in identical forms like unchanging archetypes, as if our history were already integrally written, programmed from the very first stakes, and that a dark causality, an obscure fatality, would bring one from the Inquisition's tribunals to Stalin's trials, from the ashes of Montségur to those of Auschwitz. If history appears to stutter at times, if, after long periods of latency, ancient hauntings reemerge, nothing proves that their reappearance must be inevitable: For them to return and sow terror and death, they have to be reactivated and taken hold of by new apparatuses that offer them new victims. From one era of hatred to another, there is no continuity, and the passage from one apparatus to another or the reactivation of an ancient scheme is never inevitable.

To understand the logic of hatred, I will consider it from its historical dimension by attempting to elaborate a genealogy of the exclusion and persecution apparatuses. But is this a philosopher's task? He may attempt an answer if he allows himself to be instructed by historians—without, however, substituting himself for them when it comes to uncovering what took place. The majority of philosophers who have taken persecution as an object of study have lacked this openness to history. Thus, when Levinas introduces this notion in *Otherwise Than Being*, he assimilates it to my exposition to the Other, to this "vulnerability" and "trauma" that provoke my infinite responsibility toward the other. Yet if "persecution denotes the form under which the ego affects itself" in an obsessive relationship with the other's face, then *any other* accuses and persecutes me, at every place and at every time. "My neighbor's face in its persecutory hatred" demands that I accept his accusation without reservations: It would no longer be a matter of resistance but rather a submission in the most extreme passivity since persecution is only one of the names of the ethical obligation and the destitution of the ego implied therein ("without persecution, the ego looks up . . ."). It would no longer be a historically determinate phenomenon that could be distinguished from other analogous phenomena: By considering it as a fundamental mode of the relation to the other, Levinas withholds any concrete significance from the notion of persecution, and it dissolves itself in the night where all the cows are black.

The same ahistorical abstractions are to be found in theories that abundantly invoke the "universal mechanism" of *scapegoats* or the "shunned" *homo sacer* as a unique explicative key of Western history. These are ready-made solutions that should be set aside as they do not help us to distinguish the different types of violence that we witness in history. Following Freud, René Girard focalizes on the most extreme violence, that of originary murder, of the lynching of innocent victims, and of its reiteration in sacrificial rituals. Yet he neglects the more insidious violence of exclusion, stigmatization, internment, and of expulsion that often precede persecutions and massacres and make them possible. Moreover, he does not sufficiently distinguish the blind violence of lynching, to which furious masses sometimes yield, from this other form of persecutory violence, colder, more persistent, and deliberate, that is exercised by power apparatuses — a violence that, as we shall see, "comes from atop," because it emanates from sovereign power. On his part, Agamben chooses the paradigm of the *homo sacer*, condemned to flee the city under the threat of death; and he refers to this figure of the Excluded to provide an explanation for the exterminations of the twentieth century (without understanding, as we shall see, the fundamental meaning of the *homo sacer* and its relationship with the Untouchable). And yet, to banish a *sacer* by exposing him to a *possible* death is not the same thing as relentlessly tracking down victims destined to an unavoidable death. The violence of exclusion is not identical to the persecutory violence that aims to annihilate its targets; and the limited violence of persecution that only attacks a determinate group is distinct from the limitless violence of the terror, whose victim can be anyone. Of course, different forms of violence can at times be knotted together as successive phases of a singular process. First, exclusion would start by enclosing its victims behind the unassailable walls of the leprosarium or the ghetto, and, sooner or later, this fence is then broken down and those inside wiped out . . . Yet is this radicalization inevitable? Don't we also deal with exclusion modes that indefinitely persist without them being followed up by a persecution phase? Or with murderous persecutions that seem to arise without any preliminary exclusion phase, precisely such as in the case of witch hunts? Each time, historical analysis is required if we wish to understand this passage from exclusion to persecution and terror. It is only when we cease to abstract ourselves from history or skim over it from afar — when we approach these phenomena as singular events and restitute them each time in their context and era — that we can decipher hidden affinities between them and embrace their history in its long duration. If it is true that certain analogies exist between witch hunts and the exterminations of our times, how many historians, how many thinkers have taken them into consideration? How could none of those who questioned the crimes of Stalin and Hitler have read *The Hammer of Witches*? Tenacious preconceptions have kept us from understanding the true scope of the persecution of witches. Too often, it has been considered at the same time a *universal*, *archaic*, and *marginal* phenomenon: These three errors must now be dispelled.

Nothing new under the sun. Every people, every historical period has known its shamans, magicians, spell-casters — both feared and revered — who are sometimes pestered or banished by those who believed that they were victims of their powers (as it still happens today in some parts of Africa). Certainly . . . But, with the sole exception of the Christian West, no known society has persecuted men and women en masse by accusing them of witchcraft. No other has confused beneficial magic and evil sorcery with the same hatred directed against an absolute Enemy who must be annihilated regardless of what it had done. No other has been terrified for centuries by an imaginary "sorcerers' conspiracy" to the point of exterminating all those accused of being part of it. The Prophet of Islam was not kind to sorcerers: In one of his hadiths he recommends slaying them all — and yet the Muslim world has not known any persecution of sorcerers or witches comparable to that which took place in the West. At another time, in another culture, Aldegonde's neighbor would not have brought her to court for having caused the death of his horse: He would have resorted to white magic, to a disenchantment to protect his cattle from evil spells, and perhaps also to black magic to avenge the damage he had suffered. For him to retaliate in another way, involving judges, traditional magical practices had to have been discredited and demonized; an intense fear of witches had to have been implanted in those peasants of Flanders and, with it, the certainty that only a power apparatus exterior to the village was able to fight them effectively. In a culture different from ours, a woman like Aldegonde would never have been forced to confess under torture and condemned to death for the crime of "divine lèse-majesté." What prevents us from recognizing this fact is an ethnocentric preconception: We are so deeply convinced of the superiority of our Western civilization that we cannot fathom that our persecutory rage is not to be found in other cultures.

Moreover, we are so certain of the superiority of Modern Times that we regard the witch hunt as an archaic phenomenon, discarding it into the darkness of a barbaric Middle Ages, populated by gullible peasants and fanatic monks. This is erroneous: The worst massacres took place during the time of Descartes. The elaboration of a demonological doctrine and the assimilation of magicians to heretics — which, in principle, sent them to the stake — are indeed the work of the medieval Church, but they were not accompanied by massive persecution. One has to wait until the fifteenth century for witchcraft trials to be multiplied, and the Great Hunt did not begin until the end of the subsequent century. For a long time to come, the stakes will continue to burn in several countries: "Witches" were still being burned in Augsburg in 1745, and the last to be executed was Anna Göldi in Switzerland in 1782 . . . It cannot be emphasized enough: More often than not, the repression was carried out by secular magistrates (like those judges of the bailiwick who condemned Aldegonde). When it reached its peak, it was a long time since the Inquisition and the ecclesiastical courts had lost their influence. Paradoxically, it was in the countries where the Holy Office had retained its prerogatives — namely, Italy and Spain — that the persecution was least violent. At the time when, in the French Basque Country, Judge Pierre de l'Ancre, an adviser to the Parliament of Bordeaux, unhesitatingly sent dozens of young girls to the stake, on the other side of the Pyrenees, the Inquisitor Salazar denounced the use of torture and exonerated and released most of the accused. Michelet had taken note of this: "Our magistrates," he wrote, "show themselves to be more priests than priests. By pushing back the Inquisition of France, they equal it."[6] We have to reckon the witch hunt as a *modern* phenomenon. It was not the Church but the State that implemented it, and it was carried out in the name of a *political* conception of sovereignty. The historical transition from the theological to the political, from the domination of the Church to that of the modern State, can be described as a process of secularization. What place do witch hunts occupy within such a process? Are we dealing with a still insufficient secularization, a survival of medieval beliefs that are confusedly superimposed on a more "rational" understanding of the world? As I will show, another light can be cast on this process: as the first example of mass political persecution in a society in the process of secularization. However, we must not confuse the secularization process with that of a *desacralization*, or that "disenchantment with the world" of which Max Weber spoke. Experience shows on the contrary that the secularization of certain theological schemes, their transposition to the political level, maintains certain traits of the old configuration, for example, the designation of a hidden Enemy, of the ancient figure of Satan who reappears in modern-day persecutions.

What remains astounding is that it took so many centuries for the hunt to begin. Why did the Church of the Middle Ages, which treated heretics so cruelly, spare witches? Surprisingly, the answer is that medieval theologians *did not believe* in the reality of the witches' Sabbath. The authoritative text on the subject, written around the year 900, is the *Canon Episcopi*. It evokes women who, "seduced by the illusions of demons, believe that they ride certain animals at night accompanied by Diana, goddess of the pagans"; that they make magic potions, kill and devour men. But, for the editor of the *Canon*, it went without saying that these were mere illusions — *phantasmata* — to which no credence should be given. This position was shared for centuries by all the clerics and cultivated elites. However, a turning point occurred suddenly during the fifteenth century, when the first persecutions began. From this point on, theologians and inquisitors affirm as a dogma the reality of nocturnal flights, the secret assemblies of witches, and of their crimes and their evil spells, to the point of accusing of heresy those who persisted in considering these as "phantasies"; and the secular judges who would preside over the Great Hunt would share this belief. This until the skeptics finally prevailed, and we gradually came back to the original position of denying the reality of the Sabbath. What happened? How to understand this "realistic" turn? And how did a belief that had imposed itself so massively end up disappearing?

It is the general public — and not scholars — who subscribe to the ethnocentric preconception by mistaking the witch hunt for a universal phenomenon, and to the progressist preconception, by pushing it back into the distant past. However, the third preconception is widely shared by historians. Most of them indeed consider it as a marginal phenomenon, a "fringe phenomenon" (the expression is from French historian Pierre Chaunu), an episode of the conflict of cultures that opposes the center to the periphery: the urban elites familiar with modern ideas to archaic peasant superstitions. They focused on the *village witch*, on a certain type of victim, of which Aldegonde is quite representative: poor and elderly peasant women, inadequately integrated into village communities. No doubt this was often the case. But have we sufficiently taken into account another dimension of the witch hunt, urban and not rural, where the persecution, which first attacked the poor and the marginalized — beggars and prostitutes — quickly extended to elites, clerics, and members of the ruling class? During the event known as the "Vauderie d'Arras" (1459–60), repression struck aldermen, wealthy merchants, and even a high-ranking nobleman who was a former chamberlain of the Duke of Burgundy. A century and a half later, the same phenomenon reappeared on a larger scale in Germany and some neighboring countries. In Trier, Cologne, Bamberg, Mainz, Würzburg, the victims number in the thousands. Among them, nobles, priests, academics, magistrates, and even the nephew of a prince-bishop. And it so happens that, as in Salzburg in 1680–81, the great majority of the condemned were men. In some areas, such as that of the Abbey of Obermarchtal, the town of Oppenau, or the county of Vaduz, more than 10 percent of the inhabitants were executed in a few years.[7] A little-known aspect of this persecution is revealed here, which calls into question everything we thought we knew since it affects the urban elites as well as the ordinary rural people, and men as well as women (it, therefore, seems difficult to reduce it to a "women hunt," as some feminist historians do). We are dealing with an unprecedented situation, where none of the traditional figurations of the Witch any longer hold; where, as for the totalitarian terrors of our time, the Enemy has lost all distinctive features. What distinguishes these events from the great persecutions of the twentieth century is their dispersed and sporadic character. No systematic extermination plan had been devised, and, at least in Germany, no centralized state would have been capable of implementing it. Virulent in some regions, weak or non-existent in others, the witch hunt unleashed suddenly, to cease sooner or later, and start again elsewhere . . . We can nevertheless call these moments of crisis when the persecution increases *terror phases*; moments when anyone can be accused and convicted. It is not a question here of "terror policies," those repressive strategies deliberately conducted by certain regimes to intimidate their opponents: This is not the case of an "instrumental" violence used in a controlled and limited manner in service of a policy, but of violence that only finds aim in itself and tends to increase indefinitely. An "irrational" terror, of course, but one whose *logic* can be potentially uncovered.

Once these errors are corrected, the witch hunt presents itself as an enigma. Why has the persecution taken this particular form? Why did it begin so late — only at the beginning of the modern era — when the demonological discourse and the imaginary of the "conspiracy" had already been established since the Middle Ages? Why was it so intense in some regions whereas others were mostly spared? And, another conundrum, why did it end almost as quickly as it started? Such questions are for historians to answer. It is up to them — and not philosophers — to explain what occurred: to establish the facts and to interpret the phenomena that have been discovered. On the condition, however, that their interpretations are not warped by preconceptions that prevent them from understanding the meaning of their discoveries. Many indeed consider the witch hunt as a process of "modernization," a consequence of the violent but necessary permeation of new mentalities in the backward fringes of rural society. It would have represented "the other side of Western rationalization, inseparable from the fundamental elements of the modernization of Europe, as the 'civilization process,' and of State building and secularization."[8] It comes as a surprise to see the one who had restituted the story and the name of Aldegonde de Rue, Anne Hauldecœur, and Jeanne Bachy declare without shuddering that "the multiplication of stakes for witches appears [to him] as a sign of the progress of innovating principles [. . .] an indication of the conquest of reluctant margins by the modern State."[9] We are thus dealing with a massacre that goes *in History's direction.*

Where does the blindness of these historians come from? From their philosophy. From the metaphysics of Progress to which they adhere naively: They believe that Reason progresses in History, a Reason that is embodied in the modern State and advances "by crushing many innocent flowers." For them, the sacrifice of countless victims is the price to pay for a more "rational" future. This is because they adamantly believe that there is a *positivity of the negative,* that the greatest carnage can catalyze progress. Philosophers know these arguments well, and we have learned to be wary of them. We have already encountered this dialectical ruse of Reason, this Tribunal of History more implacable than that of the Holy See, in Hegel — but the German philosopher knew perfectly well wherein this conception was rooted. He — who had taught that the incessant sacrifice of the Spirit reenacts the Passion of Christ in History — was aware that he was transposing a secularized theological doctrine into his philosophy. It is this awareness that is lacking in most of our historians. When they justify persecutions in the name of Progress, they do not see that they are taking up an old argument of the theologians: If God allows the devil to act in this world, it is in order to "do good from evil," thus preparing for the coming of the Kingdom. This belief was precisely that of the witch-hunters, who were convinced that the actions of Satan served the hidden purposes of Providence and that by inflicting the worst torments on his henchmen, they acted for the greater glory of God . . . Whether it be divine Providence, the progress of Reason, or the "Idea of Communism" that is invoked even today to absolve the crimes of Stalin and Mao, we are dealing with the same logic each time. By seeking in the will of God or an "end goal" of humanity the ultimate meaning of History, we enact violence on historical phenomena: Instead of recognizing that an event contains *in itself* its immanent meaning, we subject it to a transcendent Principle that is supposed to serve as justification. The intervention of the philosopher is required here, precisely to free the historical sciences from their implicit philosophy — from this metaphysics that sticks to their skin and hinders them from understanding what they have discovered.

When considering past persecutions, it is required, above all, to break with the logic of the persecutors. As historian Carlo Ginzburg has pointed out, the contemporary scholars' approach is often similar to that of the inquisitors and judges of the past: Despite the empathy that we may feel toward the victims, "intellectually we tend to identify with the Inquisitors [. . .] Our aims are different, but our questions largely coincide with the ones they asked."[10] If we want to give the victims justice, the time has come for a radical conversion: to stop adhering to the worldview of their murderers and to stop, as much as possible, using the same words they did.[11] We must, to achieve this, resort to the "distance-taking technique" that Ginzburg calls the "estrangement" (in Italian: *straniamento*), which helps delegitimize the version of the victors by varying perspectives, by adopting "the savage's, the peasant's, the child's, the animal's point of view," but also that of the heretics and witches. It is this decisive shift that motivates his "microhistorical" approach: It aims to "broaden downward the historical concept of the individual" by reconstituting the history of anonymous lives, subalterns, and of unknown individuals excluded from official history. As Walter Benjamin had asserted, the historian's task is *messianic* because he strives to summon the smallest existences, to cite the names of the vanquished and the dead, all of their names, so that a liberated humanity can one day gain access to all of its past. In this context, the difficulty consists in finding the right distance and in breaking with this *overview position* that leads excellent scholars to excuse the atrocities of the witch hunts or those of the Jacobin Terror. While doing their work as historians, they stay as close as possible to their object, cross-reference sources, and analyze particular cases. But as soon as they try to interpret them, they place themselves at a great distance from their object and evaluate past events in light of a Knowledge that they believe has revealed History's truth to them. This is where this coldness comes from, that is, this indifference that historians show toward so many shattered lives; and it is the same error of perspective that prevents them from understanding the facts they describe and all the implications those facts entail. This prevents them from spotting those traits that, in the persecutions of past centuries, prefigure the Great Terrors of the twentieth century.

As Merleau-Ponty has remarked, the "overview perspective" is grounded on an ontological illusion. When I settle into a position where I pretend to overlook the totality of becoming, I disregard my own situation; I forget that I am already involved in what I think I am contemplating from the outside, that I am part of it, that this story is also mine and that of all "mines." This immanent dimension under which we are always already submerged, "whereas in our body, everything counts, everything has a bearing," Merleau-Ponty calls the *"flesh of history."*[12] In this fleshly community where the most distant past is intertwined with the present, the story of Aldegonde is part of my history: What happens to each singular flesh reverberates with my own flesh. To learn to "estrange" our gaze, to abandon any position of overview, to rekindle with our belonging to the flesh of history, invites us to give up causal explanations. Historians and sociologists too often consider persecutions as the consequences of objective causes that provide the key to their understanding. These then appear as *necessary* to them, and they easily come to justify them. In doing so, they turn their eyes and cover their ears from the enigma of the event, from its partly unpredictable, incomprehensible nature. Since the witch hunt is an event as contingent as any other, it features the eruption of a persecuting hatred that resists any attempt at explanation. Like anguish or love, like the rose that "blooms because it blooms," hatred is *devoid of why*. Thus, each victim of persecution can rightfully claim: "They hated me for no reason."[13] This is what gives hatred its absurd and truly infernal character; and when men strive to create a world wholly ordered and animated by hatred, that world has all the features of hell.[14]

The search for a cause (or a series of causes) that would suffice to explain an event always risks stopping the work of thought by putting an end to the inquiry. A historian, Wolfgang Behringer, has shown that in several regions of Germany the populations did not limit themselves to obeying the orders of the authorities. Rather, they anticipated the official outbreak of the persecution by actively engaging in a hunt for so-called witches. Here he rediscovers the enigma of *voluntary servitude*, of a terror that comes from below, which seems to precede State Terror and perhaps provides it with motives. But, instead of confronting this, he prefers to resort to an "objective" explanation: The period of the witch hunts coincided with that of a great cold, the "little ice age" of the sixteenth through seventeenth centuries, and the ensuing bad weather and food shortages led the peasants to accuse so-called witches of casting spells to destroy crops. This explanation omits that harsh winters and terrible famines took place long before and after the period in question, without ever provoking witch hunts. It is time to put an end to this *lazy causality*, the designation of an external factor, whether an economic or political crisis, an epidemic or famine, that would provide an explanation for the persecutions. We know that, during the Black Death of 1348–49, Jews were accused of poisoning wells and massacred in large numbers. The case is closed: It was the panic, caused by the epidemic, that pushed the masses to seek a "scapegoat" . . . Yet the accusation precedes the Great Plague by several decades: It appeared at the beginning of the century in Switzerland and Germany, then in 1321 in southwestern France, where it was claimed that the Jews were conspiring with lepers to spread leprosy by poisoning wells. Undoubtedly, behind this is this resurgence of an old obsession, this contact phobia that had led to prohibiting all sexual relations with Jews and to prohibiting them from selling or even touching food. It is as though such accusations were reactivating very old phantasies, the fear of contagion through touch and the hatred of an intimate stranger, of an Enemy from within who threatens the integrity of a community. The ravages of the plague will only have given these phantasies an opportunity to manifest themselves in all their persecutory violence. Far from explaining it, the epidemic will have been only a simple empirical condition of the persecution: Instead of focusing on it, we should rather wonder about the persistence of these phantasies of defilement, contamination, and infection that seem to be embedded in the flesh of history. What endures over the long term are affects that change intensity and modify themselves according to their own logic, phantasies or schemes that stage them, and apparatuses that capture them to direct them toward real or fictitious targets. We will have to analyze the dynamics of these affects, the constitution of these schemes, their phases of latency and the conditions for their reactivation, the invisible hinges by which they are articulated to other schemes, and the bridges that allow them to reappear under new conditions. By renouncing any causal explanation of witch hunts, we have not given up understanding its genesis and meaning: If hatred is without a why, its *how* remains to be clarified, and to understand (should this be specified?) does not in any way serve to justify.

It is therefore not a question of rejecting the discoveries made by the historical sciences (how would we, without them, have any access to past events?), but to reject what Michelet called the *false history*, that official history that, in adopting the point of view of the victors, erases the names of victims. According to him, the historian's task consists, on the contrary, of "writing the history of those who have had no history": to *resuscitate the dead*, to rename the forgotten names of those who were reduced to silence. To reestablish between them and us a lost continuity, to keep them in our memory in order to erect a "common city between the living and the dead." He explains, in some marvelous pages from the preface to his *Histoire de France*, how he became aware of his calling after visiting Reims Cathedral. Above the altar where the coronation of kings was celebrated, he discovered this "pillory of the people," a "garland of the tormented" carved in stone.[15] He then discovered that he could not understand the "monarchical centuries" without reviving the memory of the people, that of innumerable existences whose traces were sought to be destroyed. And he knew how difficult this fight against oblivion would be: "They burned the books, burned the men, re-burned the charred bones, threw away the ashes [. . .] no names, no signs [. . .] Is it with these meager remains that I can re-create this history?"[16] These relics are those of a battle that has never ceased; for the people whose history he wants to write cannot be reduced to a passive mass: It is a force that resists, that rises against injustice and confronts the powerful, a *vanquished* people rather than victims. This life that he intends to resuscitate, the true life of the people, is defined by its capacity to create itself, by its self-generation and self-donation. What he calls *historical life* gives itself freely to itself in a "work of oneself on oneself" and self-generates continuously under ever-new forms: "Life has on itself an action of personal parturition which, from pre-existing materials, creates for us absolutely new things [. . .] Thus goes historical life, thus goes each people, making itself, engendering itself [. . .] France made France, and the fatal element of race seems to me secondary. She is the daughter of her own freedom."[17]

His interpretation of the witch hunts is aligned with this perspective. There again, he strives to bring justice to annihilated existences: "The universal martyr of the Middle Ages, the Witch says nothing, her ashes are carried by the wind" — but her martyrdom foreshadows the struggles to come. Indeed, he considers the Sabbath as a resistance movement against feudal lords and the Church, a distant omen of the French Revolution: By worshiping Satan, the serfs celebrated a "myth of freedom," the *Great Rebellious Serf*. "Fraternity of man with man, defiance of the Christians' heaven, worship of Nature's God under unnatural and perverted forms — such the inner significance of the Black Mass [. . .] Under the vague shadow of Satan, the people worshiped only the people."[18] Contemporary historians have unanimously rejected this audacious hypothesis. In fact, nothing attests to the existence of a widespread cult of the devil, and when medieval rebellions attacked the Church, it was never in the name of Satan, but of the Gospels, accusing the clergy of having betrayed the true message of Christ. And yet, although no source has confirmed this hypothesis, I consider it impossible to rule it out absolutely. How can we be sure of the nonexistence of a clandestine counterreligion since it would have precisely endeavored to hide its traces? Rather, what is problematic in Michelet's analysis is that he unhesitatingly subscribes to the accusations of the inquisitors: According to him, the nocturnal Sabbath ceremonies really took place; sexual transgressions were practiced there — including incest; Christian sacraments were desecrated and effigies of the devil venerated obscenely . . . Of course, if he takes up the persecutors' narrative, it is to invert its meaning, by providing it with a positive signification — that of a rebellion against the religion of the powerful — to what they had denounced as abject crimes. Yet never did he cast doubt on the veracity of these accusations, or on the effective reality of the representations disseminated by demonologists. Although he strives to rehabilitate the Witch, he finds himself on the same side as their torturers here. By searching for the real matrix of the witches' Sabbath in a historical experience, he did not take into account the inevitable distortion that affects this experience and the apparatuses that take hold of this experience to then disfigure it.

How can we shed light on this obscured experience? How can we allow for the phenomena of exclusion and persecution to reveal themselves in their true forms? These phenomena should be grasped under their modes of dona-tion without an effort to interpret them in the name of some historical sense, nor should they be explained by "objective" causes: We must set aside the constructions that veil them. This comes back to operating an epochē, or a phenomenological reduction: It is in this manner that we can access the truth of historical life, a life that cannot be conflated with the reality of the world or the things within the world. We are not questioning the effective reality of the witches' Sabbath — an evasive "reality" that will continue to slip out of our grasp — but this strange and paradoxical phenomenon that is a *belief* in its reality. This phenomenon-of-belief, which has appeared historically and will eventually dissipate, presents itself as a complex formation, composed of mul-tiple distinct elements: belief in demons and in the evil deeds that they allow to be carried out; belief in nocturnal flights of witches, in their metamorpho-ses into animals, in their clandestine gatherings and their criminal rituals; belief in a satanic conspiracy that tries to overthrow the power of the Church or the State . . . How did such a belief come to life? Where do these different strata come from, and how were they condensed into a single figure: that of the malevolent Witch? To gain widespread predominance for centuries, this belief required certain devices, certain *persecution apparatuses*. We must de-scribe these apparatuses that disseminated and implanted this belief by elicit-ing the compliance of numerous subjects; we must analyze the speeches that legitimized it, the concrete procedures — from the search of diabolical signs to investigative and confessional techniques — that helped the witch-hunters in identifying their targets and caused so many victims to give in to their per-secutors. And yet, this submission is not in and of itself fatal: Resistance can at times thwart the strategies of persecution, and it is its foundation in the most deeply held truth of the subjects we must investigate.

To grasp what was at stake in the Witch Hunt, a "horizontal" analysis of power relations will not suffice: It will be necessary to confront the mystery of *majesty*, of a sovereign power that can only be exerted by designating an unutterable crime, an *absolute enemy* whose threat legitimizes, in turn, its

absolute authority. By identifying the political significance of the persecution of witches and analyzing the accompanying representation of a "world
turned upside down," we will narrow toward its hidden truth and the initial
experience at its foundation. We must then ask ourselves what schemes allow
for the *demonization* of the Enemy and what malevolent figure is necessary
for the persecutory hatred to find an object: How is this projection pole for
hatred — this Adversary named Satan — constituted? It is necessary not only
to describe the phenomena of persecution but to discover their conditions of
possibility: to understand this movement from exclusion to persecution, this
mutation of affects and the apparatuses that unleash persecutory violence. Are
these murderous surges inevitable, or are they dependent upon certain particular conditions? To attempt an answer, the essential traits of exclusion and of
persecution must be uncovered by carrying out a series of *historical variations*.
This implies widening the scope of the investigation, through analyzing these
phenomena of exclusion-persecution found in different periods, ranging from
the massacre of the lepers at the end of the Middle Ages to the Reign of Terror
during the French Revolution. To know whether these phenomena pertain
only to Western history or if they have a wider reach, another variation is necessary, an *anthropological variation* that will confront them with civilizations
different from ours. Here I will limit myself to an outline; such a broad study
would exceed the frame of this work.

If we wish to unravel the enigma of persecution, these historical and anthropological analyses will nevertheless not suffice. They will not enable
our understanding of the strange persistence of persecution schemes or the
phantasies that seep through them. Where does this fear of contamination,
of defilement, of intrusion, of dissociation, of mutilation come from? From
where can we trace this obsessive fear of the *stranger in our midst*, of an enemy
from within whose threatening presence calls for persecutory violence? Such
obsessive dread brings into play primordial oppositions between the ego and
the other, the inside and the outside, the native and the stranger, that we find
in all cultures because they find their origins in our relationship with our singular body — or, more precisely, with our *flesh*. By setting aside the objective
data of the sciences and the constructions of the philosophies of history, the
first *epochē* opened us up to the domain of historical life, a life that unravels
in the world in the form of human communities. To discover the origins of
these exclusion and persecution schemes, we must go one step further and
undertake a second *epochē*, more radical than the first: to "bracket" the very
existence of the world and our existence with others in the world. It thus
appears that the immanence of historical life is not the most radical. Indeed,
the communities that are the flesh of history find their matrix in the singular

experience that each one of us makes of their own flesh. It is in this elementary experience of our embodied ego that angst, disgust, envy, hatred, but also joy, love, and all the other feelings that weave the thread of our lives are born. If the exclusion-persecution apparatuses are capable of directing these affects toward certain targets, they do not create them; they only harbor these primary feelings that take root in the life of our flesh, of our ego. Phenomena such as the persecution of witches therefore proceed from a *double genesis*. First, a historical genealogy that searches for meaning formations from which they are born within history; second, a phenomenological genesis that brings them back to the elementary experiences of the ego, experiences that underlie any contact with the world, with others, or with human history. As for the phenomena that belong on this plane of immanence, we will designate them as *primordial* phenomena. This is not to say that we are necessarily dealing with *originary* phenomena that would be present from the very first phases of their genesis. Thus, it could be that primordial affects like hate, disgust, or love are not originary; that they appear only in later phases of this genesis, following a certain distortion of experience. Let us avoid a misunderstanding: The originary to which we are referring here is not situated in worldly time, at the beginning of the history of a subject in the world. It is not a question of going back to a "primitive" phase of the psyche, and the originary ego that we discover thanks to *epochē* doesn't lead to a "primary narcissism" that is sometimes attributed to early childhood. On the worldly plane, no ego is isolated from others: Others — their voice, their desires, their actions, and their fantasies — always precede me, and my relationship with them determines entirely what I am. But it is precisely the being-in-the-world and the being-with-others that must be bracketed in order to discover *another plane*, this time more radical. This, in order to describe the primordial experiences that *give meaning* to that which happens to me on the worldly plane. This act of bringing back, beneath all others and the world, to the originary life of the ego to find the prefiguration of its existence in the world, I call *egoanalysis*.[19]

I practice the *epochē*. I bracket the objects of the world and others who surround me in the world. I do not deny that they exist: I suspend the naïve certainty that I had of their existence. Henceforth, they appear to me as simple phenomena, fluid apparitions that pass by my perceptive field. Would this mean that nothing presents itself with absolute certainty? Nothing — except for the ego who practices this *epochē*, me whose donation to myself is ceaseless, as is my experience of my own life, my sensorial impression, my affects at every moment. Is this immanent ego that is no longer a subject in the world embodied? But my body — at least my physical body, my body as an object exposed to the perception of others — is immersed in the world, and it too should be bracketed. When I operate the *epochē*, the unitary form of my body disappears and only *my flesh* remains, a flesh dispersed among countless poles that are the sites of my impressions and my elementary sensations of movement and effort. A flesh who is me and who is the originary fabric of my ego. How does this chaotic and mobile multiplicity become one body? By an *embodiment* process through which it unifies itself, circumscribes itself by de-limiting its inside and its outside, and constitutes itself as one whole composed of differentiated organs. Such a process does not stem from the everyday expe-riences that we have of things and ourselves in the world: This process must be reconstructed by operating a series of variations and by searching for concrete manifestations in our experience in order to ensure that this construction is not purely arbitrary. How does this self-embodiment of my flesh occur? It originarily begins on the tactile plane, through the fundamental experience described by Husserl where "my right hand touches my left hand," where each flesh pole is touching the other and, by letting itself be touched by the other, identifies with it, recognizing it as the flesh of its own flesh. This is the only way that my flesh gets to constitute itself in a dual mode, "all at once as flesh and as a bodily object." It gives birth to this living body that is my own by allowing it to insert itself in the world, alongside others. Merleau-Ponty calls this experience that underlies the becoming-body of my flesh the intertwining (*entrelacs*) or the fleshly *chiasma*. If this did not take place, I would not have a body; I would not be in the world. And yet, this fundamental event runs into an obstacle: Between the two sides of my flesh persists an irreducible hiatus. The discovery of this gap brought Merleau-Ponty, in the last of his Working Notes, to affirm that the coincidence of the touching and the touched "takes place in the *untouchable*," and he pondered this "central blind spot" that would be "the untouchable of the touch, the invisible of vision."[20] This enig-matic element, this Untouchable that keeps my flesh poles from completely identifying with one another, this part of my flesh that I cannot recognize as mine, we will call the *remainder*. It is the "first stranger" I experience, the "first non-me" — who is not another me, but the other *in me*. My relationship to this primordial alterity is the matrix of all my experiences of the foreigner, of all my relations with others.

Husserl rightfully observed this: My flesh "is a remarkably imperfectly constituted thing."[21] Cut across by a gap, the chiasma of the flesh collides with the resistance of the remainder. What is more, it constantly runs the risk of undoing itself, and this fissure compromises my embodiment and the becoming-body of my flesh. The same applies to all human bodies, desta-bilized by the crises of the chiasma, constantly at risk of decomposing and *disembodying* themselves. This is not an abstract hypothesis: This haunting threat of disintegration is found in the psychic life — in our nightmares and our fantasies, in the hallucinations of certain psychoses — and all the more in the historical realm, in crises that run through Collective Bodies. In my previous works, I undertook the task of describing these crises and the way in which they affect the ego and the remainder. When the chiasma unfolds, when the poles of flesh cease to mutually incarnate themselves, the remainder *disfigures* itself: It reappears within my flesh as a foreign body whose apparition provokes angst and disgust. The remainder becomes "untouchable" in a different sense: It becomes that which I cannot tolerate touching, whose contact I find repugnant. The ego thus endeavors to defend itself against the intrusion by expelling it. This act of exclusion can, however, only fail, as the remainder is not *truly* foreign to the ego: It *partakes* of it; the remainder belongs to the ego as a part of its own flesh. And the more the ego strives to repel it, the more it will come back to haunt the ego from within. This rejection changes its nature: Henceforth, it is no longer a question of expulsion, but of the destruction of that which seems to threaten the ego. So appears the affect that we call hatred. It is not derived from a bad will or a death-drive but from the ego's efforts to protect itself against an anxiogenic intrusion. At the origin of hatred, there is no "hate" in the mundane sense of the term, no aggressive instinct, no "original sadism," but rather a primordial illusion. This is what incites the ego to defend itself against an element that to it appears foreign and hostile. It would suffice, or so it seems, that this illusion dissipates for the ego to recognize this remainder as a part of its flesh and to reconcile itself with it. But how do I manage to extricate myself from an illusion that originates at the deepest depths of my flesh?

As it is accompanied by intense angst, the ego does not tolerate this hatred awakening inside it and tries to force it out by projecting it onto some outside element. Freud described in a remarkable manner the process through which the ego "purifies" itself of that which is for it a source of displeasure: It "has separated off a part of its own self, which it projects into the external world and feels as hostile," so that "at the very beginning, it seems, the external world, objects, and what is hated are identical."[22] Let us only clarify that this stranger-to-the-ego is not, in its initial form, a foreign ego but the stranger *in me*, the remainder of my flesh. The ego projects its hatred on the remainder, and this projection further aggravates its disfiguration: It seems to me, therefore, that hatred is a product of this foreign body as if it were a malevolent power trying to destroy me. It is this same process that repeats itself in the relationship between the ego and others, and we will see that this hatred projection is at work in all persecutory phenomena. However, such a projection can only be executed if it remains "unconscious." It will last, therefore, as long as the ego continues to remain blind to what concerns itself and the others. Blinded by my hatred, I do not perceive that this Evil Other is in fact a part of my flesh; that it only enters me because *it is me*. The hatred that I feel toward it is nothing but hatred toward myself: As with the other primordial affects, hatred reveals an *auto-hetero-affection* where the ego is affected by itself as if he were an other. Rooted in self-hatred, it is all at once murderous and suicidal and finds its ultimate expression (seen today in *jihadi* assassin-martyrs) in the somber pleasure of killing others by killing oneself. Here we discover a fundamental aspect of hatred: This feeling is based on an illusion, a *countertruth* where the ego is blinded from itself and, while attempting to protect itself from the "other," turns on itself.[23]

Nevertheless, this lethal disfiguration is not the sole fate of the remainder. The chiasma may reform, and each pole of flesh could begin again to embody the other pole. From here, this dead part of my flesh again comes back to life: It reincarnates itself, it is reviving, and I recognize it again as my own flesh. The remainder *transfigures* itself, and that which was the target of my hatred becomes an object of desire and love. Yet nothing keeps it from disfiguring itself once again, for love to fall into hatred again and for a reborn life to fall again into death. Throughout all of our existence, the remainder thus oscillates between phases of disfiguration and transfiguration. When this oscillation accelerates, these successive phases tend to draw closer to one another, to overlap one another, and the remainder presents itself here as an *ambivalent* object, kindling all at once hatred and love, disgust and a holy veneration. However, this is an unstable synthesis that always tends to undo itself, to bifurcate into a "good" and an "evil" object. Once again, love suits love, and hatred suits hatred as if the object the ego once again began to hate were a threatening enemy and the cause of its hatred. These phenomena are found on the historical plane; in the ambivalent relationship that humans hold with different figures of the terrestrial or celestial Sovereign and the bifurcation of this ambivalence into opposite figures, abject or holy, diabolical or divine. I expressed irony earlier about the temptation to seek ready-made terms that are used to explain everything, such as the scapegoat or the *homo sacer*. By invoking the crisis between the chiasma and remainder, would I be falling back into this old trap? However, the concepts of egoanalysis are not set forth with the intention of explaining what occurs in the world. These do not allow us to determine the objective causes of the witch hunts or the Jacobin Reign of Terror, because they are located on another plane, in the immanence of the ego and its flesh. Yet the phantasies and the schemes that take place on this plane reappear in the collective experience, and this allows us to clarify certain historical phenomena.

Far from being the result of a "mimetic rivalry" or a fight with the other for "recognition," hatred is initially a drive of the ego, a self-affection of one's immanent life that manifests itself beneath all human relationships. Of course, this primordial hatred will reappear in our relationships with others, and egoanalysis can allow us to understand this. It has often been reproached for restricting its scope to a solipsistic ego, isolated from others and the world; to be consequently incapable of opening up to the fields of politics and history. These critiques are unfounded. It is precisely to show how our being-with-others is constituted that one must begin by its abstraction, by bracketing all contacts with others. After having discovered the field of experiences immanent to the ego and the primordial alterity that haunts it, it then becomes possible to understand the formation in this field of the phenomena of an "other," within the collective phenomena of our historical lives. These two realms of experience are not separated by an impervious border, and we can describe the passage from one to the other. As Husserl has shown, I can constitute the other as an "other self" by an "analogical transfer" where I project on his body the experience that I have of my own flesh. Others present themselves as a *projection surface* where the ego transfers its own flesh and, with it, its affects, its phantasies, and the remainder of its flesh. This primordial transfer is entwined with a "countertransfer" that goes the opposite way, from the body of the other toward mine. Without our being-with-others that takes shape as early as during infancy, our body would remain "imperfectly constituted." It is my perception of the bodies of others, my *identification* with the other and his body, that allows my flesh to become body in the world: By the same movement in which I give flesh to the body of the other, he takes part in the embodiment of my flesh.

What happens if this double movement is interrupted? If the fleshly transfer fails, the body of the other ceases to be flesh; it becomes *fleshless*, appearing to me from this point forward as a hostile, foreign object, a monstrous body. Due to the countertransfer wherein our two bodies entwine, this disfiguration rebounds onto my own body, interrupting its embodiment by making it fall back to the chaos of my flesh. Phantasies of *disembodiment*, which provoke intense angst, increase all the more the rejection and hatred of the other as if he were the "cause" of my disfiguration. Hatred is rooted in a distortion of our experience of others, of strangers. To what point do these phantasies — which are ostensible in certain psychoses — concern the history of these human societies, of these apparatuses that subjugate them, and the crises that they undergo? The initial plot in action between the self and the remainder foreshadows our relationships with others: It rewinds in collective existence where the same love and the same hatred, the same phantasies of intrusion and of disintegration, the same phenomena of oscillation, of ambivalence and dissociation are all found. It is possible, therefore, at least by analogy, to speak of a "remainder" of the community. Nevertheless, it is no longer an internal foreigner or a part of myself that becomes the object of my hatred: These are very real others, and the same processes are operating in them in such a way that they also can take me as an object of hatred, notably once they have been the target of my hateful violence and seek vengeance. Thus, hatred is a highly contagious sentiment that, once it surges, tends to spread indefinitely. Spinoza understood this: "Hatred is increased by a reciprocal hatred," and it is even more intense when it is love itself that is turned into hatred . . .

If these hypotheses are correct, egoanalysis can provide an explanation for what happens when a certain group of people is apprehended as the remainder's *henchmen*. This is why I had evoked, in *The Ego and the Flesh*, a task that remains to be accomplished, the need to interrogate the experience of "pariahs, Jews, heretics, madmen, proletarians, dissidents, and of all those who were persecuted, locked, expelled, exterminated for having historically represented a figure of the remainder."[24] I had yet to confront my concepts with the data of experience, to search for concrete facts that could validate or invalidate my hypotheses. I first looked for such facts in literature, in the incomparable works of Antonin Artaud. I then saw that I must also lead a historical inquiry. The phenomenology of exclusion and persecution that I outline in this book should contribute to a reemergence of egoanalysis on a worldly plane, that is, that of political and historical communities. This also amounts to questioning egoanalysis itself. This inquiry would not have been worth an hour's effort if it stopped at "applying" a preestablished theory onto a new domain by collecting empirical data likely to illustrate it. To confront oneself with the cries of the excluded and the persecuted is to cross-examine all of one's certainties. Tested against phenomena, unanticipated questions appear, and perhaps we may better understand what occurred to so many annihilated existences. This cursed part of our history, this "still silent experience" — because we have condemned it to silence and oblivion — is what we must now revive. How else can we repay our debt to those whose names were erased?

1
"All Women Are Witches"

"Now here's a woman who is a witch," declares the soldier while pointing out Aldegonde de Rue. "Would you listen to that," she retorts, "but what is there to do: all women are said to be witches!" A brief and poignant dialogue concentrated in a few words the entire enigma of persecution. How is one identified as a "witch"—or a heretic, a suspect, or a counterrevolutionary? What features betray this absolute Enemy who can only deserve death? And how can we affirm (even in indignation) that "all women are witches"? How is this passage from a singular perception ("here's *a* woman . . .") to an assertion that presents itself as universal operated? The initial interpellation does not suffice to bring Aldegonde before her judges: It had yet to be further accompanied by another accusation, which came when her neighbor lodged a complaint against her for having "cursed" his horse. A rich farmer targets a poor peasant woman; a man targets a woman . . . Should we invoke class struggle or the conflicts between the genders? For the moment, let us simply observe that the one who accused the old woman was her *neighbor*. This comes as no surprise: Those who denounced "witches" were most often inhabitants of their village or family members. At times the brother would denounce his sister, the mother her daughter, or the daughter her mother, and the accusations of very young children sometimes sent their whole family to the stake . . . Freud designates as a "narcissism of small differences" this tendency that pushes the closest individuals or communities to fight each other with unrivaled relentlessness as if this proximity represented a threat to their identity. Among so many others, the story of Aldegonde confirms this: Persecutory hatred is not unleashed against the most distant stranger, the most different, but against the similar, the *neighbor*. Its target is a figure of the Same and not of the Other, or more precisely, of the *almost same*, since a barely perceptible difference distinguishes them. It is this "small difference," this almost invisible stigma, that the witch-hunters track down on the bodies of their victims.

What stigma allowed the soldier to identify Aldegonde as a witch? The soldier was a foreign mercenary stationed in the nearby town of Cateau-Cambrésis, and it is unlikely that he knew the old peasant woman personally. And yet he immediately *recognized* her, no doubt because of her age and her physical appearance, her looks, those traits that made up her facial expression (*faciès*). Even if he had never met her, he could easily recognize her. He had certainly not read the treatises of Bodin, Rémy, or Del Rio, and all the abundant demonological literature circulated at that time. Still, he had heard about her misdeeds in the priests' sermons and the frightening stories told at the wake. He had already seen her, disheveled and naked, riding her broom, kissing the devil's ass, or roasting little children, as in the popular almanacs and engravings of Hans Baldung Grien. It was not a woman of flesh and blood that he had identified when he saw Aldegonde but the *figure* of the Evil Witch. This figure has an uncanny property: It precedes the concrete cases to which it can be applied; it seemingly creates its object, or at the very least allows it to be seen. Where before there were only innocent peasants, the Figure gave rise to a whole cursed people. Although it presents itself as a simple statement, the statement "here's a woman who is a witch" is in truth a performative: It creates what it states — but in order to condemn it to annihilation. How to murder with words . . .

In his *Madness and Civilization*, Foucault evokes an "enunciative conscience-of-madness" that appears reducible, "without a detour by way of a knowledge," to a simple observation: *that one is mad*. He nevertheless shows that this naive conscience that presents itself as a "simple perceptive apprehension" presupposes a specific *knowledge* of madness. Indeed, it is entwined with an other conscience-of-madness: a knowing conscience that strives to name, classify, explain all its manifestations, and, more deeply, the tragic conscience of a divide, of an irreducible difference between reason and unreason. This much can be said about the statement *that one is a witch*; what appears as an immediate perception is, in fact, indissociable from a knowledge apparatus where the discourse of demonologists, theologians, and judges is grafted onto ancient popular beliefs. The conjunction that operates here is anything but immutable because this knowledge narrowly depends on the historical conditions, and the very names that stigmatize the "witch" vary from one epoch to another. A century or two earlier, Aldegonde would have been qualified as a Waldensian (Vaudoise), as so-called witches were thus designated. A few years later, a doctor might have diagnosed a case of "melancholy" (or, long afterward, a matter of "hysteria" or "demonomania") . . . As in the case of conscience-of-madness, the accusatory statement sets out a divide. To point out the madness in the other is to put it at a distance, to mark a gap where one makes sure not to be mad. To accuse a woman of being a witch is to draw a boundary between the accuser and the woman he designates as the mortal enemy of the Church and the State — but this boundary is unstable and in danger of unraveling. We will never know what the soldier was trying to exorcise by attacking the old peasant woman. We could suspect, however, that the neighbor who accuses his neighbor of having cursed his cattle, the brother who accuses his sister, the daughter who accuses her mother are more or less deliberately trying to protect themselves, to deflect toward the other an accusation that could very well be aimed at them. For the statement *here is a sorcerer/a witch* is reversible, and it can occur, as in the Stalinist purges, that the accuser finds himself shortly afterward among the accused.

How does Aldegonde respond to the soldier's question? Although she protests vehemently at first ("would you listen to that!"), she nevertheless admits that she could be the target of such an accusation: "all women are said to be witches." It is as though she understood that she was but a simple case, an example among others of a general rule, impossible to contest. She thus recognized that she was powerless to defend herself against this hearsay, this anonymous — and all the more threatening — knowledge aimed at all women indifferently. It has not always been the case: At the beginning of the persecution, the first treatises on demonology evoked a sect of *sorcerers*, and men as well as women were equally targeted. It was not until 1487 that the *Malleus maleficarum, The Hammer of Witches*, was published in Strasbourg, where, for the first time, women appeared as privileged targets. In the years that followed, the proportion of women condemned for witchcraft rose sharply, reaching 70 percent at the time of Aldegonde. Whereas the figure of the Magician continued to be valued — as attested by the literary characters of Faust and Prospero (or the favor enjoyed by certain magicians at the court of kings) — that of the Witch became utterly negative. This *feminization* of the Enemy remains an enigma that we must try to elucidate. In any case, by presuming that *all women* deserve to be accused, the statement that Aldegonde reports tends to extend the scope of persecution immeasurably since no woman can evade the accusation. During the hunt for "Waldensians" in Arras in 1459, it was claimed that "the whole town was Waldensian." It was this generalized suspicion, this almost unlimited extension of the target, that would characterize the terrors of the centuries to come. Henceforth, *anyone* could become the object of persecutory hatred.

This limitlessness could already be foreseen when the persecutions abandoned their traditional targets — heretics, Jews, or lepers — to attack a group with ill-defined borders, the "sorcerers." Unlike the leper, who was cut off from other men by the visible symptoms of his disease, or the medieval Jew, who was distinguished by his religious beliefs and the distinctive signs he was required to wear, nothing could really differentiate the so-called witch from anyone else. It follows that anyone — starting with a relative, a neighbor, etc. — can be accused. For the neighbor who denounced her, Aldegonde was a familiar figure whom he now perceived as an enemy, all the more dangerous because she was so close to him. If people's view of her has been modified, it is under the effect of the accusation, of the soldier's accusatory remarks, relayed and amplified through other accusations and a malicious rumor. Thus begins an act of exclusion, comparable to those which, in other times, cut off from society the *homo sacer*, the leper, the Jew, or, later, the insane. In the case of Aldegonde, however, this exclusion does not take the form of the traditional measures of branding, imprisonment, or expulsion: because it does not persist and is followed almost immediately by another phase during which the alleged witch is tried and executed. In a different context, she would simply have been chased out of the village, or an exorcism ceremony would have been performed to cast out her spell and reintegrate her into the community (as is still done today in some African societies). But, at the time of the witch hunt, there was no longer any question of keeping her at bay by leaving her alive, or of hoping to "correct" her through exorcism and penance. For her existence appeared to be an intolerable threat: Witchcraft was henceforth considered such a monstrous crime that the witch had to be burnt off as quickly as possible and her ashes scattered.

The initial address already made it possible to foretell what was in store for the old peasant: At the very moment when he designated her as a witch, the soldier threatened to put her to the sword or to burn her in her house. We are dealing here with a very particular form of exclusion that is immediately part of a logic of extermination. This is precisely what differentiates the victims of the witch hunt from the lepers of the Middle Ages, confined for several centuries in their sick houses before finally being massacred, or from the madmen of the classical age, whose confinement would not be followed by murderous persecution. In the case of the witch hunt, it might seem that the persecution is unleashed from the outset without being preceded by a phase of discrimination and exclusion. But this persecutory violence is, in fact, aimed at "outcasts," women who were already subject to a form of internal exclusion. Aldegonde became a stranger to her community in the wake of the accusation, and yet she remained, in spite of everything, a relative, a neighbor:

a *stranger from within*, similar to those who accused her, almost identical to them. It is this unsettling proximity that is intolerable to the inhabitants of the village since it introduces into their community the hostile presence of an *invisible enemy* that nothing (or *almost* nothing) allows unmasking. This calls into question the demarcations between the same and the other, inside and outside, inclusion and exclusion, friend and enemy. The paradoxical situation of the Witch, at the same time external and intimate: "extimate" (*extime*), as Lacan would call the object of phantasm. In the same vein, the object-of-hatred is characterized above all by its *position*, in-me-outside-of-me, very close, and nevertheless foreign. It characterizes this internal alterity that I call the remainder, this part of my flesh that I do not recognize as mine, that I apprehend in myself as a foreign thing.

How can an acquaintance, a member of the same family or the same community, appear — under certain conditions — as support of the remainder? The Other is above all my *alter ego*, one who is my likeness and with whom I can identify. By identifying myself with him, I transfer my flesh onto him, and, at the same time, I transfer to him the remainder that haunts my own flesh; so much so that our nascent community will also be, like all human communities, marked by the haunting of a remainder. It is the highly ambivalent phenomenon of the remainder that reappears in the other, transfigures her to make her an object of love or disfigures her into an object of hatred. It would be wrong to believe that it is the "wholly-other," the most distant and dissimilar, who becomes the object of my hatred: It is the *almost-same* or "other-in-the-same," my fellow man, my friend, my neighbor, the one who resembles me as a brother until he proves to be different in the closest proximity, until a "small difference" — the trace of the remainder — breaks our identification. For the object of hatred is the object of a positive identification that had already been initiated and then interrupted. Why does it then change into a repulsion that is all the more hateful as the attraction was previously intense? We have already noted the importance of identification with others and their bodies in the self-constitution of the lived body. It is precisely because the body of the other is presented within a horizon of familiarity, on the background of an original resemblance, that the discovery of dissimilarity between our two bodies — of a "foreignness" that interrupts identification — can be apprehended in a traumatic way. What attests, for example, the anguishing discovery of sexual difference, that of the absence of the mother's penis by the little boy, where Freud located the origin of the fantasm of castration and of the negative attitude toward women. Hatred, we said, is rooted in a distortion of our experience of the foreign; but hatred toward others finds its source in hatred *toward oneself*, toward an internal foreigner, a cursed part of oneself that one recognizes with horror in another. Whoever proclaims his disgust and hatred of women or homosexuals, what he hates in them is the part of femininity that he refuses to accept in himself; and Hitler, as we know, was afraid of being of Jewish origin.

Thus, persecutive hatred targets a "foreigner from within," a *foreigner among us* who represents in the world the First Foreigner *within us*. But this phenomenon manifests itself historically in different ways. During the trial of Louis XVI, Saint-Just declares that "Louis is a foreigner within us," and he calls for him to be treated "as a foreign enemy," which means "that we have not so much to judge him as to fight him," to put him to death. At the moment when the Jacobin leader rejects the former king as a member of the national community, he recognizes in spite of everything that Louis is a very singular enemy, intimately bound to the destiny of the French people, from which it is necessary to cut him off by killing him. What is valid for the king would also be valid for those tens of thousands of "suspects" whom the Terror was going to send to the guillotine: so many "agents of the foreigner" who, Saint-Just still says, "penetrated in the entrails of the Republic" and whom it is necessary to extirpate. Here, the designation of a figure of the remainder is linked to the logic of the Terror. It would be quite different half a century later, when Tocqueville described the "soft and peaceful servitude" that the "democratic despotism" generates and the fate that it reserves to those who refuse to submit to it: "The master no longer says: 'You will think like me or die.' He says: 'You are free not to think like me: your life, your goods, every-thing remains with you, but from this day on you are a foreigner among us.'" He uses exactly the same expression that Saint-Just used; and yet, in a pacified society where democratic individualism reigns, the "foreigner among us" is no longer promised to death, but to that solitude where he is condemned by the conformism and passivity of all. It is, nevertheless, a rigorous exclusion, implying the prohibition of any contact, of any promiscuity, which had struck the *"cagots,"* those "invisible lepers" who lived in the Southwest of France and Spain, for centuries — but without ever leading to massive persecution. When evoking their "miserable and abject life," an author of the seventeenth century observes that they "cannot enjoy the things common to the inhabitants of the same street or the same village: even in their own country, they are held as for-eigners." Thus, from the most extreme modes of exclusion to its most benign forms, and from exclusion to extermination, the way of treating the foreigner from within — the fate of the figures of the remainder — varies considerably according to the context and the historical conditions.

The "extimate" position of an individual or a group within a community is therefore not enough to designate them as the target of persecution. It is her neighbors who file complaints against Aldegonde and testify against her; and this is undoubtedly the result of power relations and tensions (between rich and poor peasants, between men and women, etc.) that permeate the village. Her neighbors wanted to avenge the harm, they believed she had inflicted on them by cursing their livestock, and to protect themselves against her magical powers: It was these affects that led them to denounce her to the bailiwick court, knowing full well what fate awaited her. It would be a mistake to underestimate the role played by the common people of the towns and countryside in the witch hunt. There are many cases in which hatred seems to come "from below," where the masses seem to *desire terror*. In many parts of Germany, peasants and townspeople were actively mobilized to hunt down Satan's henchmen and hand them over to the authorities. However, they were only relaying a movement that they themselves had not launched: In each case, it was the sovereign power, that of the Church or the State, that took the initiative of persecuting witches. Even if hatred always arises without reason, for it to be invested in a movement of persecution, it must be fanned, amplified by a campaign of *incitement to hatred* that comes "from above." A few years before the people of Bazuel denounced Aldegonde, the king of Spain, who ruled this region of Flanders, had issued a series of decrees calling for intensified persecution of heretics and witches. A royal decree of 1592, posted in all the villages, towns, and courts of this province, denounced the proliferation of heretics and witches that "we see in this kingdom swarming and multiplying" and enjoined the priests to "admonish the people diligently and often to beware" of these "soothsayers, enchanters, sorcerers, Waldensians." It ordered the magistrates "to have their eyes open and awake to eradicate this great wickedness" and to all subjects to denounce them to the authorities, "under penalty of attacking those who fail to do so." If Aldegonde had lived a few miles farther south, in the kingdom of France, where the persecution of witches was much less virulent, or a little farther north, in the young Republic of the Netherlands, where it had ceased entirely, her fate would no doubt have been different. Indeed, the edict of Philip II had been preceded by a series of decisions of the sovereign power — that of the Church, then that of the State — that had made the witch hunt possible. Although the medieval Church did not consider the practice of magic a crime, a significant turning point was effected in 1327, when Pope John XXII equated it with heresy and decreed that it should be punished "with all the penalties that heretics deserve"; this meant that the so-called witches were in principle destined for the stake. However, this turn was not followed by persecution for more than a century until another pope, Innocent VIII, declared relentless war on the "witch heresy" by calling for all the forces of the Church to be mobilized against it.

The state power was to take over in the following century. Without the order of Henri IV commanding him to "purge the country [of Labourd] of all the witches under the influence of the demons," Pierre de l'Ancre would not have had dozens of young women tortured and burned. And, during the possession of Loudun, Urbain Grandier would probably not have been executed without the intervention of the Cardinal of Richelieu.

This does not mean that the responsibility for the witch hunt lies solely with sovereign power. There is no evidence that the villagers of Bazuel were simply obeying an external order. Philip II's decree answered an expectation that they felt more or less confusedly: If they had not already felt hatred toward evil "enemies," his call to fight witches would have remained unanswered. How could they identify the dark object of their hauntings with this target that their ruler had pointed out to them? What does the anger of a farmer whose horse or cow died inexplicably have in common with the political decision to annihilate a conspiracy of heretics and witches? How can such different languages translate into one another? It is indeed a *translation* that allows a state policy to be grafted onto popular affects. For persecution to be initiated, several conditions are required. It is necessary that the internal conflicts and threats that a community faces push it to stigmatize some of its members; and it is also necessary that these popular passions coincide with an order that comes from above: that a decision of the sovereign legitimizes the desire to kill. If this decision is absent, we will at most have to deal with temporary explosions of hatred, with a few isolated lynchings. For persecution to take place, mass persecution that extends over a large scale and lasts, sovereign power must come into play.

We are now faced with a new enigma, that of the sovereign decision that designates the Enemy. How did a monarch reigning over an empire "where the sun never sets" come to denounce humble village diviners as the greatest enemies of his kingdom? Is there a connection between this decision and the insurrection in the United Provinces, where, a few years earlier, the "Sea Beggars" had routed the Spanish army? The mystery of sovereignty is intertwined here with that of *voluntary servitude*. When the king's order reached the peasants of Bazuel, why did they not object to it? How can we account for their active adherence to the policy of persecution? This is a question that concerns not only those who accused Aldegonde, but the victim herself. We have seen that the old woman had gone spontaneously to the executioner of Rocroi to submit to the humiliating search for the "diabolical mark." She unreservedly shared the beliefs of her accusers: Convinced that the devil really did mark his followers in their flesh, she imagined that her examination by the executioner would be enough to prove that she was not guilty. Her case is not exceptional, and the same attitude is found in many accused who believed that torture always revealed the truth and would allow them to exonerate themselves. Thus, a presumed witch of Lorraine begged her judges to submit her to torture "in order to be able to make her innocence known." It happened that, without having been accused, one denounced oneself as a witch or a sorcerer, like Madeleine des Aymards, a young peasant who declared to a judge of Riom that she had given herself to the devil, who had deflowered her and taken her to the Sabbath; or another young peasant, Jean Grenier, who accused himself before the judges of Coutras of being a werewolf and of devouring children. How to qualify this subjugation of subjects, which submits them to a policy that sends them to their death?

The story of Aldegonde is exemplary in more than one way: by the social status of the accused (a poor and elderly peasant woman, like many victims of the hunt); by the discrepancy that appears, as is often the case, between the complaints of the peasants (a few "cursed" beasts following a neighborhood quarrel) and the final indictment of the judges bringing into play the whole mythology of the Sabbath; but also because it attests to the adherence of the victim to the system of thought of her persecutors. It is not only a question of mentalities or beliefs because these representations are based on practices and institutions that give them their formidable effectiveness. Her history highlights the remarkable continuity of a procedure that begins by identifying its target, then confirms this identification by a series of ritual ordeals in which the discovery of the diabolical mark, torture, and confession play a capital role. Here we are faced with a complex set of political and judicial institutions, rituals and religious dogmas, popular beliefs, learned discourses, practical injunctions, literary and pictorial representations. It is these heterogeneous networks articulating institutions and practices, discourses, injunctions and representations, power relations, and modes of subjectivation that Foucault designates as *apparatuses of power*. A purely descriptive notion that does not aim to determine the essential nature of power, or to ground its legitimacy, but to understand "the *how* of power," to describe its different strategies, the dispositions that allow its actions, and to establish its genealogy. Here, the analyses and concepts that Foucault elaborated in this perspective seem to be fruitful and useful to me. A philosophical inquiry that confronts itself with the historical data to shed light on the phenomena of exclusion and persecution cannot avoid crossing Foucault's path — at least to a certain extent.

Let us beware, however, of a false assumption: Not all apparatuses are power apparatuses (or apparatuses of knowledge subjugated to power), and the subjectivation of individuals that they ensure is not necessarily reduced to an alienation. Thus, these *apparatuses of belief* that we call religions are not

necessarily identified with the apparatuses of power to which they are articulated and can even, in certain borderline cases, turn against them and make
possible new modes of subjectivation. It is also the case that, in times of crisis,
counterapparatuses are constituted, emancipation apparatuses that strive to
free subjects from their subjugation to power. One will also avoid assimilating
the apparatuses of power to centralized State apparatuses whose action would
be exerted only "top-down." As Foucault has shown us, power relations are
not concentrated in the central focus of political sovereignty but branch out
into the whole breadth of society. Thus, the apparatuses of power that preside
over exclusion or extermination can target "those below," but also members
of the ruling classes. In analyzing the "strategies of rejection," anthropologist
Mary Douglas has proposed classifying them according to the direction of the
"arrow of accusation," while emphasizing that the arrow can quickly change
target: "In some cases, the arrow points upward, against notables who try to
abuse their privileges; in another case, it points downward, toward the disen-
franchised majority; in the last case, toward outsiders who threaten a tight,
beleaguered community."[1]

What about the apparatus that led Aldegonde de Rue and countless other
victims to the stake? It is a very distinctive apparatus of power whose strategic
function and mode of action do not correspond to those that Foucault taught
us to recognize. Indeed, he identifies two fundamental types of apparatuses,
those of *exclusion* and those of *discipline*, grouping them under the emblem-
atic figures of leprosy and the plague. If leprosy in the Middle Ages called for
a binary division, for a massive act of separation and exclusion, which would
later serve as a model for the Great Confinement of the Insane (le Grand
Renfermement des insensés), the plague epidemics were the means of setting
up a new strategy of power, a grid of space, surveillance and control procedures, and a differential distribution of individuals, which foreshadowed the
disciplinary apparatuses of modern times, those that order the relationships
of power in our prisons, barracks, and psychiatric hospitals. The exclusion
of lepers, and the reactions of rejection that they provoked, is opposed to the
inclusion of the plague victim, and later of all "abnormal people," in a tightly
woven network where techniques of observation, recording, and normalization are used. He would later complicate this scheme by introducing the
notion of a *security apparatus*, operating through control and self-regulation
of populations. These analyses, which have become classics, describe in an
enlightening way the main apparatuses of power that, for centuries, have held
bodies and souls in their grip. But does the witch hunt fall into these categories? Here, it is not a question of disciplining bodies to make them more
docile and productive, but of breaking them by torture, then reducing them to

ashes. Nor is it a question of an exclusionary act that keeps alive those whom it rejects behind the walls of the leper colony, the ghetto, or the asylum: If so many so-called witches were imprisoned, it was to lead them sooner or later to the stake. It is strange that Foucault did not recognize the existence, next to the apparatuses of exclusion and disciplinary or security normalization, of apparatuses of a completely different type that aim neither at discriminating division nor at normalizing inclusion, but at annihilation. An omission that is undoubtedly not unrelated to one of the blind spots in his thinking: We know that he never really questioned the totalitarian terrors of the twentieth century, what differentiates them from traditional strategies of power. He never asked himself what is at stake when one moves from classic internment or disciplinary control to the extermination camp. And his elliptical reference to a "bio-power" is far from providing a clear answer to such questions.

Yet it is the Foucauldian notions of "bio-power" or "bio-politics" that several contemporary researchers have invoked in their attempts to understand contemporary persecutions and genocides. Without realizing that these are equivocal notions that Foucault applies indifferently to quite distinct problems (thinking the Nazi terror and describing the birth of liberal "governmentality"). Do they really shed light on the phenomenon of extermination? Foucault used them for the first time in 1976 to describe the emergence in the eighteenth century of a new technique of power, different from disciplinary power, but also from the traditional sovereign power, governed by the principle "allow life and bring about death" (*laissez vivre et faire mourir*) and that manifested its right to kill in "the glare of torments" (*l'éclat des supplices*). With the advent of bio-politics, it is, on the contrary, "to bring about life" (*faire vivre*), to fabricate the living, to protect and to optimize the life of the living. The whole difficulty will then consist in understanding how this power, which no longer has the function of killing, which "lets go of death" (*laisse tomber la mort*), can under certain conditions reappropriate the sovereign right to kill and organize exterminations that are much more massive than those of past centuries. It is to elucidate this paradoxical transformation of a bio-politics into thanato-politics that Foucault brings in *racism*. It would be the racism of the State, the capture by the modern State of the old narrative of the "war of races" (*guerre des races*), that would make it possible to establish a divide in the mass of the living, by dissociating those who deserve to live and those whose existence threatens the life of the species and must be eliminated. As a result, he refrains from taking into account mass persecutions such as the witch hunt, which took place *before* the appearance of bio-politics, without reference to a racist ideology, and which nonetheless possess all the features that will characterize the exterminations of the twentieth century. This difficulty seems to disappear when one decides, like Agamben, to extend the notion of bio-politics excessively, to the point of making it coincide with the sovereign power over life, such as it is deployed in the West from the Greeks right up to Auschwitz. But if all politics is bio-politics, this notion no longer has the concrete, historically circumscribed meaning that Foucault had given it: It is lost in a night where all powers are equal, where all politics merge. Whereas Foucault's conception is too restrictive to account for medieval persecutions and witch hunts, Agamben's is too indeterminate to explain anything at all. Without doubt, it is impossible to invoke bio-politics or bio-power without first questioning the original phenomenon of life. What must life be, our life, for a policy that aims to protect and increase life to plan the death of countless living people? To understand the possibility of such a reversal, it is not enough to consider the collective life, that of the species or of the "populations": It is necessary first to examine the immanent life, the most singular life, that of the living ego. It is on this level that hatred is born; that the ego, to protect itself from the intimate foreigner who seems to threaten it, can turn against itself and desire death, its own as well as that of the foreigner in it; before directing its hatred on other men in the world. In other words, a historical genealogy of the apparatuses of power must be founded on an egoanalysis.

By foregoing the confused notions of bio-politics and bio-power, I do not forego recourse to Foucault's thought. The genealogy of power apparatuses that he elaborated in the early 1970s remains very relevant for understanding the persecution phenomena. Provided, however, that we rectify it on one decisive point, by introducing a type of apparatus whose existence he had not foreseen. Let us designate these devices, whose only mission is to give death, as *persecution apparatuses*. To introduce this concept is to raise a series of questions that Foucault never asked himself. How can apparatuses of exclusion and discipline coexist with apparatuses of persecution? Are they absolutely heterogeneous, or can they join each other, perform several different functions at the same time, and even, in some cases, switch from one form to another? What happens, for example, when, after a long period of confinement of lepers in sick houses, they are massacred in the fourteenth century? Or when those in charge of psychiatric hospitals, intended to normalize and discipline the "mentally ill" with a "therapeutic" aim, submit to the order to send them to the gas chamber? How does this passage from exclusion and normalization apparatuses to the murderous violence of persecution take place? To ask such questions does not amount to justifying exclusion or disciplinary normalization, as if these apparatuses were preferable to those that persecute and kill. For these apparatuses articulate and link up with each other: By stigmatizing certain categories, exclusion procedures designate in advance

the victims of future persecutions; and there is also a violence of exclusion
that can take despicable forms. In its style and concrete consequences, however, it differs from persecutory violence. A historian who has studied the anti-
Jewish riots of Holy Week in fourteenth-century Spain shows that this periodic, ritualized, almost liturgical violence differs from the uncontrollable and
murderous violence of pogroms. By limiting themselves to throwing stones
at the walls and gates of the Jewish quarter, the rioters participated in a rite
of exclusion that reinscribed the spatial and symbolic demarcations between
Jews and Christians. In this way, they reaffirmed the necessary existence of a
community of outcasts on the margins of society and implicitly recognized
that "their history is linked to that of the Jews, that the Jews have a function
in the genealogy and existence of Christian society," so that these ritual riots
paradoxically played an "integrating role." Like carnival festivities, this violence has a cathartic function: It allows hostility toward Jews to be expressed
in a limited, channeled way, and thus defuses it. This was no longer the case
during the Great Plague or at the end of the century, when the riots took a
very different turn: Ritual violence gave way to persecutory violence, which
led to massacres and thousands of forced conversions. But this outcome was
not fatally predetermined: Exclusion and persecution do not follow the same
logic, do not mobilize the same affects or the same schemes, and the passage
from one to the other will always be random, unpredictable.

If persecution apparatuses are often constituted by grafting themselves
onto previous apparatuses, there are also cases — this is precisely the case of
the witch hunt — where persecution is initiated without passing through a
prior phase of exclusion, as if the new apparatus emerged ex nihilo, without
any relation to preexisting apparatuses . . . And if exclusion apparatuses can
sometimes be transformed into persecution apparatuses, the opposite process
is also observed: From the seventeenth century onward, the fearsome terror
apparatus that was the Spanish Inquisition gradually changed into an apparatus of disciplinary surveillance. Instead of feeding the auto-da-fé of Jews and
heretics, it was to devote itself from then on to policing morals and speech,
pursuing blasphemers, debauchees, sodomites, and the motley crowd of "abnormals." For this purpose, it maintained a vast network of informers, bureau-
crats, and archivists who were supposed to ensure the control and registration
of the entire population. In the jails where it continued to lock up supposed
Marranos, the guards meticulously recorded the prisoners' actions, their way
of sleeping, eating, and washing, hoping to discover clues to clandestine Jewish rites. If the Inquisition was no longer concerned with burning heretics and
witches, it was because it had already moved on to another plane; because
it was in the process of developing refined techniques of inspection, record

keeping, and normalization that made it the most *modern* institution of its time. We must ask ourselves whether what is being hailed as the "end of the witch hunt" does not attest to a similar mutation.

In what sense can we speak of a persecution apparatus? What makes it similar to or different from other types of apparatus? If it tends, like the apparatuses of exclusion, to operate a binary cleavage, an irreducible division between those who take part in the persecution and those whom it intends to kill, it relies, on the other hand, on practices of investigation, surveillance, and denunciation that make it similar to disciplinary apparatuses. As singular, as terrifying as its action may be, it shares with the other apparatuses several common characteristics. Each of them is an apparatus of power and knowledge, producing theories and discourses intended to justify its practices. Thus, the birth of the asylum, at the end of the eighteenth century, gave rise to techniques of observation and control, of training and restraint of bodies, and a new discourse of knowledge — that of modern psychiatry — meant to "scientifically" legitimize the internment of the "insane." Second common trait: These apparatuses function each time as devices of *subjectivation* that constitute the subjects on whom they exercise their power in order to *subjugate* them. They "identify" them, in all the senses of the word: By imposing on them an identity that makes it possible to locate them, they call for them, capture them, mark them, shape them, inscribe themselves in their bodies and their souls. But there are also, within each apparatus, lines of fracture that allow in certain cases for the subjugated subjects to resubjectify themselves in a different mode. Indeed, and this is their third essential feature, these apparatuses are at odds with adverse strategies of *resistance* that run through them and that they strive to counter, neutralize, turn in their favor.

All these characteristics are found in the apparatus that led to the witch hunt. It also presents itself as an apparatus of power-knowledge capable of mobilizing at its service many clerics, jurists, and theologians. From the beginning of the mass persecutions — in Switzerland, in the first decades of the fifteenth century — demonology treatises constructed the myth of the "Satanic sect" and advocated its extermination. One of the first descriptions of the Sabbath can be found in the *Formicarium* of the inquisitor Nider, published in Basel in 1437, and the first representation of the Witch on her broom in *Le champion des dames* by Martin Le Franc, published in the same city in 1440. Shortly afterward, the Vauderie d'Arras would in turn give rise to several writings, such as the *Invectives* of the canon Taincture. In the space of a few decades, some thirty treatises were published, followed almost immediately by countertreatises such as those by Molitor, Wier, or, later, Spee, denouncing the persecutions. It is this intense discursive production that, by breaking with the violence without phrases, the immemorial violence of lynchings, allows us to speak of an *apparatus* of persecution. In the same way that it *makes us see*, that it suddenly unveils the figure of an Enemy who was previously invisible, the apparatus also has the function of *making us say*: of arousing new statements, new narratives, new knowledge; of shifting the boundaries of the dicible by making the accused confess to a *nefandum*, a crime that is still "impossible to say." When the witch hunt began, a new kind of discourse was born, learned demonology, which intertwined testimonies drawn from trial proceedings, stories from popular folklore, as well as theological and philosophical references. For these demonologists were academics, learned scholars steeped in scholasticism and armed with syllogisms, like Sprenger and Institoris, the authors of the *Malleus*. In the following centuries, they will be cultivated magistrates, lovers of belles-lettres, like Boguet and de l'Ancre, and even a thinker of great stature like Bodin. This is what gives its particular style, both pedantic and naïve, to a treatise like *The Hammer of Witches*, which refers abundantly to Aristotle, Augustine, and Thomas Aquinas while affirming that witches possess collections of penises that they have stolen and that they "go away to deposit them in birds' nests or lock them up in boxes where they continue to move like living members"; that Satan can take on the appearance of a fly, or even a lettuce leaf; or that demons adopt a feminine form to seduce men and collect their sperm, which they reuse by taking on a masculine form in order to impregnate witches. As for Judge Boguet, he claims in all seriousness that a presumed witch copulated with the devil, who had taken the form of a chicken, and that Satan manages to speak through the vagina of women "by pretending to make sounds similar to the human voice." It is books of such high quality that served as a reference for the judges to send so many victims to their deaths. If one were to collect an anthology of these texts, it would probably have to be entitled, in homage to David Rousset, *The Buffoon Does Not Laugh*.

What characterizes this discourse is its closure, that of an apparatus of power-knowledge that dispenses with any confrontation with reality by producing through violence the "proofs" intended to legitimize it. The abundance of demonological writings is indeed based on very real practices: It consists of the confessions extracted in the torture chambers that gave their material to these treatises. The content of these confessions was dictated more or less directly to the victims by the beliefs of the judges who interrogated them, and they confirmed these beliefs in return by giving them concrete "proof," a guarantee of their truth. By attesting to the wickedness of the witches, these investigative techniques and the treaties that they fueled were to spur new persecutions. Thus, the demonologist and the torturer, the discourses of knowledge and the practices of power, are circularly justified. The closure of this system of thought also manifests itself in another way: when it disqualifies in advance any objection by attributing it to the enemy it is fighting. This is what happened in 1453 to a cleric named Guillaume Adeline, one of the first to oppose the new dogma that legitimized the witch hunt. This Benedictine preacher, a doctor of theology, had remained faithful to the old position of the Church, that of the *Canon Episcopi*: He had publicly declared that those who believed in the reality of the Sabbath were victims of an illusion. But this position could no longer be tolerated. He was accused by the Inquisition and finally admitted — presumably under torture — that he himself belonged to the "demonic sect" and that it was the devil himself who had ordered him to preach that "this sect was only an illusion, a fantasy and a daydream." The one who denies the existence of the "conspiracy of sorcerers" can only be a sorcerer himself, and his objections are valid *a contrario* as proofs of the existence of this conspiracy. This is the rhetorical strategy that all demonologists follow. "Those who affirm the opposite of the belief in witches are heretics," Sprenger and Institoris rule. Q.E.D. A heretic and sorcerer, then, the doctor Jean Wier, who dares to declare that most of the accused are in fact ill: *melancholics*. A heretic, then, the jurist Ponzinibio, one of the first to denounce the use of torture in witch trials and to question the veracity of "confessions." The judge Dietrich Flade, also a sorcerer, acquitted too many of the accused during the Great Hunt of Trier and paid with his life. By proceeding in this way, the demonological discourse immediately evades all criticism: It defuses the objection by turning it around to make it a proof of its own veracity, and sends to death those who would claim to refute it.

It is not a matter of assimilating demonology to the totalitarian ideologies that would flourish in the twentieth century, in another context and according to very different modalities. And yet, it is similar to these ideologies through certain features — in particular through the ambition to explain all events from a single Cause, from a unique Principle hidden behind the multiplicity of phenomena. The evil action of Satan and his henchmen plays here the same role as the reference to race in Nazi ideology or to the class struggle in Stalinism. Demonology also verges on these ideologies by the closure of its discourse, by its claim to verify itself through the violent forcing of reality to correspond to its logic. How can one deny the existence of the devil and witches, how can one contest the inequality of human races and the superiority of the "Aryan race," in a situation where such beliefs *really* decide the fate of countless human beings? This means that the apparatus of persecution creates its own reality, constitutes itself this Enemy that it takes on the mission of annihilating. In fact, all the apparatuses of power-knowledge proceed in this way, by constituting an "imaginary element" that they make their object and that justifies their existence and their action afterward. It is the case of the apparatus of sexuality analyzed by Foucault, or of this apparatus of exclusion that presides over the Great Confinement of the Classical Age. In the seventeenth century, the internment of the insane did not begin with them *already being identified* as such: The category of madness had to be invented, which made internment necessary by suddenly making people discover that there were insane. This gesture "produced the foreigner even where he had not been sensed"; it was "a creator of alienation." The same can be said of the apparatus of persecution. We know that the "Jew"—that is, the *mythical figure* of the profane and greedy Jew, eager to suck the blood of Christian children—did not preexist the anti-Jewish persecutions of the late Middle Ages. As for the frightening figure of the Witch, it was formed at the time the persecutions began, when demonologists reappropriated antiquated beliefs to integrate them into a new system of accusation. In this sense, it must be said that *it is the witch hunt that creates the Witch*. In fact, a multitude of witches will be discovered in Europe as long as their persecution lasts. As soon as the persecution ends, these cursed creatures that have been hunted for centuries will vanish without a trace (or will only survive in carnivals and children's stories). This will arouse the scathing irony of Voltaire, who noted that "there are no more witches since they were no longer burned."

The apparatus is thus grounded on a transcendental illusion that consists in projecting into the past the figure of the Enemy that it has created, *as if* this figure had always preceded it. This illusion is indispensable to the apparatus's functioning: It allows its agents to torture and massacre in complete innocence, as if they were merely responding to previous aggression. Whenever persecution is unleashed, the persecutors claim that they are merely defending themselves against a threat from their victims; and the more dangerous this threat appears to them, the more the scale and ferocity of the persecution are legitimized. This is exactly what Himmler tells his SS to justify the Final Solution: "We had the moral right, we had the duty toward our people to annihilate this people who wanted to annihilate us." It does not matter whether the persecutors are sincere or not, whether they are aware of this retrospective construction of an imaginary Enemy or not, as long as they actively adhere to the apparatus and implement its strategy. Moreover, most of the witch-hunters undoubtedly believed in the existence of the diabolical sect, in the formidable danger it posed to Christianity; and only Bodin, the most subtle of the demonologists, understood that it was a "beautiful lie," a fiction inscribed on power strategies. The most surprising thing about their writings is the panic they betray, the panicked certainty that Satan is triumphant; that his followers are proliferating and infiltrating everywhere; that the Conspiracy has become so powerful that it will soon be able to dominate the world. All these statements will be found in a secularized form in Hitler's imprecations or in the indictments of the prosecutor Vichinsky. This confirms Engels's judgment cast on the Terror of 1793, which applies to all forms of persecution: "We imagine it as the reign of those who spread terror; but, on the contrary, it is the reign of those who are themselves terrorized."[2] And yet fear, however intense it may be, is never enough to unleash a persecution: For it can lead just as often to moving away from the terrifying object, to fleeing from it or to trying to keep it at a distance. For the panic to turn into hatred, the *very existence* of this object must be perceived as an unbearable threat; there must be no other alternative, in the persecutor's delirium, than to destroy what terrifies him or to be destroyed himself.

As for the *Maison de force*, the prison or the asylum, the persecution apparatus ensures a function of subjectivation. This consists in identifying a target, in calling out individuals by giving them a name that qualifies them as subjects, as representatives of the malevolent Enemy. This subjugation process reaches its goal when the persecuted identify themselves with the grimacing image that the apparatus offers them: as when, before being executed, the so-called witches or the accused of the Stalinist trials "freely" confess their monstrous crimes. For it is not enough to break the bodies; the souls must also be subdued. Upon leaving the Ministry of Love, Winston Smith must finally recognize that he *loved Big Brother*. However, this subjectivation is paradoxical because it constitutes subjects only to destroy them. Unlike other devices of power, this very particular apparatus can only function by decreeing the death of those over whom it exercises its power. It, therefore, seems doomed to disappear quickly, as soon as it has annihilated its target group. To continue to exist, it will have to designate ever-new victims. From persecution that is still circumscribed, we then move on to a phase of generalized terror during which the target group expands immeasurably, to the extent that anyone can be accused of being part of it. This escalation of the apparatus, this *passage from persecution to terror*, is not an accident: It is required by the mode of subjectivation that characterizes this type of apparatus. The witch hunt offers us a remarkable example. Whereas previously a distinction had always been made between "white" and "black" magic, and only witches and wizards presumed malevolent were condemned, it was now considered that *all* deserve death. An illustrious demonologist, King James VI of Scotland, did not hesitate to declare that "when it comes to magic, those who consult magicians, those who trust them, those who witness their tricks, those who entertain them or encourage them are just as guilty as those who practice them."[3] At the height of the Great Hunt, it was sometimes enough to have had a grandmother condemned as a witch or to let oneself be called a "witch" without reacting, to possess a black cat or a rosary without a cross, to cross oneself with the left hand, to walk or dance backward, to stammer while reciting one's prayers, or to have spat out a host after taking communion, to risk ending up on the stake. An inhabitant of Val-de-Liepvre, in the Vosges, called her neighbor's son "Didier" by the wrong name. Shortly after, the child fell ill. Thus, *Didier* was an evil incantation: The "witch" will be executed. In Bergheim, in 1683, Ursula Semler, a seventy-year-old blind beggar, was sentenced to be burned alive. Under torture, the old woman had confessed to "raising fleas for the sole purpose of harassing her neighbors and spreading caterpillars in their gardens so that they would devour the vegetables." As a measure of clemency, she was not burned but hanged.[4]

It is not only subjects condemned to internment, to disciplinary training, or to extermination that the apparatuses produce: They generate at the same time the subjugated subjects, the *servants* who submit to their directives and allow them to function. At the moment when the sentence "here is a woman who is a witch" has been uttered, the outcome is already determined. A separation has taken place that assigns to each their function, divides humans into subjects destined to die and subjects destined to kill or to justify murder; and each was going to fulfill to the end the role assigned to them. The soldier who called on Aldegonde, the neighbor who denounced her, the torturers who tormented her, the magistrates who condemned her are not "monsters" or even fanatics. They are loyal subjects of the king, *citizens who respected the law* and obeyed it without hesitation, even when it became one with the death law of the apparatus. Does this also apply to the one who gave the murderous order, the sovereign who designated the Enemy? In a way, Pope Innocent VIII and King Philip II were also subjects of the apparatus. Certainly, their decision had contributed to aggravating the persecution or had oriented it differently; but they were themselves caught up in a configuration that they had not created, dependent on beliefs that had been transmitted to them, on previous decisions and strategies that they had only ratified by bending them. To recognize that persecution is at least as much a matter of an apparatus as of a decision is to admit that the sovereign decision is not the only axis or the last word of power; that sovereign power — that of the king or the pope, of the Führer or the Great Helmsman — is just as *subjugated* as that of its subjects: To a certain extent, it too does not elude the *banality of evil*.

It would be wrong, however, to believe that this decision is of no importance, that the system functions as an automaton in which human subjects are mere cogs. It is not irrelevant that a head of state chose to press onward

and intensify the witch hunt or — on the contrary — to put an end to it, as
Queen Christine of Sweden and, a little later, Louis XIV, and Maria Theresa of Austria did. Moreover, it would be a mistake to focus solely on the
decision of the sovereign. At all levels of the apparatus, microterrors relayed
the murderous order that came from above; multiple decisions constantly
intervened to radicalize, abate, or hinder it. During the great persecutions, it
is as if terror were diffused throughout society, making everyone a potential
denouncer or accomplice: giving him or her a sovereign right of life or death
over any other. At any given moment, everyone is faced with the most radical
decision, that of submitting to the command to kill or refusing to obey; and
we shall see that the most decisive blow to the apparatus would come from
one of its servants, Friedrich Spee, prison chaplain and confessor of witches.
The phenomenology of persecution thus brings us back to the fundamental
question of human freedom, of its relation to power, to the law, to evil. When
we ponder this question, it will be difficult for us to rely again on Foucault.
He considers indeed that "the individual is the result of something which precedes him," that the subjects do not preexist the subjectivation processes that
subjugate them to the apparatuses. From then on, it is difficult to see how they
could escape from the claws of these apparatuses that completely constitute
them. This limit of Foucault's thought is the one of all the *egocides*, that is,
the contemporary thinkers who maintain that the ego, the subject, the individual are inconsistent illusions, generated by anonymous instances (the Will
to Power, the Unconscious, the Structures, the Apparatuses . . .) that preexist
and radically predetermine them.[5]

No matter what — and Foucault repeatedly reminds us — resistance is possible. Apparatuses are not monolithic devices that exercise total control over
the subjects.[6] Crossed by fractures, always in a provisional and unstable equi-
librium, they are confronted with an open or latent resistance that forces them
to refine their strategies, to modify their discourses and their practices, to shift
their fields of intervention. Of course, these resistances are never in a position
of absolute exteriority to power. This does not mean, however, that they are
only a passive backlash against domination, doomed to an inevitable defeat:
They open breaches in the apparatuses, thwart the strategies of power, and
make new modes of subjectivation possible. This raises a new question: If the
relations of power suppose each time an opposite pole, if they "can exist only
in function of a multiplicity of points of resistance," should we conclude that
the resistances would be *more original* than the apparatuses? Foucault would
not have conceded this. Indeed, he rejects the quest for an absolute origin,
and, for him, it is useless to ask whether it is the action of the apparatus that
provoked resistance or whether an initial resistance triggered an apparatus

designed to counter it: Resistance and power are strictly indissociable, coex-tensive, co-originary. It is this thesis that we will eventually have to question.

"Where there is power, there is resistance." This axiom of Foucault's is equally valid for the persecution apparatuses: The most implacable extermi-nation device of modern times could not prevent the Sobibór uprising. Is this also the case for older persecutions, and in particular for the witch hunt? Admittedly, testimonies are rare. We do know, however, that the first Grand Inquisitor of Germany, the cruel Conrad of Marburg, was murdered, as were his colleagues Peter of Verona, and Peter di Ruffia in Italy, and Lopez de Cisneros, who was beaten with chains by a prisoner during an interrogation. As for one of the writers of *The Hammer of Witches*, the inquisitor Institoris, who boasted of having sent more than three hundred women to the stake, he was chased out of the city of Innsbruck and disappeared, most likely mur-dered, in Moravia, where he was hunting down heretics. The strong resis-tance of the citizens of Arras succeeded in putting an end to the massacre of the so-called Waldensians, and their accusers had to hastily leave the city. The same misfortune befell the judge de l'Ancre a century and a half later. The inhabitants of Labourd protected the accused who had fled, protested violently at the time of the executions, and declared that "the judges should rather be burned." Following a riot, the magistrate was forced to interrupt his exterminating mission. Where resistance did not reach such intensity, traces of microresistance can nevertheless be spotted — diffuse lawlessness that tried to hinder the system — as in a village in the Duchy of Luxembourg whose inhabitants were sentenced to a heavy fine because they had refused to de-liver wood for the stakes. And even when they faced their persecutors alone, without any external support, it was still possible for the victims to resist. It so happened that those accused, after confessing their "crimes" under torture, would publicly retract their confessions when they were about to be put on the scaffold (this was seen as the devil's ultimate trick); or they would leave a written testimony denouncing the lies of their accusers, as in the case of Jo-hannes Junius, the burgomaster of Bamberg, to whom we shall return. More often, their resistance remained silent: The only resource left to them was not to give in under torture, to refuse until the bitter end the ultimate hold of the apparatus over their bodies (they were then accused of using a "taciturnity spell," and their obstinacy in not confessing became the proof of their guilt). Many committed suicide in their cells (it was claimed that Satan had driven them to do so in order to avoid denouncing their accomplices). One of the ac-cused at the Arras trials, Jean Tannoye, a painter and poet, cut out his tongue to avoid confessing — but since he could read, he was forced to write down his confession. Some managed to openly defy their torturers, like the alleged witch accused of turning into a black cat who advised her judges to "take her by the tail to see who it was," or the Alsatian Maria Kintz, who sang obscene songs in the torture chamber. Some displayed that they identified with the highest figure of the innocent victim: In Raon, Lorraine, an accused declared that "Our Lord has been falsely judged and he fears that his fate will be the same" (his judges then invited him to "speak with more modesty") . . . As for Anna Armbruster, burned alive in Sélestat in 1642, she found the strength on her stake to shout to the crowd the names of her "accomplices": They were the wives of the magistrates who had condemned her — and the hunt came to an end immediately thereafter in that city.

No doubt these isolated or collective acts of resistance would have remained without effect if they had not been relayed by another type of resistance, that of certain members of the educated "elite," of those clerics, magistrates, or doctors who, at the risk of their lives, opposed the persecution apparatus. And yet, whether they came from the elite or the plebs, whether they were limited or massive, whether they asserted themselves in broad daylight or behind prison walls, by speaking out or in the silent suffering of a tortured body, each of these acts of resistance succeeded in its own way in defeating the apparatus. We find here, on the side of the victims, the same questions that we asked ourselves about the servants of the apparatus. How is resistance possible? How can subjects who have always been subjected to the power apparatuses, disciplined or terrorized by them, turn against them? If they manage to disidentify themselves, to resubjectivize themselves along a line of resistance, it is necessary to recognize that their subjugation to the apparatus was not irreversible; that an original possibility of speaking and acting by oneself escapes its grip. This parcel of freedom can also be qualified as *diabolical* — provided that we understand this term in its original sense, which is not that of the inquisitors: to understand it as that which "throws itself against" (*dia-ballein* in Greek), that which opposes or makes obstacle. This irreducible element that makes all resistance possible, how can we designate it? *Who* allows himself or herself to be called out and identified by the power apparatus without ever being reduced to this identification? Is it not the singular ego, the *true ego* of each of these subjects, which supports these processes of subjugation while resisting them? Historical experience teaches us, however, that most of the individuals, whether they are the persecutors or their victims, submit themselves most often to the injunctions of the apparatuses, even when they order them to commit atrocious acts, to betray or to denounce close relations, or to accuse themselves of imaginary crimes. If the possibility of resistance remains an enigma, that of submission is just as much so, and we still do not understand what leads men to "fight for their servitude

as if it were their freedom." To account for this subjugation, it is not enough
to describe the beliefs that are supposed to justify it: It is still necessary to understand what causes the adhesion to these beliefs, what ensures the hold of
the apparatuses on the individuals, incites them to alienate themselves body
and soul to them. The life of living individuals is their sensitive impressions,
their drives, their affects that are rooted in their flesh and decide their relation
to the world and to others. How can affects be captured by power apparatuses?
How did the inexplicable death of her neighbor's horse finally lead Aldegonde
to the stake? No doubt the farmer's anger and hatred and his desire for revenge were already predetermined by ancestral beliefs that attribute the death
of livestock to spells cast by "witches." Yet these feelings had to lead him to
file a complaint against her in court, and the judges had to torture the old
woman to force her to confess that she had gone to the Sabbath and prosti-
tuted herself to the devil. Two charges of very different origin and scope are
combined here to convict Aldegonde. There is nothing exceptional about her
case: In the minutes that have been preserved, the initial accusations made
by neighbors or relatives concern illnesses or suspicious deaths of men or
animals, rainstorms or hail that destroyed crops, and almost never mention
the alleged witch's participation in the Sabbath, her sexual transgressions,
or her diabolical counterreligion. It is during the interrogations that these
themes appear, imposed on the accused by the belief system of their judges.
The apparatus thus manages to translate the grievances of the peasants into
the language of demonology, while attributing them to the accused. We are
dealing with both a *transposition* that translates these grievances into another
discourse, that of scholarly culture, and a *disfigurement* that introduces into
the accusation a series of representations that were not present at the outset
(the profanations, the homage to Satan, the diabolic mark and coitus, etc.).
It is significant that, when they name their demon, the accused give it familiar names from popular culture — Gauwe, Vixen, Federlin, Grésil, Robin,
Verbouton, Jolibois — whereas the judges or the exorcists mobilize the entire
nomenclature of a learned demonology inspired by the Bible, such as Lucifer,
Belzebuth, Asmodeus, Leviathan, among others. How can two such dissimilar
discourses reciprocally translate one another, cross each other, graft one onto
the other? This is, however, a necessary condition for an important part of the
people of the cities and the countryside to adhere to the apparatus, to submit
to it by actively supporting the persecution.

A power apparatus is the condensation of a power dynamic, that is, a random conjunction of elements of very different status. Between these elements,
a synthesis must be possible, and it will be a *synthesis of the heterogeneous*,
since there is no preliminary affinity between old popular beliefs and a demo-

nological doctrine elaborated by theologians, between affects that come "from below" and a policy decided by the sovereign power. For it to be carried out, this synthesis requires each time an intermediary element, a hinge that allows them to be articulated, to fasten the ones to the others. What does it consist of? Perhaps an answer can be found from a philosopher who faced a similar question on a completely different plane. In his *Critique of Pure Reason*, Kant wonders how the categories of the understanding (such as substance or causality) can be applied to the given of sensible intuition, when understanding and sensibility are completely heterogeneous. For them to be able to articulate each other, "there must be a third term which is homogeneous, on the one hand, to the category and, on the other, to the phenomena." It is these "intermediate representations" that transpose in a sensible horizon the categories of understanding that he designates as *schemes*. Thus, temporal permanence is the scheme of substance, temporal succession that of causality, etc. Without their intervention, the categories would remain empty, the intuitions blind, and we would not be able to acquire any knowledge.[7] We are not dealing, as Kant will specify later, with symbols (indirect, merely analogical presentations), but with schemes that give us a direct presentation of the concept in the intuition. However, the intervention of the schemes is not enough to make objective knowledge possible: It is still necessary that the representations structured by the schemes be related to the pure form of an object in general. It is this indeterminate form of objectivity — that X which stands in front of and opposite to — that he calls "the transcendental object = X."

It seems probative to use this notion in a different context: These intermediate representations that allow a persecution apparatus to capture popular affects and beliefs by integrating them into its own belief system, let us call them *persecution schemes*. Unlike Kantian a priori schemes, which are universal representations that always assemble with the same categories, we are dealing with what Foucault sometimes refers to as *historical a prioris*. "A priori" means that they do not come from experience, because they are its condition of possibility. The schemes of persecution are not representations produced by the repression of heretics or the witch hunt: By tying popular affects to devices of power, they have made them possible. And yet, such schemes are not immutable archetypes that would travel through history without it having any hold on them: They are born in the course of history, they are modified from one era to another, and each of them is integrated into a historically determined apparatus that implements it. Paradoxically, these schemes that are the condition of the historical experience originate themselves in a certain experience, a relation to an "object-X" — a primordial Opponent — that we will have to locate and describe. Of course, these historical schemes are not limited to the persecution schemes. The other power apparatuses call upon other schemes that ensure an analogous function of capture and subjugation by bringing into play other affects. Thus, the exclusion apparatuses bring into play specific schemes that mobilize the opposition of the pure and the impure, that is, the haunting of the defilement, of the contagion of the pure by the impure. This panic fear of contamination is what motivates the acts of sharing, expulsion, or enclosure that these apparatuses accomplish; and these acts are inscribed each time in space, in the borders that the communities draw or the walls that they erect to protect themselves from contagion. The fundamental affect that this scheme mobilizes is *disgust* (of which contempt is a "sublimated" form). This affect does not necessarily incite those who feel it to destroy the object of their disgust — simply to turn away from it or to reject it, to put it aside. When this no longer suffices to overcome the anguish of contagion, when the excluded element reappears as a threat impossible to cast aside, another affect arises that aims no longer simply to reject, but to annihilate the object of one's dread. Disgust then gives way to hatred; and it is indeed hatred that the persecution schemes mobilize to put it at the service of an apparatus.[8] Other apparatuses bring into play different schemes, which mobilize other affects; and it is the same of the *counterapparatuses* that are molded during crises and revolutions when the men manage to desubjugate themselves from the power apparatuses: They bring into play *schemes of emancipation* whose fundamental feeling is *hope*.

Let us clarify: We are dealing here with schemes, not concepts or discourse or beliefs. We too often imagine that the misdeeds of a power apparatus can be explained by referring to the doctrine to which it refers. And yet, nothing in Marx's theories announces the Gulag. There is nothing in the Gospels or the Quran to account for the Inquisition or Islamic terrorism. To legitimize itself, an apparatus can appropriate any doctrine, but it is never the doctrine that mobilizes it and guides its action: It is the schemes that structure it, the phantasms that are associated with it, the affects whose capture and intensification these schemes allow. By scheme, I designate "intermediate representations," which intervene on very different planes. It is indeed advisable to distinguish *historical schemes* that hinge on affects, power apparatuses, and *originary schemes* operating at a more elementary level, in the immanent experience of the self. It can, however, sometimes be the case that the same schemes are at work on both planes. For example, the incorporation schemes allow the primordial flesh to constitute itself as an organic body by unifying itself, differentiating itself, and demarcating itself from its outside. However, the same schemes are found on the historical level, where they seize individuals to integrate them into a collective Body. The failure of these schemes provokes the same phenomena of disembodiment that are manifested in the life of the ego-flesh and in the historical communities by arousing each time an intense anguish. It is not a question of operating an "a priori deduction" of these schemes, or even of establishing an exhaustive list of them. I will limit myself to describing them as they are given in the experience of exclusion and persecution, from the most elementary schemes — of inversion, transgression, contagion, etc. — to the most differentiated ones, like the conspiracy scheme, which engage more complex figurations. Of course, these schemes are not the cause of historical phenomena and do not explain them. As such, a scheme has no power and produces no effect. It only becomes operative by being inserted into an apparatus, and its insertion is always random and precarious, because apparatuses are constantly transforming themselves by integrating new schemes, modifying or rejecting the old ones, associating them differently with each other. It is only in this way that the schemes can intervene in history: Without the schemes, the apparatuses cannot capture any affect and remain powerless to act; but, without the apparatuses that reactivate them, the schemes remain inert sediments.

What are the schemes that allow hatred to invest itself in a policy of persecution? The witch hunt gives us an example. The myth of the Sabbath is a complex formation, composed of several historically sedimented strata: belief in the devil and diabolical curses, in magical thefts and nocturnal assemblies, fear of a secret "sect" fomenting a "plot," etc.[9] Of these different elements, which is the one that makes a scheme, that mobilizes hatred and calls for persecution apparatuses? The one that will allow its most massive extension by giving it a political meaning. We find healers, diviners, and spell-casters in all human societies, both revered and dreaded for their powers, sometimes excluded and rejected in the margins. When the hunt for witches and sorcerers began in modern Europe, these familiar characters were no longer similarly apprehended. They were no longer perceived as isolated individuals, but as a *rebellious multitude*; more precisely, as a powerful *secret society* that would attempt to seize power by overthrowing the authority of the Church and the State. Since this hidden enemy is innumerable, the repression no longer targets only a marginalized few but becomes generalized, to the point of extending in certain cases to all classes of society. From the very beginning of the persecution, this conspiratorial dimension is put forward: In evoking the witch hunts that ravaged the Swiss Valais at the beginning of the fifteenth century, a contemporary chronicler reports that they "were so numerous that they thought that soon they would be able to elect a king from among themselves. And the Evil Spirit made them understand that they should become strong enough to no longer fear any power or court, but that they themselves should create a tribunal and constrain Christendom."[10] This fear of a witch's conspiracy will persist throughout the persecutions: It is found in an exacerbated form in Bodin's *Demon-Mania*, and, in the seventeenth century, the judge Boguet still worries that the witches will become "strong enough to make war on the king." This is the fundamental historical scheme that made this persecution possible. Like any scheme, it is an intermediary representation that hinges on various planes. As long as there is a *conspiracy*, it directly concerns the sovereign power: A persecution apparatus is set up because the State seems threatened by a subversive countersociety. And since we are dealing with a conspiracy of *sorcerers*, this apparatus can easily mobilize popular affects and beliefs: The immemorial fear of evil spells and the hatred of sorcerers that it inspires will lead a large number of peasants to actively support the policy of persecution.

Unlike the Kantian transcendental schemes that enable objective theoretical knowledge, the conspiracy scheme, like the other exclusion and persecution schemes, produces only false knowledge, and this one has, above all, a practical bearing. By claiming to explain seemingly inexplicable natural phenomena, from the death of a horse to an epidemic of plague, or unpredictable historical events — attacks, wars, or popular revolts — such a scheme brings everything back to a single imaginary Cause, to the maleficent will of a hidden enemy that it is then a question of unmasking and annihilating.[11] I must say that, when I began this investigation, I did not expect to find in the persecutions of a distant past this conspiracy scheme, which plays such an important role in the totalitarian ideologies of our time. We would unduly honor it by referring to it as a "conspiracy theory": It is not a theory in the strict sense of the word — a coherent set of concepts intended to explain or understand a certain type of phenomenon — but a scheme, an imaginary representation that acts as a hinge between affects and apparatuses of power. Excellent scholars affirm that the conspiracy haunting appeared for the first time during the French Revolution. I was surprised to discover that it is much older, that it even predates the witch hunt since it already motivates the persecution of lepers in 1321. We are dealing with a prevalent scheme that crosses the centuries without ever fading away and functions each time to legitimize persecutions and massacres. If it sometimes loses its intensity, it always ends up being reactivated by investing itself into new apparatuses. This scheme thus assures a more decisive function in the long duration of persecutions than demonological beliefs or racist ideology. Who still believes today that there are witches who change into black cats, who suck the blood of children and copulate with Satan, or that blond dolichocephalic races are more intelligent than brown brachycephalic ones? While so many of our contemporaries are thoroughly convinced that the secret society of the Illuminati or the "Zionist lobby" secretly rule the world . . .

A scheme is a *synthetic* representation, unifying several heterogeneous elements, and *dynamic*, because it is able to modify itself through association with other representations. This is the case of the scheme that motivates the witch hunt. To an initial nucleus, of which the motifs of the multitude, the conspiracy, and the secret form the principal components, several other elements are aggregated. The "sect of witches" was accused of all the infamies that for centuries had been imputed to heretics (devil worship in animal form, sexual transgressions) and to Jews (desecration of Christian sacraments and ritual murder of children).[12] The very old belief in magical flights and nocturnal assemblies then took on an evil meaning that it did not previously possess: They were now presented as the ritual ceremonies of a diabolical counterreligion. The black legend of the Sabbath was born, and it was to last for centuries without much alteration. The very names given to these assemblies reveal the historical origin of these accusations: First they were called *"vauderies,"* after the heresy of the Vaudois (Waldensians), a religious dissidence persecuted by the Church since the end of the twelfth century; or "synagogues" (in 1440, the poet Martin Le Franc evokes the witches who go at night to the "whore synagogue"); and, a little later, "sabbaths," a term that was finally to become established and that is none other than the *shabbat*, the holy day that the Jews dedicate to God. The main features of the Witches' Sabbath thus derive from earlier persecution apparatuses that were aimed at other targets. It is, therefore, not its constitutive elements that make this scheme so singular, but rather its unique way of articulating them, of condensing them into a single Figure: of taking a new enemy as a target, of figuring it and disfiguring it.

Indeed, each historical scheme operates as a mode of (dis)figuration. Like the Kantian transcendental scheme, it consists in a sensitive transposition, which makes it possible to *aim* at a target: It makes visible what would otherwise remain invisible. Integrated in an apparatus of persecution, the conspiracy scheme opens a horizon where it becomes possible to discover innumerable enemies. And yet, this scheme that makes it possible to see is not itself visible: In order to designate the target of persecution, it must *portray* it. According to Kant, the scheme is what "provides a concept with its image": It generates for this purpose image-schemes or, more exactly, *figure-schemes* — for they are not limited to visual images only — that present the concept by portraying it in a sensible intuition. The historical schemes are also manifested in differentiated figure-schemes. Thus, the scheme of contagion can be represented in several ways: as a voluntary or involuntary contamination, at a distance or through fleshly contact, as an evil that spreads by penetrating

the body (this is the case of the possessed and the vampires) or by poisoning —
an old accusation of which different groups have been the target. As for the
scheme of the conspiracy, it does not have the same meaning if it is a conspiracy of witches, Jews, or Freemasons. In each case, a certain figure-scheme
is associated with other representations to give this imaginary plot its specific
content. What is true for the historical schemes is also true for the originary
schemes that unfold on the plane of immanence of the self. The primordial figurations of these schemes take most often the form of *fantasms*, representations that mobilize primary affects (of anguish, of disgust, of hatred, of
love . . .) by relating them to an "image of the body," or rather to a figuration
of the flesh, of the relation of the ego-flesh to the remainder. These phantasms
of intrusion, of rejection, of scission, of mutilation, of parceling out, etc. are
formed below any relation to others. They are the immanent matrix of the
psychological *fantasms* where the ego portrays itself on the plan of the world
in various "scenarios" — most often sexual — staging its relations with others.
These elementary phantasms and these psychic fantasms intertwine with one
another and articulate themselves with the schemes that they portray to produce aesthetic representations, beliefs, myths that the apparatuses diffuse and
that orient their action.

What makes the statement "here is a woman who is a witch" possible, what
makes it possible to identify the enemy, is a figure-scheme of the witch that
appears in stories and tales, literary and pictorial representations? One of the
first artists to depict witches at the Sabbath was a disciple of Dürer, Hans Baldung Grien, who lived in Strasbourg at the beginning of the sixteenth century,
where *The Hammer of Witches* had just been published. He represents them
naked, surrounded by skulls and bones, preparing their devilish potions. Some
of them carry dishes with the remains of men or children on them; and they
roast on skewers strings of long sausages where some historians thought they
saw penises (they were suspected of stealing phalluses by means of magic).[13]
Baldung does not refrain from painting young witches with desirable bodies,
multiplying allusions to their sexual perversions. Thus, one of them presents
her rump to the mouth of a dragon whose tongue is stretched out to penetrate
her from behind (witches were accused of practicing sodomy on the Sabbath).[14] This staging of transgressive sexuality, these images of mutilated and
dismembered bodies, of infanticide and cannibalistic devouring, these grimacing images of demons and hybrid beings, half-man and half-beast, situate
the figures of the Witch and the Devil in the dimension of the phantasm, in a
certain representation of the body, of a monstrous or hybrid body, in danger of
being disincorporated. It will be necessary for us to question these figurations
of the body, to try to understand how the historical schemes of persecution

are rooted in original schemes of incorporation and disincorporation. By depicting the witch, these image-schemes disfigure her: As the caricatures of the *Stürmer* will do, they present the accused of the witch trials as repulsive creatures, guilty of the most despicable crimes, which allows their murderers to be absolved in advance.

This disfigurement is also exercised on another plane: in the specific operation that allows us to identify the Witch, to recognize her under the appearance of virtue and piety that most often conceals her. Dis-figuring, then, means substituting another figure for an initial one, presented as the *only true one*. In 1519, an Italian peasant woman named Chiara Signorini, accused of witchcraft by another peasant, appeared before the Inquisition of Modena. She began by denying all the accusations and declared that the Holy Virgin had appeared to her several times, "beautiful and young and dressed in white," that she "embraced her with great veneration" and "felt her soft as silk and warm." By insidiously questioning her, the inquisitor led her to recognize that this rather un-Catholic Virgin had commanded her "to give her soul and body to her," promising to avenge her of those who had wronged her and that Chiara had paid her homage by offering her the soul and body of her son. The inquisitor decided to put her to "the *quaestio*." She then "confessed" that she was a witch and that in truth it was Satan who had asked her to worship him and had avenged her of her enemies.[15] Less cruel than the secular judges who were to rule in France and Germany, the inquisitors did not condemn her to the stake, but to life in prison. The physical violence of torture is here at the service of more radical violence, of a dis-figuration act that authorizes the agent of the apparatus to interpret the testimony of the accused by turning it into its opposite (and by forcing the victim to state this substitution herself): instead of the soft and warm caress of Mary, the cold embrace of the devil. What authorizes the inquisitor to substitute this diabolical figure for that of the Virgin is a theological doctrine affirming that Satan can "disguise himself as an angel of light," taking on the appearance of someone sent from Heaven. By making the devil a *simulacrum of God*, Christian theology has established a hermeneutic of suspicion: It becomes very difficult to distinguish a divine miracle from a demonic manifestation because the same visions, the same stigmata, the same prodigies qualify the saint and the witch in the same way. A sovereign decision is then required to *decide through the undecidable*, to differentiate between friend and foe, the Lord's chosen one and the devil's whore. And this decision, because it is totally arbitrary, is also reversible: Joan of Arc was burned as a witch before being venerated as a saint.

This analysis would not be complete without taking into account a third function of the persecution scheme. To be able to exclaim "here is a woman who is a witch!" the soldier had to have already seen images or heard stories featuring the diabolical Witch — but he also had to consider them as more than mere fictions: that these figurations refer to a real experience; that he remembers having already met other, similar old women, other "witches," or at least that he expects to encounter them. Adherence to a belief would be impossible (or inoperative) if the scheme that underlies it did not make it possible to identify in reality a series of concrete cases that validate this belief. Long before the soldier met Aldegonde, the scheme had predetermined their meeting so that he could identify her without error, and the old woman's confession will confirm this identification after the fact. Thus, the figuration provided by the scheme is from the outset a *pre-figuration*, a *pre-vision*. It is this that ensures the closure of the demonological discourse and of all the ideologies of persecution by conferring on it the absolute certainty of a knowledge that determines in advance everything that happens and will always be confirmed by the facts. What "verifies" the belief is the scheme's *identificatory function*, which allows one to recognize past phenomena and to anticipate future phenomena as the same as the present one. By allowing themselves to be identified by the scheme, individuals become mere cases, examples among others of a general rule ordained by the apparatus. It was up to Aldegonde herself to enunciate this rule: "they say that all women are witches." By prefiguring and identifying in advance all the phenomena that would confirm it, the scheme makes it possible to pass from a particular statement to an affirmation that is intended to be universal. The whole city of Arras is Waldensian, all the Jews are greedy and lecherous, all the Vendeans are counterrevolutionary rebels; or again, as the executioner of Bamberg will declare to Junius, all the witch trials happen in the same way, and, whatever they may have done, all the accused will end up on the stake. It is this operation performed by the scheme that allows the apparatus of the persecution to extend its target almost without limit.

The scheme thus manages — by preforming experience and reinterpreting it — to protect the discourse of the persecutors from any breach of the real. Does this mean that it is entirely closed in on itself, that it constitutes from end to end the "reality" to which it refers? However, in medieval Europe, long before mass persecution began, there were Jewish communities, religious dissidents condemned as heretics, or patients suffering from leprosy. In each case, the apparatuses simply designated groups that already existed as absolute enemies to be annihilated. In the case of the witch hunts, however, no identifiable groups existed prior to the persecution, only isolated individuals practicing magic. When the witch-hunters attacked an innumerable "sect," was this a purely fictitious construction of an imaginary enemy to justify the persecution? Or is this fantasy rooted in an actual experience, while at the same time disfiguring it? How could a belief be so massively accepted if it did not refer to a certain experience, however remote and obscured it might be: if it was not rooted in a "kernel of historical truth"? This is the expression that Freud used to qualify this part of the truth that he spotted in the delusions of psychotics and the dogmas of religions by underlining that this truth undergoes each time a "deformation" that makes it unrecognizable. Even if he reduces this "kernel" a little too much by insisting on the illusory and pathological character of religions — unlike Lacan, who has better apprehended what he calls "the truth of God." Would the schemes of persecution also have their kernel of truth? The old quarrel between the historians who affirm the reality of the Sabbath and those who deny it could have lasted indefinitely if an unexpected discovery had not changed the situation. While working on the archives of the Friuli region, Carlo Ginzburg indeed discovered certain facts that had not attracted the attention of historians. In 1580, the inquisitor of the diocese of Aquileia had summoned two villagers, Gasparutto and Moduco, who were said to have gone "wandering at night in the company of witches and goblins. The two men confess to him that they are Benandanti (literally, "good-goers," those who "go for the good"). On certain dates, they fly away "in spirit" in the night, armed with fennel branches, to fight "for Christ" against Malandanti, evil sorcerers armed with sorghum stalks. If the Benandanti win this fight, the harvests will be abundant; if not, it will be a year of famine. Disconcerted by these strange "sorcerers" who claim to be fighting other sorcerers in the name of Christ, the inquisitor tries to apply his own reading grid to their story, the one provided by the persecution scheme. When Gasparutto tells him that he is called to battle by "an angel from heaven all in gold," the inquisitor asks him if this angel has promised him food and women, if he is being worshipped, if he is leading him "to the other angel sitting on a throne." After having strongly disputed it, Gasparutto will end up admitting that he "believes that the appearance of this angel was a temptation of the devil, since you told me that he could transform himself into an angel." In the years that followed, several other peasants would in turn confess that they were Benandanti. But their certainty that they were acting for the good would gradually crumble under the pressure of the inquisitors, and eventually they would admit without any hesitation that their nighttime wanderings were in fact leading them to the Sabbath, where they worshipped Satan.[16] Their story shows, once again, the formidable effectiveness of the schemes of persecution that manage to implant themselves in the consciousness of the accused, disfiguring their beliefs in order to integrate them into the thought system of their persecutors. It also reveals that these schemes do not completely create their object, since the belief in magical flights and witchcraft assemblies has its source in ancient popular traditions. It is the survivals of these fertility rites that, disfigured by the demonological discourse, would have given rise to the myth of the Sabbath.

Although most of the victims of the hunt were probably unaware of it, the accusatory narratives that led them to the stake were not mere fictions forged by their executioners: They refer to a forgotten experience that shows through behind the distorting screen of schemes and fantasies. This archaic layer that sometimes emerges in the confessions of the accused, Ginzburg was to explore, and he discovered similar beliefs in many other regions of Europe.[17] The ritual ecstasies, the nocturnal escapades, and the magical battles would be the expression of rites of shamanic origin staging a journey into the world of the spirits and the dead. For the trance of the Benandanti and their departure "in spirit" to the other world are themselves akin to death, and the sorcerers against whom they fight can be likened to the "wild hunt," the troop of the dead who wander through the night. By rooting it in an original experience, he has profoundly renewed our understanding of the Sabbath. But do his discoveries allow us to understand the political dimension of this scheme, that is, the belief in a *conspiracy* of witches? Here, it is no longer a question of ritual combat for the fertility of the fields but of a conspiracy infiltrated at all levels of the State . . . At least he identified a fundamental trait of the schemes of persecution: their *plasticity*. He indeed proposes a very convincing genealogy of the witch hunt. The theme of the conspiracy against Christianity appeared for the first time in 1321 in the Southwest of France, during the persecution of lepers, accused of conspiring with Jews to spread their disease by poisoning wells. It resurfaced during the Great Plague of 1348, once again focusing on the Jews, before taking on its definitive form in Switzerland at the beginning of the fifteenth century, where the Waldensian heretics were first incriminated, followed by the "new sect" of witches.[18] To the primitive core of the scheme, other motives were progressively added, such as night robberies, an homage to Satan, infanticide, and sexual transgressions. However, this condensation of heterogeneous motifs is accompanied by several changes in the target, as it moves from lepers to witches, heretics, and Jews. Freud considered condensation and displacement as the main unconscious processes of "dream work." We see that they characterize as much what we could call the *work of the schema*.

Yet, despite the transformations that affect it, its kernel remains unchanged. This tendency to persist, to maintain itself in the slow rhythm of the long term, we define as the *prevalence* of the scheme. Far from being opposed to their plasticity, it is its condition: It is because the schemes have this power to travel through the ages while always remaining identical that they can merge with other motifs without disintegrating. Paradoxically, the designation of a new target does not seem to affect this prevailing structure, as if the different faces of the Enemy possessed common traits that made them interchangeable. This is because they have already been pre-figured and dis-figured by the scheme that identifies them as a single Figure. The names "heretic," "Jew," or "sorcerer" then become simple synonyms, and the scheme passes from one to the other, charging them indifferently with the same accusations, even if the historical configuration in which they had appeared has been profoundly modified or has disappeared. This is how the accusation directed in the Middle Ages against Jewish doctors, denounced as poisoners, will reappear in the twentieth century in Stalin's USSR, where Jewish doctors will be accused of being part of a "Doctors' Plot" aimed at assassinating Party leaders. In both cases, the accusation is based on the scheme of the conspiracy, on the denunciation of an imaginary conspiracy to subvert the established order. On the surface, everything opposes the medieval society in which this scheme was formed and the modern, secularized Soviet society; but the resurgence of the same scheme reveals "anachronistic" proximity between these two societies, hidden connivance between the Inquisition of the Middle Ages and the Stalinist secret police. If the *prevalence (prégnance)* of the scheme defines its general capacity to maintain itself through different historical configurations, I will use *remanence* to designate its capacity to reappear when the configuration in which it was constituted has completely disappeared.[19] It then resurfaces as a specter of the past, and its spectral resurrection profoundly affects the new configuration. We shall see that this haunting of the fallen monarchy as a *phantom member* of the Republic plays a decisive role in the Terror of 1793.

We are beginning to understand the relationship that ties the schemes to the apparatuses of power. Of course, the schemes can only operate by investing themselves in apparatuses that offer them the human agents, the techniques and the institutions, the knowledge, and the discourses of legitimation that allow them to implement. But any apparatus is the condensation of an unstable and shifting power dynamic: It is born and transformed according to the situation, disappears, and is reconstituted under another form. It presents itself as a variable without a constant — or, more precisely, as a variable whose only constant element is its scheme. The apparatus that presided over the massacre of the lepers is not the same as that which, in the following centuries, would attack the "witches," and the latter differs greatly from the one that would exterminate the Jews of Europe; but all three repeat similar accusations, because they bring into play the same schemes while giving them new targets. Indeed, the plastic character of the scheme authorizes it to invest itself in very different apparatuses while preserving identical features. This allows us to understand that the appearance of persecution schemes can precede that of the apparatus that will implement them; or that certain schemes reappear, always identical to themselves, at other eras, in other cultures. One should be careful not to confuse a historical scheme with the discourses of knowledge elaborated by the apparatus to legitimize its action. In the Nazi apparatus, racist ideology is part of the legitimating discourses, of the pseudoscientific knowledge that it has appropriated; but the haunting of the Conspiracy is a founding scheme, inherited from a long series of persecutions, which gives the movement its raison d'être by determining its internal organization and its secret objectives. As Hannah Arendt has pointed out, the Nazi movement takes its model from the imaginary "Jewish conspiracy" described in the *Protocols* by giving itself the same goal, the domination of the world through the manipulation of the masses and through terror.[20] If the discourses of knowledge are produced by the apparatus, the apparatus is founded on the scheme that precedes it and will outlive it. When Foucault, though so concerned with identifying ruptures and discontinuities, insists on the role played by the secular fear of leprosy in the Great Confinement of the Insane, and then in the birth of the modern asylum,[21] he assigned to the account of a "resistance of the imaginary" what in fact is the prevalence of a scheme. It must be possible to describe the genesis of such schemes: to go back upstream in search of the *Urstiftung*, of the original institution that gave birth to them; to locate the time when, as the historian Robert Moore writes, the Christian West "became a society of persecution."

Unless this quest for an origin is doomed to failure: Perhaps the advent of these persecution schemes in the twelfth and thirteenth centuries is not a true historical creation; perhaps they merely perpetuate older schemes, ordering them differently so that they aim at other targets. If this were the case, what conclusions should be drawn? The analysis of the schemes brings to light deep continuities — "anachronies" — that most often go unnoticed. How can we account for the astonishing prevalence of these schemes, which seem to straddle epochal differences and give the impression that all attempts to invent something new are merely a recurrence of bygone hauntings? How is it that the Renaissance reconstituted and radicalized the persecution apparatuses of the Middle Ages? And, as Michelet and Quinet affirmed, how did the Jacobin Terror come to resurrect the medieval Inquisition? The enigma with which we are confronted is that of the *resurrection of the dead* evoked by Marx in the famous preface to *The Eighteenth Brumaire of Louis Bonaparte*: "The tradition of all dead generations weighs like a nightmare on the brains of the living. And just as they seem to be occupied with revolutionizing themselves and things, creating something that did not exist before, precisely in such epochs of revolutionary crisis they anxiously conjure up the spirits of the past to their service, borrowing from them names, battle slogans, and costumes in order to present this new scene in world history in time-honored disguise and borrowed language." There are thus two very different modes of the resurrection of the dead: that which is, according to Michelet, the proper task of the historian and allows us to hear their voice reduced to silence; and this spectral resurgence of the past, evoked by Marx, where "the dead seizes the living" and repeats itself indefinitely through it. How can we understand the reappearance of old persecution schemes under such different historical conditions? Should we see in it a kind of inertia, that dull resistance that the "traditions of dead generations" oppose to change? Husserl admirably described this process of *sedimentation* where the new formations of meaning are deposited and petrify, concealing the lived experience where they were instituted.[22] However, he notices that their persistence under a sedimented form is what makes possible the reactivation of their initial meaning. In this manner, a historical tradition is founded: It is not only the dead weight of the past crushing the present but also the bedrock and the flesh of history that allows the past to interweave with the present while opening itself to the future. A historical scheme would be nothing other than a sedimented formation of meaning, surviving as tradition and always capable of being reactivated if a new conjuncture authorizes it. Just as there is a tradition of science, just as there is a "tradition of the oppressed," there is a *tradition of hatred*,[23] a tradition of the persecutors that is instituted, petrified, and that appears to be lost and then reappears under new forms.

This hypothesis would be the most plausible if these persecution schemes belonged to a single historical tradition or if they were only the mortifying heritage of Western history. On the other hand, if similar schemes were found elsewhere, in different historical contexts and other cultures, it would become difficult to consider them as mere historical sediments. We could no longer be satisfied with looking in our history for the initial institution from which they originate: We would have to try to discover their hidden underpinnings, the primordial experience from which they draw their meaning. Such an experience would not belong to any particular tradition: It would no longer belong to world history. We would no longer be dealing with a historical a priori but with what Husserl characterizes as the a priori *of* history. What can be this experience — at once singular and universal — wherein these schemes take consistency, and that gives them the strength to travel across borders and centuries? Egoanalysis provides an answer to this question. For human beings always and everywhere live as *egos*, singular individuals incarnated in their bodies. Although their concrete forms can vary, their primordial relation to their body remains the same each time, and it tends to repeat itself on the wider plane of collective existence. The event of embodiment, where this relation is tied up, and that of disembodiment, where it is altered, are thus the matrices of our historical experience. It is possible to designate them also as schemes; but it is then a question of *originary schemes* and no longer of historical schemes, and their genesis does not coincide with the historical genealogy of meaning formations. This does not mean that they are "atemporal," but only that their temporality is not the same as that of our historical life in the world.

A historian like Ginzburg, paving a distinct path, asked himself similar questions and came to very similar conclusions. Having identified "discon-certing analogies" between phenomena located in very distant times and cultural spheres, such as the beliefs of the Italian Benandanti of the seven-teenth century and the magical rituals of the Siberian shamans, he had at first assumed that these resemblances referred to "typological connections," symbolic structures independent of historical influences. He goes a step fur-ther in *The Witches' Sabbath* by asserting that these connections are rooted in "primary experiences of a bodily character." More precisely, they are fun-damental bodily representations (as that of the envelopment) and borderline experiences where the image of the body is altered (such as in metamorphosis, mutilation, death) and that "operate similarly to schemes" by generating "po-tentially universal symbolic configurations."[24] A fertile hypothesis that would help him to overcome the tensions between microhistory and long duration, between the singularity of the experience and its universality, and to elucidate several features of the myth of the Sabbath. But does it help us in understand-ing the intensity of the hatred that this mythical representation has inspired? For this, a historical approach, however enlightening, is not enough. If we want to describe the logic of hatred, we must bracket our worldly existence to recapture our ego's immanent life, below any relation with others. On this plane, in the ambivalent relation of the ego to the remainder of its flesh, are born primordial affects like love and hate, anguish, disgust, and fear of dy-ing. This is where the original schemes of incorporation and disincorporation crystallize, where they take on these affects to transpose them on the plane of community and history. The analysis of this original schematism — which is one of the tasks of the egoanalysis — allows us to answer some fundamental questions with which phenomenology has been confronted. How does the transcendence of the world originate in the immanence of life? In what way does the immanent life, a life each time singular, our life, manage to make itself world? By schematizing itself, by transposing the schemes coming from our most originary experiences so that they are deployed on the level of the collective existence. It is thus that our affects can ground some objects in the

world, and, carried by these schemes and invested by their affective load, deploy apparatuses of exclusion, persecution, normalization, or emancipation.

What is gained by adopting this approach? How might an analysis focused
on power apparatuses and historical schemes account for the beginning, the
surge, and the end of the witch hunt? It seemed that the persecution had
begun ex nihilo, by creating an altogether imaginary enemy. We now realize
that the witch hunt proceeded from a tradition of hatred that predated it by
centuries and that would persist under different forms. Moreover, that the
apparatuses it implements have reappropriated already constituted schemes
to give them a new object. And finally, that they have pre-figured their target by seizing elements that already exist to recompose them by de-figuring
them, and that these schemes find their origin and their affective charge in a
primordial experience. And yet, these schemes are not immutable: In the long
tradition of the persecutors, ruptures occur, new figures of the Enemy appear,
like that of the evil "conspiracy," and are exerted by undergoing historical
transformations. A further question then arises. If we are really dealing with
prevalent schemes, capable of persisting over a very long period of time, how
is it that this persecution was able to come to an end despite everything, that
the witches' stakes ended up being extinguished after two or three centuries?
What is at issue is not only the termination of this or that localized persecution, whose apparatus depends closely on a given power dynamic: They come
to an end when the circumstances that were favorable to them change for
one reason or another, as a result of an intervention by the sovereign power or
when the ruling classes feel directly threatened by the outbreak of terror. But
we must also ponder the end of witch-hunting as such, the process that led to
the decriminalization of witchcraft in Europe (from the beginning of the seventeenth century in the Netherlands, in 1682 in France, some sixty years later
in Germany), thus putting an end to prosecutions and executions. Although
historians are divided when it comes to explaining this phenomenon, this
episode is unanimously celebrated as decisive progress of the Enlightenment
and of Reason. Indeed, it is difficult to understand how the arguments of his
opponents, those of Adeline, Wier, Cyrano, or Spee, which had had almost
no echo for several centuries, suddenly asserted themselves as incontrovertible
evidence. Too often, a naive and idealistic explanation is given, invoking an
intellectual "paradigm shift," the "decline of the magical worldview": The end
of the witch hunt, says a historian, is "the victory of Descartes." This gives a
lot of weight to ideas . . . Is it not, on the contrary, the end of the persecution
that would have brought about this change in mentalities by making obsolete
the discourses in charge of legitimizing it? By invoking the progress of the
Enlightenment, one forgets once again that the persecution of witches was not

an "archaic" phenomenon, and one refrains from identifying the muted persistence of the same schemes, the same hauntings in an "enlightened" society.
If it is true that this specific apparatus that governed the Great Hunt eventually
disappeared, one may wonder whether the schemes that supported it were not
reinvested in other apparatuses that took on new objects and very different
modes of action. Certainly, witches and possessed women now survive only
in literature and cinema; but their hidden stigmata, their contortions and
their cries, would reappear by coming to mark other female bodies on another
stage. When he observed how difficult it is for us to "give up a pleasure which
[we] have once experienced," Freud lucidly recognized that "we can never
give anything up; we only exchange one thing for another. What appears to
be a renunciation is really the formation of a substitute or surrogate."[25] The
same applies to hatred, to the obscure *jouissance* of hatred that men never
renounce. Far from disappearing when persecution ceases, the apparatuses
that had conducted it try to perpetuate by reactivating the same schemes in
"substitute formations."

It is undoubtedly advisable to refine the analysis by distinguishing the
changes of target operated by the persecution apparatuses and the internal mutations that affect them by transforming them into apparatuses of an entirely
different kind. We have seen that, from lepers to Jews, and then to witches,
the conspiracy scheme could be applied to a whole series of successive targets;
and this plasticity would allow it to adapt to different targets without having
to modify its structure of prevalence. At the beginning of the seventeenth
century, an apocryphal document entitled "Secret Instructions of the Society
of Jesus" circulated in Europe, claiming to reveal a conspiracy hatched by the
Jesuits in order to ensure their universal domination. A few years later, a new
target would appear, destined to a long posterity. Shortly after witchcraft had
been decriminalized in France, an anonymous pamphlet published in London attacked a "diabolical sect that had recently appeared," accusing these
"followers of the Antichrist" of conspiring to overthrow the British monarchy:
It was Freemasonry. A century later, Abbé Barruel accused it of having fo-
mented the French Revolution, and Abbé Fiard asserted that "the Jacobins,
Freemasons and Illuminati" were all "demonolaters" who had "made a pact
with hell" to overthrow the monarchy.[26] The Nazis associated them with the
"world Jewish conspiracy," and they were made responsible for the 1914–18 war
and the Russian Revolution, for the crimes of Jack the Ripper and the Ken-
nedy assassination. Still assimilated today to the mythical "Illuminati sect,"
the Masons were to represent one of the major figures of the Hidden Enemy.

Another change in targets, less often observed, occurred at the same time
in Central Europe. Since remote times, in different parts of Europe, there

were various kinds of shamans with magical powers analogous to those of the Italian Benandanti: They were said to be able to change into animals to fight against evil sorcerers and to fly "in spirit" during ritual trances that left their bodies in a state similar to death. At the end of the seventeenth century, as the witch hunt spread throughout Europe, these figures were presented in a more sinister light. It is said that they survive in their tombs in the state of the undead and emerge — sometimes in animal form — to drain the blood of men and cattle, and around 1750 they begin to be referred to by the Hungarian term *vampire*.[27] A novel figure of the Enemy was born, retaining some of the attributes of the ancient shamans (notably their undead state) while associating them with certain characteristics of witches and Jews, who were also accused of drinking the blood of their victims during ritual murders. Armed with their swords, the vampire-hunters took over from the witch-hunters, but this new belief did not lead to massive persecution. No doubt because, unlike witches, Jews, or Freemasons, vampires were never suspected of conspiring to seize power. It is as if the old scheme had disintegrated into its constitutive elements, only to be reconstituted almost immediately in different forms, sometimes emphasizing the theme of conspiracy and sometimes that of bloodthirsty monsters. It is this recomposition that is innocently celebrated as the end of the witch hunt.

Foucault notes in *Discipline and Punish* that, from the nineteenth century onward, the strategies of power that he had distinguished — the model of leprosy and that of the plague, the apparatuses of exclusion and discipline — now tend to come become similar, to merge. It seems that this lability of the apparatuses, which corresponds to the plasticity of their fundamental schemes, is more radical still: In certain cases, the apparatus itself is affected by a mutation where it is transformed into another type of apparatus. This is the case of what is called the "end of the witch hunt." For a crime of extreme gravity, a "crime of exception" such as witchcraft, to have been decriminalized, it had to be reconfigured: translated into another language, transposed into another kind of discourse where its monstrous aspects and its supernatural dimension would have disappeared. This task would be carried out by medicine. In a sense, the doctor is the designated rival of the "witch," since the latter is often a village healer, the bearer of immemorial knowledge on diseases and their remedies. In order for modern medicine, originating from urban (and male) elites, to take root in the countryside, this ancestral knowledge had to be discredited as "diabolical magic," and those who passed it on had to be burned at the stake.[28] However, the doctors were not partaking in the witch hunts. On the contrary, the hunters were concerned about their growing influence on the witch trials. As a famous demonologist, the Jesuit Del Rio, declared,

"If doctors are allowed to give their opinion, no one will be burned anymore." Their first interventions in witchcraft trials were, however, very limited. Their expertise was sought in certain cases of possession; and when scrupulous judges were not satisfied with the services of a butcher or a torturer, doctors were asked to search the bodies of the accused for the stigma that would prove their guilt. But doctors would not be satisfied for long with this subordinate position.

In 1563, Johann Wier, the Duke of Cleves's physician, published his *Five Books on the Imposture and Deceit of the Devils*, which were to provoke a heated debate. Under attack from all sides, denounced as a sorcerer by his opponents, he probably only survived thanks to the support of his powerful protector. Like all the men of his time, Wier believed in the existence of the devil and was convinced that there were "infamous magicians" who were devoted to him. However, he tried to distinguish from the real henchmen of Satan those old women "feeble, stupid and of wavering spirit" who imagine that the devil transports them to the Sabbath and allows them to accomplish evil spells. Vain illusions: They are only *phantasmata*, imaginary representations similar to those which affect patients "whose senses are disturbed when the melancholic humor seizes their brain." The word makes its appearance: *melancholy*. It is the sick excess of this humor that, by acting on the imagination, would explain the hallucinated visions of the Sabbath. However, Wier's position is more ambiguous. Indeed, the reveries of the so-called witches are the effects of an imagination derailed by melancholy, but it is Satan himself who derails it. The devil knows that melancholics have a fragile mind and manages to influence them by "disturbing the source of the nerves which is in the brain" in order to imprint illusory images. What is at issue is no longer criminals, but the passive victims of a demonic illusion.[29] As melancholy is both a disease and the action of the devil, its treatment is as much the art of the exorcist as the skill of the doctor. Far from wanting to sideline the priest, the judge, and the torturer, Wier only asks that the doctor be given an equally important place in the apparatus. Nevertheless, he opened a breach that his more daring successors were to enter. Since the hallucinations suffered by the "witches" could be explained naturally, the intervention of the devil would become superfluous. It was already some time ago that the judges of the Parliament of Paris had overturned several death sentences on appeal, considering that the accused were suffering from melancholy or idiocy: As Voltaire wrote, "it was finally understood that one should not burn imbeciles." A few more years and melancholy would give way to new concepts, promised to a bright future. At the time of the possession of Loudun, in 1632, a doctor maintained that "it would be better to speak of hysteromania or erotomania," because the so-called possessed women were "tortured by the urges of the flesh, and in reality what they need is a carnal remedy."[30] We can see the distance that has been traveled since the *Malleus*. If the demonologists attributed to witches unbridled sexuality and vile perversions, they saw it as a simple consequence of their subjection to Satan. On the contrary, the doctor detected in the sexual frustration of the nuns of Loudun the natural cause of their affabulations. From now on, the "devil" is nothing other than sex.

This profound mutation of the discourse and practices is attested by a significant episode that occurred during another case of possession. In 1599, the demon Beelzebub spoke in coarse Latin through the voice of a certain Marthe Brossier and amused the audience by making the young woman perform "extraordinary jumps and convulsions." The archbishop of Paris summoned to her bedside an exorcist, Father Séraphin, and a doctor, a skeptic named Marescot, who was convinced that "the actions of Marthe Brossier should not be attributed to the devil." As Marthe's body contorted violently, the exorcist with the angelic name challenged the doctor:

> Then Father Séraphin said aloud: "If there is anyone who doubts, let him try at the peril of his life to stop this demon." At once, Marescot got up and, putting his hand on Marthe's head, pressed it down and restrained all the movements of her body. Marthe, not having the strength to move, said that the spirit had withdrawn, which Father Séraphin confirmed. To which Marescot added: "I have cast out the demon!"[31]

The doctor's victory had immediate consequences: The very next day, the Parliament of Paris ordered Marthe's arrest and imprisonment in order to "put an end to the imposture." The most remarkable thing about this anthological scene is that Marescot imitates the traditional techniques of exorcism, the hand-to-hand combat between the priest and the possessed in which physical contact played an essential role. However, if he mimics this cathartic ritual, it is to better substitute another apparatus. When he announces to the audience that he has "cast out the demon," he does not mean, as Father Séraphin would have done, that he has expelled a real entity from Martha's body: He reveals that the possession was only a lure, that *the devil did not exist*. What Marescot exorcises is the ritual of the exorcism. The magistrates will draw the necessary conclusion: In cases of possession or witchcraft, priests and demonologists have lost all legitimacy, so that witchcraft ceases to be a diabolical crime that calls for an exceptional procedure. If it is an imposture, it becomes a simple offense, punishable by the ordinary courts. If it is a disease, it will be up to the doctor to intervene.

Thus, the compromise Wier proposed did not hold. Henceforth, the physician, the new thaumaturge, would completely replace the exorcist; and his competence would soon extend to the deaths attributed to the evil spells of so-called witches. Around 1620, while the stakes were still burning all over Europe, an Instruction from the Roman Inquisition recommended that "expert physicians" be called in to determine whether the suspected death "had occurred by natural or supernatural means."[32] Soon, it would be the "witches" themselves who would come under the purview of medicine, and a new apparatus would supplant the witch hunt. In fact, no persecution apparatus is self-extinguishing: if it eventually faced a crisis and disappeared, it is because the methods of the witch-hunters and the "knowledge" that legitimized their action had been called into question both by the resistance of their victims and by the converging criticisms of doctors, magistrates, priests, and thinkers. Behind the seemingly impersonal processes in which apparatuses of power decompose and recompose, one must also hear the muffled cries of their victims and the "roars of battle." In a sense, their resistance will not have been in vain, since "witches" will no longer be burned — but it is to another apparatus, just as implacable, that it will henceforth fall to treat those who have escaped the stake. It has not been sufficiently pointed out that it was at the moment when the witch hunt stopped that workhouses were opened all over Europe, where beggars and lunatics, charlatans, blasphemers, and libertines were locked up pell-mell. In France, the creation of the General Hospital by Louis XIV (in 1656) preceded the decree of the same king decriminalizing witchcraft (1682) by only a few years. The instructions of his police lieutenant on "false soothsayers and so-called witches" leave no doubt on this point: Those who would have been sent to the stake some time earlier would henceforth be locked up at Bicêtre or at the Salpêtrière. Not to be treated there — internment had no therapeutic purpose at that time — but because they were included, like so many others, in the moral condemnation of insanity. It was not until more than a century later that they were no longer considered as mountebanks to be punished, but as sick people to be treated, by institutionalizing them in this new apparatus destined to normalize the abnormal, the psychiatric hospital. There we find the heiresses of the possessed and the witches of the Renaissance, whose case is now a matter of "mental pathology." In a treatise from 1814, the great alienist Esquirol describes a particular form of "religious monomania" that he calls *demon-mania* and that is characterized by the delirious certainty of being possessed by the devil.[33] Charcot, Esquirol's successor at the Salpêtrière, continued his work by describing "demonic attacks" in some of his patients and by re-creating under hypnosis all of their manifestations (convulsions, insensitive zones, hallucinatory episodes . . .) that were once observed in possessed women. Thus, modern medicine has succeeded, he wrote, in "giving their true name to the demoniacs": hysterics. Perhaps the Hysteric is not the only heir of the witches and the possessed of the past. For the witch was characterized by sexual transgressions (sodomy, bestiality, incest . . .) and abject crimes (notably infanticide and anthropophagy) that she committed on the Sabbath. However, the nascent psychiatry tried to circumscribe the type of the *monster*, the exceptional criminal, who is defined precisely by the same features; and it tried to account for its monstrosity by interpreting it as an extreme form of mental pathology: by making the Monster an "abnormal," a *pervert*.[34] From the "devil's whore" who was destined to be burned at the stake to the "criminal lunatics" who are interned in asylums, the same scheme persists, the same tale of horror where a transgressive sexuality is hidden within an evil countersociety. Is the clandestine "pedophile network" not the ultimate avatar of the Satanic Conspiracy that the witch-hunters were tracking down?

Thus, we come full circle: Everything that had been related to demonology was reinterpreted in the discourse of medical science. By assigning a cause (mental alienation) and a univocal meaning to possession and witchcraft, by designating the Pervert and/or the Hysteric as the true name of "witches," this discourse claims to give the definitive explanation for witchcraft and possession, to unveil their hidden truth that would have been ignored in obscure times. Should we see in this, as everyone nowadays believes, a decisive progress of reason and science? Is this proximity, or rather this identity between the demonic and the insane, a discovery of modern psychiatry? By no means. As early as the Middle Ages — and already among the Church Fathers — heresy is assimilated to *insania*, to a form of madness; and it is the identification of witches with these heretical lunatics that, by making them the target of the Inquisition, made the Great Hunt possible. The very term *demon-mania* has a long history, and Jean Bodin, a resolute supporter of the hunt, had already used it in the title of his treatise.[35] Let us not be misled: For him, it referred to the madness that is the submission of witches to Satan, and, far from exonerating them, their demonic "mania" destined them to the stake. In Esquirol's case, it simply described a delusional belief. And yet, despite this shift in meaning, the reappearance of this notion attests that the discourses that had legitimized the persecution did not disappear with the end of the hunt. By choosing the same word, the Renaissance demonologist and the chief physician of the Salpêtrière gave themselves the same object: the *devil's madmen* (les fous du diable), those whom Satan had driven mad. Of course, this "madness" does not have an identical meaning in both cases, since Bodin and his contemporaries believed in the real existence of demons, whereas

Esquirol and Charcot only see it as a delusional idea, a *fantasy*. But the very notion of fantasy—inherited from Aristotle and his theory of imagination (*phantasia*)—already played a major role in the theories of demonologists. Let us open this classic manual of witch-hunters, the *Malleus maleficarum*. According to its authors, the prodigies attributed to the devil are only vain illusions, because only God is capable of performing miracles. They are nevertheless *real illusions*, or at least capable of producing effects in reality. Indeed, the devil can "act on the soul through fantasies" and thus distort our judgment.[36] When witches extract virile limbs, it is only an illusion; and however, "the eyes that see, the hands that touch" perceive effectively the absence of a penis . . . Freudian theory *avant la lettre*: The castration that they inflict is *at once* true and false, "true for the imagination, although it is not in reality,"[37] as is according to Freud the hallucinated perception of the mother's penis by the young boy. The satanic spell is an imaginary truth, a true fiction, the very thing we continue to define as fantasy or phantasm. It does not matter, then, that Renaissance demonologists believed in the real existence of the devil and the Sabbath, whereas modern physicians no longer do—since they agree on the same conception of diabolic illusion, that fantasy that is both real and unreal, caused by a disease of the imagination, and use similar methods to detect this madness.

An enthusiastic student of Charcot had already noticed this. In 1897, Freud questioned himself at length about the witch hunt, the meaning of the Sabbath, and Satanic coitus. He read the *Malleus* "with ardor" and went so far as to affirm in a letter to his friend Fliess that "the medieval theory of possession, supported by the courts of the Church, was identical" to the theory of neuroses that he himself was developing. It is not the victims that he identifies with here, it should be noted, but with their torturers: "Why do the confessions extracted by torture resemble so much the accounts of my patients during treatment? [. . .] And now the inquisitors are using their pins again to uncover the diabolical stigmata, and the victims are again inventing the same cruel stories"; and he adds in another letter that he "now understands the rigorous therapy that the judges applied to witches."[38] These new inquisitors, of whom Freud says he is a member, are the psychiatrists, the disciples of his master Charcot; and he recognizes in the methods they apply to hysterics the same technique that the witch-hunters used to unmask their victims: the search for areas of the skin that are insensitive to pain, to which they give the same name, the old word *stigma*. Adopting the point of view of the persecutors always comes at the cost of certain blindness, and the young Freud is no exception. He still believed that the scenes of seduction and sadistic practices of which his patients said they had been victims in childhood had really taken place.

He, therefore, came to suspect the existence of an ancient satanic cult that was maintained in secret and that exercised its obscene rites on children. In order for him to become Freud, the founder of psychoanalysis and no longer Charcot's pupil, he would have to stop giving credence to the complaints of the hysterics; he would have to understand at last that the scenes of infantile seduction that they describe are only fantasies in which they project their own incestuous desires onto their father.

Thus, in the space of a few years, Freud once again travels the path that leads from *The Hammer of Witches* to Wier and Spee, from the belief in the real existence of the Sabbath to the questioning of its reality. And yet, when he sees a strange kinship between the confessions extracted under torture and those whispered in the therapist's office, he is not led astray. Indeed, the psychiatrists of the nineteenth century share with the inquisitors and judges of the past the same objective: to obtain the *confession of truth*, the confession supposed to deliver the witch from the grip of the demon, just as it should, by bringing the insane to admit that she is mad, cure her of her delirium.[39] These are the techniques of truth that psychoanalysis has inherited and that it has been able to turn into a liberating anamnesis. Should we then consider the demonologists as distant precursors of scientific psychiatry? Rather, a survival of the beliefs and rites that accompanied the persecution of witches should be recognized in the theories and practices of the medicine of the mind: a "resurrection of the dead," a resurgence of sedimented meanings, transposed into the field of modern science. This is how an apparatus of persecution was transformed over the centuries into an exclusion apparatus of insanity, before being integrated into the new disciplinary apparatuses of the treatment of madness.

At least, one could reply, this mutation allowed innocent people to escape from the flames of the stakes. I will not be so bold as to deny it. Although the fate reserved for the insane — chained up their whole life in the dungeons of the workhouses, then forced into straitjackets in our modern asylums — is not so enviable . . . But if there was undoubtedly an improvement, it was paid for at a high price; and above all for all those who were hunted down as "witches" and "sorcerers" in the belief that they themselves possessed mysterious powers. Spell-casters and disenchanters, werewolves, Benandanti and Kresniki, the transmission of a secret or a birthmark had made them special beings, capable of predicting the future and curing diseases, of changing into animals and conversing with the dead, of fighting the forces of evil in order to save the crops. If they were doomed to the worst torments and death, their atrocious end was still part of this supernatural experience that had given meaning to their lives. From *Macbeth* to *Faust*, from Baldung Grien's engravings to Goya's *Caprices*, so many works of art bear witness to the intense fascination aroused by their hallucinatory visions and cosmic adventures. When the belief in bewitchments and nocturnal battles has ceased, stripped of their ancient powers, they will have joined the dark crowd of the demented recluse behind the walls of the asylums. By saving them from the stake, the mutation of the apparatus deprived them, at the same time, of their prestige and freedom. The freedom attributed to them by the demonologists was ambiguous, however. The witch had to be free; otherwise, it would have been impossible to judge and punish her. But they only conceded her the freedom to let herself be seduced, to give in to the great Tempter: Totally free at the moment when she signed the pact or let herself be penetrated and marked by the devil, the next moment she became totally subjugated to the power of the Wicked One. It is the equivocation of this freedom, its tragic dimension and its mystery, that the new apparatuses have tried to dissipate. By considering the so-called sorcerer as a vulgar charlatan, the policemen of the classical age reduced his powers to the derisory tricks of a fairground entertainer. By making the insane captives of their delirium, modern psychiatry locks them into an implacable determinism. When Charcot and his disciples modeled the bodies of their patients as they wished, when they made stigmata and convulsions appear or disappear under hypnosis, the doctor no longer assumed the role of the exorcist who delivered the possessed woman, but also that of the demon who haunted her. On this stage afforded by science, the Hysteric alienates herself as surely to the will of the therapist as the Witch had once enslaved herself to that of Satan. To exchange one alienation against another, by passing from the scaffold to the asylum: Here is what we hail a little hastily as a major progress of modern times.

Let there be no mistake: I am not nostalgic for the days of the stake. I only seek to understand what happened behind the reassuring fable of the "end of the witch hunt." Above all, I see a reconfiguration of the persecution apparatuses that, underpinned by the same schemes, by the same obsession with contagion, intrusion, and the evil conspiracy, reconstitute themselves by finding new enemies. I also see a mutation of these apparatuses that keep their old targets — witches and the possessed — by transforming themselves to integrate into the new apparatuses of exclusion and normalization of the insane. But this analysis needs to be extended: It may be that the decriminalization of witchcraft and the end of persecution are the manifestations of a historical dynamic that has profoundly transformed our relationship to the Body politic, to the law, to sovereign power. However, before addressing this question, we need to understand how the persecution apparatus operated in practice; and where these techniques of truth that modern psychiatry has inherited from the witch hunt come from — in the naive belief that they have a scientific value.

The story of Aldegonde de Rue has not yet revealed all its secrets. On the path that led her from her initial arrest to the stake, the mark of the devil had to be discovered on her body, and the torturer had to torment her so that she would confess the unspeakable. The signs that allow one to identify the heretic, the Jew, or the witch are always ambiguous: External appearance and allure are not enough, and the accusation needs to be supported by more solid evidence. The apparatus then turns to the body of its victim in search of a clue that was lacking, the visible or hidden mark that will make the difference, and it is then that Aldegonde falls into the hands of her persecutors.

2

A Death Mark

What defines a "witch"? At the time of the Great Hunt, it was first and foremost a *stigmatized* woman. This expression bears several meanings, both as a bodily marking and as a symbolic gesture of exclusion. Long before being accused and judged, Aldegonde had been the object of stigmatization: designated as a witch by the soldier, rejected to the margins of the village community by her social status and the muffled rumor that had latched onto her. For her to be burned at the stake, however, another stigma had to come into play, the mark that the torturer of Rocroi was to discover on her left shoulder. No longer dealing with a derived and metaphorical meaning of the stigma, we are now faced with a real trace, inscribed in the flesh, that confirms and accrues the previous stigmatization of which the old woman was a victim. What, then, is a stigma? What happens when one "stigmatizes" an individual or a group, or when one complains about being "unfairly stigmatized"? How did this word — which in Antiquity referred to the awl, the brand engraved with a red iron on the skin, the mark of infamy of condemned men and fugitive slaves — become in the Middle Ages the preserve of the greatest saints, before becoming today the attribute of the excluded, the abnormal, and the reprobate? Where do the *stigmata diaboli* — that witch-hunters claimed to find on the bodies of their victims — fit in this history? Seldom practiced in the early days of the hunt (the *Malleus* never mentions it), the search for the diabolical mark indeed appears beginning in the sixteenth century as the decisive criterion for identifying the witch with certainty. What does it consist of, and what role does it play in the persecution apparatus?

We have learned from Foucault that all power deals with the body. Every power apparatus connects itself directly to bodies, to constrain them, mark them, shape them, train them, make them more docile and productive. He established a typology of the different "corporeal devices" that allow the apparatuses to perform this function: devices of guarantee and trial, devices for extracting the truth, disciplinary devices of restraint . . .[1] One way or another, whether they hinder or mutilate, punish or train, all devices of power produce stigmata; but it is particularly the case of these "devices of marking and torture" that he evokes: By imprinting themselves on the tortured flesh, they manifest the omnipotence of a sovereign power over the bodies of its subjects. The stigma of the condemned is undoubtedly part of this type of device: When he marks Milady's shoulder with a fleur-de-lis, the executioner of Bethune there inscribes the seal of the king's justice. But this is not the case with the stigma of the witches, which the apparatus does not imprint on their bodies but rather seeks to uncover, as an *already present* but hidden trace of their subjection to Satan. Whence comes this haunting of a hidden mark that obsesses judges and executioners? If the apparatus took over an older element by altering its meaning, what previous practices were replaced by the search for the diabolical mark? If we want to understand its genesis, we need to write a history of the stigma. I will limit myself here to identifying a few milestones.

In 1610, cases of demonic possession multiplied among the Ursulines of Sainte-Baume. When the exorcists were called in, two of the possessed women accused their confessor, Louis Gauffridi, of being the "prince of sorcerers" and of having seduced them by magic to lead them to the Sabbath. Confronted by the young women, the priest from Marseille firmly rejected their accusations. The inquisitor Michaëlis then appealed to the authority of science: He sent for Doctor Fontaine, from the Faculty of Medicine in Aix-en-Provence. After having blindfolded Gauffridi, the eminent practitioner thrust long needles into his body — "in more than thirty places" — until he discovered on his kidneys an "enormous and deep mark of lust": an insensitive area where the patient did not seem to feel the prick. The evidence had been established; he was lost. Subjected to the *quaestio,* or interrogation by torture, Gauffridi confessed. He would be burned alive in Aix on April 30, 1611. According to an eyewitness, the crowd surrounding the stake was "large and enthusiastic," gathering more than three thousand people.[2] The same scenario reoccurred in 1634 during the possession of Loudun. This time, it was the demon Asmodeus himself who, speaking through the mouth of Mother Jeanne des Anges, guided the surgeon's hand and enabled him to find painless areas on Urbain Grandier's skin and sex. The body had spoken: Despite his denials, Grandier ended up on the stake. The two priests were thus added to the already long list of victims whom the ominous mark had sent to their deaths.

For about a century this practice had become established throughout Europe. According to an immutable ritual, the accused are stripped naked and completely shaved. Their bodies are carefully examined for any visible mark (a spot on the pupil, a wart, a nevus, or even a simple scar might do the trick); and if the test proves inconclusive, they are pricked with needles, sometimes reaching the bone in search of an invisible mark. As the theologian Jacques d'Autun explains, this mark presents itself as a "part [of the body] that seems dead or insensitive, since all the iron of an awl that is plunged into it causes neither water nor blood to come out, nor causes any pain to the sorcerer."[3] When dealing with suspects less well known than Gauffridi or Grandier, the judges did not necessarily resort to doctors, but to more or less improvised "prickers" (who could sometimes be butchers or torturers, chosen for their knowledge of anatomy). The judge de l'Ancre found this spectacle so entertaining that he would invite his friends to attend. The discovery of a spot insensitive to pain or that did not bleed through pricking was enough to convict the accused, even if he did not confess his "crimes" under torture. This is indeed deemed the "devil's point," the seal that he imprints on the bodies of his followers when they pledge allegiance to him. Why is insensitivity to pain an infallible criterion of a demonic character? A sixteenth-century author gives a significant answer: He recalls that to find out if a man was suffering from leprosy, the doctors used to stick an awl (a *stigma*) into the sole of his foot, looking for an area made insensitive by the disease; and this is still today, he adds, "a means of incurring the guilt of *sorcerers as well as scoundrels* [*ladres*]."[4] A profound continuity is thus revealed between the medieval persecution of lepers and the witch hunt. Before giving way to doctors, Renaissance judges had borrowed from them this technique that aims to detect a hidden evil. But the diabolical mark cannot be reduced to a single determination: Like the dream or the symptom, it is an overdetermined phenomenon, a skein of intertwined meanings that we must attempt to unravel.

If witch-hunters confer so much importance on this mark, it is because they are looking for concrete proof of the accused's guilt, a more reliable testament than mere rumors or confessions extracted under torture. The mark has the advantage of being inscribed in the reality of the body: By confirming that there was physical contact between Satan and the accused, it testifies irrefutably to the existence of the devil and the "witch's" crime. However negligible it may be, it is the *point of reality* that offers grounding for the whole system of accusation. It would be wrong to see there a superstition inherited from the Middle Ages. For the medieval Church, the very notion of a diabolical stigma was inconceivable: The only "stigmata" recognized were those of the Passion, or later those of mystics and saints. Like the use of torture, the search for the mark bears witness to a break with the old judicial rituals, to the emergence of another relationship to truth, where an "objective" experiment entrusted to experts substitutes the hazardous trials of God's Judgment. It thus testifies to a mutation in the history of truth and of the apparatuses intended to uncover it, but also to a profound transformation of the figure of the Enemy. What characterizes the diabolical mark above all is that it conceals itself, as befits the signature of the Great Deceiver. An obvious trace would not have been worthwhile: It is its elusive character that calls for the science of surgeons or the know-how of prickers. The search for the mark is thus part of the new *techniques of unveiling*, which appeared in the thirteenth century and which strive to dis-cover a truth that is evasive, to wrest it from an accused who refuses to confess it. It attests, in any case, the fact that the adversary of the sovereign power has ceased to be easily identifiable, that we are now dealing with a *hidden enemy*.

Indeed, this trace that is legible on the body will be as difficult to decipher as the divine will in the medieval ritual. The diabolical marks are not easily recognizable, and de l'Ancre raged against the cunning of the Evil One, who "often imprints them in parts so dirty that one is loath to go and look for them there," so that "the body would have to be torn apart to find [them]."[5] It is not only a question of discovering hidden marks but also of interpreting highly equivocal clues. Most demonologists agree that it is very difficult to distinguish diabolical stigmata from simple birthmarks or marks of accidental origin, and judges are sometimes deceived by impostors or unscrupulous prickers who use rigged needles. After having Aldegonde and many other women sentenced to death, the torturer of Rocroi was finally convicted of fraud and sent to the galleys. A similar misfortune befell two famous Scottish prickers, and their arrest put an end to the Great Hunt of 1661–62. In both cases, the justice system showed little mercy toward its auxiliaries: After all, they had only applied in their own way a fundamental principle of the apparatus, which creates each time the object over which it exercises its power. In a sense, every diabolical mark is a fabricated mark, a trace invested with meaning by the investigators — and it is not the signature of the devil, but that of the apparatus that invents it by claiming to discover it. Paradoxically, the equivocal character of the mark and the impostures of the prickers were not enough to discredit this practice, which would last as long as the witchcraft trials themselves. No doubt because it originates in deeply engrained beliefs, it brings into play the relationship of each subject to his or her body and subjective identity, the possibility of drawing a line between the same and the other, the proper and the foreign, the benevolent and the malevolent, the normal and the abnormal.

In Riom, in 1606, the young Madeleine des Aymards, aged thirteen, spontaneously confessed to a judge. She told him that she had met Satan, that he had ordered her to renounce God and the Church and had taken her to the Sabbath. After having copulated with her — which "caused her great pain" — the devil told her "that she was one of his own and that he wanted her marked [. . .] and, in fact, the said devil bit with his teeth into the right eye of the said deponent, and since that time the said deponent has seen very little from the said eye."[6] This exemplary account of stigmatization reveals different aspects of the satanic mark. Whether it is of natural, diabolical, or even divine origin, a stigma always imprints itself violently on the body, undermining its integrity: It suggests the threat of total destruction of the body, of its disincorporation. In Madeleine's case, this violence is almost akin to mutilation. During the first trials, the judges looked for traces of injury or amputation, since the demon was supposed to ask his followers for a part of their body, a finger, an arm, a leg.[7] In the centuries that followed, this sacrificial gift became a pact between two partners, from the mutilated body to the marked body, from the search for an apparent lesion to that of a trace that was most often invisible. To what mutation of the relationship to the body and to the malefic Other do these transformations bear witness? Would the mark be the substitute of a more radical lesion (a castration?) whose representation had become intolerable? Is it the trace of a forbidden *jouissance* that can only be experienced in suffering (coitus with the devil is considered excruciatingly painful) or in a total absence of sensations (like an insensitive area of the skin)? In any case, it is a signature, the seal that authenticates a transaction. The devil's *claw* is a paraph affixed to the skin, an equivalent, among illiterate peasants, of the pact attested by stories spread in cultured circles; and it is not indifferent that such a pact must be signed in blood. In fact, the literary theme of the pact with the devil is older than the search for the mark: It can already be found in the twelfth and thirteenth centuries in various versions of the *Miracle of Theophilus*. It is as if, at a certain epoch, the letter of the pact had come to be inscribed directly in the body. The archives of persecution sometimes attest to this shift: Indeed, a Swiss "wizard," arrested in Vevey in 1448, declares that he carries inside his body the parchment of the pact, which the devil had sewn between his flesh and his skin . . . Whether a bodily stigma or a contract, we are dealing in all cases with a sign of allegiance to Satan, which is also a sign of belonging to the community of his followers: The devil stigmatizes Madeleine because he "wanted her to be his." By marking her, he attests that he *owns* her, including sexually. For the judges, the witches' mark is incontrovertible proof of copulation with the devil, and this *coitus diabolicus* is a tacit pact in which the witch submits unreservedly to her master. In the end, the diabolic stigma has the same meaning as that which royal justice inflicts on the condemned. Whether it is the monarch or Satan, each time a sovereign power sanctions its domination by a bodily marking that identifies a man or a woman as its subject.

The demonological discourse hinges here on immemorial beliefs and practices, widespread in many cultures, where bodily marks play a decisive role in determining personal and collective identity. When dealing with a birthmark, it is often interpreted as a sign of election, an indication of royal or divine ancestry. If it is an acquired mark, it refers to those initiation rituals that, by imposing *symbolic wounds* (tattoos, incisions, or circumcision), define membership in a social category, a clan, an ethnic group. This initiatory value is present in the case of the stigma of witches: Their marking in fact ratifies their rupture with the Church, the mystical body of Christ, and their incorporation into another collective body, that of the satanic sect. This act of allegiance is accompanied by other gestures whose meaning is identical. By giving them a new name — most often a derisory sobriquet — Satan parodically renames his followers in order to erase the name baptism had conferred on them. He thus tries to eradicate God from his sovereign place, that of the *Father who names*, of the One in whose name the child receives his own name ("I baptize you in the name of the Father . . ."). The diabolic stigma thus has the meaning of a *countermark*, meant to replace the initial marking of baptism. This did not escape the attention of demonologists: As one of them declares, Satan marks his new followers with his "brand of slavery" in place of the Christian sacrament, "just as thieves change the brand on stolen cattle to their own mark."[8] The search for the mark thus takes on its full meaning: If stigmatization proves an initiation ritual, the discovery of the hidden stigma and the torture sessions that follow are a *counterritual* in which the power apparatus marks them in turn with its imprint. Since the stigma claims to replace the sign of Christ, by piercing the skin of their victims and breaking their limbs, judges and executioners reinscribe in their flesh the seal of the divine Master. Torture is then equivalent to a new baptism where the Church takes possession of the lost sheep: The supplicated body of the witch is this battlefield where God and the devil compete with successive markings that in turn are covered and erased.

The devil's sign is a countermark for yet another reason. In numerous myths, birthmarks are miraculous signs that allow one to recognize the royal or divine origin of heroes by conferring supernatural powers on them: invulnerability, the gift of prophecy, or the ability to heal. Whether it is the solar wheel visible on the soles of the feet of the ancient monarchs of India and Persia, the marks of Zarathustra and Buddha, the "seal of prophecy" of Mohammed (a wart between the shoulders), the "cross of the Royals of France," the sign on the right shoulder worn by the Capetian kings (said to have allowed Joan of Arc to recognize the future Charles VII), or the mark "in the shape of a crown and a lion" of James I of England, each time *the sovereign body is a marked body*.[9] How, then, can we distinguish it from the body of the condemned man or the henchman of Satan? The stigma appears indeed as an ambivalent sign, where the sacred and the abject, the mark of the sovereign power and that of its enemy, are at risk of becoming indistinguishable. In order to reduce its ambivalence, a network of symbolic oppositions intended to fix the stigma must be called upon, to assign it a univocal meaning. What differentiates the signs of the election of prophets and kings from the diabolic stigmata is not only the fact that they are visible, whereas the mark of Satan is most often invisible, or that they are birthmarks, whereas that of the devil is acquired. At stake is also their location on the body: The glorious mark is on the right side, whereas the devil almost always marks his followers on the left side. The difference between the divine and the demonic is thus inscribed directly on the body, in the spatial difference of left and right, whose symbolic meaning is the same in all human cultures. As the legendary stories about sacred or royal marks are much older than the search for a demonic mark, one can assume that the persecution apparatus appropriated an earlier element from folklore and myths. But it could only integrate this element into its belief system by inverting its meaning, giving an evil value to what was once the sign of a divine election; and this inversion manifests itself in the displacement that transfers it to the *sinister* side of the body (or in the lower and impure parts such as the vagina or the anus). Thus, the body of the witch appears as an inverted replica of the body of the divine king or hero, just as Satan appears as a counterfigure of God, his malevolent simulacrum, ruling over an inverted world.

Surely this inversion of meaning was favored by the existence of another kind of acquired mark, very different from the initiatory signs of recognition: the marks of infamy that the Ancients precisely called "stigmata." After having disappeared at the beginning of the Christian era, they reappeared and spread massively from the thirteenth century onward, but they were no longer engraved on the skin. From then on, they were insignia of clothing, the wearing of a particular attire: the yellow *rouelle* and pointed hat of the Jews, the "lazar's robe" and the clapper of lepers, and other lesser-known emblems sometimes imposed on madmen, prostitutes, heretics, and numerous categories of penitents and convicts. The *Manual* of the inquisitor Bernard Gui mentions the red cloth of slanderers and false witnesses, the yellow felt crosses of perjurers, and, in the case of priests accused of "charms and evil spells" or "misuse of sacraments," the obligation to wear a badge in the form of a host.[10] From these marks of infamy to the diabolical stigma of the witches, the lineage is not self-evident; because they are visually given, whereas the stigma is dissimulated, and they are external marks, symbols sewn on clothes, whereas the seal of the devil is inscribed directly in the body, taking after the ancient techniques of hot-iron branding. Why did they reappear — first in symbolic form — at the end of the Middle Ages? To what haunting does this *return of the stigma* attest? And how did we return from the garment to the skin or from the text of the pact to the corporal inscription of the mark, that is, from the symbolic to the real of the body, thus reviving practices that had disappeared for centuries?

One of the essential innovations of Christianity had indeed consisted in breaking with all religious forms of bodily marking, with the Hebrew rite of circumcision, but also with the scarifications and ritual castrations of the worshippers of Cybele and other pagan cults. If baptism resembles an initiation ceremony, it leaves no trace on the skin. The mark of Christ must remain invisible, purely spiritual because it signals the belonging to a community with a universal vocation, where there is henceforth "neither Jew nor Greek, neither man nor woman, neither free man nor slave." This very radical gesture of *de-marking*, of the abolition of all distinctive marks, will also lead to the prohibition of corporal stigmatization of convicts and slaves. Hereafter, it will be forbidden to harm the human face, the visible image of the divine Face. Marking practices would then be rejected to the side of evil and sin: Unlike birthmarks, all acquired marks tended to become marks of infamy, and they would retain this meaning when the practice of marking was reinstituted. They would only reappear about a thousand years later, when the Church decided in 1215, at the Fourth Lateran Council, to impose on Jews the wearing of insignia to distinguish them from Christians. Indeed, the decree states, in many regions "there is such confusion that nothing differentiates them. Whence it sometimes results that, thus deceived, Christian men unite with Jewish women, Jewish men with Christian women."[11] It is therefore a question of *re-marking a difference* that tends to disappear. It was to ward off this undifferentiation (of which sexual promiscuity was a major consequence), to better identify a figure of the *almost-same* — of the internal foreigner — that Jews were forced to wear the yellow *rouelle*. In France, the pious King Louis IX made it compulsory in 1269. This stigmatization was accompanied by several other discriminatory measures: It was at the same time that the first "jeweries" — the separate districts where Jews were forced to reside — appeared in the West and they were forbidden to practice the same trades as Christians, while accusations of ritual murder and profanation of the sacraments accrued. At the same time, analogous measures of marking and segregation were applied to lepers and prostitutes. There, too, it was the haunting of undifferentiation, of sexual promiscuity, of contagion through contact that motivated these exclusionary

practices. It seems that the decision taken by Louis IX in 1256 to confine prostitutes to their *bordeaux* and to enforce a distinctive sign on them was motivated
by a misadventure that happened to his wife. At church, Queen Marguerite
was said to have inadvertently given the kiss of peace to a prostitute "who did
not distinguish herself in any way from other women."[12] The diabolical mark
that witch-hunters tracked down is inscribed in this long history: It admits
the inversion of the meaning of the sign of election of heroes and kings, the
negative meaning of the symptoms of leprosy, and that of the signs of infamy
of Antiquity and of the Middle Ages, which are condensed to constitute a
new stigma.

Yet it is still necessary to understand how these *visible* marks of exclusion
were able to reappear during the witch hunt in the form of a *hidden* stigma.
Let us attempt a hypothesis: If the sign of difference has become invisible, it
is precisely because it tends to fade away as the exclusion apparatuses put in
place in the twelfth and thirteenth centuries — of which symbolic marking
was an essential component — *did not hold*. Whether applied to lepers or Jews,
the measures of discrimination that forced them into the closed space of the
jeweries and sick houses were not enough to ward off the threat of contagion
and undifferentiation. In the following century, on the occasion of a crisis for
which I will offer an analysis, exclusion would turn into persecution, and the
great massacre of lepers would be accompanied by numerous pogroms aimed
at their Jewish "accomplices." By passing from the yellow star and the ghetto
to the Final Solution in a matter of months, the Nazis repeated a curtailed
process that had already been experienced in Europe in the Middle Ages,
but in the very different context of a planned and centralized extermination
program. The transformation of exclusion apparatuses into persecution apparatuses thus implies a *failure of the mark*, a crisis of the differences and signs of
differentiation that drew a boundary between the inside and the outside, the
pure and the impure, the proper and the foreign. This erasure of the earlier
signs of exclusion will favor the unlimited extension of persecution: Since no
mark holds, it becomes impossible to distinguish and isolate the Enemy. It
seems then that the Enemy proliferates and infiltrates everywhere. All women
are witches, everyone is a suspect, that is, guilty, and nothing can stop the
dynamics of persecution any longer. Nothing, except a sign, a new stigma,
which would be able to identify the threat and thus circumscribe it. The
punctum diaboli plays here the role of a *point of fixation of hatred*: By allowing
the apparatus to identify its targets, it prevents the persecution from extending
indefinitely. In this sense, the appearance of this new stigma is equivalent to
a *re-marking* gesture, an attempt to reinscribe in the body a mark that falters
and keeps fading away. This attempt is doomed to failure, however, because

it goes against a more powerful dynamic that runs through the history of the West: This gesture of de-marking, of undifferentiation, this rejection of all stigmatization that the Christian faith holds out the promise.

After all, one would expect, in a religion where the Son of God was put to death on a cross, the stigma to take on a completely different meaning: that it would become a sign of glory and no longer of abjection since it can now be identified with the wounds of Christ. The Apostle Paul already hinted at this when he said in the Epistle to the Galatians that he "bears in [his] body the stigmata of Jesus." However, it was not until the beginning of the thirteenth century that fervent Christians, such as the beguine Marie d'Oignies, saw the bloody marks of the Passion imprinted on their own bodies. In 1224, during an ecstasy on Mount Verna, Francis of Assisi in turn received the Five Stigmata of the Crucified. Today, we can hardly measure the astonishment and incredulity of his contemporaries, who were confronted with a miracle that introduced an unprecedented form of bodily marking within a religion that had always condemned this practice. Among the admirable frescoes in the Basilica of Assisi that Giotto dedicated to the life of the Poverello, we can discover the scene of the "verification of the stigmata" where a layman, probably a doctor, kneeling next to the corpse of Francis, palpates the wound on his right flank. The authenticity of his stigmata had been violently contested by the opponents of the Franciscans: Some even claimed that they were lesions caused by leprosy. It took no fewer than nine papal bulls — and several posthumous appearances by the saint — to silence his detractors . . . It is worth noting that this return of the stigma in the Christian religion was contemporaneous with the decision to impose a distinctive mark on Jews. In both cases, we are witnessing a re-marking, an attempt to reinscribe marks in the visible, whether those of exclusion or those of election. This gesture becomes dangerously equivocal because the mark is henceforth divided between the glorious stigma of the saint and the sign of infamy of the Jew, the leper, and, later, the witch. This ambiguity would not leave the meaning of the diabolic mark unaltered. If mystics and saints are also marked, it becomes very difficult to distinguish the stigma of witches from those of divine origin that, like the wounds of Christ, also appear on the hand or the left flank. Could an objection be that, unlike the diabolical mark, the sacred stigmata visibly manifest themselves? Yet, sometimes the latter remained invisible, like the stigmata of Catherine of Siena, which would not be revealed until after her death. The two variants of the stigma appear more and more indistinguishable. No criterion is absolutely infallible, and nothing allows us to differentiate with certainty the saint from the witch, the Lord's elected from the devil's servant. There would come a time when victorious science would indiscriminately define all stigmata, diabolical or divine, as symptoms of hysteria. Charcot and his disciples will thus only ratify this becoming-undecidable of the stigma that condemns the search for the satanic mark to an inevitable failure.

From Golgotha to the Salpêtrière, we have traveled — much too quickly — through Western history to discover the origins and meaning of the witches' mark. Is this enough to elucidate its enigma? For the different forms of stigmata, tattoos, incisions, scarifications, piercings, with their ambivalent, evil or sacred, initiatory, punitive, or even erotic value, to be found in so many eras and cultures, they must be rooted in primordial experiences that are replayed in the history of each subject. To the historical genealogy of the stigma, we must articulate another approach, a phenomenological analysis that takes into account the relation of the ego to its body, to this bodily envelope that is its skin, to the orifices that pierce it, to the secretions that pass through it, to the traces that are inscribed on it. Unlike the witch's schemata-figures, which play such an important role in the persecution apparatus, the diabolic mark is almost always invisible. Where there is no trace left to be seen, it is up to the touch to reveal the hidden stigma. However, this is an insensitive area of the skin, which is not accessible to any tactile sensation. At this point where the touch comes up against its limit, the ego experiences the *untouchable*. By engraving itself in the flesh, the stigma reveals its most secret dimension, that part of my flesh that I cannot recognize as mine, that elusive, enigmatic phenomenon that is the invisible of my vision, but also the untouchable of my touch. The stigma is a *bodily inscription of the remainder*.

How can the remainder present itself in this very particular historical experience as the "devil's point," the imprint that Satan inscribes in the flesh? The recourse to egoanalysis proves necessary: It teaches us that the remainder can be disfigured, appear in my flesh like a dead thing, foreign to my flesh, thus awakening disgust and hatred; that the ego defends itself against this threat by rejecting the disfigured remainder outside and by projecting all its hatred on it. It is these phantasms that surface in the writings of the demonologists. According to them, the diabolical stigma can be recognized by two features that place it in relation to blood (it does not bleed through pricking) and death. A certain relationship to blood, as we shall see, plays a fundamental role in the exclusion and persecution schemata, as if its ambivalent value made it a privileged representative of the remainder. The most characteristic feature of the stigma, however, is its insensitivity to pain, anesthesia that makes it look like a "dead part" of the body, a "mark of death." These are the terms used by the theologian Jacques d'Autun as well as by the physician Fontaine: It is a question, says the latter, of "dead parts made such by the malice of the devil, who only vies for the death of our soul and body." What has been mortified by Satan can, nevertheless, be resurrected by the grace of God, as attested by the case of one of the possessed of Sainte-Baume whose diabolic stigmata miraculously disappeared on the blessed day of Easter. This proves, he concludes, that God has "the capacity to erase the marks [. . .] by breathing life into the parts which were already dead."[13] One would be wrong to neglect such indications: As strange and ludicrous as it may seem, the "knowledge" of the apparatus contains a kernel of truth. It expresses original schemata and experiences in a deformed way, and what Fontaine affirms about the witch or the possessed is, in a certain sense, valid for each of us. All flesh is a battlefield where are confronted a force of death — an Opponent that might conceivably be called *Satan* — and a more powerful principle of resurrection and life. In the case he describes, this primordial battle is manifested by the appearance and disappearance of a stigma, of a piece of flesh, apparently dead, that comes back to life; and it can take many other forms, which thought, art, or faith have tried to name. But we no longer need to look for an external cause for such phenomena, to attribute them to the action of a transcendent Principle that would imprint itself from outside on the bodies. It is in the immanence of the ego and its flesh, in the mutations of the remainder, its disfigurations and transfigurations that originate the oscillations between hatred and love, the passage from life to death, from death to resurrection of the flesh. Perhaps we understand better how the diabolic or divine nature of the stigma became undecidable. On the plane of immanence, the force of life and the force of death are one and the same: It is the same phenomenon, the primordial phenomenon of the remainder, that manifests itself in two opposite forms.

Nevertheless, if egoanalysis allows one to describe its immanent genesis, it cannot tell us anything about the historical destiny of the figures of the remainder. To know what happened to its bodily inscription in the form of the stigma, we had to resort to a historical genealogy. This showed us that the signs of exclusion and persecution that appeared historically come to fade away; that no stigma could resist this movement that carries through the history of the West, this *de-marking* of all distinctive marks, this process of de-differentiation, of disincorporation of collective Bodies that continues for centuries under various forms. One can thus understand that the witch-hunt apparatus failed to re-mark its victims, to reinscribe on the tactile plane the signs of infamy that were already fading on the visible plane. At the apogee of persecution, the most lucid demonologists had already realized that the stigma always eludes one's grasp. According to Bodin, "the greatest sorcerers are not marked, or else in such a secret place that it is impossible to discover." As for Judge Boguet, he acknowledged that he had never been able to find a single one of these marks. Therefrom he concludes that "the devil most often erases the marks of witches as soon as they are imprisoned," and he recommends that they be condemned to death, even if no trace of the diabolical stigma is found on them.[14] Charcot, three centuries later, would echo them: "All these stigmata are constant in hysteria, but, in spite of their constancy, I have to admit that it often happens that we do not find them all or even, in rare cases, that we find none at all."[15] The search for the satanic mark, which the demonologists presented as irrefutable proof, is therefore no longer sufficient to unmask the witch: It will be necessary to have recourse to other practices, even more cruel, to force the accused to confess the ineffable.

3

Confessing the Truth

By the time Doctor Fontaine had discovered the devil's mark on his ribs, Louis Gauffridi would undergo "the *quaestio*."[1] According to his interrogation's transcript, Judge Ollivier demanded that "he tell the truth or face torment." Given his answer that he had already told the truth, they began to torture him, asking him, "if some devil is keeping him from saying the truth." He shouted: "I will tell you, *Messieurs*! [. . .] I met Madeleine at the synagogue, yet I had known her before." They tortured him yet again so that he would betray his accomplices: "[We] attached a big rock to his feet. [He] said that the devil had taken away his memory. [We] ordered that he be brought up to the great Gehenna [. . .] [He] said, screaming: 'No, I'll say everything!' and again: 'I do not know why you torment me. No, I do not know. Ah! *Monsieur* Ollivier, you are a devil!' Admonished to tell the truth, hung from the highest point [. . .] [He] said that he would tell the truth once brought down [. . .] [He] was warned that, now that he had been brought down, he must tell the truth [. . .] [He] said that he knew of no accomplices. Was ordered that he be hoisted up a third time. [He] said: 'I'll say it!' [. . .] He was hoisted up once more. He was given the strappado [. . .] Having been brought down [he] said: 'No, you torment me! I waive my place in paradise if I know one!'"[2]

How does this text inform us on the practice of torture? Every time he is questioned, Gauffridi admits to his crimes; he acknowledges that he has sexually "known" Madeleine de la Palud, one of the two possessed charging him with witchcraft—whom he had brought to the "Synagogue," that is, the Sabbath (it is precisely this confession that sends him at the stake)—and he promises to denounce his accomplices. At the first sign of reprieve, he takes back his confessions if only to give in once more as the torture starts anew. We begin here to see the distance that separates us from the men of the seventeenth century. Indeed, it seems clear to us that such confessions, extorted under torture, have no value. Yet the magistrates leading the interrogation are convinced of the opposite: For them, the tortured is telling the truth at the moment of his agony, and he is once more lying — or falls under the devil's sway — as soon as his suffering is eased. The tools of torture are truth-producing machines. Whether they force Gauffridi to admit it, or he promises to tell it, or the devil forces his silencing of it, the word "truth" reappears obsessively throughout the interrogation. The commonplace nature of this atrocious scene, for its time, tells us that torture is exercised *in the name of the truth*. The judges interrogating him are part of a long-lived tradition: Ulpian, a third-century Roman jurist, had already defined the *quaestio* as "the torments and sufferings of the body" that were to be inflicted *ad eruendam veritatem*, "to discover the truth" — or, better yet, to wrench or extract it, with the verb *eruere* always implying a degree of violence (*ruée* and "eruption" are lexical cognates). Would the use of torture during the classical age be a survival — the barbaric heritage — of less enlightened epochs? In no way. Historians teach us conversely that, for the longest time, the Middle Ages had little recourse to torture. As for the witch hunts and the quest for the devil's mark, the systematic use of the *quaestio* is a properly modern phenomenon. What's at stake here is not torture as a punitive practice, which remains widespread throughout history, but "interrogative" torture, or the *quaestio*, as a tool for extracting confessions from its victims. Admitted with great restrictions under Roman law, it would completely disappear by the Empire's end. Denounced by the Church Fathers, ignored by the Franks and Germanics, the *quaestio* remained proscribed for about seven centuries. As such, in 866, Pope Nicholas I would remind that it was "contrary to divine and human laws" and that extorted confessions bore no value. It would only be reintroduced within the judiciary proceedings at the beginning of the thirteenth century, before massively spreading about in the following centuries. It appears patent that the *quaestio* was in large part responsible for the intensity of the witch hunts, since the confessions of the victims who were ordered to denounce their "accomplices" entailed the arresting of other victims who would, in turn, denounce others. Indeed, during the Great Witch Hunt of Bamberg, Margreth Kerner, tortured through an entire night, gave up the names of 126 "witches." This is how the apparatus gets carried away and persecution gives way to generalized terror. Yet in countries like England where judiciary torture was not common practice, persecution never quite rose to such magnitudes, and when Denmark forbade the use of the *quaestio*, the mass execution of "witches" ceased immediately.

It was a reform of the judiciary proceedings that brought judges to reintroduce this long-forgotten practice. For centuries, the tribunals were aligned with an "accusatory" procedure. At the end of the twelfth century, this gave way to a new "inquisitorial" procedure that became slowly but surely established throughout most of Europe. What had characterized the accusatory procedure was the possibility for a private person to set forth the accusation. Throughout the trial, the judge was to stay an impartial arbiter, never substituting himself for the accuser. The confession of the accused was not considered sufficient ground for their conviction as the judge was not looking for *proofs* of their guilt: He arbitrated a trial whose victorious party was by the same token exculpated. This is why he often resorted to a trial by ordeal, by "God's judgment." These trials could take the form of a trial by combat to the death (as God would ineluctably make the truthful victorious) or a ritual trial: The accused was to hold a red-hot iron or pass through a blaze without burning himself, or he was trussed and thrown in a river blessed by a priest: If he were to float without sinking, it meant that the water refused to welcome the guilty and he would be condemned. As if a religious ritual were at play, the priest's involvement proved indispensable. By forbidding in 1215, during the Fourth Council of the Lateran, the consecration of the instruments of the ordeal, the Church struck a devastating blow to divine judgment and to the entire procedure to which it would put an end. The inquisitorial procedure that would replace the accusatory one entailed several major innovations. Henceforth, the judge and not the plaintiff would begin procedures; he would be within his rights to do so without a submitted complaint, on the basis of mere rumor, or of the "bad reputation" (*infamia*) of the accused. And above all, it would no longer be incumbent on the ordeal to establish the truth; instead, the *inquisition* was destined to unveil it, this *inquisitio* that gives its name to the procedure. How does one account for such transformations? It could be that this transformation mainly sanctioned the difficulty of interpreting the trial as attributing without ambiguity the results of the ordeal to God. The authors of the *Malleus* condemned the trial of red-hot iron for this reason in cases of witchcraft: as the demon "could invisibly lodge something between the hand and the red-hot iron to preserve the hand from burning."[3] As for the stigma of witches or saints, as for the cases of possession some centuries later, the ordeal—sign of God or cunning of the Devil—had risked becoming *indecisive*. Paramount, then, was the need to replace it with a more reliable method: to establish the truth through rational means by searching for actual proofs of the accused's guilt or innocence. By supplanting the ordeal's ritual magic, the institution of the *inquisitio* partook in the "disenchantment of the world": It bore witness to a rationalization of juridical procedures and coincided with the process of secularization of law. And, paradoxically, this same progress of rationality would reintroduce torture in judiciary procedure and foster the persecution of "witches" in the subsequent centuries . . .

With the advent of the *inquisitio*, Foucault recognized a new exercise of power and knowledge that would mark Western history to this day. He assigned two different sources for its emergence: a political origin, linked to the consolidation of the Medieval State; and a religious one, ecclesial, wherein the *inquisitio* is firstly a spiritual inquiry on the sins for their atonement.[4] According to him, the *quaestio* and the confession are the mise-en-scène of a *sovereignty rite*. He is right to insist on their political meaning: As the history of Roman law already suggests, the extension of judiciary torture is inseparable from the "lèse-majesté crime," that is, the affirmation of the sovereignty of the State.[5] Yet we may ask ourselves whether Foucault took into account an essential aspect of this process. Through the passage from the "ordeal game" to the "inquiry system" in the thirteenth century, God's judgment is replaced by that of men — or rather of a man, a magistrate who accuses, leads the inquiry, and sentences. Endowed with all powers, the human judge takes the place of the divine Judge. What appeared as a simple reform of judiciary procedures attests in fact to a radical mutation in the relationship with truth, and this would affect the totality of the apparatuses of power. By going from God to Man, the truth changed subjects but also its criteria and modality of unveiling because this mutation displays the relation between juri-diction and veri-diction, between the power of distinguishing the just and the unjust and that of articulating the truth. In the accusatory system, God is the guarantor of law, because he is the *subject of truth*, the omniscient Eye that "probes the kidneys and the hearts." The truth always comes from the Other — the divine Subject — and this is why a man's confession isn't a conclusive proof; or, at the very least, it is less significant than the result of the ordeal. The judge is not an investigator aiming to establish the truth by himself: He is a hermeneut, entrusted to interpret the forever ambiguous signs of divine Will, to evaluate if the accused has sunk quickly enough to the bottom of the river or if the burn is deep enough. Through the new procedure, Man would become the subject of truth, yet this subject becomes immediately twofold since he is both the judge who tracks down the truth but also he who knows the truth and yet refuses to reveal it to the judge: the accused himself.

The inquiry system called for a *wresting of the truth* where confessions became a decisive proof, so that an accused who would refuse to confess could not be condemned. The judge would thus exert himself to obtain confessions by wresting the truth, notably in the case of "secret crimes" where material proofs were lacking. Yet in this new configuration, *all* major crimes could be considered as unutterable (*nefanda*), secret crimes for which the confession must be wrested by force. If the accused must be compelled to tell the truth, it's because he is dissimulating it—that the concealed truth demands to unveil: The inquiry system thus presumed a *principle of dissimulation* that justified the recourse to *inquisitio* techniques, including the cruelest ones. This principle would play an essential role in the new apparatuses and techniques of unveiling that they in turn implement. Their apparition would indeed be accompanied by a redefinition of what constitutes a secret and a new figuration of the enemy, represented thus forth as the *hidden enemy*. When the enemy was apprehended as countless multitudes, a shift would occur from the confession of secret crimes committed by isolated individuals to the tracking down of a criminal *secret society* conspiring against Church and State. In both cases, the recourse to the *quaestio* proves necessary to obtain the Secret's confession. From an etymological view, *inquisitio* and *quaestio* are cognates, and both practices are historically inseparable. In fact, the ban on trials by ordeal by the Lateran Council would be quickly followed by the legalization of the *quaestio*, which would gain a foothold during the thirteenth century. We can designate the process—characteristic of modernity—which dispossesses God of his prerogatives and transfers them to the human subject as a phenomenon of *secularization*. Thus, the rehabilitation of torture is but a consequence of the progressive secularization of truth, power, and law. We find a remarkable counterexample in regions where this secularization had not taken place: If judicial torture was never imposed in Islamic lands, it was precisely because of a religious motive, since the human judge cannot take the place of God by seeking to probe the hidden motivations of the accused. This is why a *qadi* who executed an accused party after obtaining his confession under torture risked being himself, in turn, sentenced to death.[6] Yet the judge-inquisitor would henceforth supplant not only God; by sustaining the accusation throughout the procedure, he equally occupied the function of another character that the religious tradition had finally distinguished from God, that of "Satan," the *Accuser* in the literal sense, the Prosecutor who pleads against Job before the celestial Judge. It is surely not by chance that the *quaestio* (or rather one of its phases) was designated by one of the age-old names for hell, the "Gehenna": By attributing to a single magistrate the charge of judge and accuser, by allowing him to embody both God and Satan, the new procedure would soon unleash hell on earth. Perhaps Gauffridi had foreseen this when, attached to the trestle, he shouted, "*Monsieur* Ollivier, you are a devil!"

The role played by the Church in the abolition of a ritual that abolished God's judgment may come as a surprise. Perhaps the Church only consecrated an ongoing mutation since secular jurists had been the first to question the ordeal, and the inquiry system had already intruded on civil jurisdiction.

Instead of confronting the new procedure, the Church would strive to sway it for its own end by integrating it into its own power apparatuses. And this in two distinct ways: by creating a new judicial institution so intricately meshed with the *inquisitio* that the Church would later borrow its name; and by inventing, outside the field of law, a new form of inquiry, a new apparatus of subjectivation grounded on a particular confessional technique. In 1231, Pope Gregory IX instituted an extraordinary tribunal operating according to the inquisitorial method in order to fight against the Cathar heresy. This tribunal was chaired by clerics, directly appointed by the Holy See, who took the title of inquisitors. Most of these clerics were Dominican members of the Order of Preachers created just after Lateran IV, and their motto (unsurprisingly) was *Veritas*. Admittedly, the founder of the order, Dominic de Guzmán, had sought to combat heresy by nonviolent means and by the sole virtue of predication. Yet before the rooster crowed, his disciples would betray Dominic's message by agreeing, shortly after his death, to take charge of the Inquisition's trials . . . From the start, we are clearly dealing with an exceptional jurisdiction, freed from the mooring that restricted the other courts, because it was intended to combat a crime itself exceptional: the "divine lèse-majesté crime" of heresy. The Inquisition did not, therefore, invent the inquisitorial procedure, as is often believed: The procedure, through its generalization, would pave the way for the creation of an institution commissioned to ensure its practice in the domain of faith — and it is the logic of this procedure that would move the Inquisition toward the use of torture. In 1252, Pope Innocent IV authorized the recourse to the *quaestio*, but the canonical rule *Ecclesia abhorret a sanguine* (the Church abhors shedding blood) forbade clerics to participate in the act of torture. The pope would parry by authorizing the inquisitors to take turns torturing and absolving each other from this offense . . . Soon after, the saint king Louis IX would legitimize the use of the *quaestio* by secular tribunals of the French kingdom. A *right to torture* was born that would last five hundred years[7] — and this new right and the procedures that it would authorize would play a major role during witch hunts. It would soon become quite perilous to contest the recourse to the *quaestio* during witchcraft trials: For having contested it, the Italian jurist Ponzinibio would be accused of "heresy" by the Inquisition. Taking into account the function that assured the use of torture and the confession of the "truth," here we must narrow the analysis of the apparatuses of persecution. By this term, I designate the apparatuses of power that do not seek either the exclusion of the public sphere, or to discipline through normalization, but to locate their targets and to annihilate them. Now, we recognize that these apparatuses have taken different forms, for which the totalitarian terrors of the twentieth century have provided new examples. We must here distinguish strategies of persecution that aim at the pure and simple extermination of their victims and the ones that seek their subjugation by bringing them to renounce themselves in the form of a "confession" or "autocritique" before putting them to death. If the former ones are satisfied with destroying the bodies, the latter intend to dominate the souls, to extend their dominion over the deep interiority of their victims' consciousness. While the extermination of Armenians, Jews, and Tutsis belongs to the first mode of persecution, the witch hunts, as Stalin's terror, belong to the second type of apparatus. We must now ask which fundamental positions underlie and differentiate judicial terror from exterminating terror.

This is a secularization process, a transfer from God to Man of the power of stating the truth that reintroduced the *quaestio* in the judicial inquiry: In this sense, the use of torture is an eminent manifestation of modern Humanism. However, there remain no clear demarcations between the ancestral logic of God's Judgment and the "modern" use of torture. Each time, we witness a confrontation between the accused and the institution judging him, and it is upon the body of the accused — in its resistance to torture or the traces inscribed on it by the ordeal — that can be deciphered signs of guilt or innocence. In both cases, this event presents itself as a *trial of truth*, ruled by ritual procedures in which a power apparatus maintains its grip on the body. This is why Foucault would claim that the confession is "one of the remnants of the accusatorial procedure transferred within the inquisitorial procedure."[8] Some authors insist on this dimension of the *quaestio*, that of a spiritual trial where the truth is unveiled: They present it as a kind of asceticism, a cathartic ritual where the confession of truth would *purify* the accused, thus giving him back his true freedom. Lorraine's "plague of witches," the bloodthirsty prosecutor Nicolas Rémy, also maintained that the sufferings of the *quaestio* would be for the accused "the starting point of salvation": "Through this, God would purify them of their wrongdoings," and he would insist that "they were unanimous in reiterating that their first day of freedom was, in their misery, when the judge unleashed the terrifying violence of torture upon them."[9] This belief was largely upheld by the accused themselves: Thus a so-called witch of Moyemont in the Vosges implored her judges to inflict the *quaestio* on her as she "wished so adamantly to be purged of her crime that if we were to send her back free and honest to her dwelling, she would refuse to go, so staunchly she desired purgation."[10] Whether it appeals to the Judgment of God or to the justice of men, whether it presents itself as a spiritual trial or as a rational proof, it is always in the name of the truth that the ritual is implemented, of a truth that must be engraved in the flesh in letters of blood. As for the ordeal, the *quaestio* is inscribed in the long-lasting history of truth, a history of rituals and techniques that allow the apparatuses of power to decipher it on the bodies and to extract it from the souls, to extort it through cunning or violence, to have it confessed. And it is the same will to truth that will provoke the abandonment of the *quaestio* during the eighteenth century: The jurist Thomasius would dispute it in his *Essay on Torture* — which would lead to its abolition in the Prussian kingdom — not for humanitarian reasons but in the name of a justice that would be fairer because it would be *more truthful* and would be based on more reliable means of establishing the truth. Indeed, he rejected torture as a "deceptive mean of uncovering the truth," to such an extent that "after having applied it, the judge would have no more certainty with regard to the crime than prior to its use."[11] Henceforth dissociated from the "barbaric" practice of the *quaestio*, the inquisitorial techniques and the rituals of confession would maintain their grasp through new forms, in more subtle strategies of control, discipline, and normalization. Only until Stalin's secret police, a worthy heir of the Inquisition, would once more dignify torture and confession as instruments of mass terror.

However, whether the use of torture played a decisive role in the ritual of confession remains a question. It seems that a large number of so-called witches — perhaps a majority — would "spontaneously" admit their belonging to a satanic cult, without having undergone the *quaestio*. Would the simple fear of torture incite their confession? The judges willingly practiced the *quaestio ad terrendum*, exhibiting — through an elaborate mise-en-scène — the instruments of torment in order to "terrify" the accused, and it sometimes sufficed to break him, as was the case for Galileo . . . Or perhaps, as René Girard has done, a "mimetic drive" should be invoked where the accused would identify himself to his judge?[12] It would be an affront to the victims to presume that they confessed simply because they wanted to "imitate" their persecutors; this all-purpose explanation does not clarify what is concretely at stake in the ritual of the confession and what specific strategies made it possible. One of the last trials in France serves as a significant example. Shortly before a decree from Louis XIV decriminalized witchcraft, the fires of immolation glowed in the summer of 1679 in the village of Bouvignies in Flanders. Before being put to death, Jeanne Goguillon had denounced other villagers, among them a peasant named Jeanne Bachy. The latter represented herself before the judges and confronted her accusers by energetically rejecting the accusations made against her: "*Hé bien*, if I am a witch, I pray God would have allowed me knowledge of it!"[13] To the judges pressing her to reveal the name of her familiar spirit, she retorted that they "compel her to say more than she knows." And yet without even being tortured she slowly lost her confidence and admitted a few days later that she "knows well deep down that she has something to say [. . .] without knowing what it could be." Her entire body was shaved, pierced with needles by the prickers, and its most intimate parts scrutinized. Although no marks of the devil were found on her body, this humiliating ritual had unsettled her, as she would confess that "she had noticed, since being shaved, that she was afraid of being a witch." What tormented her, she declared, was that she belonged to "a lineage that could never confess," since her mother had been erstwhile accused of witchcraft. It is yet another ritual that would break her resistance. Indeed, during the trial, she recounted that she heard "something around her that troubles and scares her" at night in solitary confinement and that she addressed this prayer to it: "Tell me if you are my Familiar. Tell me your name. They always ask me, and I cannot answer them." It is not to the God of her forefathers that she addressed her prayers; rather, the request Jeanne formulated from the depths of her cell shares an uncanny resemblance with that of Moses when confronted with the burning bush, as if the knowledge of the secret name of the Other, be it God or the devil, were at each time at stake. The judges, having concluded that a demon haunted her and hindered the confession, would have her repeatedly exorcised. She would collapse at that moment: She declared "that she had been damned, that she needed neither priest nor justice, that she would only ask for her executioner, that she had nothing left to say." Paradoxically, it is the ritual meant to expel the devil from her body that succeeded in injecting the poison of self-accusation in her soul, to implant the Great Accuser, *Satan*, in her. She then revealed her ultimate secret to her judges, the name of her devil, that is to say, *Verbouton* . . . She would be burned at the stake, after having denounced ten of her "accomplices," a few of whom would also be executed.

It is always difficult to locate, for the human subject, the breaking point where resistance capitulates and is inverted into submission. Orwell admirably described the crossing of this abjection point, which brought Winston, in the chamber of torture of the Love Ministry, to renounce himself and love *Big Brother*.[14] We will never know what exactly — in the apparatus that held her under its sway — led Jeanne Bachy to relinquish herself. Had it been the anxiety that took hold of her when she recounted her lineal guilt? She had been taught that there were cursed families, "races of smoke" destined to the stake; and she had to expiate her mother's crime as if she had been mysteriously contaminated by her. Of course, Jeanne shared with her accusers the same system of belief, which would forbid her to contest the grounds of the accusation. Besides, we know that during the period of the witch hunts, none of the accused ever questioned the fundamental belief in the existence of the devil, a devil capable of manifesting itself to humans, of seducing them, of "possessing" or copulating with them by imprinting its mark, as this belief was an essential component of their Christian faith. Yet this set of beliefs would remain inoperative had they not materialized themselves in a series of rituals that would give them consistency through their inscription on the bodies. A bare and shaved body, larded with needles and scrutinized in its most intimate parts, a body exorcised by the old rite of conjuration that strives to root out a sinister Other. Thus, doctored by the surgeons and the priests, the body of the accused lost all its force of resistance without even having to call for a torturer. Yet these beliefs and rituals would have most likely not sufficed to break her down had she not possessed the deeply instilled certainty that there was "something she had to say." Surely, she had not yet known what she had to say, but she knew nevertheless that she had to say it, to reveal the name of the unnameable: And the only way she could exempt herself from the lineal malediction — of a lineage that "cannot confess anything" — would require her to confess. What trapped Jeanne, what subdued her body and soul to the exorcists and judges, was her shared will to the truth with her accusers and the formulas and rituals necessary for its expression that had been instilled in her since infancy. She knew that the confession of guilt would be essential to salvation.

As Foucault has shown, since the Middle Ages, "confession has become one of the Western societies' most valuable techniques for the production of truth": In his literature, justice, medicine, love relationships, Western man "has become a confessing animal."[15] Witch hunts would certainly not have assumed such magnitude if so many of the accused had not rushed to confess their misdeeds and designate "accomplices," and they would not have done it with such docility had the Church not subjected them to this particular avowal technique: the confession ritual. It has not been underscored enough that the same Fourth Council of the Lateran that had forbidden the ordeal also made possible a surge in inquisitorial procedures and imposed on each believer, since the age of seven, the obligation to confess sins to a priest at least once a year. This was a novel measure, unprecedented in the history of Christianity, and entailed an imperative obligation: The priests would also receive the order to denounce to their bishop the faithful who would try to avoid it . . . If the adoption of the inquisitorial procedure — and the torture legislation that "accompanied it like a shadow" — sanctioned the apparition of a new truth technique, we must recognize that this applied simultaneously in two domains. In the cries that resonated across torture chambers and the mumblings of confession, the same science of avowal is at play. Whether it is the "external forum," that is to say, the apparatus of the judicial inquiry, or the internal forum of a conscience that aspires to penance and forgiveness, it is the same lexicon that characterizes them, that is to say, *forum* or court.

The theologians would also strive to translate the successive steps of penitence in strictly juridical terms: Confessions — as trials — begin with interrogation and correspond to the avowal of the accused, as the priest's absolution would be analogous to the accused's acquittal. The Church during the thirteenth century thus invented an *internal Inquisition* that would become far more efficient than the Holy Office's judges and torturers when it came time for probing consciences and redressing them for voluntary servitude.

Our purpose here is not to retrace the long history of the Sacrament of Penance, meant to absolve the sinner after reconciliation and remission of sins. The sacrament, which first appeared during the early days of the Church, was based on Christ's gift of the "keys of the kingdom" to Peter the Apostle — that is to say, the power to unbind and forgive sins. This sacrament was dispensed in various manners: At times the confession was public, in front of an assembly of the faithful, and at times private, imposing a merely material reparation as a form of penitence or insisting instead on the "heart's contrition" as a necessary step for a veritable spiritual conversion. However, the sacrament never became an obligation. Another form of confession, infinitely more rigorous, was long in the making in the silence of cloisters. In the discipline schools that were monasteries, a new figure appeared, that of the *director of the conscience*: the abbot or the "elder" to whom the monk was required to confess each of his thoughts, each of his actions, to the point of having to reveal to him "the number of steps he takes in his cell and the number of drops of water that he drinks, to know if in that he does not sin."[16] This monasterial rule of frequent and detailed confessions, with the immense disciplinary power it gave the confessor, would be imposed on all Christians by Lateran IV. By instituting a periodical "conscience examination," the Church would implant the obsession with sins in the Christian Western world, thus developing and refining techniques of self-accusation, introspection, and self-control — and appropriating for itself the exclusive mastery of these techniques, *ad majorem gloriam Ecclesiae*. Beforehand, it had been quite possible for a secular person to receive a confession and give absolution. By making confessions mandatory, imposing their regular and repeated use, and reserving the power of absolving sins to priests alone, the decisions of the Council conferred a crushing authority on the Church. A significant modification of the sacramental rite attests to this evolution: For centuries, the confessor would absolve in the name of God, uttering *Deus te absolvat a peccatis tuis* (God absolves you of your sins). After Lateran IV, this becomes *ego te absolvo* . . . (I absolve you . . .): hereafter, it is not for God to forgive, but the Church's priest as the unique beholder of the *power of the keys*.[17] We find on this plane the same turning point, the same transfer of power from God to the human Subject that we had already recognized in legal proceedings — and yet again, this secularization process, far from liberating men, subjugates them through a more implacable apparatus.

Nothing could resist the holy alliance of the confessor and the torturer. A proof of this formidable alliance's effectiveness? While *none* of the Cathar or Waldensian heretics had recognized the charges made against them (worshiping the devil, profanation of the sacraments, cannibalism, infanticide . . .), the vast majority of "wizards" and "witches" arrested and questioned in the following centuries would end up confessing to the same crimes. Thus, the new techniques of unveiling had pushed back the limits of the unutterable: What appeared as a *crimen nefandum*, an offense "impossible to name," so monstrous that it could not even be formulated, would be precisely what the inquisitors and confessors would wrest in confession. What does this unutterable crime concern? Since Ancient Rome, two types of infractions were considered *nefanda*, those regarding major sexual transgressions, viz. incest, and those infringing on the *majestas*, human or divine sovereignty — so-called crimes "of lèse-majesté." The new apparatus would seek confession for these two crimes. Whereas the inquisitors and judges pursued all offenses to the majesty of the Church or the King, the confessors concentrated their efforts on sexuality. Innumerable manuals of confession would orient the confession ritual toward sexual practices, compelling penitents to describe their dreams and most intimate behavior in accurate detail; there is every reason to believe that our imaginings of sex, our science of sexuality, and even our erotic techniques take root in this confessional literature. Yet what defined the crime of witchcraft since the end of the Middle Ages was its position at the convergences of these two major transgressions. Assimilated to heresy, that is, a "divine lèse-majesté" crime, witchcraft was also condemned, as we will see, as a political crime, as an attack on royal majesty. At the same time, witchcraft also belonged to the other modality of the *nefandum* as a sexual crime: and what we call a witch hunt was foremost a *sex hunt*, the unflagging hunt for sexual transgressions and the veiled truth of sex. For judges, a witch is not only a caster of spells whose curses provoke poor harvest and cattle's death: She is the one who participates — in the shadows of Sabbath — in frenzied orgies, sodomy, and incest; before all things she is the perpetrator of the *coitus diabolicus*, offering herself sexually to the devil and bearing his mark on her flesh as a result. Doubly aimed, both as a rebel to all majesties and as the "devil's whore" (as Luther had named her), she would be the elected target of a bilateral use of the apparatus. That the persecution of wizards quickly became witch hunts is explained by this very fact. The Church had long ago designated the Woman as the instigator of the sexual Sin; demonologists would make her an accomplice of forbidden *jouissance*: the cold and cruel *jouissance* they called *Satan*.

Thus, two power-knowledge devices, two functions of the same apparatus, combine efforts to flush out the witch and force her to confess: Whereas one torments the body, the other breaks the soul. The judge and the confessor are both convinced that the accused is under a demon's spell that impedes the confession: They regard her as a *possessed* who must be exorcised. Hence all means used to extract the truth from her benefit her soul's salvation. Too often have rural witches and the possessed of cities or convents been opposed: The former freely gave herself up to the devil, whereas the latter was insidiously penetrated by the devil; one is burned at the stake, whereas the other can be exorcised and saved. What's lost is that both figures appear most often indissociable: as is the case for the witch Rolande du Vernois, whose execution Judge Boguet ordered in September 1600, even though an exorcist had taken out the demon in her mouth in the form of a black slug.[18] Likewise, the Great Witch Hunt that swept over Germany was accompanied by massive possession phenomena affecting both sexes and people of all conditions: Nearly 150 males possessed in the small town of Friedeberg . . . In fact, what distinguishes the witch from the possessed is their respective place in the apparatus designed to extort the truth. If a witch is one whom another witch (or public rumor) has denounced as such, the possessed *is the one who denounces* another as a wizard or witch, as in the case of sisters of Sainte-Baume who accused Gauffridi or those of Loudun who sent Urbain Grandier to the stake. Whereas the witch has to be constrained to confess the "truth," the possessed utters it herself, proclaims it loud and clear with the demon's voice that speaks through her. In this terrifying voice that substitutes itself with her own voice, we clearly recognize that of the Accuser, of the inner Inquisition that the apparatus has implanted in her. As penitent, the possessed is an exemplary *confessing animal* by virtue of actively consenting to her subjugation. By yielding to the exorcist's injunctions and crying out the name of the "witches" whom she is sending to their deaths, she bears witness through her contorted body of the triumph of the new techniques intended to ease the unveiling of the truth.

The apparatus wouldn't be perturbed by the resistance of its victims, prepared for revealing the truth by their confessors or broken by their tormentors: Rather, it would be contested from the inside by a witches' confessor meant to serve it loyally, Friedrich Spee. In the persecution schema, the final confession held an essential role. After forcing the accused to confess under torture, they were to "freely" reiterate their confession the day prior to their execution. They would thus, in their death, be reconciled with the Church, that is to say, vanquished twice and entirely subdued by their persecutors. A doctor of theology and a poet, the Jesuit Spee was named chaplain of Würzburg's prisons in 1627, at a time when witch hunts were intensifying in the city, claiming 1,200 victims in a few years. He had visited every condemned held in solitary confinement and had followed them to the stake. He had been convinced — by collecting their final words — of their innocence. "Grief has turned my hair white, grief on account of the witches whom I have accompanied to the stake and whose innocence I recognized," he would write. He had asked to attend torture sessions and found out by what means their confessions had been extracted from them. He then decided to testify: In 1631, he published a book titled *Cautio criminalis*, "Warning to criminal lawyers on the excesses that creep into witchcraft trials."[19] While reaffirming his belief in the devil's existence and a "witchcraft crime," he attacked the judges' methods and contested confessions' juridical value: "We aren't all cast as witches and wizards because we haven't undergone torture." He questioned all the arguments put forward by the judges to inflict the *quaestio*, the legitimacy they allowed rumors and denunciations, their recourse to the concepts of "secret crime" and "exceptional crime," the absence of a lawyer, the subterfuge of investigators who fabricated evidence, the relentlessness of some confessors to make the accused confess just before they go to the stake . . . Unlike Wier and other doctors, Spee did not vilify the apparatus's power techniques and its deceptive "knowledge" in the name of medical science, a new apparatus that would soon supplant the former. His denunciation took shape *in the name of truth*; the same "quest for truth" that had been incessantly invoked by judges and torturers would be turned against the apparatus itself. *Cautio criminalis* was published anonymously, but the identity of its author would be quickly divulged, and Spee faced abundant attacks against himself and his "pestiferous" book (as a bishop had referred to it). His book, however, would cause an unparalleled stir: It is through his influence that the archbishops of Trier and Mainz — centers of intense witch hunts — followed by Queen Christina of Sweden would decide to ban the death convictions for witchcraft; finally, Pope Innocent X officially disapproved in 1657 "the barbaric use of torture and other irregular and cruel procedures of which [the judges] bear guilt in such trials."

Of course, many other writings had already denounced the practice of the *quaestio*. Yet the publication of Spee's book marked a turning point, mainly because of its author's singular position. As a confessor of "witches," he had not limited himself, as had his peers, to simply having them repeat confessions obtained under torture, thus making his role merely ancillary to that of the torturer. He was also driven by unveiling the truth, but his quest led him to where no one else was looking, in the victims' unmoored speech — and this truth would be far different from the self-accusations extorted by the victims' persecutors. Through this process, he claimed, "I have found nothing else but that those who were made guilty were truly innocent." By lending an ear to the so-called witches, Spee recovered the true and initial meaning of confession, what the Gospels had called the "power of the keys," a cathartic dimension of confession and pardoning that had been diverted for centuries and that had been transformed into a technique of subservience for the devices of power. He recognized the difference between a "truth" wrested by force, intimidation, cunning, the subdued violence of rituals, and truth freely confessed without violence or constriction. He discovered a truth other than that of the inquisitors and executioners. He understood that an official "truth" is not the only possible one or, rather, that it is *nothing* like a truth: that the noun "truth," consistently invoked by judges and confessors alike, only signaled a system of *countertruths*, an array of lies produced and conveyed by the power. Henceforth, it would become impossible to justify witch hunts by the accused's confessions, and the entire grounding of the apparatus would be left irremediably damaged. Spee's action would cause a decisive rift: By negating the lie at the basis of the apparatus, its self-legitimization through the "truth" of confessions, he revealed that the techniques of truth can lend themselves to countertruths. That the truth can, under certain conditions, become a moment of falsehood. This entails that the truth is profoundly divided — and this division sets the scene for struggles between strategies of power and those that endeavor to undermine them. What could resist the countertruths of power, unmasking the lie and the madness of its so-called truth? Only truth itself, irrupting as this *other truth*, occulted, stifled by the apparatus's power. By holding the words of the condemned as truthful, Spee succeeded, at the risk of his own life, in disrupting the system. And yet, he never shared these words of truth that grounded his indignation and revolt: Never would he cite in his book what the victims had confessed to him. How to attest to this persecuted truth? Without archives, without witnesses, stories, and letters that sometimes survive extermination, nothing could interrupt the unending monologue of the persecutors.

What makes finding traces so difficult is not only the judges' persistence in erasing the trials' archives by throwing them in the same flames burning the body of the accused. What also impedes this recovery is the social condition of a majority of the accused, most of whom were illiterate peasants whose cries for help didn't pierce through the walls of their cells. Nevertheless, we know that when the persecution runs amok, members of the dominant class can also become targets — noblemen, magistrates, priests, and men generally capable of leaving a written trace of their trials. An example of this is found in Bamberg, where a particularly ferocious witch hunt between 1626 and 1630 led by Prince Bishop Dornheim claimed as many as 700 victims. He had directed the construction of a torture center, the Malefizhaus, where the accused were kept for indeterminate lengths and endlessly interrogated. In June 1626, the city's mayor, Johannes Junius, was arrested because of a "blueish mark, similar to a cloverleaf" found on his body that seemed unresponsive to pricking. Despite undergoing the *quaestio*, he resisted multiple torture sessions without confessing. However, a few days later he would come around: He admitted that he had been seduced by a female demon named Vixen under the shape of a goat; that they fornicated and that he had offered her sacramental bread; that he had renounced God and recognized Satan as his god; that he had gone to the Sabbath on the back of a black dog and that he had participated with the Chancellor and other notables in an assembly of wizards in the Great Council Hall. His demon had ordered him to kill his son and daughter, but he had refused to obey. He was burned at the stake after having given the names of some thirty "accomplices." He nevertheless successfully handed down a secret letter to his daughter: a few leaflets of trembling handwriting, hardly legible as his hand had been crushed in a thumbscrew. This is one of the rare testimonies of a victim of witch hunts that has reached us.

"Innocent have I come into prison, innocent have I been tortured, innocent must I die. For whoever comes into the prison of witches must become a witch or be tortured until he invents something out of his head and bethinks him of something." After having described the torments that were inflicted on him, Junius explains what had finally led to his confession: "The executioner came to see me in prison and said: 'Sir, I beg you, for God's sake confess something, whether it be true or not. Invent something, for you cannot endure the torture which you will be put to; and, even if you bear it all, yet you will not escape, not even if you were a count, but one torture will follow after another until you say you are a wizard. Not before that,' he said, 'will they let you go, as you may see by all their trials, for one is just like another.'" And Junius adds: "I must say that I am a wizard, though I am not and must now renounce God, though I have never done it before. Day and night, I was deeply troubled, but at last there came to me an idea [. . .] I would myself invent something and say it. It were surely better that I just say it without conviction (*nur mit dem mauhl und worten* [only with mouth and words]), even though I had not really done it; and afterward I would confess it to the priest, and let those who compel me to do it answer for it [. . .] And so I made my confession, but it was all a lie."[20] This document provides precious testimony on the manner in which the persecution apparatus functioned and on the possibilities for a subject to resist. It isn't only this perspective — veritably infernal — of an unending agony that would break Junius's resistance: It's the certainty of the apparatus's forgone conclusion. The Bamberg executioner revealed to him that trials are all alike:

None of them take facts into account, nor the social position and the personality of the accused; they all obey the same logic of hatred, always rephrasing the same charges and accusations, obtaining identical confessions that lead the victim to the stake every time, according to the same implacable ritual. Yet Junius's example shows that some resistance is possible. At the moment when he appeared to submit, he wrote a letter that *disavowed* his avowals, and this was enough to disrupt the apparatus. He confessed "only with mouth and words," but in his soul, he had not conceded. He persisted in not liking Big Brother.

This text sends us to another document, written under similar circumstances by Bukharin in 1937, before being shot on Stalin's orders. The former general secretary of the Comintern knew enough history to identify all the similarities between the methods of Stalin's secret police and those of the Inquisition. To Vichinsky — his prosecutor who had summoned him to confess — he had promptly responded that "confessions of the accused were a medieval juridical principle." And yet like the others accused during the Moscow trials, he ended up admitting to his "crimes." All the endless interrogations, sleep deprivation, threats against his relatives and loved ones, would probably not have sufficed to break him had he not been subjected to an apparatus that demanded his total obedience. Like the victims of the witch hunts brought to confess, he had been prepared to face communism's self-criticism ritual and to accuse himself. Like the former victims, he was a prisoner of a system of beliefs from which he could not break free and that justified itself in anticipation of his confessions. He was ready to sacrifice himself in the name of a transcendent Truth — not the Church's truth, but the Communist Party's, the Party that is "always right" and whose orders cannot be questioned, "because History has given no other means to exercise the truth."[21] But here this omnipotent apparatus would hit an obstacle. Subjugated unreservedly in appearance to the apparatus's infallible authority, Bukharin wrote a letter whose content his wife would memorize. He admits therein his "helplessness against the infernal machine that, with its medieval methods, produces a series of falsehoods," and he calls for "the future generation of Party leaders" in the hope that "the historical truth would cleanse [his] tarnished name."[22] When his Party had demanded his self-repudiation, the Russian revolutionary retaliated in the same way as had done Bamberg's burgomaster. As Junius had, he pretended to submit, to give in to his accusers if only better to thwart this apparatus's trap. In a context where it is impossible to openly protest against the power's falsehoods, the *courage of the truth* can only be expressed through secrecy and cunning. Compelled to lie in the name of the truth, both men refused to become what the Psalmist calls "false witnesses." They respond by a clandestine truth that contradicts confessions' false "truth" and reveals its imposture. It is at this hefty cost that they manage to free themselves, that their words can testify to the resistance of a subject, of a true self that escapes the apparatus's grip.

Thus, it is erroneous to suppose that the ego or the individual does not preexist the power apparatuses that subjugate it: If it were so, that is, if a kernel of the ego did not preexist its alienating identification, individuals would be wholly alienated from the apparatuses that constitute them and incapable of resisting them. It is just as misguided to reduce the truth to "games of truth" (as Foucault does so often), to techniques of truth-statement production that depend entirely on power relations. What Spee, Junius, and Bukharin show us is the possibility of dividing the truth and turning it against the falsehoods of power: to resist, in the name of truth, the apparatus's falsified "truth." As powerless and desperate as it may seem, this resistance has a major significance. As Arendt has claimed, no world could exist without men and women ready to bear witness to what *truly* happened.[23] A world where falsehood has become law, where the heroes of the October Revolution confess to being Nazi spies and where burgomasters can ride black dogs and fornicate with succubi — such a world abolishes the limits between truth and falsehood, reality and illusion, abolishing all benchmarks that orient us within reality; this generalized falsehood goes so far as to put the existence of a human community in peril. Perhaps what's at stake here is not "falsehood" in the ordinary sense, of a narrowed deception that would oppose the truth on such or such a particular point. Indeed, the persecution apparatus presents itself as a coherent system of *countertruths* that tend to entirely rebuild the world by placing the truth as but a moment of falsehood. In such a world where, as Arendt said, "organized lies tend to destroy everything that they negate," where the confession ritual is a simple prelude to murder, no one is immune to accusations, and neither the living nor the dead are ever sheltered. The experience of witch hunts and modern-day terrors attest to the essential link between countertruths and hatred. These persecutions schemas redirect hatred toward imaginary enemies; and the more the apparatus blights the truth, the more this hatred is unmoored. We must now ask ourselves what is this fundamental truth that the power strives to cover and why this veiling must be accompanied by persecution and terror. Yet this question could not have even been formulated had men and women not decided — in solitude and facing death — to bear witness to the truth.

4

The Capital Enemy

What had convinced Johannes Junius to confess was not the torture he had undergone in the Malefizhaus, but the fear of seeing them endlessly repeated: the prospect of ceaseless torment, which resembled medieval representations of hell. Yet when the *quaestio* was reintroduced into the judicial process during the thirteenth century, precise rules were laid down to protect the accused from the arbitrariness of the judges: The accusations had to be confirmed by at least two witnesses; these witnesses were not to be close to the accused; and, above all, the number of torture sessions was strictly limited, and their duration had to be kept short. However, as confirmed by Junius's letter, all these restrictions had been abolished in the context of the witch hunt, so much so that the executioner of Bamberg could threaten to torture him relentlessly until he confessed. One of his colleagues had said it more harshly and cynically to another defendant: "I do not take you for one, two, three, not for eight days, nor for a few weeks, but for half a year or a year, for your whole life, until you confess: and if you will not confess, I shall torture you to death, and you shall be burned after all."[1] How did we move from a stringently enforced and limited practice to the arbitrary exercise of unlimited power? What makes the emergence of an *exceptional procedure* possible — one that gives itself the right to transgress all the rules of law and makes the accused an *exlex*, an "outlaw," whom no legal guarantee can protect? What turns an exceptional judicial apparatus (whose creation may be legitimate in certain circumstances) into a persecution apparatus, in a strict sense? The motivation behind the introduction of the *quaestio* into the judicial inquiry was to "extract the truth" where it remained hidden: if the material evidence of the crime remained invisible; or if the crime was so monstrous that it was almost impossible to state. The recourse to torture therefore applied to secret crimes and to those that were unutterable — the unmentionable crimes that Roman law designated, as we have seen, as *nefanda*, acts that were "impossible to put into words": certain sexual crimes and those that attacked the divine or human *majestas*, the crimes of "lèse-majesté." It was this limit of the unspeakable that, from the thirteenth century onward, new techniques of power such as the *inquisitio* and the *quaestio* were striving to transgress. From then on, it was important to make the *nefandum* confess by all means, as if it were necessary "for the unspeakable to be said so that a certain type of power could assert itself without a divide."[2] What kind of power? The one that defines itself as the object and the stake of the crime of lèse-majesté: a power that claims to personify the *majestas*, the sovereignty of the State.

When, in 1307, Philip the Fair had the principal dignitaries of the Order of the Temple imprisoned, the arrest warrant multiplied periphrases by refraining from immediately naming the crime that would lead them to the stake: They were dealing with "a bitter thing, a deplorable thing, a thing certainly horrible to think, terrible to hear, a loathsome crime, an execrable deed, an abominable act, an awful infamy, a completely inhuman thing," that they could not hear "without shuddering with violent horror."[3] We will find the same rhetorical precautions in the indictment of the Waldensians of Arras or when a demonologist like Bodin refused to transcribe in his treatise the "damnable invocations" of the witches so as not to risk "cursing" his readers. Unnameable, the crime of the Templars or that of the witches is certainly so by its content, but also by its mode of enunciation. They are cursed words that can only be uttered in secret, rites so monstrous that they must remain clandestine, protected by the walls of the Templar commanderies or the darkness of the Sabbath. The horror of their crimes coincides here with their secrecy, and it is both to reveal hidden crimes and to make people confess to unmentionable crimes that the apparatuses of power must resort to the new techniques of compelling the truth. Atrociously tortured, the Knights Templar would eventually confess the unspeakable, confessing that they were sodomites, blasphemers, heretics, and devil worshippers. This was probably the first time that an official institution, respected for centuries throughout Christendom, was accused of being a satanic "secret society" disguised as loyalty and piety. The unfortunate Templars will remain, in the imagination of the conspiracy, the model of the evil and clandestine sect perpetuating itself through the ages. A few years after their trial, the same accusations were made against lepers, Jews, and then "witches," before finding other targets during the terrors of modern times. The emergence of new techniques of inquiry and confession has a political significance. It allows one to redefine and to extend the sphere

of secrecy by placing it in direct relation to political sovereignty. It responds
to the threat that the *nefandum* poses to the royal power: The majesty of the
State retaliates in this way to the crime of lèse-majesté, a crime that allows it
to define itself, to assert itself as a sovereign power. When these apparatuses
wrest the "truth" from broken bodies and subjugated souls, they push back the
limits of the sayable in order to offer the power a total grasp on the word and
the body of its subjects. They allow him to deploy himself without hindrance,
by freeing himself from all the rules of right, from all submission to a superior
authority: like an absolute power, a sovereign power.

There were three crimes that fell under the *nefandum* category, and, from
what he confessed, Junius had perpetrated all three. He was thus charged
with maximum defilement. He had committed a major sexual transgression
by fornicating with a succubus (and since she took an animal shape, he com-
pounded his case by practicing *coitus diabolicus* and zoophilia at the same
time . . .). He had sinned against the divine majesty by denying the Christian
religion to adore the devil, and this apostasy was coupled with sacrilege since
he had profaned a host by offering it to the devil. Finally, he had committed
a crime against political majesty by conspiring against the authority of the
prince-bishop. Indeed, he declared that he had participated with Chancellor
Georg Haan in a "sorcerers' assembly" in the Grand Council Chamber, the
very seat of municipal power, clear evidence of a rebellion of the magistrates
against their sovereign. In truth, this "conspiracy" was not entirely imaginary:
One historian tells us that Chancellor Haan was concerned about the extent
of the witch hunt in Bamberg and intervened at the highest legal authority
of the Empire, the High Court of Speyer, to denounce the arbitrary arrests
and to impeach the prince-bishop.[4] By having Junius arrested and tortured so
that he would accuse the chancellor of being the leader of a conspiracy, the
bishop's men were trying to eliminate a dangerous adversary who was guilty
of opposing the onslaught of persecution. Those who try to oppose mass terror
often become its victims: Like Danton and the Indulgents in 1794, Chancellor
Haan was to end up on the scaffold, condemned both on grounds of "witchcraft" and "high treason." But the justice of the prince-bishop of Bamberg was
crueler and more implacable than that of the Jacobins, since the chancellor's
wife, Katharina, and three of their children — Katharina Röhm, Adam, and
Maria Ursula — were in turn accused, tortured, and executed as "witches." It
would be wrong, however, to consider the trials of Junius and Haan as purely
political trials disguised as witchcraft trials. For their political significance is
inseparable from their demonological dimension: At the time of the witch
hunt, a political strategy intended to defend the sovereign power takes the
form of the accusation of participating in a "diabolic conspiracy."

It is not without significance that Haan and Junius were accused of conspiracy. This accusation resurfaces whenever sovereignty seems threatened. This is because it is a historical a priori, a scheme that is both prevalent and plastic, and that mobilizes different persecution apparatuses in order to put them at the service of a sovereign power. It may be that other types of apparatus, for example those disciplinary devices analyzed by Foucault, engage another relationship with power; that we must, if we want to describe them, turn away from the central focus of sovereignty and delve into the depths of the "social," where the fine-meshed networks of disciplinary micropowers are shaped. But a persecution apparatus is constituted each time in a certain relation to sovereignty: For there to be mass persecution, sovereignty must be at work. The analysis of such apparatuses can therefore no longer be limited to a "horizontal" microphysics of power relations: It must also take into account the "vertical" dimension of political sovereignty, which has always eluded Foucault. This does not mean that central power is always at the origin of movements of persecution; they can also arise on the periphery, where a local center of power is threatened, where a rebellion allows itself to be hijacked, captured by an apparatus that designates another target for its revolt. However, such movements remain mostly sporadic and diffuse. In order for these lynchings, these more or less spontaneous pogroms, to be organized and to last; in order for them to fit together as a true *apparatus* by elaborating long-term strategies and the knowledge discourses that justify them; for the persecution to grow, to take the form of a generalized terror, it is necessary that the sovereign power gets involved in the apparatus. What is more, it must settle on the target that it has given itself or designate another target, and that it actively support it by implementing exceptional procedures that allow it to unfold without limits.

The crime of witchcraft of which Junius is accused encompasses several kinds of transgressions — sexual, religious, political — whose implications are at first sight very different: Similar to the "thoughtcrime" of which Orwell speaks, it is a *crime that contains all crimes*. It is exactly in these terms that it was defined by the author of *Demon-Mania*: For Jean Bodin (1529–1596), witchcraft is "the crime of divine and human *lèse-majesté* that includes all the other crimes imaginable."[5] He concludes therefrom that it is a "crime of exception," which requires the use of an exceptional procedure, and in particular the suspension of all legal guarantees meant to protect the accused. The crime of the sorcerers is so extreme that it justifies the paradox of a *law of exception*: in this case, "it is rightly in the spirit of the law to abandon the rule of law" (200). Bodin proposes, for example, against all the established rules, that one accepts the testimonies that very young children could bring against their parents ("it is necessary to take the young girls of the sorcerers [. . .]: in the tender age, they will be easy to persuade and to rectify with promises of impunity"). He considers that, for witchery, the "common noise," that is to say the rumor, is worth as an "almost infallible" proof, even in the absence of witnesses. He recommends to the judges that they accept anonymous denunciations (which were until then considered inadmissible under French law) and that they lie to the accused by making false promises to entice them to confess. Since he deplored that interrogations were less severe in France than in Germany, he did not hesitate to advocate torture methods that he considered more effective, such as sleep deprivation or nails driven underneath the fingernails, "which is the most excellent Gehenna of all." However, unlike Institoris or Rémy, who took pride in having hundreds of accused executed, this man had little blood on his hands. He had admittedly sent to the stake a few unfortunate women, such as Jeanne Harvilliers, whom he had condemned when he was the king's prosecutor in Laon, but his writings would claim many more victims. He was above all an *ink criminal*.

The man who wrote this witch-hunting handbook was not a fanatical inquisitor like the authors of the *Malleus*, nor an obscure subordinate magistrate like Boguet, Rémy, or de l'Ancre: He had written a major work on modern political theory, the *Six Books of the Republic*, and he was one of the most remarkable thinkers of his time, who was nicknamed "the Montesquieu of the sixteenth century." Jurist, philosopher, economist, he had been for some time an influential adviser to King Henry III. He was also a humanist, one of the first supporters of the abolition of slavery and an ardent defender of freedom of conscience and religious tolerance who advocated the reconciliation of Catholics and Protestants. Suspected of sympathy for the Reformed, his life was threatened during the St. Bartholomew's Massacre; and his very last book, *The Colloquium of the Seven Wise Men*, is a plea for a universal religion that would "harmoniously" overcome the conflicts between the different revealed religions. How could a thinker of such stature, such an enlightened mind, write this breviary of hatred? Such paradoxes have ceased to surprise us: We have seen a philosopher who tried to think about the originary freedom and the authenticity of existence call for submission to Hitler; another, known for his analyses of resistance to power, celebrate without reservations Ayatollah Khomeini's victory; yet another—theorist of the events of truth and faithful to the May '68 revolt—praise the Khmer Rouge regime. At least they did not theorize these positions and make them an essential element of their thought. Is this also the case for Bodin? How should we interpret this scandalous work, the *Demon-Mania of Sorcerers*?

For a long time, it was thought that this was only a circumstantial writing. On the contrary, it seems that this treatise also has its place in the systematic unity of his work, as a necessary continuation of his theories on the *Republic*. When Bodin calls for an exceptional procedure to punish the "crime of lèse-majesté" of which the sorcerers would be guilty, he is applying only one of his fundamental theses. His main contribution to political thought consists indeed in defining the concept of *sovereignty*. By this term (which translates the Roman notion of *majestas*), he designates the power of the State under-stood as absolute, perpetual, one and indivisible power, excluding any right of resistance. Defined in this way, sovereign power was freed from the set of restrictions that had previously limited the king's authority, and in particular from his submission to the divine will embodied by the Church. It also eman-cipates itself from the subordination to an Idea of the Good, which, since the Greeks, had characterized classical political theories. Henceforth, subjects were no longer expected to obey the will of the Prince because he wanted the common Good, and *only* insofar as he wanted what was Good. They obey him because his will is sovereign and precisely thereby calls for an unconditional submission. Like his contemporary Machiavelli, but from a very different per-spective, Bodin thus strives to free political power from all external authority, whether theological, legal, or ethical. The significance of the *Republic* is too often misunderstood as an apologia for monarchical absolutism. In fact, Bo-din's great invention is that of the modern State: He gave us the founding the-ory of those *State democracies* of which we are citizens and that always refer to the principle of State sovereignty.[6] His essential operation consists in ordering the multiple to the One, in subordinating the multitude to the unity of the sov-ereign will by erecting the latter as the absolute foundation of the State — of a State that threatens to decompose, if this One Will is lacking. Bodin's main successors would simply take up his conception of sovereignty by legitimizing it through the fiction of a contract. Thus, when Rousseau transferred the site of political sovereignty from the King to the People, he continued to define it in the same terms, as an absolute will that "is always what it must be" and tolerates no right of resistance.

Ut Deus, sic Princeps: The earthly sovereign is similar to God. It is this sec-ularization of a theological concept, its transposition to the political level, that grounds the absolute character of its sovereignty and thus sets it free from any submission to the divine will. Now, the fundamental attribute of the sovereign power — whether divine or human — consists in the power to give the law *and to exempt itself from it*, to derogate from its own laws: "that is why the law says that the Prince is exempted from the laws."[7] *Deus est exlex*, says Luther, God is outside the law. He is the one who, by performing a miracle, can suspend the laws that He himself has established; and the political ruler is in the image of such a God, since he has the power to decree a *state of exception* during which the laws are suspended. This is precisely what happened during the witch hunt, an exemplary manifestation of the new political sovereignty. For Bodin, "the person of the sovereign is always exempted in terms of law."[8] We find at the pole of sovereignty the same situation of exception that characterizes, at the other pole, the accused of the witch hunt. These are two figures of the *exlex*, the head of State because his majesty puts him above the law, the "sorcerer" because he has been dispossessed of all legal status, because he is no longer a subject of law, but an outlaw handed over to the unlimited arbitrariness of judges and torturers. The Sorcerer (or rather the Witch: "for one sorcerer," says Bodin, "we find fifty witches") is presented here as a figure symmetrical to the Sovereign, a *counterfigure of the sovereign exception*. We are dealing here again with a thesis of theological origin that is maintained, unaltered, by being transposed to a political level: For divine sovereignty also presupposes a counterfigure, an antagonist named Satan whose opposition is required as a necessary element of God's providential plan. When secularized, this doctrine will take on a new meaning: It will make it possible to demonize the enemies of the State, to base political sovereignty on an opposition between Friend and Enemy as radical as the antagonism between God and Satan. This shows that the secularization of theological schemes does not necessarily coincide with a desacralization, a "disenchantment" of politics; on the contrary, it preserves these ancient schemes at the very moment when it translates them into political terms. If it is true, as Schmitt claims, that all our political concepts are in fact secularized theological concepts, then the question arises as to what a radical desacralization might be, one that would break with all the concepts and schemes derived from theological representations of power and sovereignty.

The *Demon-Mania* thus confirms the analyses of the *Republic*, while bringing an essential complement to them. In the *Republic*, Bodin had defined the notion of sovereignty as the power to exempt oneself from the law; but he had not sufficiently determined in which cases this "exemption" becomes necessary. The *Demon-Mania* gives us the answer: In order to decide on a procedure of exception, the sovereign must be confronted with what Bodin calls the *capital enemy*, an enemy that calls into question the very exercise of sovereignty (we know that "capital" comes from *caput*, qualifying the head of the Body Politic, the head [*chef*] of the State). To be sovereign is to have the power to designate such an enemy and to set him outside of the law. The figure of the Sovereign appears here to be inextricably linked to his counterfigure, to this Other whom he sets up as an absolute enemy in order to be able to assert himself as a sovereign power. Such is the role that the Witch plays for Bodin, that of a rebel who threatens the existence of the State. He indeed likens the witches' revolt against God and the rebellion against the sovereign of the State, and even tends to identify them.[9] If the Witch can be designated as the capital enemy of the State, it is because her alliance with the devil has a directly political bearing: Satan is the great Rebel, the primordial Enemy of the divine sovereignty, and to oppose God is to oppose at the same time the "earthbound God" that is the State. Hence, he can affirm that "Satan has nothing in greater recommendation than [. . .] to stir up seditions between subjects or civil wars" (233). Since the fourteenth century, witchcraft had been assimilated by the Church to heresy, that is to say, to a crime of divine lèse-majesté. Henceforth, it is also defined as a crime of political lèse-majesté, which makes it an absolute crime that contains all crimes.

Bodin has understood that it was impossible to secularize the figure of the Sovereign, to transpose it from the theological register to the political register, without also transposing the counterfigure of the Enemy to make of it a political opponent. However, this *secularization of the Enemy* remains partial, unfinished, since it retains an equivocal status, both theological and political, medieval and modern, that of a heretic worshipper of Satan and a rebel standing against the State. But this is what makes the accusation so formidable in its effectiveness. By characterizing the Witch as the enemy of God and the Prince, he was calling for all the forces of Church and State to be united against her. His appeal was to be heeded: While his book, buoyed by the prestige of its author, enjoyed considerable success (several dozen reprints and translations in just a few years), repression quickly increased to reach its apex. Indeed, most demonologists were soon to adopt Bodin's theological-political approach: While Binsfeld, bishop of Trier at the time of the Great Hunt, denounced the accused as "traitors to the fatherland," the Puritan preacher Perkins did not hesitate to call the accused "the most notorious traitor and rebel that can be."[10] This made one historian (Trevor-Roper) say that the *Demon-Mania* "is the book that, more than any other, rekindled the witch-burnings in Europe." A few more years and the Church would recognize that witches and possessed women were not only under its authority, but that this was first and foremost a political matter concerning the power of the State. During the possession at Loudun, in 1632, one of the exorcists commends the intervention of royal justice by declaring that the battle against the devil "is a work of God since it is the work of the king." This case shows, he wrote, "that the demons can only be driven out by the power of the scepter and that the crosier would not suffice to break this dragon's head."[11]

How did such an astute politician as Bodin come to designate obscure village witches as the worst enemies of the State? His work is embedded in his time — a time of crisis, persecution, and civil war — and it is part of a precise political strategy; but this strategy is not easy to decipher. As with Plato's *Republic* or Machiavelli's *Prince*, his writings are encrypted texts, belonging to an "art of writing" intended to thwart censorship: They conceal their true aims, multiplying false leads and apparent contradictions, while resorting to allusive clues to guide the reader to their hidden truth. The *Demon-Mania* is no exception. Bodin had discovered that sovereignty is founded and strengthened by naming a capital enemy. Since he wanted the wars of religion to end, this enemy could not be the one denounced by the Church and the king's entourage, that is, the Protestants. It was thus necessary for him to designate *another figure of the enemy*, in order to deflect toward it all the hostility of the Prince and the people. This enemy had to appear as a serious threat to the State and a credible opponent for all the rival factions. This is exactly the function he assigns to the sorcerers' conspiracy. By calling for its eradication, he set out to reconcile Catholics and Protestants, leaguers and partisans of the king, by offering them a common target: This manual for witch-hunters had an ecumenical aim. It is wrong to contrast the "humanist" Bodin of the *Republic* and the *Colloquium of the Seven Wise Men* with the author of the *Demon-Mania*: It is precisely because he was a supporter of religious tolerance and civil peace that he wanted to intensify the witch hunt — but by giving "witchcraft" a completely new meaning, that of a major crime endangering the sovereignty of the State.

He reaffirms this fact throughout his treatise: A State that tolerates the presence of witches in its midst is heading for ruin. It is difficult to see, however, how the spells cast by a few miserable peasant women could jeopardize sovereign power . . . What then allows him to turn the witch into a capital enemy? To this question, he gives several answers that may seem contradictory. To make them a formidable threat, he has to exaggerate their number and influence. He assures us that witches and sorcerers are "as numerous as the army of the great Xerxes": more than a million in the kingdom of France . . . Underlying this argument is the fear of a rebellious multitude that refuses to submit to the sovereignty of the One, and we will have to examine the kernel of truth in such a depiction. He also maintains that it is the people who demand their punishment and that it is important to satisfy this call, "otherwise there is a danger that the people will stone both magistrates and sorcerers" (185). He moreover rebukes Charles IX for having been too lenient toward them, by thus allowing them to proliferate in all the kingdom. We recognize there an argument often invoked by those who claim that the fundamental affect of the multitude is hatred, the desire for murder, because they try to justify the persecutions in the name of the will of the people. Behind the figure of the weak Prince, incapable of defending the State, Bodin, however, suggests another, more worrying, figure, that of a Prince who himself has been contaminated by evil. Indeed, "there is nothing so holy and so sacred which is not defiled and infected by Satan and his henchmen" (72): Satan is the very name of a *principle of contagion* from which no one can escape. This is why the *Demon-Mania* is unleashed against the witch-priests, the witch-doctors (those who, like Wier, consider the accused as sick people who should be treated), and the witch-magistrates (who are recognized precisely because they refuse to condemn the sorcerers); before attacking the "sorcerers of the Court" who come to "infect the sovereign Prince" (232). This is the ultimate victory of the devil, which will fatally lead to civil war and the ruin of the State, since "God makes the subjects rebel against the sorcerer Princes" (185). A surprising conclusion to say the least: He who had denied to the subjects any right of resistance, who seemed to fear a popular revolt against a king too indulgent toward the sorcerers, now justifies an insurrection against a king "infected" by the devil . . .

Let us stop for a moment to consider this strange figure of the *sorcerer-prince*, this conceptual oxymoron that condenses in one person the image of God and the devil's deputy, the worst abjection and sacred sovereignty. What changes in the imaginary of power does it reflect? How could such antinomic elements merge? And *who* is Bodin aiming at with this locution? Here again, the context sheds light on this allusive and cryptic writing. When he published the *Republic* in 1576, he still enjoyed the favor of the king. However, shortly afterward, Henri III decided to go to war again against the Protestants, and Bodin opposed it. Having fallen from grace, he became close to the moderate Catholics gathered around the king's brother, the Duke of Alençon, who wanted to reconcile with the Protestants. Of course, it was not out of the goodness of his heart that a political figure like Bodin advocated religious tolerance: It was because he was a statesman that he sought above all to strengthen the sovereign authority of the State, which he believed required reconciliation and an end to the civil war. It is in this context that he writes the *Demon-Mania*. Indeed, he implied to the most subtle of his readers that the "Sorcerer-Prince" was none other than Henri III, whom he accused of letting himself be "bewitched" by the *sorcerer-priests*, that is, the Jesuits and the most extreme Catholics. The same accusation was to be taken up again a few years later, more vehemently, by Bodin's political opponents, those fanatical Catholics grouped in the Holy League. After the king had their leader, the Duke of Guise, assassinated, the Ligueurs went on a rampage against Henri III, who was accused of being an atheist, a hermaphrodite (*sic*), a pederast, an incestuous man, a "sorcerer, the son of a sorcerer," of sacrificing children to the devil, and even of being an "incarnate devil."[12] Countless engravings and pamphlets represent him under the

features of a ferocious beast — king-lion or king-wolf — or of a demon. These
attacks will only cease after the death of the king, assassinated by the monk
Jacques Clément. It is necessary to question the figure of the sorcerer-king,
incestuous, sacrilegious, vampire, and cannibal: Perpetuated for centuries by
a clandestine "counterhistory" that opposes the official history of the kings
and the powerful, this figure plays an essential role in the logic of hatred.
Among these accusations, we can note that of murdering children in order to
bathe in their blood. Before being attributed to witches, this charge had been
directed against heretics, lepers, and Jews. It is this *nefandum*, this monstrous
crime, that legendary accounts attributed to the pharaoh or to King Herod, of
which the Ligueurs accuse the king (to the point of making his name, Henri
de Valois, an anagram of "vile Herod" (*vilain Hérode*), and we shall see that,
at the onset of the French Revolution, the same infamy would be imputed to
one of his successors. Admittedly, Bodin does not openly take up this slander,
but by recalling that sorcerers are bloodthirsty infanticides and by suggesting
that Henry III is a sorcerer, he subscribes to the same logic. In the long history
of this scheme, his *Demon-Mania* occupies a special place. The first theorist
of political sovereignty, he also discovered its *reversible* character: If the figure
of the Sovereign and its counterfigure are indissociable, it can happen that the
holder of sovereignty is cast in the place of the Enemy, to the extent of taking
on all the attributes of the malevolent Other. By turning the old scheme of
the witch-prince against the king, he tried to exploit this reversibility, this
ambivalence of the figures of the sovereign.

At first blush, there was nothing new about such accusations. Throughout
the Middle Ages, the incessant conflicts between the pope's partisans and
those of the German emperor or the king of France often led the two parties
to accuse their opponents of being sodomites, heretics, or of practicing black
magic, as was the case with Emperor Frederick II and Pope Boniface VIII.
But this was done in a polemical way, in the context of a power struggle,
and without ever evoking a demonic conspiracy. Bodin's masterstroke consisted in combining the two accusations, in associating — perhaps for the first
time — the scheme of the sorcerer-prince and that of the conspiracy. In this
respect, the *Demon-Mania* is an innovative piece of writing. The need to
defend Christianity against a "conspiracy" had already been invoked in the
past, during the persecutions of the Jews and the lepers. However, this was
only a threat, for the men of the Middle Ages did not even imagine that the
hidden enemy had already seized power; that the conspiracy had succeeded
in reaching the top of the Church and the State. A few centuries later, Bodin would not hesitate to take the step. When he attacked a conspiracy of
sorcerers infiltrated in the magistracy, the clergy, the Court, and of which

the king himself was the accomplice or the leader, he provided us with a new representation of sovereign power, that of an occult power, all the more dangerous because it remained concealed. He who had elaborated the modern notion of sovereignty by liberating it from its subordination to the Good, knew how to forge at the same time its counterfigure, a sovereign will, but one fundamentally *evil*, capable of secretly occupying the place of absolute power. This representation was to enjoy considerable success in the following centuries: There is not a historical upheaval that the myth of the conspiracy has not been entrusted with "explaining," not a persecution that it has not legitimized. If the conspiracy scheme is still so popular today, it is because the dynamics of modern democracy have profoundly transformed the traditional representations of sovereign power. In a divided and unstable society, where the figurations of the political Body tend to unravel, to disembody, where the exercise of power is regularly questioned, it may seem that legal power is reduced to a mere appearance, an inconsistent simulacrum that obscures the reality of genuine power. The elected leader of a democratic State is always too *normal* to embody the majesty of the sovereign exception. Despite the disembodiment and desacralization of power, the theological-political representation of an all-powerful and above-the-law Sovereign persists to this day, but in the phantasmatic form of the secret society, the "hidden masters of the world" who "pull the strings" in the shadows.

From the *Demon-Mania* to the *Protocols of the Elders of Zion*, it is this same scheme that continues to justify the vilest massacres. And yet, Bodin was probably more lucid, more cynical than the average inquisitor, witch-hunter, and world conspiracy ideologue who naively believe in the reality of the wicked Enemy that they denounce. He discreetly indicates that the sorcerers' conspiracy is merely a fiction. At the moment when he advises the judges to make false promises to the accused in order to obtain their confessions, he evokes indeed "Plato and Xenophon [who] allowed the magistrates to lie to govern a people, as is done to the sick and to small children" (192). No doubt he thus suggests to perspicacious readers that the conspiracy of the sorcerers is only a "beautiful lie"; that he himself did not believe in the existence of this innumerable sect that penetrated the heart of the State; that he consciously constructed this myth for a political purpose, in order to put an end to the religious wars by diverting hatred toward an imaginary enemy. Some of his contemporaries did not miss this point: As one of them wrote, "Bodin's *Demon-Mania* is worth nothing at all; he did not believe in it himself and only made this book so that one would believe that he believed in it."[13] If Bodin undertook to secularize the figure of the Sorcerer, to make it a rebel, an enemy of the State and not only of the Church, it is because he was trying to neutralize the theological field, the privileged place of confrontations in the sixteenth century; to move the conflict onto a political ground where the sovereign power could be refounded by designating its capital enemy. As one of his disciples would write, the modern State "is essentially the product of a religious civil war, and precisely of the overcoming by neutralization and secularization of the confessional fronts, that is, detheologization."[14] It is the paradox of Bodin, an audacious thinker and a prisoner of his time, that he only undertook to detheologize the figure of the Enemy by having recourse to the myths of medieval theology. In order to give the modern State a worthy adversary, he had to feign war on the henchmen of Satan, on werewolves and succubi. Politically, this strategy would have formidable consequences. By declaring "that there have been several Popes, Emperors and other Princes who have allowed themselves to be tricked by Sorcerers and finally to have been precipitated unfortunately by Satan" (preface, iv), he shifted the traditional focus of the witch hunt: Instead of limiting it to the margins of society, he refocused it on the highest spheres of power. But he did not stop there. As he also maintained that "Satan has loyal subjects of all states and qualities" and that he refused to distinguish them by the presence of a diabolical mark (one remembers that, according to him, "the greatest sorcerers are not marked"), he incited the judges to suspect anyone. He, who gave his wise advice to the torturers, had confidence in the virtues of torture to discover the guilty everywhere. He considers furthermore that the denunciation of his or her "accomplices" by an accused can be sufficient proof to convict them all, and, he specifies, "we only need to catch one to accuse an infinity of them" (166). Here, it is no longer just a question of intensifying the hunt for witches, but of extending the scope of persecution without limit. Thus, the first theorist of State sovereignty is also the first ideologist of State terror.

Should we conclude that sovereignty necessarily leads to terror? That sovereign power is always based, as Agamben assures us, on a state of exception by designating each time a *homo sacer*, a "bare life," is exposed to extermination? No absolute sovereignty without an absolute enemy . . . According to a historian, the witch hunt was necessary to found the absolute monarchy, which would explain why demonological theories "accompanied the rise of the theory of divine right and declined at the same time as it."[15] Yet it was one of the most eminent representatives of absolutism, King Louis XIV, who was to put an end to the witch hunt in France by decriminalizing witchcraft; and his example was to be followed by most of the European "enlightened despots" such as Maria Theresa of Austria or Frederick II of Prussia . . . It is a mistake to believe that the exercise of political sovereignty necessarily implies recourse to persecution and terror. It is not sovereignty per se that calls for the apparatuses of persecution: It is the threatened sovereignty, the sovereignty *in crisis* that tries to relegitimize itself. That of the Church at the beginning of the witch hunt, thwarted by royal power, torn by the Great Schism, and distressed by heresies; that of the Duchy of Burgundy at the time of the Vauderie d'Arras, undermined by the rebellion of the Flemish cities and the hegemonic ambitions of the kings of France; that of the Kingdom of France at the time of the Wars of Religion or of the German States at the beginning of the following century. It is in such a context that Bodin sought to establish a new persecution apparatus on a purely political basis, for he hoped that this State terror would make it possible to refound sovereign power. In a sense, his project was to fail entirely. The accession to the throne of Henry IV would lead to the end of the civil war and the reestablishment of the authority of the State, without the Great Hunt that Bodin had been calling for being unleashed in France. His strategy was to clash with the defenders of legal norms and the rule of law. If the persecution of witches was not very intense in seventeenth-century France, this was, above all, because the magistrates of the Parliament of Paris had decided to annul on appeal most of the death sentences for witchcraft pronounced by lower courts. They had taken into account the critiques of the opponents of the witch hunt: The motives of the accusation seemed to them inconsistent and the methods of the accusers illegal. Without bothering to contradict Bodin, they refuted him de facto by showing that it was possible to preserve the sovereignty of the State in strict compliance with the law, without resorting to exceptional procedures. The lesson is worth bearing in mind: Even if recourse to the law is not enough to prevent persecution, contempt for the rule of law and the justification of the state of exception always pave the way for it.

We would be wrong, however, to underestimate Bodin's legacy to modernity. He not only spelled out the theoretical justifications of State terror by legitimizing the state of exception and secularizing the figure of the Enemy, but he also contributed to the elaboration of the *imaginary of terror*, the schemes that underlie it and give it its affective intensity and its mortifying rage. Of course, he did not invent the sorcerers' plot out of thin air. He merely transformed a medieval belief into a modern myth, by installing this malefic conspiracy at the head of the State. He thus allowed this scheme to adapt to the new persecution apparatuses that would sow death in the centuries to come. Where does this conspiracy haunting come from? We have seen that it was triggered by the appearance, in the thirteenth century, of new techniques of unveiling the "truth." These techniques presuppose a principle of concealment that tends to make every major crime a secret crime and every political enemy a hidden enemy. When one represents this enemy as a rebellious multitude, it will thus take the form of a secret society conspiring against the throne and the altar. Perhaps this analysis is insufficient: Perhaps the scheme of the conspiracy is rooted in the phenomenon of sovereignty, in the way it manifests itself. We know that the persecution apparatuses constitute the capital enemy as a counterfigure of the Sovereign. The sorcerer is the evil double of the monarch, also marked by a bodily stigma and endowed like him with powers of supernatural origin; but this is a dark sovereignty that opposes that of the king and reflects his inverted model. What characterizes sovereign power in the West is that it *gives itself to sight*, constantly exposed in its emblems and ceremonies, endlessly reproducing the face or body of the Prince on coins, statues, paintings (and today on screens). This is precisely what differentiates it from those Eastern or African monarchies where the body of the sovereign must be absolutely hidden from the sight of his subjects. Such a mode of manifestation undoubtedly has a theological origin; for the Christian monarch claims to be an *image of God*, an "imitator of Christ": By making a spectacle of himself, he strives to imitate a God who has chosen to be incarnated in a visible body. From then on, we can understand that his counterfigure presents itself, on the contrary, as an *invisible* power whose every act is a *nefandum* that must be kept secret.

And yet, this opposition between a Sovereign who shows himself in the visible and his invisible Enemy does not by itself give us the key to the enigma. For this sovereignty that displays itself through its images preserves at the same time a part of irreducible opacity, what the medieval legists called the *arcana imperii*, the "arcana" of power. This notion, which evoked in ancient Rome the occult rites of the brotherhoods of initiates, then the "holy mysteries" of the Christian religion, ended up designating the most secret center of the monarchic State.[16] It is, moreover, Bodin who, in his treatise *Method of History*, introduced this concept into modern political philosophy. It is not a question here of State secrets, in the restricted sense of the term, but of this ultimate Secret, this Mystery that is the State. If the modern concept of sovereignty transposes into the political domain a theological conception of divine sovereignty, the mystery of the State finds its source in this relationship to the divine, in the unfathomable abyss of God's will, and its secret character is inseparable from its sacred dimension. Nevertheless, it is a Christian God, a God who reveals himself here below under the features of Jesus Christ, and the mysterious power that proceeds from him must also be embodied in a visible body, that of the monarch, the head of State. This is a paradoxical representation of a power that is both visible and invisible and that can only reign by making itself visible, while at the same time concealing itself, by withdrawing into the invisible home of the "mystical foundation" of its sovereignty.

The most powerful, the most dissimulated of the "conspiracies," and often the only one that really exists, is the State itself . . . The conspiracy scheme is thus inscribed in the representation of the sovereign power proper to the Christian West, in its double human and divine nature, immanent and transcendent, manifest and hidden. Since he remains invisible, the Sovereign occupies no assignable place: Like God, he is everywhere and nowhere. This is why the legists attributed to him a sort of symbolic ubiquity: Wherever justice is administered in his name, wherever his representatives or only his portraits are found, the king is present.[17] We now understand why the capital enemy can only be a hidden enemy: He is an imaginary replica of the *arcana* of royal sovereignty; he reflects in the other pole the divine mystery of the State by giving it a diabolical meaning. For those who adhere to this scheme, it is a question of unmasking this evil sovereign, but also of competing with him, of *imitating* him in order to better supplant him. As he declared to one of his followers, it was such a project that Hitler devised after reading the *Protocols*: "The concealment of the enemy and his ubiquity! I suddenly understood that we had to copy it in our own way [. . .] What a struggle between them and us! What is at stake is quite simply the fate of the world."[18]

Let us try to determine more precisely the features of the enemy that a sovereignty in crisis strives to reconstitute, this capital enemy that becomes the target of the persecution apparatus. We are dealing with an *absolute enemy*, that is to say, an *irreducible* enemy with whom no reconciliation is possible; with a *hidden enemy* who conceals himself deviously; and, finally, with an *inhuman enemy*, a ferocious beast or a monster that can be exterminated without committing a crime. It is to one of Bodin's most faithful followers that we owe the notion of the "absolute enemy." In his early work, Carl Schmitt made the demarcation between friend and foe the criterion and essence of politics: For him, the fundamental act of political sovereignty is a "decision of hostility" that consists in designating the enemy of the State. But the sovereign is also defined as "the one who decides on the state of exception," the one who gives himself the right to transgress all legal norms. The designation of an enemy as *exlex* and the situation of exception that it entails characterize, as we have seen, the action of persecution apparatuses. Schmitt thus tends to reduce the field of politics to the sole exercise of persecution, which makes it possible to understand why he was able to actively adhere to one of the most murderous extermination enterprises of the twentieth century. When he questioned himself again, after the defeat of Nazism, on the concept of politics, he modified his theory on an essential point. The enemy is defined henceforth as "our own question as *Gestalt*," as this Other who allows me to determine myself; so much so that I must not seek to eliminate him, but to "contend with him in battle, in order to assure my own standard [*Maß*], my own limits, my own Gestalt."[19] This leads him to recognize — a statement that is heavy with meaning for a former supporter of Hitler — that "all extermination is only a self-destruction." It is therefore important to search for a "principle of limitation of hostility" that can prevent the political struggle from becoming radicalized into absolute hostility. It is for this reason that Schmitt comes to distinguish between the *real enemy* and the *absolute enemy*. If the real enemy is a target delimited in space and time, a provisional adversary who may have been a friend or ally before, and who may become one again later, the absolute enemy, on the other hand, presents itself as the object of unlimited hostility, as an "enemy of the human race," a "sub-categorical monster, one who must not only be defended against but definitively annihilated."[20] While the designation of the real enemy aims simply at pushing him back beyond a border or a spatial limit, that of an absolute enemy leads to pursuing him beyond any assignable limit, to *per-secute* him, and it inevitably leads to a war of extermination. Indeed, such an enemy does not oppose us for contingent reasons, but because it is hostile to us by nature; so that our antagonism will continue without end, as long as it has not been eradicated. It is strange that Schmitt considers that this "passage from the real enemy to the absolute enemy" — which he now condemns unreservedly — occurs only in the twentieth century, as a drift that he imputes both to the communists and to the "humanitarian wars" waged by liberal democracies. We should rather consider the absolute enemy as a scheme that runs through the ages and reappears in very different persecution apparatuses. Schmitt notes, moreover, that this policy of absolute hostility finds its source far upstream of our modernity: It has a theological origin; it refers, by secularizing it, to the antagonism between God and the devil, or, more precisely, to the Gnostic dualism of the good and the bad Principle.[21] The designation of an absolute enemy implies indeed a *demonization* of the enemy, the determination of an evil essence, that of a being who can only do evil. This is exactly how Bodin described the Witch.

In many cultures, when evil sorcerers have been identified, they are not punished but, rather, subjected to certain cathartic rites that allow them to be disentangled, to be purged of the evil forces that inhabit them. Among the Nyakyusa of Tanzania, the one who is accused of being a sorcerer must empty himself of the "great serpent" that he carries within him: In order to be reintegrated into his tribe, he must expel the evil out of himself, spit, vomit, and utter out loud the feelings of resentment and hatred that had made him evil . . . For Bodin, on the other hand, "if a Witch has been condemned as a Witch, she will always be reputed to be a Witch, and consequently presumed guilty of all the impiety with which sorcerers are noted" (*Demon-Mania*, 209). On this point, he does not really innovate: During the persecutions of the thirteenth century, heretics had already been qualified as "incorrigible." Similarly, as one of the inquisitors of Arras wrote in the early days of the hunt, sorcerers "cannot be corrected because of the nature of this accursed sect to which they have given themselves once and for all."[22] There would thus be a Fault impossible to expunge, an inexpiable crime that no ritual, no punishment, no later conversion can redeem. It is a question of an occult quality, of a being-sorcerer that sticks to the skin of the accused, from which they will never manage to be delivered. It is worth highlighting the fact that this representation is foreign to the Christian conception of sin, which considers it as a voluntary fault that can be absolved through confession and penance. Even if the meaning of confession was distorted when the medieval Church integrated it into the apparatuses of discipline and persecution, the ritual of confession still bears witness to the power to forgive, to release from guilt that Jesus had transmitted to his apostles. What Christian theology has retained from Augustine's fight against the Manicheans is his conviction that there is no evil nature in us that can compel us to sin. He proclaimed this in a text of admirable rigor in which he opposed the followers of Mani in these terms: "According to you, there is no sin. The race of darkness (*gens tenebrarum*) does not sin, since it fulfills its nature; and the nature of light does not sin, since what it does, it is forced to do. Therefore, there is no sin that can be cured by penance. But if there is penance, there is also fault; if there is fault, there is also will; if there is will in sin, there is no nature that compels us."[23] It is of course the young Augustine who defends an ethical conception of evil, pondered as a free decision of the human will, which he would later renounce by elaborating a doctrine of predestination and a "quasi-gnostic" vision of original sin.[24] When he rejected the Manichean notion of a "race of darkness," he reaffirmed a fundamental message of the Christian faith: that "no man should be called soiled or impure";[25] that redemption and salvation are offered to all. Insofar as the Church has remained faithful to it, this message has prevented it from splitting humanity into two irremediably hostile blocs. For Manicheism does not only consist in hypostasizing evil by making it a transcendent Principle, eternally opposed to the Principle of good: It transposes their antagonism within humanity by dividing it into a race of light predestined to good and a race of darkness doomed by nature to evil. One should avoid giving its modern "racist" meaning to this term: Here *gens tenebrarum* designates the demons and the men who are subjected to them because of their evil nature. When Bodin and the other demonologists claim that witches are *incorrigible* criminals, they unknowingly break with the teaching of the Church to adopt the position of the Manicheans; and this "Gnostic recidivism" was to be repeated in the persecution apparatuses of modern times.

Our demonologists also deviate from the classic rules of law, which establish that the judge can only rule on acts actually performed. By attributing a malefic nature to witches, they dissociate the actions carried out by the accused from her hidden essence, and allow themselves to condemn her *whatever she may have done*. However, since ancient times, it was customary to distinguish between "white" and "black" magic and to punish only those who practiced evil magic. When Emperor Charles V promulgated a penal code in 1532, he still prescribed that only those magicians "who have done harm to others by means of a spell or curse" should be burned at the stake. However, this distinction tended to disappear more and more as the witch hunt intensified throughout Europe. Some forty years later, the Saxon penal code condemned any witch to death, "even if she has done no harm with her art." One step further, and it was soon considered that beneficial magic was *worse* than the other. This is the opinion held by an English theologian: For him, "the good witch is a more horrible and detestable monster than the bad one"; she causes "a thousand times greater harm," because the bad one "strikes only the body," whereas the good one, "by curing the body, causes the death of the soul."[26] This means that the evil essence of the Witch is always at work, even when she seems to be acting for the good, and *especially* when she does so, because her diabolical nature is all the better hidden under this deceitful mask. Satan, as we know, sometimes disguises himself as an angel of light, and the same is true of his followers, who multiply the signs of piety in order to avoid any suspicion. Thus, Madeleine des Aymards tells her judge that an envoy of the devil "exhorted her to feign great devotion and to frequent the churches often, so that it would not be known that they were witches."[27] As for Bodin, he evokes the abbess of a Spanish convent, venerated by all as a saint, until she confessed that she had given herself to Satan and that the miracles she performed were the work of the devil. The more impious one is, the more condemnable one is; but the more pious one is, the more one is suspected of being secretly impious . . . Spee will denounce this unstoppable argument, this double contradictory accusation where the accuser wins at every turn: If the accused "is of bad character," "here is a violent indication of her alleged witchcraft"; "if on the contrary she has been of good character, the indication is not less. For they say that it is the characteristic of the witches to cover themselves thus by the appearance of a virtuous character."[28]

The maleficent side of the mystery of the royal sovereignty, the capital enemy is always a hidden enemy; but this determination is charged here with a moral significance: If he remains invisible, it is because he hides himself that he is a "hypocrite." *The uncovered muzzle of the great hypocrite of France:* This is the title of an engraving distributed by the Holy League after the assassination of the Duke of Guise. It represents Henri III in front of the corpse of the duke, dressed in a monk's robe and holding a rosary to show his piety; but his hood lets glimpse pointed ears of a demon.[29] In a very different context, we will find this accusation when the Jacobins attack the "lies" of Louis XVI and declare the "war on hypocrisy." When Saint-Just denounces "the party that conceals," when he affirms that "the counterrevolutionaries of today, no longer daring to show themselves, have more than once taken the forms of patriotism,"[30] he adopts the same discourse, submits to the same scheme as Bodin and the witch-hunters. And the consequences will be the same: From now on, acts, opinions, appearance, or social status are no longer enough to identify the absolute enemy. If the miscreant is a "witch" but also the devout, the virtuous as well as the debauched, the rich burgomaster as well as the miserable peasant, if the most ardent Sans-Culotte is "suspect" in the same way as the aristocrat or the Girondin, no one will be able to elude the accusation anymore. The haunting of a faceless enemy, of an omnipresent threat, characterizes these phases of terror where the persecution extends without limit.

There is, however, a remarkable difference between the apparatuses of terror: between those that aim simply at the physical extermination of their victims and those that seek first to subdue them by extracting from them the admission of their guilt. Perhaps this difference in strategy refers to two distinct conceptions of the absolute enemy. For one, its malevolent and hostile character attests to a fundamentally evil nature that it would be useless to try to change: The "race of darkness" can only do evil, and the only possible response will be the stake or the gas chamber. For the other, the enemy of the Church or of the Party can still be corrected by the confession or self-criticism that must precede his death; this presupposes that his malevolent character comes from a free decision, from a *freedom to commit evil* that could, however, be straightened out and saved, turned toward good. At the risk of anachronism, I would say that the first conception is Gnostic (or Manichean) and the second, Augustinian.[31] Demonologists seem to agree with the second position. Contrary to the possessed, whom the demon has taken possession of in spite of herself, the witch voluntarily devotes herself to Satan: She is therefore responsible for her misdeeds and can be judged and condemned; but they also maintain that her freedom disappears irrevocably as soon as she submits to him, and that is what makes her incorrigible. Thus, the line between the two positions tends to blur, since this wicked freedom can will *only* evil, which means that it is *not free* and can be attributed to an innate nature. When the witch-hunters sent whole families to the stake, when the Stalinist regime persecuted the parents and children of the "enemies of the people," they too postulated that the fault was rooted in an inherited evil nature. In this perspective, it is no longer a voluntary decision, but an atavistic and unchangeable character, a stain that corrupts both the accused and their relatives. Stalinist ideologists would coin the category of "objective enemy" to designate those who, *without even knowing,* played into the hands of the "imperialist enemy" and therefore deserved death. An analogous concept had already appeared at the height of the witch hunt: It surfaced in the panic-stricken interrogations of those who saw themselves accused without understanding what they were accused of. The theologian Jacques d'Autun thus evokes a condemned who begs his judges to tell him "whether one can be a sorcerer unwittingly, for if that be possible, I may be of that miserable sect, though I know it not."[32]

How can a defilement be communicated without those who spread it being aware of it? In the same way that evil spells are transmitted: through bodily contact. Boguet speaks of a witch who, when she wanted to kill an animal, struck it with her wand saying, *I touch you to kill you*; and some judges were so afraid of being bewitched that, during interrogations, they wore loose-fitting clothes with long sleeves in order to avoid the slightest contact with the accused . . . However, the two privileged forms of contact that transmit the curse are sexual union and the primordial relationship between the mother and her child. A witch is the one who has fornicated with the devil, but also the one whose mother has been condemned as a witch. The belief in the hereditary dimension of being a witch was anchored in the people's mentalities, so much so that certain families were designated as "races of smoke" destined to be burned at the stake. The authors of the *Malleus* already maintained that the children of witches were "inclined to malevolence until the end of their lives": Through the mother's crime, "the whole offspring is infected." Bodin endorses this belief, which allows him to extend the field of persecution by creating a new category, that of the *witch-child*: "if the mother is a witch, so is the daughter, the rule is almost infallible." He therefore advocates pursuing them "up to three generations" and putting to death the children and grandchildren of witches, provided that they have reached the age of twelve. Other demonologists were less lenient: Boguet even recommends "kill[ing] also the one who is still a baby, if one recognizes that there is malice in him."[33] These were not simple threats without consequences. In the early days of the hunt, the judges were content to order that the children of "witches" attend the torture of their parents. The bailiff of Luxeuil thus mentions two children of eight and nine years of age whom he had "condemned to be present at the executions, one of his father, the other of his mother, each loaded with a small burden of thorns, and to throw them into the fire where their father and mother were to burn."[34] As the persecution intensified, these measures of "clemency" were abandoned. In several regions, very young children were executed (some as young as two years old were sent to the stake). By 1629–30, in Molsheim, Alsace, there were thirty-three child victims. Among them, Peter Lichtenauer, aged eleven, and his sister Barbara, aged nine, whose father sat on the court that sentenced them to death . . . In the bourg of Bouchain, in Flanders, several children were put to death, until a royal decree in 1612 forbade the execution of those condemned before they had reached puberty. Thus, little Anne Hauldecœur, arrested and tried at the age of seven, was imprisoned for five years before being burned at the stake.[35]

The insistence of demonologists on the hereditary transmission of witchcraft is quite surprising at a time when no racist doctrine had yet been developed in the modern, bio-political sense of the term. Of course, Bodin does not mention a hereditary contagion: He simply maintains that witches pervert their daughters by bringing them to the Sabbath. Yet his colleague Rémy acts as a precursor when he calls for their children to be put to death at an early age, because "*degenerate blood* bears the mark of its first origin."[36] It is this aspect of the witch hunt that most directly anticipates the "racial" persecutions of the twentieth century. Under what conditions did this belief in a hereditary curse, which could be transmitted by blood, appear? It is astonishing that the society of the Middle Ages, which was based on the heredity of powers, functions, and professions, did not attempt to justify this principle that constitutes its basis. Nonetheless, it seems to have ignored the notion of a natural hierarchy between castes, peoples, or human "races." It is only in the fourteenth century that the notion of "noble blood," of "royal blood," is imposed in France, and the word "race" appears for the first time in our language in 1480, in a treaty on hunting dogs . . . Medieval civilization was indeed steeped in the Christian conception of the equality of all the children of Adam. This is the grandiose vision of a universal Mystical Body in which there is "neither Jew nor Greek, neither slave nor free man, neither man nor woman," and in which all human beings are members in power or in action. It is possible to situate very precisely the time and the country where the opposite conception resurfaces, the one that I have qualified as "Gnostic." In fifteenth-century Spain, a large number of Jews had converted to Christianity — either willingly or often by force — and their descendants occupied an increasingly important place in the ruling classes. It was to limit their growing influence that the City of Toledo adopted statutes in 1449 that excluded these "new Christians" from most official functions. This was a decisive break with the traditional view that the water of baptism purified the new converts and their descendants from their

"Judaic defilement" forever, making it impossible to distinguish them from
the "old Christians." Contemporaries were aware of this: Shortly afterward,
Alonso de Cartagena, bishop of Burgos, published *Defense of Christian Unity*,
in which he declared that the Statutes of Toledo were contrary to the principles of the Catholic faith. In spite of vigorous resistance, the new doctrine of
"purity of blood" (*limpieza del sangre*) quickly gained acceptance throughout
Spain, to the point of being adopted a century later as an almost general rule.
Henceforth, it was impossible to hold public office, to exercise many professions, or to be admitted to the army, the university, or religious orders if one
did not provide "proof of purity" going back up to ten generations. And these
discriminatory measures were extended to the children and grandchildren
of anyone condemned by the Inquisition. In the words of one historian, the
Inquisition had become an "agency for the investigation of blood purity" and
published registers of infamy with lists of families suspected of impurity. As
one inquisitor stated, despite baptism or even "ennoblement by the Prince,
the (Jews') macula remains intact. Nothing can erase their defilement which
spreads through the seed and sticks to the bones. It is something natural and
unchangeable."[37] For it is not only blood that transmits the Jewish curse, but
also other bodily fluids, sperm or milk. In 1644 in Valladolid, an aristocrat
named Lope de Vera y Alarcon was suspected of having secretly converted
to Judaism. The archivists of the Inquisition found no suspicious traces in
his family tree, but it was discovered that the nurse who had breastfed him in
the past was of "infected blood" (that is, of Jewish origin). QED: The noble
hidalgo ends up at the stake.

Admittedly, this was an exclusionary apparatus rather than a persecutory
one, and this fear of the "hidden Jews" did not lead to mass extermination.
Yet the emergence at the end of the Middle Ages of the doctrine of the *limpieza del sangre* calls into question several commonly accepted theses. It is
no longer possible to maintain that "racial" anti-Semitism is only a recent
phenomenon, appearing in the nineteenth century and that has nothing in
common with medieval anti-Judaism. And it becomes difficult to affirm, with
Foucault and his followers, that the exterminations of our time are the result
of a "bio-political paradigm" that began to prevail only two centuries ago, associating politics with the preservation of the living. Unless we admit that this
paradigm is anchored upstream, in originary schemes where the anguish of
the defilement and its ambivalent relation to blood and to other bodily fluids
plays a major role. In any event, it is not irrelevant that the obsession with
the purity of blood began to manifest itself in Spain at the same time when,
in other countries, "races of witches" began to be hunted down. Rather than
a bio-political turn, we are dealing with a *Gnostic turn*: In both cases, these

apparatuses of exclusion and persecution generate a new figure of the absolute enemy, a new version of the Manichean race of darkness, whose wickedness originates in a hereditary and unerasable stain. It is not the life of the living that is at stake with this turn: It is above all directed against the humanity of human beings, by dissociating them into races opposed by nature, and against human freedom by crushing it under the weight of an obscure fatality. Some authors believe to have discovered in the "political religions" of the twentieth century a resurgence of the ancient Gnosticism that would reappears in a secularized society.[38] But the position that I qualify here as Gnostic should not be considered as a particular doctrine. It is a historical a priori that mobilizes a primordial scheme, that of defilement, of its propagation by contact, of its hereditary transmission. This scheme appears in various forms in all human societies, and we shall see that it plays a decisive role in the exclusionary mechanisms that structure Indian society. In truth, the Gnostic position is not limited to this one scheme. It preserves most often the fundamental character of ancient gnosis, which presented itself as a knowledge (*gnôsis* in Greek) that was both esoteric and redemptive, the revelation of an ultimate Secret. It affirms that the Creator of the world is not a God of goodness, but an evil demigod hidden under the mask of "God." By revealing the true nature of this demigod (that is, the God of Israel . . .), the Gnostic revelation allows its initiates to understand his wicked plan and opens the way to salvation. Now, these are the same features that we find at the end of the Middle Ages, when the first versions of the conspiracy scheme appear. What still gives this scheme its strength today is the pleasure of unmasking the Enemy, of uncovering the maneuvers of the "masters of the world" in order to thwart them. When the two major themes of the Gnostic position come together again, when the scheme of the cursed race merges with that of the conspiracy, their conjunction will prove to be particularly deadly. It was no doubt favored by the fact that it is a race *of darkness*, that is to say, a hidden enemy. It should also be noted that, according to some linguists, the word "race" comes from the Latin *ratio* via the medieval Occitan *rassa*, which means precisely "conspiracy, conjuration."

If one can find obvious traces of this gnostic recurrence in the totalitarian movements of our time, its effects were first felt in another domain. It has not been stressed enough that nineteenth-century medicine and psychiatry, when they postulate the existence of "hereditary defects" and "criminals by birth," when they invoke an atavism or a "degeneration" to explain "mental alienations," only take up again the old belief in an evil nature, giving it a pseudoscientific basis. From the incorrigible Witch, we have simply passed to the incurable Abnormal. With the consequences that this implies: If we are dealing with sick people who cannot be cured, passive victims of their pathological heredity, it becomes absurd to judge them for their acts and useless to try to cure them. All that remains is to exclude them, to lock them up for life, to sterilize them, even to eliminate them. Foucault is not wrong in affirming that the exterminating racism of the twentieth century was "born of psychiatry"; or, more exactly, that it results from the fusion of this eugenic medical racism and an ethnic racism.[39] I will simply add that their conjunction was made possible by the same schemes and same neo-Gnostic orientation that underpin these two racisms of different origin. In both cases, the notion of "race" designates a hereditary predisposition, a blind determinism, meant to explain all the acts of an individual. As Barrès declared, "that Dreyfus is capable of betraying, I conclude from his race." Indeed, the shift from a theological to a medical perspective had begun much earlier, even before exorcists began to give way to physicians. From the seventeenth century onward, a shift took place within the system of persecution: From the Witch — who was totally at fault, because she had freely given herself to Satan — the Possessed was now distinguished, and the latter was no longer responsible for an evil that had come to her from outside. In a context still marked by the Augustinian position, the involuntary character of her possession allows her to be exonerated, since she is only an innocent prey of the devil. Yet after modern science's decisive victory, such considerations will no longer apply, and the Possessed, having now become the Hysteric (or the "démonomane"), will dissipate in the anonymous mass of the abnormals consigned to straitjackets, to electroconvulsive therapy, and to lobotomies and programs of sterilization and euthanasia.

Have we adequately determined the features of the absolute enemy, this wicked Other, always concealed and incorrigible? When Schmitt refers to him as an *inhuman monster*, he is indicating another of his fundamental traits. What characterizes the position I call "Manichean" is that it divides humanity into two races that are opposed in essence, as light is opposed to darkness and good to evil. If their antagonism is based on their nature, it must be possible, in order to account for it, to have recourse to the most obvious natural difference, the one that distinguishes humanity from other living species. Ultimately, there is no longer any question of two *human* races, because they do not belong to the same species: Either the race of light is presented as superhuman, of quasi-divine essence, as certain Gnostics already did;[40] or the race of darkness is rejected as outside and below humanity, considering it as an animal species, *bestializing* it. The conjunction of these two gestures, the opposition that it entails between a supposedly superior race and races of *Untermenschen* destined to servitude or death, will be a major theme of Nazi ideology; but it is already announced in the "biological" racism of the nineteenth century. Barrès could then declare that the "Indo-European race" and the "Semitic race" are in fact "different species" and conclude that it was useless to judge Captain Dreyfus, that there was only need to slaughter him, because "there is no justice except within the same species."[41] This passage from the struggle between two human *races* to an antagonism between two different and hostile *species* will have formidable consequences. It fixes hostility forever at its most intense degree, transforms it into a war without mercy, without possible armistice or reconciliation, since no agreement is possible between men and "monsters" foreign to the human species. Such antagonism sooner or later leads to extermination, because these evil beasts must be annihilated, without their killing being considered a crime. At most, it is an act of self-defense, even of simple hygiene, all the more so when they are no longer considered as ferocious beasts, as animals to be slaughtered, but as repulsive creatures, parasites, vermin. Without a doubt, the genocide in Rwanda would not have been carried out with an unruffled good conscience by so many honest citizens had a powerful apparatus not persuaded them that the Tutsis were both dangerous "agents of the foreigner" and "cockroaches" that needed to be eradicated.

It would be wrong to believe that this bestialization of the enemy only appeared in modern times. The Werewolf, Agamben reminds us, is first and foremost the *wargus*, the ancient German equivalent of *homo sacer*: the banished one, condemned to roam the forests and whom anyone has the right to kill. It should come as no surprise that the same figure of the wolf-man also appears in the opposite pole, that of political sovereignty. Since Plato's *Republic*, an entire tradition assimilates the political enemy par excellence — the evil ruler, the tyrant — to a wild beast, a wolf thirsty for human blood. At times of crisis, this identification has led to the representation of a monarch under animal traits: those of a dreaded beast, like Henry III in the pamphlets of the Holy League, or of a vile beast, a king-pig, like Louis XVI in revolutionary caricatures. However, these are only polemical representations intended to belittle the opponent, and no Sans-Culotte has ever believed that Louis Capet really turned into a pig. The same is not true when certain authors of the late Middle Ages claim that Jews have a small tail and that their wives can give birth to pigs. In this case, bestialization seems to be real . . .[42] There is another figure of the enemy who is not only characterized by partial traits of animality but who can be transformed entirely into an animal, namely the Witch. For a long time, there were stories of witches who could transform themselves into evil animals, usually into wolves or cats. They were said to be wounded by a hunter in their animal form and, having regained their human form, their wound would betray them, like a stigma allowing the discovery of the spell. However, it was not until the time of the witch hunt that people began to question the reality of these metamorphoses and that some judges made them a charge that could lead to the burning of the accused. From the sixteenth century onward, trials were brought against alleged werewolves, but they rarely resulted in convictions. We have seen that in 1603, a young peasant named Jean Grenier declared that he and his father turned into wolves and that he sometimes devoured little girls. Although he was condemned in the first instance to be strangled and burned as a sorcerer, this judgment was overturned on appeal by the Parliament of Bordeaux, which considered, after having consulted doctors, that this "stupid and dazed" teenager was a "melancholic" and that this was nothing more than an "imaginary metamorphosis."[43] Most of the judges and demonologists agree with the authors of the *Malleus*, who consider these metamorphoses as simple illusions, the fantasies of an imagination derailed by the devil.[44] Bodin is one of the only ones to make an exception, since he maintains on the contrary that "the evil angels have the power to transmute our bodies" and consequently considers lycanthropy as "a very certain, true and indubitable event" (*Demon-Mania*, 112–13). At any rate, he pretends to believe this. He knew his classics well enough to know that bestiality also has a political significance, that it is an effective means of making an adversary a capital enemy of the State. The bloodthirsty werewolf that roams the night can convincingly represent such an enemy: As a contemporary writes, "man being a divine and political animal, the lycanthrope is a wild animal [. . .] enemy of the sun, that is to say of the king, himself an image of God."[45]

The political dimension of this belief, the role it can play in exclusion and persecution, should not be underestimated. When Ginzburg evokes the transformations of the Benandanti into animals or reports the testimony of an old Livonian peasant who said he changed into a wolf to fight troops of sorcerers, he sees in them survivals of immemorial traditions on the powers of shamans, brotherhoods of warrior-bears and warrior-wolves who "fight in ecstasy" by putting on animal skins that make them invulnerable. This is because he is only interested in cases where men claim to *change themselves* into animals, without taking into account those very different situations where *other men and women are accused* of doing so. As with the other primordial schemes, the scheme of metamorphosis can be applied just as much to the magical warrior as to the widely hated and rejected wargus. The figure of the man changed into a beast is, at the outset, as ambivalent as those of the magician and the ecstatic undead (or even those of the Jew and the leper). When this ambivalence is undone, they take on a purely evil meaning and give way to the werewolf, the diabolical witch, the vampire. Whereas they had once aroused sacred veneration and terror, they now only provoke horror and hatred. What is decisive in this scheme is the very process of metamorphosis, with the de-figuration that it implies: that moment when the face is deformed into a muzzle or a beak, when claws and fangs emerge, when the skin is covered with thick fur or a shell. A moment of terror evoked in fairy tales or in Ovid's poem, and that is also the moment when Gregor Samsa wakes up "transformed into a monstrous vermin." The fascination of this scene lies in the fact that it reveals the fragility of the human form, its disquieting proximity to animal forms, be they terrifying or abject. Between the two kingdoms, the border proves to be strangely permeable, and a simple accentuation of certain features can make one pass through to the other side. Aristotle thus evokes the curvature of the nose that, by becoming slightly cambered or convex, "remains no less beautiful and pleasant to look at"; but "if we accentuate this tendency excessively . . . finally the deformation will be such that there will not even be the appearance of a nose":[46] We then pass from the human face to the animal face. Between the beautiful straightness of the nose and the bestial ugliness of the muzzle or the snout, there is only a difference of degree. And yet it entails a change of nature, the passage to another species, which can be a harmful species that it will be necessary to eliminate. From what degree of curvature does a nose that is too hooked make its owner a subhuman? Some, as we know, have paid for it with their lives . . . The fabulous stories of witch-cats and sorcerer-wolves remind us that "the figure of the enemy coincides with that of a body or a set of bodies to be destroyed."[47] And it is most often an abnormal or deformed body, marked by the visible or hidden sign of a difference. Neither human nor animal, *both* man and repulsive or ferocious beast, the enemy's body is always a hybrid, a mixture. It is therefore not surprising if he presents both masculine and feminine traits, as we shall see in the case of the devil; and if he is also an undead. From the shaman or the Benandante to the bloodthirsty vampire, the same scheme persists that designates in the enemy the presence of death, the threatening intrusion of death into the living. This is what Céline denounced in his hallucinatory imprecations in which he attacks the Jew, projecting all his disgust, rage and hatred onto him: "He is only rotten, rotting. He has only one authentic thing at the bottom of his scum substance, it is his hatred for us, his contempt, his rage to make us sink lower and lower, into a mass grave."[48]

What about the body in the witch hunt, in all the persecution apparatuses? What do these monstrously deformed bodies mean, half-man half-beast, male and female, the revolting bodies of the possessed, bodies lacerated by the devil's claw or mutilated by a curse, representations of which are rife in the persecution's imaginary? First of all, we can see the designation of very real targets that are identified with singular bodies. These stigmatized bodies are the anchoring point of the apparatuses: It is by producing a "knowledge" on the body of the enemy, by putting it into practice in the rites of exorcism and the torture chambers, that the apparatuses of persecution ensure their hold on their victims. They are also the figurations of a collective Body: The bodies that are deformed, torn apart, or let themselves be penetrated by a hostile entity are so many metaphors of the Great Body of the Church or of the State that the apparatuses must defend against the Stranger who threatens them. If mass persecutions always involve sovereign power, we are dealing each time with a sovereignty in crisis, endangered by an external aggression, a revolt or a civil war, that tries to rebuild itself. It is this sovereignty that is represented as a body attacked by a hostile force, a body in the process of being disfigured, of being disembodied. The real body of the enemy — its cursed part, its abject waste, what can be designated as the "remainder" of the community — then appears as a sick part that must be cut off from the Great Body. There is yet another way of representing this heterogeneous element. Since Christ is the head of the Mystical Body of the Church, some theologians maintain that his enemies are part of *another body* opposed to him, of a *Corpus diaboli* of which Satan is the head. The body of the witch is then much more than a simple human body: It is one of the "members of the devil," a living incarnation of the Anti-Body of the absolute enemy.[49]

This organic representation of the community as an immense Body of which each individual is a member does not only belong to Christian theology. It can already be found in Plato and Aristotle, and it reappears in the political philosophers of modern times, after the conception of the Church as a mystical Body has been secularized and transferred to the Kingdom, the State, the Nation. It can also be found in other civilizations, for example, in India, where it plays an essential role in legitimizing the caste system. Such representations are not simple metaphors: To take up a Kantian distinction, they are not *symbols* (analogical representations external to what they illustrate), but *schemes*, modes of figuration of a community where the latter gives itself consistency by presenting itself to itself. Such a prevalent mode of figuration cannot come from a cultural tradition or a particular doctrine. For it to have asserted itself in so many different times and cultures, it must be rooted in a primordial experience affecting each human subject: It must find its source in the original schemes that allow each of us to constitute his or her own body, to unify the heterogeneous multitude of his or her flesh impressions under the stable form of a body. Such is the function that the incorporation schemes assure in the genesis of our individual body: They unify the dispersed carnal poles by arranging them like so many parts of a total body. Flesh poles live henceforth like parts of a whole, like differentiated and hierarchical organs, while the inside of the body distinguishes itself from its outside, the top from the bottom, the right side from the left side, the head from the other members; and that a heterogeneous residue, a remainder, dissociates itself from this total body. The genesis of the community replays on the intersubjective level that of the singular individual: The same schemes that had transformed my flesh poles into bodily organs take hold of my body and of *the bodies of others* to make of them the members of a transcendent Great Body.[50] When I recognize others as an *alter ego*, when I insert myself with them into a community, we can hardly avoid submitting ourselves to this scheme, to merge imaginatively into a unique Body. Is it not the ideal of love, this fantasy of a flesh fusion where our individuality would abolish itself? Of course, this collective embodiment can be more or less intense and fusional, but it tends to be reproduced in different forms in all human communities. It is then necessary to ask ourselves if these will always take the form of a unique body; if it is possible to withdraw from this scheme; if a disembodied community could exist and maintain itself without submitting to the prevailing form of a body.

Claude Lefort's work provides some elements of answer: For him, modern democracy is based precisely on a "dynamic of disembodiment" that, since the French Revolution and the execution of the king, strives to undo all the representations of a collective Body, by exposing the social to the test of division, of indeterminacy, of an incessant questioning. He notices that, in societies shaped by this dynamic, the totalitarian attempts to "remake" the body only succeed in reconstituting a deformed representation of the Great Body, where "the attraction of the whole is not dissociated any more from that of the fragmentation."[51] We may regret, however, that he did not sufficiently question the ambivalent meaning of disembodiment. If we want to understand its advent on the level of the community, it is necessary to return to the level of immanence of the ego-flesh, to resort to egoanalysis. We discover then that this process announces itself in the originary experience of our singular ego, where our incorporation is never definitively acquired, where it must unceasingly start again, reconstitute itself by resisting to an adverse tendency. If it is so, it is because its flesh underpinning is precarious; that the chiasma in which my flesh is knotted to itself risks unraveling again and again; that it generates a remainder that does not find its place in the body and resists being embodied. We have seen that the anguish of disembodiment increases even more when the double transference where I give flesh to the body of the other is interrupted, and where it allows in return my flesh to become body. While the body of the other becomes defleshed and disfigured, my own body no longer manages to identify itself with it and in turn becomes disfigured. It is in this primordial experience that the representations of monstrous bodies, at the same time men and beasts, living and dead, masculine and feminine, that we discovered in the persecution imaginary, originate. This monstrously deformed body is the body of another disfigured by the rupture of the flesh transfer; but it is also my body that decomposes and appears to me now like a stranger. The possibility of disembodiment thus presents itself on this level as a terrifying threat. If it is most often occluded in our daily experience, it transpires in certain borderline states, through phantasms of intrusion, of fragmentation, of self-mutilation, of self-destruction, that haunt our nightmares and obsess certain psychotics to the point of delirium. However, such phantasms are also manifested on the level of the community, long before the democratic revolutions of the modern times. Often, the classical representations of the Great Body describe it as a sick body, "swollen with humours" (Plato) or affected by gangrene, or as a deformed body where the disproportion of the organs compromises the unity of the whole. Far from carrying the promise of a collective emancipation, the perspective of disembodiment appears at first as a disaster. In the traditional reading of the Body politic, it is the stable hierarchy of its members and their submission to the head that allows it to sustain itself while avoiding decomposition. According to Aquinas, "the body of man, like that of any animal, would fall apart if there were not in it a certain guiding force, ordered to the common good of all the members [. . .] It is therefore necessary that there be in any multitude a guiding principle charged with governing."[52] By allowing itself to be incorporated in the form of a unique body, the multitude subordinates itself to a single sovereign will: In this perspective, the political body is no more than an inert matter, entirely submitted to the guiding principle that unifies and animates it. What this theory refuses to consider is that a multitude can cohere *by itself*, without submitting to a master, to a transcendent Other, unifying itself without submitting to the scheme of the Great Body, to the sovereignty of the One.

It should come as no surprise that Bodin remains faithful to this tradition when he uses an analogous image to illustrate the necessary subordination of the Republic to its Sovereign. Just as "the ship is no more than wood, without the form of a vessel, when the keel that supports the sides, the bow, the stern and the upper deck is removed, the Republic without sovereign power that unites all its members and parts [. . .] into one body is no longer a Republic."[53] The vessel is here only a metaphor for the organic unity of the body: For Bodin, as for so many other thinkers, political sovereignty is founded in an incorporation scheme. It thus takes the form of a *politics of the Body*, and this one legitimizes the persecution: When the "conspiracy of the sorcerers" threatens the "body of a Republic," "it is necessary to apply to it the cauteries and hot irons, and to cut off the putrefied parts" (*Demon-Mania*, 184). That the amputation of a gangrenous member is required to save the whole body, that it is sometimes necessary to sacrifice a part of the City for the good of the whole, was already a lesson found in Plato.[54] And we will find this figure-scheme (or the very similar one of the purge) in the inquisitors of the Middle Ages, when they call for the annihilation of heretics in order to save the Mystical Body of the Church; but also, as we shall see, in a Jacobin like Billaud-Varenne, when he intends to justify the Terror of 1793, or in the rhetoric of the Stalinist trials. The reason why the discourse of persecution so often has recourse to it is that it brings into play the expulsion of a heterogeneous element, the excision of a remainder that allows a body to constitute itself as a unique, total body. The capital enemy, whatever his name, presents himself each time as a figure of the remainder, and that is what destines him to expulsion or extermination.

Another passage in the *Six Books of the Republic* suggests a different way of representing the remainder. At the moment when he evokes the civil wars that are the "capital plague of the Republics," Bodin compares them to a body struck by madness to the point of tearing itself apart: "If it were to happen that (the limbs) were to *become hateful toward one another* and that one hand were to cut off the other [. . .] and each limb were to prevent its neighbor, it is quite certain that the body would finally remain truncated and mutilated [. . .] The Republic will suffer from it and will happen to it what it was to the virgin, for whom, as Plutarch says, the pursuers entered in such jealousy and passion that they dismembered her in pieces."[55] It is no longer a question of the disintegration of an organism deprived of its unifying principle: Here we are confronted with the mad rebellion of a body that "becomes hateful" *against itself*, of which each limb turns against the others and seeks to destroy them. Phantasm of a fragmented body, or rather of a body that mutilates and parcels out itself, as if it was struggling against an internal "bad object" impossible to circumscribe. This internal enemy is still the remainder, but it presents itself here under a more diffuse and worrying aspect. Instead of being fixed in an organ that one can amputate, it spreads throughout the whole body by identifying itself with each of its parts; this no longer justifies only the persecution of a determined enemy, but calls for a terror without limits. Such a phantasm is situated below the organic body, on the elementary plane of the flesh, that of an ego-flesh that is anxious to discover in itself a stranger and make it the object of its hatred. Since this thing seems to emerge from within its flesh, the hatred that it arouses is presented as a hatred of oneself, a self-destructive rage. Like the classical metaphors of purging and amputation, this phantasm of self-mutilation attempts to figure an unfigurable phenomenon, the initial exclusion of the remainder. No doubt it is *closer to the truth* of the remainder than such metaphors; for the remainder is constituted on the plane of the primordial flesh, even before being embodied in the form of a body composed of distinct parts. This is how it appears in the imaginary of persecutions as an undifferentiated threat, a hostile entity impossible to delimit, which spreads everywhere like an evil contagion. And certainly, on the immanent plane of the ego-flesh, the remainder is impossible to circumscribe, since it is a part of my flesh appearing to me as both a heterogeneous element and as belonging to my flesh and haunting me like an internal stranger. This text thus makes it possible to approach the most original matrix of the hatred, a hatred that finds its source in our primordial relation to the remainder.

If Bodin wrote the *Demon-Mania*, it was with a political aim. He tried to put an end to the religious wars, to reconcile opponents by providing them with a common enemy; but it was also to escape from a phantasm: from the haunting vision — emerging in the *Republic* — of a body that dismembers itself. It is a bodily scheme, that of amputation, that, joined to the conspiracy scheme, will allow him to overcome this haunting. From the *Republic* to the *Demon-Mania*, the landscape has been profoundly transformed. For the madness of a body whose every organ went to war against the others, another representation was substituted, that of a *reembodied body*, reconciled with itself and consistent enough to support, if it is necessary, "the cauteries and hot irons" in order to amputate some of its members. It is still a question of mutilation, but it only concerns a small number of organs that must be cut off for the good of all the others. It is as if the hatred, previously spread throughout the body, has now been concentrated in one point. The meaning of this operation has also changed: It is no longer a primordial panic that pushes the body to self-mutilation. It is the intervention of an Other distinct from this body that motivates the amputation, that of the doctor, the wise ruler whose science authorizes him to cut into the flesh, to decide which members of the people have the right to live or die. The wild rebellion of a body that unleashes its hatred against itself is superseded by the reassuring vision of a well-ordered Republic where sovereign power is exercised by designating the enemy that must be extirpated from the Great Body.

This enemy represents each time a figure of the remainder, and this is why it becomes the focus of all the hate. And yet the remainder is not only a source of anguish, disgust, or hatred: It is an ambivalent phenomenon that can, by being transfigured, become an object of love. Whomever a whole community sets up as the only object of love, to the point of alienating themselves to him, of submitting themselves lovingly to his power, is the sovereign of this community: the divine or human leader, invisible or visible, whose subjects imagine constituting the Great Body and ordering it toward the Good. Freud has brought to light the role of the loving identification with the leader who cements the masses and the social institutions; so much so that, if this identification fails, the mass, falling prey to a "panic anguish," immediately disperses. He spotted — without examining it sufficiently — the possibility of a *negative identification* where hatred assures the same function as love in the positive identifications.[56] On this point, egoanalysis brings a complement to the discoveries of psychoanalysis: It affirms indeed that, loving or hateful, these identifications that underlie human communities originate in a primordial self-identification, that which unites the ego to the remainder of its flesh. Everything opposes, at first sight, the glorious body of the sovereign and the abject body of the enemy, this stigmatized body, dedicated to torments and death. However, these two antagonistic poles result from the splitting of the same ambivalent phenomenon: They represent on the level of the community two opposite aspects of the remainder. This allows us to understand that they are reversible, that love can change into hatred, and sometimes hatred into love. Before taking on the monstrous features of the werewolf, the evil sorcerer, or the vampire, the wolf-man and the shaman had been the object of sacred veneration; and the same reversibility affects the figure of the monarch when he transforms himself into a sorcerer-king, a fawn-king, or a pig-king. Michelet had intuited it: If the French were able to commit a regicide, it is because "no people had loved its kings as much," and we know that hatred is never as intense as when it takes its source in love. We will have to return to this decisive moment when the sense of identification is reversed, when "the king, this god, this idol, becomes an object of horror." This passage from love to hatred is not always immediate: In some cases, the object of love goes through an intermediate phase where it is not yet a question of annihilating it, but only of pushing it aside, of expelling it like waste. What was a pole of attraction becomes the target of an intense repulsion, which is not hatred, but disgust. Bataille tried to found a *heterology* — a "science of the heterogeneous element" — on the affirmation of "the subjective elementary identity of excrements (sperm, menses, urine, fecal matter) and of all that could be considered as sacred, divine or marvelous."[57] He considers in this perspective the royal sovereignty as one of the modes of this heterogeneous element that carries out an "imperative exclusion" of its other mode by turning it into an object of disgust. Thus, "the world of the sovereignty has as an elementary function to define the world of misery as untouchable and unnameable, as *defiled* and *impure*."[58] His analysis thus completes that of Schmitt: More original than the political demarcation between friend and enemy would be this demarcation between the noble and the ignoble, which is itself based on the initial ambivalence of the sacred and the defiled. It is for this reason that, more often than not, the phases of exclusion of the impure precede the phases of persecution

and extermination of the enemy. If Schmitt allows us to understand the apparatuses of persecution, Bataille, on the other hand, gives us the key to the
apparatuses of exclusion. It is then a question of articulating these two theories
in order to understand the intimate relationship that is established between
these two types of apparatuses.

How can one escape this original ambivalence — this oscillation between
attraction and repulsion, desire and disgust, love and hate? How can a community free itself from its love of the Sovereign, its disgust and hatred of the
Stranger? In his last works, Derrida had begun a *deconstruction of sovereignty*,
a "never-ending" task, he said, intended to open the horizon of a "democracy
to come." This deconstruction seems necessary if we want to resist the logic
of hatred: The persecution apparatuses, we know, are linked to the sovereign
power. Their mission is to capture hatred, to concentrate it on a figure of the
enemy in order to defend a sovereignty in crisis, to protect a political body that
threatens to disintegrate. But has Derrida really given himself the means to
accomplish this task, given that he never addresses the question of the political
Body? The "messianic" politics that he tries to elaborate remains suspended
on ethical imperatives of justice and hospitality, without ever anchoring itself
in a phenomenology of the flesh and the body, or, moreover, confronting
the genealogy of the power apparatuses. For a community to free itself from
its alienating identifications, it would have to manage to disembody itself, to
withdraw from the figurations of the Great Body without immediately disintegrating. This implies that it finds its consistency in itself, in an element
that preexists the political Body. What is this originary element? If I operate
the *epochē*, if I put out of play the world and my existence with the others in
the world, "I find my own flesh (*Leib*) distinguishing itself from all the others
(bodies) by a unique particularity; it is indeed the only body (*Körper*) which
is not only body, but precisely also flesh."[59] This primordial corporeality that
I feel in my touch, my listening, my vision, in my sensations of movement, of
effort and resistance to effort, of anguish, of pleasure, of pain, this arch-body of
affects, of impulses and of primary sensations, that is my flesh. Between flesh
and body, there is an essential difference: The unity of my flesh is not given
to me at once. I apprehend it as a moving multiplicity of fragmentary impressions, of dispersed flesh poles. By identifying themselves with each other, by
embodying each other, these multiple poles intertwine to compose a flesh
community that supports my body and animates it throughout my life. Insofar
as it manages to unify itself without submitting to an *arkhē*, to the authority of
a superior principle, the flesh is an an-archic multiplicity. It is only in a later
phase of its genesis that the schemes of embodiment will constitute it as an
organic body. The phenomenological difference between flesh and body has

thus a political significance. If it is true that the individual body is founded on the base of its flesh, it is necessary to admit that the figures of the collective Body are also founded on a more original community of flesh.

This prebodily community, "acephalous" and an-archic, how to detect it under the corporal figurations and the sedimented institutions that conceal it? It remains the unthought of political philosophy, for this philosophy has been elaborated since Plato and Aristotle *from the point of view of the Body*, in order to legitimize each time a figure of the Great Body, the hierarchy of its organs, the sovereignty of its directing Principle; and it can only envision a disembodiment of this Body as a disaster, a panic dispersion. And yet, if there is a flesh of history, an arch-community of flesh that configures itself in the form of a political Body, it should be able to free itself from the schemes of embodiment, to maintain itself in spite of the crises of this Body. In truth, the flesh of the community does not have the same status, the same consistency as the flesh of individuals. When I transfer my flesh onto a foreign body in order to constitute it as another embodied entity, the site of an *alter ego*, it is only a question, Husserl warns us, of an "analogical transposition": Between my life and that of another, an unbridgeable barrier persists, and each of us will remain forever a monad without doors or windows. In spite of everything, the flesh transfer takes place; in spite of the irreducible distance that separates our lived experiences, it makes possible a universal historical community that "embraces all the monads and the groups of monads of which one could imagine the coexistence."[60] It is this underpinning of flesh covered and dissimulated by the stature of the collective Bodies that is the flesh of the history. It is, however, only a *quasi-flesh* derived by projection and transfer of each singular flesh. What follows for the collective Bodies that are built on the basis of this community? If they submit to the same schemes, reproduce the same structure, their status differs deeply from that of the individual body. While the primordial flesh is constituted through the chiasm "both as flesh and as a corporeal thing," objectifies itself in a body while remaining flesh, the same is not true on the collective level. Deprived of this chiasm, of this living presence of my flesh to itself that gives its foundation to my body, the Great Body remains unstable and precarious. Either it threatens to disintegrate by sinking into chaos, or it deincarnates by transforming itself into an abstract entity, incapable of structuring and animating a human community (it is this tendency to deincarnate that most often characterizes contemporary societies).

In this respect, the demarcation between flesh and body can thus take the form of a radical opposition. Whence does the Great Body derive its power and the illusory appearance of its life? From individual flesh bodies, whose flesh it captures by incarnating it. This, a young and daring thinker had dis-

covered while questioning the enigma of *voluntary servitude*. When La Boétie
wonders how a "great and infinite number of men" can actively consent to
their servitude, he answers by describing a donation of flesh, an alienating
transfer where a multitude of flesh poles project themselves onto the figure
of a single transcendent Body and identify with it: "From where did it take
so many eyes from which it spies on you, if you do not give them to it? How
can he have so many hands with which to strike you, if he does not take them
from you? How can he have any power over you, except through you?" It is the
hidden truth of the Body politic that he unveils here. And he draws the necessary conclusion: Since the sovereign "has no power but that which is given
to him," it is enough to "give him nothing," to interrupt this transfer, to cease
to be embodied in the Body of the One — "and you will see it, like a great
colossus whose base has been removed, collapse into itself and break."[61] La
Boétie thus reveals to us the emancipatory scope of disembodiment, and we
discover that it has a very different meaning on the individual and collective
planes. When it is a question of the own body, of our bodies of living flesh, the
perspective of its disintegration is only a terrifying phantasm. In the case of the
political Body, it carries, on the contrary, the promise of a utopian (or, if one
wants, messianic) community, a disembodied community without sovereign
principle and without enemy.

So what are the obstacles that prevent this community from arising? Here
again, La Boétie gives us some elements of an answer. If he was able to uncover the *arcana* of sovereign power, the fundamental apparatus that allows
it to victoriously resist seditions and revolts, it is because he lived and wrote
in the immediate vicinity of a peasant insurrection and that he was acutely
aware of its limits. He wrote his *Discourse on Voluntary Servitude* in 1548,
when the revolt that had set his province on fire had just been defeated by
the royal army. It is this radical refusal of all servitude, this will to disembody
totally from the Great Body, that the insurgent peasants lacked. Their revolt
remained partial, reactive, limited to demanding the abolition of the salt tax,
without questioning all the privileges and apparatuses of power. After seizing Bordeaux, they simply appealed "very humbly" to the king's "mercy" to
listen to their demands.[62] Henry II responded by sending his army to crush
the uprising. The repression was to be ruthless: It is said that, after having
executed hundreds of "leaders," the king's soldiers tortured the leader of the
revolting peasants by driving a crown of red-hot iron into his skull. According
to one contemporary, they did this to imprint on his body "the mark of the
sovereignty he had usurped."[63] By refusing to attack directly the focus of sovereign power, by continuing to submit to the figure of the Prince, the rebels
had allowed themselves, as La Boétie admirably wrote, "to be fascinated and,

as it were, bewitched by the name of the One." This capture by the name and in the body of the One condemned their revolt to an inevitable defeat. It would be mistaken to simply oppose revolt and servitude: What the *Discourse* reminds us of is that the processes that maintain servitude, the representations that justify it, are always at work within the rebellion itself. It could be that they persist even when the rebellion is victorious; that the figure of the Body-One tends to reconstitute itself within the revolutionary process by reproducing in other forms the same apparatuses of exclusion and persecution, the same logic of hate. Such is the question that the revolutions of modern times raise for us, and I will try to confront it in the discussion that follows. One difficulty remains, however. We are beginning to understand how popular revolts have been demonized: It is the schemes of persecution that the power apparatuses have projected onto them that have presented them as a threat to the unity of the Great Body, as figures of the absolute enemy, justifying in advance the bloodiest repressions. On the other hand, it remains difficult to understand how so many innocent victims, accused of being witches, could be stigmatized as the "worst of the rebels," how these so-called heretics, enemies of God and the Church, ended up appearing also as the capital enemy of the Prince. If it should not be underestimated, Bodin's influence is not sufficient to explain this turn. One must then ask oneself what the kernel of truth of such representations is, and if there is not an essential relation between the myth of the witches' Sabbath and these rebellions that confront the sovereignty of the State. These popular revolts are indeed presented in the same way as the Sabbath: as the grotesque and disquieting representation of an upside-down world.

5
The World Upside Down

Contribution to a Phenomenology of Multitudes

What is the Witch? A figure of the absolute enemy. A terrifying threat that needs to be fought relentlessly until she is annihilated. First an enemy of the Church, since the practice of magic has been assimilated to heresy, she has also become the enemy of the State, since Bodin and his kind have designated her as the "ultimate rebel." As a counterfigure of sovereign power, the "sect of sorcerers" is often presented as a countersociety as ordered and hierarchical as that of which it is the replica. It is therefore not surprising that, like the ruffians of the Court of Miracles, the sorcerers have their "king" and their "queen" (after all, didn't the possessed of Sainte-Baume accuse Gauffridi of being the "prince of sorcerers"?) and that, in certain descriptions of the Sabbath, the master-sorcerers arrive in a carriage and are served by servants in livery. Nevertheless, demonologists sometimes accuse him of systematically inverting all the customs in place: of being an *upside-down world*. Thus Rémy is incensed by the "extravagant morals" of witches and sorcerers at the Sabbath, who sign with their left hand, dance backward, back-to-back, move "backward like crabs," and "behave in all things in a manner opposite to that of other men"; and de l'Ancre maintains that, during black masses, the officiant is "raised in the air with his feet up and his head down before the devil" since "the devil, who loves only disorder, wants all things to be done in reverse."[1] In some cases, the simple fact of having danced or walked backward could lead an accused to the stake . . . It could be shown that *all* the rites of the Sabbath are a parodic inversion of the customs and ceremonies of Christian society: By kissing the demon's anus, his followers parody the feudal ritual of the kiss of homage to the suzerain; when they enumerate their misdeeds in front of their master, who congratulates them, they imitate the ritual of confession by inverting its meaning. There are satanic incantations that consist in reciting Catholic prayers in reverse; and the imposition of the diabolical mark, followed by the attribution of a new name, is a simulacrum of baptism. An engraving by Hans Baldung Grien presents a striking image of this reversal of perspective that defines the world of the Sabbath: A naked witch with her back to us puts her head between her spread legs, as close to her sex as possible, and looks at us upside down . . . Let us not forget, however, that in the persecution imaginary, this representation coexists with others. Superimposed on the caricature of an upside-down world is a faceless haunting, that of a foul, proliferating Thing, which awakens the old panics of contamination, gangrene, and epidemic. It is this that Bodin calls to eradicate by the cauteries and the hot irons; it is this "vermin" that Boguet evokes, "which has pullulated for a long time, and which would have infected many places" without the energetic action of the witch-hunters. How can such heterogeneous representations coexist? Would the figuration of a world turned upside down be only a *screen-image* that protects from a terrifying threat?

It is this imaginary construction of the upside-down world that we should first analyze. As one historian observes, the category of "witch" is a topology: It is defined "by a strict polar opposition" to the dominant norms and values and "by the spatial metaphor of inversion."[2] It is impossible to understand its meaning without inscribing it in a network of symbolic polarities, in the system of oppositions between the sacred and the profane, the beneficent and the maleficent, the pure and the impure, the proper and the foreigner, the masculine and the feminine, the human and the animal, the order and the disorder, the day and the night, etc., which can be found in various forms in all human cultures. Among these pairs of opposites, several refer to the fundamental polarities of the human body, to those dual relationships that characterize the different dimensions of our body, such as up and down, inside and outside, front and back, right and left side. These polarities are presented as dissymmetrical, hierarchical relations, where one of the poles dominates the other: They are inserted in apparatuses that allow the dominant pole to subjugate or exclude the subaltern pole. The diabolical inversion that presides over the Sabbath consists precisely in reversing this hierarchy, and Satan is the name that designates this *principle of inversion of polarities*. It is not surprising, therefore, that his worshippers perform their rites left-handed or upside down, using excrement and impure substances — and that most of them are women. Indeed, the opposition of masculine and feminine in the general system of symbolic polarities tends to associate femininity with the subordinate, impure, and wicked side, so that the inversion of the system could only be done by *witches*. One of the main grounds for the "feminization" of the

Sabbath appears here: It is the logic of the dominant symbolic oppositions that has progressively oriented the apparatus of persecution toward women. Where does this *scheme of inversion* come from? What can be the historical origin of these representations? And in which original schemes do they find their source?

Historians have traced the origin of most of the elements that make up the myth of the Sabbath. When witches are accused of worshipping Satan, desecrating the sacraments, practicing sodomy, incest, and infanticide, these are accusations that have been directed for centuries against heretics and Jews, and that have simply been transferred to a new target group. As for animal metamorphoses, night flights, and night assemblies, Ginzburg has shown that these representations are rooted in popular beliefs linked to ancient rites of shamanic origin. However, there are two features attributed to the "diabolic sect" that do not seem to be linked to any known belief, to any identifiable historical phenomenon: its representation as a hostile multitude and that of the upside-down world. But how can we render this fact? We know that the inversion scheme is found in other cultures, where it is used in religious rites. In several North American Native cultures, there are "ritual clowns," incarnations of divine tricksters, who are supposed to transgress all taboos, to speak and act in a way opposite to what they mean, to dress as women, to swallow excrement and urine . . . Is it possible to find such practices in Western civilization? A historian tells us about a strange service celebrated in the chapel of the convent of the Cordeliers in Antibes: The officiants "sit in the choir stalls instead of the religious priests; the priestly ornaments are ripped and turned upside down; the books are turned upside down and read backward, with obstructed glasses, or only the frames; masses and psalms are mumbled with confused cries."[3] We are not dealing with blasphemers, heretics fighting against the Church, but with monks: "minor brothers" of the convent, usually employed in subordinate tasks and who were allowed to celebrate every year the "feast of the fools" or "of the donkey," according to an ancient medieval tradition that lingered for centuries. During these burlesque ceremonies, under the leadership of the "Bishop of the Children" or the "Abbot of the Fools," the mass is celebrated wearing masks or women's clothes, singing bawdy songs, and burning garbage to replace the incense. After the ceremony, the officiants parade through the streets throwing garbage and excrement at the crowd and "blessing" them with urine-filled *aspergillum*. During the feast of the donkey, the animal was brought near the altar, dressed in priestly clothes, while the audience imitated its braying.

These transgressions, reversals, and buffoonish masquerades are found on a larger scale in the popular carnival. There, it is no longer only members

of the Church who mock their hierarchical superiors, but men of all conditions who joyfully break norms and prohibitions. For a few days, the world
upside down ceases to be a simple allegory: By cross-dressing, dressing up as
a woman, wearing devil or animal masks, the major distinctions of masculine
and feminine, human and animal, divine (of man created "in the image of
God") and demonic were challenged. Indeed, in the Middle Ages, the carnival was closely associated with *diableries*, grotesque representations of the
devil and demons, and a construction called the Inferno was often exhibited
in the parades, then burned at the end of the festival. Bakhtin could see there
a "carnivalization of hell" aiming at demystifying, at overcoming by laughter
the frightening representation of the eternal punishment. It would be wrong
to underestimate the subversive scope of this festival and the opposition it
could entail. Like the festivals of the fools, the masquerades of the carnival
would be condemned by the Church in increasingly virulent terms. In 1444,
the Faculty of Theology of Paris solemnly declared that those who took part
in the festival of the fools "imitated pagans, profaned the sacraments and were
to be treated as heretics"; and the editors of the *Malleus* did not hesitate to
associate the carnival with pagan bacchanals and the witches' Sabbath.[4] Two
centuries later, an author still attacks Satan, "who introduced Carnival in
the middle of penance" and "dishonored Lent by his pomp and his works."[5]
Thus the "carnivalization of hell" has given rise in return to a demonization
of carnival, and this coincides with the formation of the myth of the Sabbath.
In the stories of the demonologists, we see these parodic inversions reappear,
but they are now charged with a purely evil meaning. It is as though, at the
moment when the Church condemned them as diabolical manifestations,
the carnival transgressions were projected out of social reality, transposed into
an imaginary representation where the figure of the devil, mocked in the
masquerades, regained its terrifying dimension.

  We usually think of the carnival as an innocent folkloric revelry, forgetting
that this word is related to *carnage* and *carnal*. However, it would be a mistake
to ignore the violence and cruelty of this celebration. It ends with the killing
of the "Carnival King," a straw dummy or a man made of cardboard who will
be dismembered, burned, or thrown into a river; and one can see in it the
substitute for a human victim who, in older times, would have been sacrificed
during agrarian rites celebrating the end of the winter. In the Middle Ages —
as Hugo recalled in *Notre-Dame de Paris* — the crowd would often appoint a
poor man as the king of the feast before "dethroning" him by insulting and
beating him. In the Rome of the Renaissance, it was the Jews who were forced
to participate half-naked in humiliating trials. Perhaps the carnival festivities
also have a funereal meaning: Some anthropologists consider them to be a

survival of the ancient festivals dedicated to the dead — the Greek Anthesteria, the Roman Feralia — which took place at the same time of the year and where the dead came out of the kingdom of darkness to receive offerings. One of the main accessories of carnival, the mask, was in Rome the attribute of the deceased, before being condemned by the Church as a diabolical symbol; and the Latin terms that designate it (*larva, masca*) ended up characterizing the ghosts, the witches, the demons.[6] Carnival parades would have initially staged the procession of the dead back to earth: the irruption of death into life and the victory of life over death. Yet it is precisely a representation of the world of the dead that constitutes, according to Ginzburg, the core of the myth of the Sabbath. According to him, the magical flights attributed to the Benandanti and the witches in fact refer to shamanic ecstasies, namely to a journey to the land of the dead, and this hypothesis allows him to shed light on the most enigmatic features of the "sect of witches." If the latter is presented as a hostile multitude, it is because the dead are an innumerable mass, sometimes referred to as an immense army ready to attack the living. Since it remains invisible, it can easily be associated with the scheme of the conspiracy, of the subversive secret society. This hypothesis could also account for the motif of the upside-down world. At times, indeed, we imagine the afterlife as the inverted image of our world, as a reversal of the hierarchies that structure the society of the living. This is how Lucian's *Menippus* and Rabelais's *Pantagruel* describe it: In the underworld, King Xerxes is a mustard seller and Alexander the Great mends old shoes, whereas "those who had been destitute in this world were great lords there in their turn." This theme is found again in a more dramatic way in the Hindu tradition. The Brahmanas tell us of the vision of the sage Bhrigu, who sees men dismembering and devouring other men; this means that the beasts and plants killed and eaten here below by men will in turn devour them in the hereafter: "whatever flesh a man eats in this world, it will eat him in the next."

As with the carnival, the inverted world of the Sabbath is an allegory of the world of the dead, a world where "the first will come last," where the dead will take revenge on those who made them suffer during their lifetime. How, then, can we understand that the myth of the Sabbath took on a political meaning from the very first days of the witch hunt? It seems that, in addition to the ancient representations of the afterlife as an upside-down world, inhabited by a crowd hostile to the living, a different representation was superimposed in the fourteenth and fifteenth centuries, that of a rebellion that endangered sovereign power, of a conspiracy seeking to conquer the world. It is the conjunction of these two themes, their explosive fusion, that gave impetus to the new persecution apparatuses, first targeting lepers and Jews, and then "witches."

Is this rebellion, which threatens the sovereignty of Church and State, only an inconsistent fantasy? I do not think so. As a historian observes, the same scheme of inversion characterizes both the popular festivals, the representations of the witches' Sabbath and those of the peasant revolts.[7] And indeed, the period preceding the witch hunt was a time of intense political and religious effervescence, an era of uprisings and civil wars. Michelet was right to link the medieval jacqueries and the witches' Sabbath, even though he was wrong to imagine that these popular revolts could really have been based on a counterreligion, a popular devil worship. In fact, when the rebels challenged the authority of the Church, it was in the name of a return to the "true faith" of the Gospels, like the Lollards in fourteenth-century England, the Czech Hussites in the following century, or the followers of Thomas Münzer during the Great Peasants' Revolt in the sixteenth century. It is their opponents who accuse them of being heretics, of being Satan's henchmen, and denounce this "diabolical" subversion of political and social hierarchies. "And the times lament: / You see the world turn'd upside down": During the English Revolution, the partisans of the monarchy thus attacked those who wanted "to put the world upside down," "the head instead of the foot, the foot instead of the head."[8] This allegory has often been used to designate popular rebellions by associating them with the triumph of the devil. A print bears the following caption: "The world is turned upside down . . . / Hell commands and the Lord entreats; / The rich weep, the poor laugh / The mountain is down, the plain in the clouds."[9] Many of these images recall the carnivalesque inversions of up and down, human and animal, masculine and feminine, dominant and dominated, showing us, for example, humans mounted by donkeys or horses, or men plying the distaff and women carrying swords, or a peasant on a horse alongside a king walking on foot. Sometimes, the more lucid ones forgo the caricature, stop depicting witches dancing backward and mice chasing cats to let us see what worries the powerful so much. A fifteenth-century cleric predicted what would happen if the witch cult were not quickly exterminated: "All will be in confusion and disarray [. . .] The wicked will usurp the lordships and governments [. . .] the villains will attack the nobles. We will see among the cities only execrable evil, rebellions and dissents."[10] In the following century, a chronicler evokes in these terms the uprising of the Limousin countryfolk: "They went so far as to believe that the king would not be their master, that they would make brand-new laws. They gave terror and fright to many; it seemed that the world was overturned."[11] The imaginary representation of the Sabbath thus obeys a schema of inversion because it figures the "upside-down world" of the popular uprisings.

We finally understand how this conspiracy scheme, always at work in the

great persecutions, was constituted. We have seen that it condenses into a
single representation (*a*) the motif of the hidden enemy, brought about by the
appearance of new techniques of unveiling, (*b*) that of an invisible counterfigure of the royal majesty, and (*c*) the haunting of an innumerable and hostile
crowd. We now discover where this last haunting comes from: The wizards'
conspiracy is the shadow cast by the rebellious multitude. Such is the authentic meaning of Michelet's intuition, the kernel of truth of the myth of
the Sabbath. He identified, genially, its hidden political significance, that of
a rebellion against the feudal and monarchical order, but he went too far in
projecting into reality what is undoubtedly only a distorted representation of
real events. There is no evidence that the rebels in the countryside or among
the common people in the cities really adhered to a satanic cult — but the
dominant classes perceived them as such, and the clerics forged the myth of
the Sabbath by integrating into it certain features of the popular revolts that
seemed to them particularly strange and disturbing. We know, for example,
that the most radical fringe of the Hussite dissidents, the Adamites of Bohemia, advocated sexual community and practiced their rites by dancing naked
around a fire. And when the *Malleus* attacks "archer-sorcerers" from Switzerland, accusing them of monstrous crimes and profanations, it is possible to see
an allusion to the role played by Swiss archers in the victories of the insurgent
peasants who had just defeated the army of Charles the Bold. They were also
archers who, half a century earlier, had allowed the Hussites — accused by
the Church of profaning the sacraments — to defeat the army of Emperor
Sigismund.[12] By reappearing in a distorted way in the Sabbath's imaginary,
these popular rebellions came to be seen as satanic plots. There is truth in the
delirium of the demonologists when they evoke an evil sect "as numerous as
the army of the great Xerxes": It is thus that the dominants perceive popular
rebellions, like the uprising of an innumerable multitude. As they seem inexplicable, they try to explain them by attributing them to an obscure conjuration. The witch hunt would thus be a backlash of these revolts, a deferred
revenge, the bloody reprisals with which the dominant classes will answer the
popular rebellions. Moreover, it is often in the regions where the uprisings
had been the most violent that the persecution was the most intense. The
rebellion of the Flemish cities against the Duke of Burgundy preceded the
repression of the Vauderie d'Arras by about ten years. In Rouergue and in
the Vivarais, the witch trials followed almost immediately the revolt of the *croquants*. In sixteenth-century Alsace, the extension of the peasant insurrection
of the Bundschuh coincided more or less with that of the subsequent witch
hunt; and, like the latter, it stopped at the gates of Strasbourg and spared the
city. In Germany, if the region of Würzburg or Westphalia were the focus of

a long and cruel hunt, they had previously been the scene of powerful millenarian movements, and similar phenomena were observed in England.[13]
As for the decree of Philip II, which revived the witch hunt in Flanders and
was to decide the fate of Aldegonde de Rue, how could one fail to see in it a
response to the recent victory of the insurgents of the United Provinces over
the Spanish armies?

Why did the ruling classes take revenge for popular revolts by burning
tens of thousands of innocent women at the stake? For the very same "reason" that the Nazis responded to the workers' uprisings of 1918–21 and to the
crisis of 1929 by murdering millions of victims a few years later. Hate has its
reasons that reason does not know. It is obviously not a question of pointing
to popular rebellions as the determining cause of the witch hunt. It is not the
rebellions themselves, but their profoundly altered memory, that contributed
to forging the myth of the Sabbath, by feeding that imaginary of terror that
accompanies the persecution and gives it meaning. Moreover, the relationship between the two events is not immediate, and an interval of several years
almost always separates the jacqueries from the beginning of the persecutions. It is as though it took a certain amount of time for the memory of the
uprisings, initially repressed, to return in a deformed way to the "knowledge"
of the apparatus. The uprisings would thus have been punished twice, once
when the troops of the lords or the royal armies crushed them in blood, and
again a few years later, when new victims would pay the price of these revolts
at the stake. We understand better how harmless village dwellers could be
stigmatized as dangerous rebels. Innocent victims, the so-called witches were
undoubtedly so, but they can also be considered as *defeated*, because their
torment is in some way the continuation of a fight. It was the battles lost by
their forefathers that signed their belonging to the same community, that of
the "capital enemies" of sovereign power, of those *races of smoke* destined
from generation to generation to extermination. Hatred is without a why, and
it would be futile to look for an objective cause in reality that would suffice
to "explain" this or that persecution — yet it is not without meaning: It has
its own logic and hidden signification, and if the witch hunt suddenly sets
Europe ablaze, it also does so in response to a diffuse threat that haunts the
memory of the dominants. What the demonologists tell us, these prayers recited backward by ass-over-head officiants, this obscene homage paid to the
devil, these unbridled sarabands that end in orgies, these child sacrifices and
profaned hosts, all of this obviously has no relation to the historical reality of
popular uprisings. For the memory of the revolts, cartoonishly distorted, is
associated with other representations where it is no longer a question of an
upheaval of the political order, but of symbolic inversions and transgressions

of fundamental prohibitions. In the upside-down world of the Sabbath, the haunting of the peasant jacqueries and the masquerades of the festival of the fools and the carnival are thus superimposed.

What made it possible to associate them is the subversive aspect of these festivals. According to some historians, the feast of the fools was an opportunity to challenge the ecclesiastical hierarchy, since the lower-ranking clerics and altar boys took the place of consecrated priests by officiating in their stead.[14] By exalting the humble, the weak, the children, while mocking the authorities of the Church, these parodic inversions prove to be faithful to the message of the Gospels ("the last will be first, and the first last," "whoever will exalt himself will be humbled and whoever will humble himself will be exalted"). We find an analogous gesture in the burlesque rites of the carnival. If the dethronement of the king of the festival and the killing of the carnival *bonhomme* are probably the survivals of a sacrificial ritual, we can also consider them as an act of resistance, a symbolic challenge to the political and religious authorities. To stage the fight of King Carnival and Mother Lent was to protest the period of fasting and sexual abstinence that followed Mardi Gras and, ultimately, against all the prohibitions imposed by the Church. It is from this perspective that Bakhtin considers it in his study of Rabelais: By inverting hierarchies and abolishing social distinctions, the "carnivalesque culture" of the Middle Ages would manifest the revolt of the people of the cities and the countryside, their ironic contestation of the clerical and feudal order, their dreams of freedom, equality, abundance. The "other life of the people" thus breaks into the festival, by freeing itself from the standards of an alienated daily existence.[15] However, let us not be mistaken: It is not a genuine revolt that we are dealing with, but a periodic inversion-transgression rite, the provisional institution of a counterorder that does not really threaten the order that it reverses. By enabling the participants to unload an overflow of affects, to carry out a latent revolt that could have manifested itself in more radical forms, these ritual transgressions reinforce, on the contrary, the authority that they seemed to contest. Once the festivities are over, everything will return to normal: Everyone will meekly resume their place, with a more intense awareness of the norms and prohibitions that had been suspended for a while.

These inversions and these parodical transgressions have nevertheless a subversive impact, and the monarchic State was going to try, from the seventeenth century, to defuse it by transforming the carnival into an inoffensive popular festivity. When they invert the domination of the sacred over the soiled, of high over low, of front over back, of the masculine over the feminine, of the wise over the fool, etc., the grotesque ceremonies of the festival of the fools and of the carnival certainly maintain these symbolic polarities — but, at the same time, they destabilize them. They reveal that these polar oppositions are not absolute, that the domination of the "superior" terms is precarious and always reversible. They can thus pave the way for authentic revolts. Between celebration and riot, it is sometimes difficult to draw a line. Sometimes popular uprisings imitated carnival parades, and the rebels wore masks or headdresses with bells (for example, during the riots against the tax authorities in Aix and Dijon in 1630), or disguised themselves as women (during the revolt in Guéret in 1705 or the "War of the Maidens" in Ariège). Other times, however, a carnival suddenly turns into a riot and ends in a bloodbath, as in Nuremberg in 1539 or in Romans in 1580.[16] Whether it is a simple festival or a real sedition, the overthrow of the dominant hierarchies is apprehended as a threat by the power, denounced as a satanic demonstration. It is this upside-down world that demonologists have transposed into the myth of the Sabbath by burdening it with the worst infamies, infanticide, cannibalism, incest . . . As if they wanted to ward off the excesses of the festival and the fury of the revolt by deporting them into this darkness where the inversion of order culminates in the adoration of an Anti-God. By *demonizing* the carnival or the jacquerie, the persecution apparatus strikes a double blow: Not only can it condemn the so-called witches as "the worst of the rebels," but it also manages to denounce the real rebels as henchmen of the devil.

In traditional societies, social hierarchies are always based on an image of the body, on incorporation schemes that lead the dominated to consider themselves as "inferior organs," subordinate to the sovereign authority of the Head. It is this figuration that enters crisis when revolts shake the "natural" hierarchy of the Great Body. This is why they so often appear in the phantasms of the dominant in the form of a monstrous body or a body in struggle against itself, each member of which would seek to take the place of the others. The defenders of the organic hierarchy of the City or the Church have never ceased to condemn the possibility of a secession of the organs, of their unjust revolt against the rest of the body. We have already met in Bodin the haunting of a body whose members would become their own objects of hatred and would go so far as to mutilate and tear itself apart; and when a certain Morrison publishes, after the uprising of 1536 against Henry VIII, a *Remedy for Sedition*, he also attacks this "insane and unheard-of thing that the foot says 'I want to wear a hat, as well as the head'; that the knee says it wants to have eyes [. . .] that the heels want to go in front, the toes behind."[17] These are, however, only phantasms, the distorted image that their opponents make of the revolts; and these counterfigurations of the body are found just as much on the other side, in the representations that the rebellions and the popular festivals make of themselves, of their ritual or violent challenge to the dominant hierarchies. It is precisely what Bakhtin identifies in the "grotesque image of the body" that characterizes the carnival counterculture. It is indeed about an *inverted body*, which subverts all the organic differentiations, "puts the top in the place of the bottom, the backside in the place of the face"; but this reversal is accompanied here by a disfiguration that destabilizes the shape of the organic body. In the imagery of the carnival and the work of Rabelais that is the literary expression of it, one deals with a deformed body, or rather one without form, infinitely plastic, that transgresses the demarcations of the inside and the outside, of the same and the other, of the ego and the world. What explains the privilege granted to the orifices and to the protrusions of the body — to the mouth, to the anus, to the sexual organs — and to all the practices that cross the bodily limits, to the gestures of swallowing, vomiting, urinating, defecating.[18] Bakhtin insists on the obscene, excremental character of this body that exhibits its lower parts, its dejections; what allows one, according to him, to understand the importance of the *diableries* of the carnival: Because "the particular traits of the devil (above all his ambivalence and his bond with the material and corporal 'bottom') explain very well why he became a figure of the popular comedy."[19] The medieval representation of the devil, with its rear face whose mouth is in the place of the anus, illustrates this inversion of the noble and the ignoble that characterizes the carnivalesque body. By inverting the hierarchy of the symbolic oppositions, these counter-figurations reveal the ambivalence that is attached to the "low body." For these obscene parts, these ridiculous or filthy wastes are also, underlines Bakhtin, "what fecundates and gives birth," what soils and destroys, but to create, to generate new forms of life. What can be the origin of these ambivalent figures, at the same time sacred and soiled, diabolic and divine? In the buffoonish parodies of the Christian rites, he thought he had discovered the persistence of a primitive cult where this original unity of the upper and the lower, of the pure and the impure, manifested itself, a cult that was later condemned and repressed by the dominant religion. This is an appealing hypothesis that is also found in Bataille (and to a certain extent in Freud). And yet, nothing attests to the historical existence of this primitive religion that would not have dissociated the sacred and the abject.

How to make sense of this ambivalence? By leaving the plane of history for a more original plane where historical phenomena find their immanent matrix and their meaning. Behind these images-screens of a world inverted, of a body upside-down, we can locate phenomena of disembodiment of the collective bodies; and this must be understood as a *dis-embodiment* in the strict sense: as the motion by which an original element withdraws from its embodiment, from its alienating capture in the form of a body. The primordial dimension that precedes our body and allows it to constitute itself, I named, after Husserl, the *flesh*. It is probable that the word "carnival" comes from the Italian *carne*, which, by a curious coincidence, means precisely the flesh, because it identifies the period that precedes the Great Lent, that when *carne vale*, where it is still allowed to eat flesh. The "flesh" in question here is obviously the animal meat, prohibited in a time of penance. By playing on the etymology, I would like to also evince the resurgence of this other flesh, the flesh of history, the carnal dimension of the community that emerges in the carnival body, just as it reappears in a different way in the riots and insurrections. What is revealed during the crises of the Great Body is the heterogeneous element, rebellious to any embodiment, that haunts the flesh of the community: the *resistance of the remainder*. This manifests itself originally on our plane of immanence, where the remainder resists the carnal chiasm and the becoming-body of our flesh. It is possible to find the same phenomenon on the collective plane where appears what we can call the "remainder" of the community. Revolts and popular festivals show us the different forms that its resistance to the embodiment in a collective Body can take. How to characterize more precisely the original carnal dimension where the remainder is constituted? When the *epochē* brackets the unitary form of our body, it reveals to us a diffracted multiplicity of carnal impressions that is our flesh. When this *an-archic* multiplicity resurfaces on the plane of collective existence, it presents itself as a *multitude*. This term is appropriate to designate the affirmation of the multiple that confronts the One of the sovereign power. It is, as we have seen, the term used by Thomas Aquinas to name the disintegrated mass in which the political Body risks dissolving if its sovereign principle fails. Hobbes will give it a similar meaning, associating it more closely with the threat of a rebellion — necessarily illegitimate — against the Sovereign; and it is still in this way that Spinoza understands it, but by seeing on the contrary in the "power of the multitude" the possible foundation of a democratic politics.[20]

For Merleau-Ponty, the flesh of history is the primordial element of historical experience, the common medium where the past and the present are indissociably intertwined. This invisible hinge, this hidden armature that spans the difference of eras, we first envisaged as a community of the living and the dead, a community that we cannot contemplate from the outside, from the false neutrality of an overhead position, because its destiny concerns us, because we co-own it as if we were of the same flesh. It never gives itself as an anonymous, undifferentiated *milieu*: On this still indistinct background, we have seen singular individualities stand out. Each time, what is at stake were victims, unjustly accused innocents, appallingly tortured bodies, choked cries. Now it presents itself in another form, that of a living community, of a rebellious multitude that is the flesh of politics, the flesh of history. Henceforth, these massacres, these tortures, these stakes that occupied the front of the scene appear as a backlash, the murderous retort of the dominant to these uprisings that challenged their power. This flesh is thus given in different ways, as a multitude that asserts itself and gives itself to itself, but also as these atomized, enslaved masses, from which occasionally emerge the face and name of a victim. Even under this form, it remains the focus of a potential threat: As alienated as they may be, the subjugated masses belong to the flesh of history, and it is always possible for them to tear themselves away from their passivity, from their alienation, by rediscovering the affirmative power of a multitude. The flesh of history is this carnal base that La Boétie had glimpsed, a primordial community where, by a series of transfers, the collective Bodies draw all their strength. It is this power, sometimes passive, sometimes active, that the power apparatuses try each time to divert or to break, to reincorporate in a Great Body. Each apparatus is the condensation of a power relation: of the relation which, in a given conjuncture, is instituted between the affirmation of a multitude and the power that resists it. Whether they operate by exclusion, by disciplinary normalization or by persecution and extermination, these apparatuses are each time destined to annihilate the power of the multitude, to submit it to the sovereign authority of the One.

If my hypothesis is correct, if the witch hunt and many other persecution apparatuses are indeed a response of power to the rebellion of a multitude, we will have to reexamine Foucault's thesis on the relationship between power and resistance. For him, there is no power without resistance, *but there is no resistance without power either*, without these power apparatuses in which the resistance finds a fulcrum, investing or circumventing them, while they modify their strategy and their action. This does not mean, he specifies, that the initiative would return to power each time, that each resistance would be only a desperate counterattack, always doomed to failure, in front of an almighty power. When he says that resistances are immanent to power relations, he means that they are intertwined in a battle that has never ceased, without power or resistance being the ultimate origin of this struggle. And yet, if we consider a certain historical sequence, for example, that which goes from the peasant insurrections to the burning of witches, we must recognize that *resistance comes first;*[21] that the persecution apparatuses are only constituted to resist a preceding resistance. Therefore, it is better to speak here of a revolt, rebellion, or uprising of a multitude, rather than a resistance. If it is true that a "resistance" is always a reaction to an action that precedes it, it is only the power that resists, deploys its apparatuses to oppose what it apprehends as a threat.

Let us specify that a multitude is not defined in a quantitative manner (there are immense crowds that remain alienated and passive), but by its way of manifesting itself. Whatever its antecedent conditions and the objective causes that would pretend to explain it, it is each time an *originary phenomenon* that thwarts any calculation and any forecast. No multitude preexists the event of its appearance: Before it emerges, there was at most an inconsistent multiplicity, subjugated subjects, alienated to predetermined roles, passively accomplishing the tasks that were assigned to them by the power relations. By disalienating them, by resubjectivizing them in order to make them the subjects of a revolt, by transforming an atomized mass into a community, the appearance of a multitude makes something new happen in history. Power simply perseveres in its being, perpetuates itself indefinitely by adapting its strategies and its apparatuses to new situations. But the multitude makes caesura: It seems to arise ex nihilo by breaking the course of time, and its appearance is a *condition of possibility* in an eminent sense. It opens possibilities, it is the sketch of a possible world, of new forms of life, irreducible to the alienated life subjected to power apparatuses. As Bakhtin underlines, "during the carnival, it is the life itself which plays and interprets then [. . .] another free form of its accomplishment." This notion of a *life form* is particularly important to think the deployment of the life within the transcendence of the world. If immanent life is an affective and impulsive matter, movement without form and thrust without goal, it cannot be inscribed in a world without taking a differentiated form, without figuring itself in various ways. It is here that the schemes intervene that give it form and configure it, bring its indeterminate drive to invest itself in desires and affects oriented toward objects. By yielding to the same *schemes*, by sharing the same form of life, by aiming at the same objects of love and hate, a great number of individuals can integrate themselves in a single historical community.

Up to now, I have only examined schemes of exclusion and persecution, invested by negative affects of disgust and hate. But the drive of the life also generates other affects, which lend their affective load to very different schemes. The uprisings of the multitudes reveal the existence of *emancipation schemes* that mobilize the hope of a "different life," of a historical world better than this one. By reversing the hierarchies and by transgressing the prohibitions, by abolishing any difference between spectators and actors of the festival, the reversed world of the carnival sketches the utopia of a community of equal men. This is the same utopia that an English chronicler attacked after the Great Jacquerie of 1381, by attacking "envy and the devil," who "preach to men of Plato, and prove it by Seneca, / That all things under heaven ought to be in common." He no doubt remembered the combat chant of the rebellious

serfs ("When Adam delved and Eve span, / Who was then a gentleman?")
and their leader John Ball declaring that "things cannot go well in England
until all property is shared and there is neither villain nor gentleman, but
we are all one."[22] The same demand for equality was found among the most
radical of the Czech Hussites, the German Anabaptists, the Diggers of the
English Revolution and, later, the Enragés of the French Revolution. The
equality that these rebels claim is their way of life, the way that a multitude
asserts itself through an emancipation schema. In their most radical forms, the
rebellions of the multitudes thus make appear this original, disincorporated,
an-archic community, which is the flesh of history. Most popular revolts have
more limited objectives: They are primarily about righting a specific wrong,
about taking revenge on a cruel or unjust master, about abolishing a tax or a
privilege deemed illegitimate, without the rebels calling into question the very
foundations of domination. We must surely distinguish, from these *reactive
multitudes*, riveted to their particular wrong, *affirmative multitudes*, capable
of universalizing the wrong, of extending their rebellion, of joining other multitudes in the perspective of universal emancipation. In any case, whatever
its objectives, the uprising of a multitude always disrupts power relations; it
tends to disincorporate the Great Body, to deconstruct those schemata that
reproduce and justify hierarchy and inequality among men. By its mere appearance, each multitude carries the promise of a community delivered from
injustice and domination. Here lies the utopian dimension of the multitudes
and their messianic horizon.

What stands in the way of the advent of such a community? How is it that
it has been constantly postponed, to the point of becoming a "utopian" ideal
in the wrong sense of the term, an inconsistent fiction, a chimera? For classical political philosophy — with the exception of Spinoza — the multitude
is defined precisely by its inconsistency, by its impotence to want, to act, to
create stable institutions. This is the meaning of the distinction that Hobbes
establishes, for example, between the unity of will and action of the people
represented by its sovereign and the "hundred-headed hydra" of the multitude, to which "no action whatsoever must be attributed"; so that, when a
multitude appears to act, we are not dealing with a real action, but only with
a "conspiracy" of "seditious persons."[23] For the author of *Leviathan*, the intervention of a multitude is thus equivalent to a conspiracy . . . Certainly, the existence of the multitude is precarious: Always threatened, it lasts as long as the
revolt and seems to disappear with it, without leaving any trace. And yet, if the
circumstances allow it, it can take more consistent forms, inventing counterapparatuses, new ways of thinking and acting, multiform networks capable of
confronting the apparatuses of power. As there is a tradition of the dominant,

a tradition of the persecutors, there is also a "lost treasure," a secular tradition of seditions and insurrections. An interrupted tradition, crushed each time in blood, broken by its successive defeats, stigmatized by the official history written by the victors. If this an-archic community, this *democracy of the multitudes* has never managed to institute itself and to last, it is perhaps because, unlike our singular flesh, the flesh of the community remains a quasi-flesh incapable of taking on a body, of constituting itself "at the same time as flesh and as a corporeal thing": of remaining a living community while being inscribed in stable institutions. But it is also necessary to see there the effect of the power apparatuses, whose essential function is to resist to the irruption of the multitudes. To the emancipation schemes that underlie it, they oppose their own schemes, try to capture the affects of the multitude by directing them toward new objects. They try to convert them into other affects that weaken it, divide it, divert it toward imaginary targets or make it fall back into passivity, servitude. This is how the multitudes find themselves dissociated from their power to act, how their process of disembodiment is interrupted, how they allow themselves to be reembodied into a figure of the Great Body.

We must, however, avoid idealizing the revolt of the multitudes by overlooking the charge of hatred that so often runs through them, the desire for terror that can animate them. Spinoza knew this: There can be "ferocious multitudes" who behave like the "worst of the barbarians."[24] The multitudes are immediately confronted by violence and hatred, the thirst for vengeance because their revolt always has a target that necessarily presents a face, that of the gendarme who must be driven out of the village, of the hated informer, the noncommissioned officer or the foreman, of the lord or the tyrant against whom they rise; without forgetting the face of their brothers, of their friends imprisoned, tortured, assassinated, whom they wish to avenge. This does not mean that the multitudes are by nature persecutory, driven by a murderous "mimetic violence" that would inevitably push them to massacre an innocent "scapegoat." It is the dominant ones who represent them in this way, as savage crowds thirsty for blood, animated only by hatred, envy, and resentment, which allows them to justify repression. What constitutes a multitude is not a death-drive, but the feeling of injustice. When revolt breaks out, it is always to oppose a *wrong* (tort), what the revolted perceive as an intolerable abuse: a new tax, a police provocation, the imprisonment or murder of an opponent, or that rotten meat that the sailors on the *Potemkin* refused. In a sense, this wrong does not preexist the nascent community that rises up against it. Without the formation of this multitude, there would be no wrong, but a simple indifferent element in the long chain of calculations and strategies of power. The uprising breaks this chain: It subtracts an element-X from it to constitute it as a wrong, and it is the shared consciousness of this wrong that resubjectifies the subjugated subjects and gathers them into a community.[25]

The collective awareness of an injustice is accompanied by very intense affects, and these will become a decisive stake in the confrontation between the rebellion and the power apparatuses. These feelings are *indignation* and *anger*, to which is often added the desire for *vengeance*. Such affects are not only a matter of psychological analysis: They are fundamental tonalities of our lives, and each of them gives it a singular style, a horizon where our openness to the world and to others is at stake. Cicero gives an excellent definition of anger by associating it precisely with the feeling of an injustice: He characterizes it as "the desire to punish the one who seems to have caused us an unjust damage." It is because it involves justice and injustice that, in another tradition, this affect has been attributed to God: The "Day of the Lord" will be the *dies irae*, the day when his anger will be unleashed against the unjust. As for indignation, Spinoza has shown how it allows enslaved individuals to overcome their isolation and their fear of the master, to discover that collective resistance is possible. It can go as far as overthrowing political authority, when "the fear felt in common by the greatest number of citizens is transformed into indignation" and incites them to rebel.[26] It therefore seems possible to distinguish between revolts motivated by legitimate indignation, by righteous anger, and a mob motivated only by hatred. Unlike anger, hatred is an affect that aims only at destroying its object, without any consideration of what is just and unjust. In order to distinguish between a hateful mob and the revolt of a multitude, it would be necessary, however, that indignation, anger, and revenge be clearly dissociated from hatred, whereas they often tend to ally themselves with it, to merge with it. This is not surprising if it is true that these affects find their origin in hatred, of which they would be only simple variants. This is Spinoza's position: For him, "indignation is a hatred towards someone who has done harm to another," while anger is nothing other than "the effort to do harm to the one we hate."[27] Rather, let us say that, as legitimate as it is at the beginning, anger can change into fury, into destructive rage, and finally into hatred.[28] By giving in to the desire to annihilate by all means its target, it then turns into hatred. And if there are just vengeances, inspired by the will to repair an injustice, it is still a question of a limit-affect that hinges on revolt and hatred (I will have the occasion to show it in the case of the revolutionary Terror). Thus, these affects never manage to escape entirely from the logic of hatred: "envy [. . .] contempt, anger, revenge and the other affections that are related to hatred or are born from it are bad things,"[29] and this is why power apparatuses can so easily capture them and divert them to the service of a politics of persecution.

How does this captivation take place? In their indignation and anger, the multitude tries to discern what is at the origin of the wrong they have suffered, to discover the real enemy who is the cause and their *real enemy*. By rising up against him, the revolted seek to take revenge on him, to repair the injustice he has inflicted on them. However, as soon as their feelings of revolt turn to hatred, this objective takes a back seat. From now on, they wish above all to destroy the one they hate, whatever he may have done. When they project their hatred onto him, when they attribute to him their own desire for destruction and murder, his representation changes, and he now appears to them as an *absolute enemy*, a fundamentally hostile being who arouses the most intense aversion. The persecution apparatuses favor this transformation of the real enemy into an absolute enemy: By mobilizing the schemes at their disposal, they demonize the enemy, impute to him the most infamous transgressions, these sexual and religious *nefanda* that make him a monster unworthy of living among men. This evil Other who deserves only death is no longer the real enemy that the multitude had targeted, but an imaginary enemy. His fictitious nature allows him to be portrayed as one pleases, by loading him with all the negative traits that arouse disgust and hatred. The operation succeeds when the multitude abandons its initial target to attack the one that the persecution schemes have designated. This is what happened, for example, to the Shepherds' Crusade. Starting in Normandy in 1320, this uprising of poor peasants invaded Paris and defied the king's authority by opening the doors of the prisons. They descended en masse to the South, pillaging castles and rich abbeys. As the inquisitor Bernard Gui wrote, "they had planned to rise up against the clergy and monks who possessed wealth and to seize their possessions"; that is why "the mention of their name provoked terror and horror [. . .] among princes, prelates and the rich." When they arrived in the Southwest, their movement changed its target, and they began to massacre the Jews . . . What had made this change possible? The Jews of France were neither richer nor more powerful than the ordinary people of the countryside and the cities; but they enjoyed a paradoxical privilege: They had been considered for centuries as "serfs of the king," as his personal property, and were therefore under his protection. In attacking the Jews, the Shepherds had not ceased to attack the sovereign power, but they were now doing so in a derivative and indirect form. At a time when it was unthinkable to challenge the royal majesty, this shift of focus to an envied and hated minority made their revolt more acceptable.[30] Michelet sometimes interprets the witch hunt in this perspective as a *diversion* to protect the dominant classes from the revolts that threatened them: "Excellent popular weapon to tame the people, admirable diversion. The storm was going to be redirected on the witches this time, as it had been turned on the Jews in 1349 and on so many other occasions."[31] He had already understood the importance of "scapegoating" phenomena, but he does not make it an invariable universal mechanism: He describes specific *diversion strategies*, carried out by power apparatuses that manage to capture the rebellion of a multitude in order to divert it to another target. When a rebellious multitude stops targeting the ruling elites to attack another subaltern group, the apparatuses have served their purpose: From now on, its action can only reinforce the power against which it was rebelling.

Bodin demonstrated that he had perfectly understood such a strategy, when he exhorted the magistrates to intensify the persecution of the sorcerers, without which "there is danger that the people will stone the magistrates." It is to protect themselves from this threat and to protect the apparatus of which they are the agents that the judges are called upon to divert the people's anger toward the alleged witches . . . The analysis of these diversion strategies thus allows us to shed light on one of the most enigmatic features of the witch hunt. Historians tell us that the first accusations did not appear in the remote countryside, but at the heart of sovereign power; and it was not poor peasant women whom they targeted, but an emperor of Germany, bishops and popes, dignitaries of religious orders, such as the Templars. Men, not women, rich and powerful men who had come into conflict with other centers of power. The first recorded witchcraft trial involved a woman, but it was an Irish aristocrat, Lady Alice Kyteler. Accused in 1324 of having cursed her deceased husband, of having sacrificed children to Satan, and of having fornicated with a demon, she managed to escape, while one of her servants ended up on the stake . . . From the fifteenth century onward, the axis of persecution gradually shifted from the center to the periphery, from the cities to the countryside, from men to women, from the ruling classes to the lower classes. It is as if the new persecution apparatuses were constituted in order to protect the sovereign power, to move the target of hatred by diverting it always further toward the fringes of the society, toward these marginal, declassed, defenseless beings, these "races of smoke" destined to end up on the stakes. Insofar as these are *strategies*, a set of decisions that are part of power relations, this detour of the accusation is, however, reversible. All it takes is for the apparatus to get out of hand, for the enemy's features to fade, for persecution to return to its source, from the margins to the center, striking men again and not just women, notables, priests, judges; and for it to come dangerously close to the focus of sovereign power, resurrecting the very ancient figure of the witch-king, the child-killing vampire-king . . .

Between the revolts that are misled by the lures of power and those that succeed in thwarting them, where is the difference? The truth. The capacity of a multitude to assert itself in truth, to free itself as much as possible from the hatred that blinds it, from this countertruth that is at the heart of hatred. But how can they do this? If they are fanned by the power apparatuses, the hateful affects originate in our primordial flesh, in the disfiguration of the remainder. It is its initial ambivalence, its incessant oscillation between love and hatred that reappears on the world plane, in the historical life of communities. It would be wrong to believe that the disembodiment of political bodies would be enough to deliver human societies from these fundamental passions, since they find their source upstream, below any incorporation. When they burst into history, they invest themselves in schemes and apparatuses that give them their objects. This is how the multitudes allow themselves to be carried away by the love of the Leader and the hatred of the Enemy: by the figure of a Sovereign who concentrates on himself all the veneration and love, and that of an absolute Enemy who becomes the focus of an unlimited hatred. If the persecution schemes find their emotional charge in the flesh of history, it is understandable that they are so prevalent. This raises a formidable question: Are not all communities subject to schemes of exclusion and persecution that lead them to make an enemy of the Foreigner, whether internal or external, and to demonize him or her? And if this is the case, how is a messianic community possible, which would manage to reconcile itself with the remainder of its flesh?

6

Behind the Devil's Mask

Car enfin d'où sortit Satan? / Pourquoi ce double et cet écho? (Then from where came Satan? / Why this double and this echo?)

ANTONIN ARTAUD, SUPPÔT ET SUPPLICATIONS

Thus God wears the devil's mask [*larvam diaboli induit*], and the Devil likewise sheweth himself behind God's mask: and God will be known behind the devil's mask, and will have the devil known behind the mask of God.

MARTIN LUTHER, A COMMENTARY ON
ST. PAUL'S EPISTLE TO THE GALATIANS

In *The Origins of Totalitarianism*, Hannah Arendt classifies the three types of concentration camps invented during the twentieth century according to "three basic Western conceptions of a life after death: Hades, Purgatory, and Hell." If Purgatory might be compared to Stalin's work camps, "Hell in the most literal sense was embodied by those types of camps perfected by the Nazis, in which the whole of life was thoroughly and systematically organized with a view to the greatest possible torment."[1] Paradoxically, it would be modern men — freed from the belief in the immortality of the soul, the devil, and hell — who would be tasked with carrying out purgatory or hell on Earth . . . Yet it remains equally paradoxical and incomprehensible to see men who believed in the devil, who dedicated their entire lives to fighting the devil, seeking to replicate hell in this world. The torments inflicted in Bamberg's Malefizhaus or other torture centers weren't the only elements that seemed inspired by medieval descriptions of hell. As we have seen, the torturers also

sought to evoke the fear of endless torments, the infernal representation of an
"eternity of suffering," in their victims. Assured that they embodied the fight
of good against evil, that they defended a religion of charity and love against a
wicked Enemy, they did not realize that they were following the model of the
adversary they claimed to confront. Perhaps some of their victims had realized
this: We remember Gauffridi's apostrophe "Ah! *Monsieur* Ollivier, you are a
devil!" when his judge inflicted the *great Gehenna* on him. In any case, this
paradox did not elude one of the most lucid adversaries of witch hunts. As a
devout Christian, Friedrich Spee also believed in the devil's existence, yet it
was not in the so-called witches that he detected his presence but rather in
the cold cruelty of judges and torturers: For him, Satan "hid behind denunciations, jealousy and hatred, in envy and the lust of the people, among scholars,
priests and confessors who only saw the devil in their victims, the witches, but
did not feel his action in their hearts."[2]

Differing from so many learned demonologists, Spee perfectly understood
the true meaning of *the devil*. He acknowledged that Satan is, before all else,
he who accuses and condemns. The "diabolical" affects of hatred, envy, and
joy in others' suffering are on the side of the persecutors. They attribute these
base passions — that motivate their actions although they do not detect them
"in their hearts" — to their victims by accusing them of abominable crimes. In
fact, it is *because* they don't recognize these lethal affects in themselves that
they then project them onto other men. Thus, Spee glimpsed an essential
character of the logic of hatred: It always implies a *projection* where the ego
expels outward its hateful affects, which it locates in an Other. Certainly, at
work here are persecution apparatuses that orient indignation, anger, and the
desire for vengeance toward the designated targets. These derivation strategies
would, however, remain inoperative were they not grounded in deeper tendencies, present in every human subject: on the disfigurement of the remainder that awakens hatred in us, on the external projection of this disfigured
remainder, on the intervention of certain schemata that provide an object
for this hatred. This hatred-driven projection would indeed be impossible
(or at least a large part of its destructive force would be mollified) if it did not
polarize a certain figure of the malevolent Other: that of a fundamentally evil
principle whose human enemies would be agents. An ancient tradition designates him as the par excellence Adversary, the primordial Enemy, or Satan.
The devil is not the Great Persecutor (it is the priests and the demonologists
who represent him as such): He is the *vector of persecution*, that is, what allows
the apparatuses to focus on real targets by making them representatives of the
Absolute Enemy. Indeed, for centuries, no persecution had been possible in
the West without *demonizing* the enemy; and this still seems to be covertly

operative in our enlightened era when men have ceased to believe in the existence of the devil, without giving up on demonizing their enemies.

Of course, if the devil is the vector of hatred that orients the persecution, it is only from the apparatus's point of view. From the victims' point of view, in contrast, it is the persecutors' zeal that seems "diabolical." Under certain conditions, Satan may even appear as a *resistance principle* or become a symbol of an insurgent mob — a multitude that haunts the dreams of the ruling classes (this figure of the Great Rebel would later be celebrated by Michelet and the Romantics) — against the sovereign authority of the One. At times this resistance principle takes a more concrete form through its direct inscription on the body, as evidenced by the experience of possession where the diabolical principle manifests itself in all its ambiguity. When the exorcists force the demon to reveal, through the voice of the possessed, the name of the sorcerer who bewitched her, she is thus *possessed* by the persecution apparatus that has seeped into her and speaks through her mouth. Here, Satan remains the Great Accuser, the agent of this apparatus that forces the accused to confess the "truth." And yet, at the same time, the possessed never ceases to resist him: The convulsions shaking her when the exorcist approaches her with the holy bread, the invincible force preventing her from joining her hands in prayer or making her spit out the host, the "horrible voice" coming out of her mouth as she screams, "I renounce God, I scorn him,"[3] all of this attests to her desperate effort to elude the apparatus's power. Foucault observed this: The body of the possessed is an "invested and besieged citadel," the battlefield "between the part of the possessed that resists and the part of herself that oppositely gives way and betrays her."[4] The "demon" under whose spell she remains *also* points at a resistance force, her freedom's ultimate resource. When the accused refuses to give in under torture and the judges consider that it is the devil who prevents him from confessing, the tormentors recognize, under the name of Satan, the adverse principle hindering their power. Satan regains his primary role of the Opponent by resisting the apparatus and by preventing it from extorting a confession or intruding into bodies and souls: He escapes the persecutors' thought system to put himself at the service of their victims. It is rather this "God" of vengeance — and the one invoked by inquisitors and judges to justify torture and to fuel the fire of the stakes — that presents himself as a satanic principle, and, in this sense, Luther was not wrong to assert that the devil can present himself behind the mask of God.

Who thus hides behind the devil's mask? Who, then, is Satan? And how did he come to impose his mask on so many human faces? How does the *demonization process* concretely take place? Medieval persecutions offer several examples. When the Church undertook the annihilation of the Cathars and

Waldensians, these religious dissidents were denounced as "Satan worshippers" and accused of worshipping him in a sacrilegious and obscene manner during nocturnal assemblies. The demonization of Jews would be more radical: From the thirteenth century, when accusations of desecration of holy bread and ritual crime multiplied, the representation of the "Jew" would undergo a remarkable mutation. Although in the iconography of the preceding centuries nothing distinguished them from Christians, Jews were now assigned a particular physiognomy where crooked noses and pointed beards became predominant. Soon after, they were attributed horns and tails through proximity with animals associated with the devil, namely, goats, scorpions, and bats. Conversely, the devil would be represented with a crooked nose and wearing the Jewish *rouelle* badge.[5] They are no longer only considered as worshippers of the devil but are *identified* with him. By the end of this process, Luther could proclaim that Jews are "worse than all demons." As was the case for heretics, a religious minority already present within medieval society would become disfigured by new persecution apparatuses that assigned satanic traits to it. In the case of the "conspiracy of the sorcerers," the apparatus would strive to exterminate an enemy it had itself invented. Here, the demonization process does not consist of projecting certain schemata on a real group to make them a target but of creating the target group from a preexisting schema: this schema of a malevolent Other that Christian theology had named Satan.

All the traits that the persecutors then attributed to the Witch had indeed characterized the figure of the devil for a while. We have seen that from the start of the hunt, wizards and witches were denounced as *rebels*, members of a powerful *conspiracy* against Church and State. A plot whose followers proliferate, this is a rebellion of an innumerable *multitude*. Their "sect" being secret, they are accused of being *dissimulators* hiding their infamous practices under the guise of piety. Finally, unlike the Jews, who were offered the possibility of conversion and salvation — at least before the invention of a "blood purity" criterion — the witches are not allowed redemption at any cost, since their crimes attest to an evil nature rendering them *irredeemable*. Yet these characteristics are precisely those which, for centuries, identified Satan. Since Augustine and the Church Fathers, his Fall had been explained by his pride and by his will to equal his Creator. Head of the fallen angels who had mutinied against God, he had also been considered as a symbol of the rebel and the felonious vassal during the Middle Ages. From the thirteenth century — with the apparition of the new techniques of unveiling previously analyzed — the political enemy began to be apprehended as a hidden enemy or conspirator. The bygone accusations of treachery and pride are then replaced by a more "modern" accusation, as seen when the theologian Guillaume d'Auvergne,

Saint Louis's counselor and confessor, designated the angels' mutiny as a *conspiratio* that sought to establish an "other king" in the legitimate suzerain's place. Demonologists also insisted on the colossal number of infernal cohorts: According to one of them, there were 7,409,127 demons, under the rule of 79 princes . . . What characterizes a conspirator is his aptitude for dissimulation, and in fact Satan often disguises himself as an angel of light.[6] Finally, although originally he had been created as benevolent, he had devoted himself irrevocably to evil since his Fall; and we find here the paradox of freedom that can only want evil and thus resembles an evil nature. Of course, theologians such as Origen of Alexandria and Gregory of Nyssa had maintained that, at the end of time, Satan would be forgiven and hell would disappear. Yet this doctrine of *apokatastasis* — of the final restoration of unity and universal reconciliation — had been condemned as early as the sixth century by the Church. Affirming the incorrigible or "unrepentant" character of the devil thus limits God's forgiveness and infinite goodness. There is yet another trait through which the devil's figure foreshadows that of the Witch. The latter has the power to morph into a beast, and Satan, who can take the shape of a black cat, a goat, or any other animal, also possesses this power. Luther thus claimed that the Evil One constantly harassed him under the guise of a black dog or a swarm of flies . . . Through all these traits — rebellion and conspiracy, dissimulation, "unrepentance," bestialization — the devil's figure remained the *Urbild*, the Pre-Figure, that made it possible to forge those of the Jew or the Witch and marked the fate of countless victims.

A genealogy of persecution apparatuses is tasked with analyzing the schemata underlying these apparatuses, the figures constituted by these schemata and that provide targets for the persecutors. However, in the case of the witch hunts — or already during prior medieval persecutions of heretics and Jews — we discover that these figures trace their origin to a theological schema. When they appear as political schemata at work in power apparatuses, the Absolute Enemy and the Conspiracy are the result of the secularization process of a previous figure, that of Satan. Does theology — or more precisely a secularized theology — then hold the key to understanding persecutions and exterminations? Secularized theology only yields one of the sources since these schemata proceed from a second genesis at the same time; they find their sources in the most elementary phenomena of our lives, in the intrigue of the ego and the remainder. Here, on our plane of immanence, schemata and phantasms that structure our experience of the stranger take form: our relation to others and this modality of the stranger that we call God. In this sense, theological schemata also partake in egoanalysis. Yet this phenomenological genesis does not suffice to account for it. For the apparition of their historical imaginings, these original schemata are intertwined with historical ones that are modified from one epoch to the other and do not take the same forms within different human cultures.

Undoubtedly, the devil of Christian theology is one among many possible figurations of a malevolent entity, bearing different names elsewhere. If we wish to understand how this Enemy could take the name and traits of Satan in the Western world, a genealogy of the devil should be established: His first apparition in late scriptures of the Hebraic Bible; his metamorphosis into a wicked character, a leader of the rebellious angels, in several marginal currents of ancient Judaism; and his ulterior transformations in the history of Christian theology should be analyzed. The birth of Satan indeed supposes a cleavage, a polarization of the religious experience, under a particular form that is not found in all human cultures. It is not enough to postulate a hostility between gods and demons: This hostility must still be concentrated in a fundamental opposition between a single divine principle and an antagonistic principle. Surely, the so-called "polytheistic" religions recognize ferocious and perfidious divinities (the savage Rudra in Vedic mythology, the deceitful Loki of the Scandinavian *saga*, Seth, Osiris's murderer in the Ancient Egyptian religion . . .) or divine *tricksters* transgressing rules and laws; yet these divinities remain ambivalent, they are as benevolent as they can be destructive (Rudra is another name for Shiva the Benefactor and the Egyptians celebrated the cult of Seth), and they never unified under *a single* malevolent figure. For Satan to appear within history, faith had to have been placed in a single God whose unicity determined that of his Adversary. All monotheism thus carries the possibility of *monodevilism*. Nevertheless, the most coherent monotheism does not permit the differentiation of a Satan from God because it affirms the absolute and exclusive unity of the divine principle, to the point of situating the origin of evil in God himself.[7] This God of justice and love is also a "devouring fire," a jealous and vengeful God, a God of wrath whose negative affects, however, never turn into hatred. It is only in a later phase, when the monotheistic demand abates, that this dark Ground in God—the focal point of his anger—can detach itself from him and appear as an evil principle: Satan. In evoking the "dark Ground," it is to Schelling, the only philosopher who took the devil seriously, that I am referring. Of course, according to him, this *Grund* is not an evil principle: It is the "remainder which never hatches" or "what in God is not yet God himself."[8] Yet this remainder becomes so when it dissociates itself from God and conquers a separate existence, that of an "inverted god."

As long as the Ground remains subordinate to the divine principle, the fundamental affirmation of monotheism is nevertheless maintained. This is no longer the case when it presents itself as power wholly independent and equal to God, as is the case in a Manichean dualism: The way is then paved for a division of humanity into two "races" opposed by nature, of which one would be the irrevocable subject of evil—a conception against which the three monotheistic religions have always fought. Christianity, however, is alone in attributing such great importance to the devil, to the extent of seeing in him the "Prince of this world." This comes as no surprise: By proclaiming that "God is love" and identifying him with the Sovereign Good, one inevitably tends to dissociate his Ground from him, to transform it into a hotbed of hatred under Satan's name. That the devil emerged out of the fissure within the divine principle is attested by iconography. Our image of a tall, dark figure with goat horns and bat wings looming in the darkness of Sabbath is only a late invention. Conversely, during the first centuries of the Christian era, his celestial origin was emphasized: On a mosaic from the fifth century of Saint-Apollinaris of Ravenna—just as much as in the oldest medieval miniatures—he is depicted as a young man with angel wings, without any diabolical attributes. Since Satan is of divine origins, like all creatures, he is subject to the will of his Creator and can in no way threaten the reign of God. The Church Fathers had unanimously proclaimed that through his sacrifice and his resurrection, Jesus had forever annihilated the devil's dominion. Origen even maintained that Satan had been "duped by the Cross," tricked by the cunning of God who allowed his Son to be crucified in order to better triumph over his Enemy . . . This representation of the *duped devil* permeated medieval folklore, and numerous fabliaux portrayed him as a stupid and ridiculous being that can be easily fooled. As the devil of the High Medieval period was not an object of apprehension, his followers, if any, could not inspire fear. This explains why, for centuries, the Church refused to give credence to the Sabbath and did not reprimand the practice of magic. Yet at the beginning of the fourteenth century, the devil's representations began to change: His monstrous traits, as well as signs of his power, would be underscored. The emphasis placed on his malevolent character would indeed accompany his rise in majesty. His size would grow disproportionately, and he was then presented as King Lucifer, "the Emperor of the kingdom dolorous," as Dante called him—endowed with a crown, a scepter, and sitting on his throne, surrounded by his court of demons.[9] This significant transformation does not find its source in popular culture, but in knowledge and power apparatuses that are constituted within the ruling classes. Generated by theologians and disseminated through the sermons of preachers and the works of artists, this transformation had clear political significance. Indeed, it accompanied the consolidation and sacralization of monarchical power. Satan—if he continued to be considered as the Adversary of God—then also appeared as a counterfigure to the King or State, a symbol of illegitimate power. By rebelling against his Lord, "he wanted," writes Honorius of Autun, "to reign by means of tyranny"; and the remarkable *Allegory of Good and Bad Government* Siena fresco panels of 1338 show us the allegory of Tyrannia on her throne with fangs and horns . . . The *devil's demonization* simultaneously transformed him into a monstrous figure and an absolute political enemy. There, too, the modification of his image foreshadowed that of his henchmen: It is because wizards and witches are believed to serve this satanic counterpower that they will be accused of "lèse-majesté crimes" and denounced as the "worst rebels."

This metamorphosis of Satan is also found on a theological level. A triumphant devil who extends his hold over the world without resistance succeeds this deceived and vanquished devil—the miserable adversary whom the intercession of the Virgin or a saint was enough to rout. This mutation is all the more astonishing when we consider that the Church was engaged in a merciless fight against the heirs of the ancient Manicheans, the Cathars, whose most radical currents considered the devil as "another God," an eternal principle of evil as powerful as the good God. Now, once heresy had been vanquished and the last Cathars exterminated, eminent members of the clergy seemed to adhere to this same theory they had so violently opposed. Yet, once the heresy was vanquished and the last Cathars exterminated, eminent clergy members seemed to adhere to a theory they had so violently opposed. Of course, the official Church doctrine continued to affirm that the devil was created by God, that he had remained subject to his Creator and had only become evil by rebelling against him; however, reading the treatises on demonology, it seems that Satan reigned supreme over a world deserted by God. For demonologists, Spee underlines ironically, all evil stems from witches, because "God no longer does anything, nor nature, but everything is done by witches."[10] Thus, a *Gnostic recidivism* affected Christendom by the end of the Middle Ages. As in the times of Augustine and the Church Fathers, "anti-Gnosticism became quasi-Gnosticism."[11] Let's turn to *The Hammer of Witches* once more: Whenever God is mentioned, he only appears as the one who grants the devil *permission* to do evil. The worst mischiefs attributed to witches—incest, poisonings, infanticides, etc.—are always accomplished "by the devil's power with God's permission," an expression repeated ad nauseam throughout the book (recall that it was written by two inquisitors personally backed by the pope). Since the Church Fathers, this notion of "divine permission" was to account for the existence of evil in a world created and governed by a benevolent God: He would have the power to prevent evil but would permit the devil's actions in order to "do good from evil," according to his Providence's mysterious designs. Nevertheless, this permission was intended solely for the possibility of sinning in general and not any particular sin. The authors of the *Malleus* would maintain instead that God grants special "permission" for "all the elements and all the things composed of those elements,"[12] to witches and Satan; that "the permission of God is greater when by means of a renunciation of the Faith a creature dedicated to God co-operates in further horrible crimes";[13] that he accepts, for example, that witches steal and devour a newborn baby to punish a pregnant woman who had uttered, "I wish I were carrying the Devil."[14] All of this amounts to making God the accomplice of Satan and his crimes. Sprenger and Institoris thus tend to erase any difference between God as permissive and persecutor. The God of the *Malleus* is perverse: He wittingly authorizes evil in order to punish it afterward by making men suffer. Yet such a "god" becomes nearly identical to Satan himself, the Manichean principle of Darkness, or the "Being-Supreme-in-Wickedness" of the Sadian libertine. It is as if God and Christ had been replaced by Satan, as if he had become the *last god* of the Christian West. The more the inquisitors insisted on fighting him, the more they recognized a quasi-divine power in him—what he had once been, before being dissociated from God and hypostatized as a malevolent principle. Demonology is a dark theology where, in the torture chambers and the flames of the stakes, the witch-hunters celebrate in their own way the worship of the Anti-God, all the while denying that this god of darkness is God. Thus, "nothing could stop Satan from being divine, but this enduring truth was denied with the rigors of torment."[15]

How, then, should this Gnostic turn, or rather recidivism, be interpreted? This does not concern only Catholic theology: Some fifty years later, Luther would follow the path set by the old Gnostic treatises. For him, "we are all subject to the devil both in body and goods [. . .] the bread which we eat, the drink which we drink, the garments which we wear, yea the air and whatsoever we live by in the flesh, is under his dominion."[16] This turning point is not a simple doctrinal evolution: The theological dogmas and the schemata that underlie it are rooted in power apparatuses to which they turn to legitimize their action. The new persecution apparatuses that appear between the thirteenth and fourteenth centuries, further radicalized in the following centuries, call for certain schemata and representations of the enemy that seem more apt than others to legitimize them. In the traditional Christian doctrine (which I have qualified as "Augustinian"), the possibility of repentance and forgiveness remains open to all, and, consequently, the Mystical Body of Christ can in principle extend to all of humanity. Given that the origin of evil is in each of us, the devil's figure initially occupies only a marginal place in dogma. Yet to uphold the new strategies of persecution, this position turns out to be less effective than neo-Gnostic conceptions where the principle of evil subjects the world to its grip; where the *Corpus mysticum* is directly opposed to a diabolical Anti-Body, where a countless multitude of men belong to "races of darkness" due to their impure blood and predestination to evil. The omnipresence of Satan and his plethoric henchmen then justifies the limitless extension of persecutions, and their irredeemable character justifies their extermination.

Nonetheless, it must be recognized that the Church's traditional position already permitted the legitimization of persecutions. How did it define the devil? As God's intimate foe, created by him to then rebel against him, as God's "rival" or "ape." This mimetic character is that of the double, perversely trying to imitate his Creator. The devil is *God's counterfigure*, his simulacrum, which is inseparable from him as a reflection is from its model, and his irreducible adversary since the Double is always a rival trying to supplant what it imitates. A counterfigure inversely reflects its template, and the devil is precisely defined as an *inversion principle*. For the devil to appear as God's ape, a difference in hierarchy must persist between the model and the simulacrum as they cannot be at the same rank (as is the case in Manicheism). The opposition must remain dissymmetric: One pole should precede and dominate the other, so that this domination's reversal should be seen as a wicked perversion. This is why Satan reigns over the reversed world of the riots and popular festivities, presides over the inversion of all norms in the universe of carnival and Sabbath, and himself appears as an inverted body. This counterfigure is a *phantasma*, a simulacrum in the Platonic sense, and a misleading copy that insidiously dissimulates its difference with its model to usurp its place. If Satan can take any shape at will, it is because he doesn't have any proper form of his own: The counterfiguration of God is equivalent, thus, to a radical dis-figuration and a disappearance of all determinate figure. *Inconsistency*, according to Pierre de l'Ancre, is the main trait of this "master of metamorphoses": "he has no constant shape, all his actions are movements riddled with uncertainty, illusion, deception, and imposture." When an accused was asked by his judges to describe Satan, he answered, "it seemed like flies dancing around a candle" (had he known that Beelzebub means "Lord of the Flies" in Hebrew?).[17] And a young Basque "witch," Marie Daguerre, would describe him to de l'Ancre as "an obscure and tall tree trunk, armless and faceless." A faceless X, a shapeless mass, a fleeting shadow, a whirlwind of darkness . . . Infinitely plastic, he may seem identical to all things he mimes, or rather, *nearly* identical. Indeed, Deleuze reminds us that dissemblance alone does not define the *phantasma* but the minute gap — the nearly imperceptible distortion of the real image — that allows the simulacrum to *double* its model and to replace it.[18] How was Satan assimilated to the Platonic simulacrum? Surely, the Church Fathers' theology was rife with Neoplatonism, yet invoking doctrinal influences would not suffice to account for this. We have seen that, among the different figures of the stranger, the one that evokes the most intense anxiety and hatred—and unleashes the most ferocious persecutions—is not the ultimate Other or the absolute strangeness: It is the almost-same, the *stranger within*, so similar to us that nothing (or *almost* nothing) can distinguish it from us. It thus comes as no surprise that this hotbed of hatred named Satan could have occupied such a place.

And yet, the simulacrum fails to imitate exactly its model, to ape it to the point of blending entirely with it. Neither Paul nor Luther tells us how to identify Satan when he manifests himself as an angel of light or behind the mask of God. However, many tales and fabliaux teach us how to recognize him when he presents himself in human form. Indeed, the Evil One appears quite similar to the one he imitates, except for one detail that may result in his eventual uncovering. This can be a deformed foot that evokes a hoof, split lips, red teeth, markedly pointed ears, a nose that is too hooked, the strange touch of a too-cold limb—even of a sex—that does not look like human flesh . . . An engraving by Lucas van Leyde evokes the moment of anguish where the Enemy slips out of his disguise: In this rendering of the *Temptation of Saint Anthony*, a young and pleasant woman, lavishly dressed, is standing in front of the anchorite and offering him a present. Not allowing himself to be misled, the saint gestures refusal or conjuration: Surely, he has perceived, under her headdress, the two extruding small horns.[19] In the end, the devil will always unveil himself. If he could perfectly imitate the work of God, if the "small gap" between the simulacrum and the model disappeared, he would become identical to his model: Satan would be God. We measure here the distance that separates the Manichean or Cathar position—wherein the benevolent God and the evil Principle are opposed in all points—from the opposing position that affirms both their antagonism and their proximity, their almost total similitude within a most radical opposition. On this point as on others, it is the same with Satan as with the Jew, the heretic, or the witch. As an eminent figure of the Other-in-the-Same and the intimate stranger, he prefigures these human targets that the apparatuses send to the stake. What so many legends and confessions wrested out under torture evoke is this unsettling proximity: a fading difference, a demarcation between the same and the other, the divine and the diabolical, the saint and the witch, which is always at risk of being erased and that must be *re-marked* and violently reinscribed on the body. Indeed, this representation of the devil determines in advance what will be the persecutors' methods. Long before witch-hunters sought them out on the bodies of their victims, the discovery of a corporeal clue — of a hidden *stigma* — had allowed the demon's cunning to be thwarted. Therefore, the persecution apparatuses do not hesitate to resort to widely varying schemata. They retain, from the Gnostic position, the triumphant omnipresence of the devil and the certainty that there are cursed races who are irremediably doomed. From the Catholic position, they take the dread of a hidden Enemy that *almost nothing* can help identify.

What happens when the Adversary removes his mask, when the almost-same suddenly reveals itself as absolute-other and Absolute Enemy? Then, the difference seemingly can no longer stabilize: Like so many signs of his monstrosity, the stigmata proliferate on Satan's body. There is an "unlimited becoming-mad," a "becoming always other" in the simulacrum, as Deleuze noted, that thwarts any assignment to a stable identity; so much so that the diabolical counterfigure will never stop disfiguring itself by deviating further and further from the image and likeness of God. At the end of the seventeenth century, the painter Christoph Haizmann would attest to this growing disfigurement through his paintings that represented the demon tormenting him: As Freud reports, if the first drawing depicts him as an "honest elderly citizen," in the following "his appearance grows more and more terrifying — more mythological one might say. He is equipped with horns, eagle's claw and bat's wings."[20] Most often, of course, Satan is differentiated from the human form by a trait belonging to the animal realm: horns, forked hoof, tail, or claws. We also know that certain animals — the goat, the cat, the snake, the toad, the bat, etc. — are particularly inclined to lend the devil their form or attributes. These traits are multiplied in Haizmann's drawings: Like so many other images and stories, they attest to a *bestialization* of the diabolical figure, that is to say of its dehumanization and an erasure of the fundamental demarcation between man and animal, with the anguish that this undifferentiation entails.

Yet the devil's figuration also comes to transgress another major demarcation. Whereas in Haizmann's first drawing he appears as a middle-aged man, in the second he bears two womanly breasts. Here again, the signs of dissimilarity are increasingly ostensible, and the figuration of breasts will multiply in the following representations. Satan's bestialization here accompanied his *feminization*, as if the image's transformations took note of the historical mutation that had transformed the persecution apparatus into a *witch* hunt. Yet the demon, the painter's object of obsession, does not entirely transform into a woman: Freud observes that in addition to the numerous breasts, he has "a large penis ending in a snake."[21] *At once* man, woman, and beast, he is thus *neither* one *nor* the other: by concentrating all their attributes in one body, he erases what could help to distinguish them. The monstrosity of the diabolical body is that of the mixture and the hybrid, in other words, the unclassifiable, the undifferentiated, which in every culture evokes disgust and fright.[22] He defies God's creative work, which consisted in differentiating, classifying, and inserting an order in the chaos separating light from darkness, then distinguishing the living between animals and human beings, and finally men and women since the first days of his Creation . . . Most of the attributes that characterize the devil follow this fundamental logic: His bat wings denote the animal's mixed nature as a mammal that flies like a bird. When "witches" accused of fornicating with him tell their judges that Satan's sperm is glacial, they do so because the diabolical body transgresses the opposition between masculine and feminine. It must consequently invert the semen's symbolic determinations as a principle of virile fecundity, always associated with heat and life, whereas the feminine body — and foremost the impure blood of the menstrual body — is associated with cold and death.[23] It is worth noting that malevolent spirits of Chinese mythology are also endowed with horns, bat wings, and breasts of a woman: This is a schema that goes beyond historical and cultural differences.

Yet the demon is not simply a principle of inversion of polarities: By inverting them, he subverts their opposition. In the figuration of the diabolical body, the masculine and feminine as well as the human and the animal aren't the only differences abolished; so too are the differences between up and down, front and back, noble and depraved (he is often represented with a "behind's face" where his anus, which his worshippers kiss during Sabbath, is placed where his mouth should be). As a principle of undifferentiation, inversion, and a transgression of all opposition, the figure of Satan shows us the dissolution of all constitutive differences that shape our identity, the uncanny and anxiogenic image of a *body in disembodiment*. A disfigured figuration of the human body whose origins lie in the rupture of transference, wherein my flesh is entwined with the other's body and, yet more profoundly, in the crises of the fleshly chiasma as the matrix of hatred. This representation of a monstrous body can easily be associated with that of the great Rebel, instigator of seditions and popular revolts. Indeed, the powerful fear most the disembodiment of the collective Body as they apprehend the threat of a destruction of hierarchies, of the collapse of social order. However, Satan's cannot be reduced to this unstable assembly of contradictory attributes. Unlike the Mystical Body of Christ, effectively present in the host, the satanic Anti-Body is not a body of flesh, but a disembodied pseudobody. It is precisely because he lacks a body that the Evil One tries to *embody* (taking up all the meanings of the word) the witches or the possessed. The Apostle was unequivocal: "For we are not fighting against flesh-and-blood enemies, but against evil rulers and

authorities of the unseen world [. . .] against evil spirits."[24] Satan — fallen yet
of angelic nature — remains forever deprived of flesh and sex, and the *coitus
diabolicus* is merely an illusion wherein he offers his harlots a simulacrum of
jouissance. Yet this theological dogma contradicts staunchly the main charge
of the witchcraft trials, where so-called witches were sent to their deaths on the
grounds that they had actually copulated with the devil. This guilt was attested
by looking for physical traces of the copulation. This contradiction affects all
treatises on demonology: They are obliged to simultaneously affirm that, on
the one hand, the body of the devil and his evil deeds are real (otherwise it
would be absurd to want to chastise his followers) and, on the other, that they
are only imaginary representations (otherwise he would be made a material
entity, an evil substance, as the Manicheans held). This equivocal conception, of a *phantasm* at once real and unreal, imaginary and true, cannot be
maintained to its logical end. The theory supposed to ground the persecution
apparatus is also its Achilles' heel; and when the contradiction is unraveled,
the demonic simulacrum will appear as a simple illusion.

Why were the witch-hunters so determined to assert the reality of the Sabbath and diabolical copulations, desperately seeking to reconcile this assertion
with the Church doctrine? Although the Church had declared for centuries
that the magical flights and nocturnal assemblies of witches were mere illusions, its claim, henceforth, was that they actually took place; neither limited to imagination nor dreams, witches united "through flesh" with demons.
Where did this demonological realism — this new insistence on the reality of
the *Corpus* and *coitus diaboli* — come from? To the extent that Satan is God's
counterfigure, the modifications that affect him may well find their source in
those rooted in a belief in God. Yet a few decades earlier, a "realistic" turn had
affected Christian theology. For a long time, controversies over the nature of
the Eucharist had agitated the Church. The major turning point again took
place in 1215, at the Fourth Lateran Council, which ratified the doctrine of
transubstantiation: From that moment it was argued that, in the Eucharist, a
total change of substance takes place in which bread and consecrated wine
truly become the body and blood of Christ. This was not only a theological
quibble. At the moment when, during the communion, the faithful absorb
the body of the Christ, they allow themselves to be absorbed in this body, in
this community of believers that defines itself precisely as the Mystical Body of
Christ. Attesting the "real presence" of Christ in the host amounts to positing
the reality of a collective Body that is the Church.[25] The Eucharist is an *incorporation rite* that reconstitutes the unity of the *Corpus mysticum* each time
and makes it possible to counter these tendencies toward disintegration and
disembodiment that are at work in all collective Bodies. It is not an accident

that the same council that reaffirms the reality and the unity of the Mystical Body of the Church is also the one that marks the visible borders of this Body by ordering the Jews to wear a distinctive sign; it is also at the same time that the Church adopts the inquisitorial procedure and imposes obligatory confessions. All these processes strive in different ways to reincorporate the Great Body, with the dogma of transubstantiation as their key.

It would be difficult to overestimate the importance of this doctrinal turn. A Eucharistic devotion was born with its doctrinaires, mystics, and miracles, when blood gushed out of a holy bread pierced by so-called profaners (first in Bolsena in 1264, then in Paris in 1290) . . . Jews were the first to be accused of this sacrilege, and such accusations would multiply, associated with those of infanticide — or "ritual crime" — which spread at the same time. Condensing both accusations into a single image, it was also claimed that the profaned host sometimes appeared in the form of a small bloodied little child . . . The new dogma, in anchoring the flesh and blood of Christ in material reality, requires for its confirmation equally real proofs of this metamorphosis: The blood that flows from the stabbed host would be the visible proof of transubstantiation.[26] This "Eucharistic realism" would profoundly change the representation that the faithful had of their fundamental rite. Henceforth, communion would consist of *actually* devouring the flesh of their god and drinking his blood. The celebration of Mass can be experienced as an archaic sacrificial rite at the intersection of cannibalistic and vampiric phantasms. From Christianity's earliest days, this rite served as a commemoration of the Passion of Christ without resorting to a bloody sacrifice. Thus, the commemoration had been alleviated of the anguish and the horror that follow the murder of a god. It is this protective symbolism, this *sublimation* of sacrificial violence that would disappear in a realistic interpretation of the Eucharist. The Communion rite then takes on a phantasmatic dimension that can be accompanied by extreme anguish. When Catholic soldiers summoned him to choose between conversion and the stake, the Huguenot poet Agrippa d'Aubigné replied that "the horror of the mass abated away that of the fire." To endure the anguish of murder and consumption, many believers would be left with no alternatives but to project their phantasm on external targets by accusing the Jews (and later the "witches") of killing children — who are here substitutes for the Son-of-God. Moreover, these crimes are supposedly committed on Easter, and the Jews are accused of crucifying their victims and drinking their blood . . .[27] The fiction of the diabolical Sabbath condenses these two accusations; since Satan's worshippers allegedly profane the Cross and sacraments while also sacrificing children to drink their blood and devour their flesh.

The demonological realism that motivated witch hunts would thus be a consequence of the Fourth Lateran Council turn. It comes as no surprise, then, that Institoris, after having participated in composing the *Malleus*, would write a treatise to defend the dogma of transubstantiation. Only a step separates the belief of a real presence of Christ in the host from that of the reality of the *Corpus diaboli* and copulation of flesh, and, in the apparatus's "knowledge," these beliefs mutually bolster one another. Underlying the Sabbath's myth is a phantasm tied to the fundamental rite of the Christian religion, consisting in the Church's commemoration, with an offering of bread and wine, of the murder of an innocent victim. According to the demonologists' delirium, Satan's worshippers would fruitlessly attempt to imitate this rite, which grounds the unity of the Mystical Body. They reenact the mystery of the Blessed Sacrament by immolating children whose flesh they devour and blood they drink; they try to incorporate in their own flesh the power of the Anti-God by allowing themselves to be penetrated by the devil's sex, as if these rituals could uphold a diabolical Anti-Body. All these efforts are to no avail because Satan will always fail to take shape and generate a body: Not only is the *coitus diabolicus* unable to result in childbearing, but the devil does not succeed in incarnating himself in a real body, to give his community of followers the consistency of a Body like that of the Church or State. Is this the inevitable defeat to which Boguet alludes when he evokes the final episode of the Sabbath, where the demon "sets himself on fire and is reduced to ashes which the sorcerers gather and hide"? The *Corpus diaboli* will never be more than a simulacrum, and, when it vanishes in the early morning, only the body of the witch remains onstage, this stigmatized and humiliated body destined to suffer the torments of the question and the flames of the stake.

Satan's Anti-Body counters not only the Mystical Body of Christ but also that of his mother. In 1477, an inhabitant of Saint-Jorioz in Savoie called Antoinette Rose "confessed" under torture to having participated in a "heretics synagogue" with devil worshippers who ordered her to renounce God and "that brothel keeper [*maquerelle*] Virgin Mary." And when Niklas Fiedler, Trier's burgomaster, met the devil and pledged allegiance to him, what did his new master demand from him? That he "should help him commit murder and to renounce God, Jesus the Crucified, and his mother whom he had called a whore." Or at least this is what Fiedler declared under torture before being executed in 1591.[28] According to demonologists, Satan and his followers foster a particularly intense hatred for the Virgin Mary as she is often presented as the ultimate defender of men and their most efficient auxiliary in the fight against the devil. In *The Miracle of Theophilus*, it is her intercession that delivers Theophilus, who had sold his soul to Satan, and it is in her sanctuary that the painter Haizmann sought refuge. The inquisitor Sprenger, one of the authors of the *Malleus*, devoutly observed the Marian cult. So too did the archbishop Ferdinand of Bavaria, who sent more than two thousand women to the stake during the Great Witch Hunts of Cologne after he had made a pact with Mary by signing it with his own blood . . . How did the Holy Virgin come to represent such an antidiabolical principle? Precisely because she is *the Virgin*, a symbol of the untouched body that resists all breaches. It is for this very reason that she was depicted with a vast blue coat enfolding countless men and women and was celebrated as the protector of city walls. An ancient hymn of the Byzantine liturgy would invoke her as such: "Rejoice, steadfast rampart of the City [. . .] / Rejoice, unmarried bride." Contrasting this forever virgin body are those of the "devil's whores." As the *coitus diabolicus* is deemed sterile, the opposition is total between Mary, who becomes a mother while remaining a virgin, and the Witch, who prostitutes herself to Satan without being able to bear children. The unfathomable irony of the devil can only be admired — or rather that of the judges and confessors, who whisper these "confessions" to Antoinette or Fiedler — when the Evil One inverts the accusation by calling the Virgin a whore.

Mary's body — virginal, sealed off on itself, like a maternal membrane that envelops and protects — is the exact antithesis of the satanic Anti-Body. Indeed, the latter presented itself as an *intrusion principle*, a foreign element penetrating other bodies in order to brand and possess them. Judge de l'Ancre would purport that Satan's penis is divided thrice, in order to simultaneously penetrate his followers' vaginas, anuses, and mouths . . . The devil's penis, its size, and the quality of the *jouissance* it could arouse was of great interest among demonologists. Rémy thus claimed that his "dimensions were equal to the clouds formed by chimney smoke," and de l'Ancre would not miss the chance to mock the small size of the satanic penis as described by Boguet. His Basque witches, said indeed that it is "of beautiful shape and measure," so that they "are better sated by Satan than the women of Franche-Comté." All testimonies concur on one point: Copulation with the devil is extremely painful. Not only is his semen as cold as ice, but his phallus — bristling with spikes or scales — violently tears their flesh. As stated by Chrétienne Parmentier, executed in 1624 at the age of twenty-three, by deflowering her "he would have done her great harm, feeling great cold and great pain, as if there had been thorns between her legs, so much so that she was sick for a fortnight."[29] Satan's penis is the emblem of an unattainable *jouissance*, for it is immediately inverted into atrocious suffering. This *jouissance* transgresses major forbiddances: involving sodomy, bestiality, incest, yet carrying its own punishment by providing a glimpse into the torments of hell. A *jouissance* so desirable, nonetheless, that demonologists had to represent it as a terrifying agony. We

have asked ourselves what possession could possibly make a miserable peasant
like Aldegonde de Rue an object of envy to her persecutors, an envy that "is
nothing other than hatred itself." Perhaps they were envious of the *jouissance*
that they suspect in their victims—for which they would make them pay.

With the devil as a metaphor for *jouissance* we finally find a common
thread passing through all these stories. This metaphor is an essential element
of the logic of hatred. Whether it is the Witch, the Sodomite, or even the
Medieval Leper, the persecution apparatuses' target is always presented as a
subject supposed to be indulging in jouissance. This is also the case in our era
with its own targets of racism: Black, Arab, and Jew. "The Jew is naturally a
pornographer," would write an anti-Semite author of the nineteenth century.[30]
And Louis-Ferdinand Céline's anti-Semitic pamphlet *Bagatelles pour un massacre* is wholly entrenched in the rage and envy of this purported *jouissance*
of the Jew. Why would their persecutors suppose this intense *jouissance* in
those they hate? Would it be *their own jouissance*—the somber *jouissance* of
hatred—that they deny in themselves and project onto their victims? Here,
the genealogical approach is strained to its limits. It would no longer suffice
to describe the historical transformations of beliefs and myths: We have to understand the persecutors' phantasms, and, for this, recourse to psychoanalysis
becomes unavoidable. Who is the true subject of this abject *jouissance* we
call "Satan"? To this question, Freud believed that he had found a definitive
answer: The devil is a *substitute for the father*. He is the mythical Father of
the primitive horde mentioned in *Totem and Taboo*, a cruel, incestuous, and
castrating Father whose murder by his rebellious sons would be the founda-
tional moment at the root of all human religions and cultures. It is he who
reappears in the guise of God, but also of the devil, who is initially identical
to him. This Father figure would in fact present itself in primitive religions as
a "unique personality," object of both love and hatred, who "would be later
riven into two figures each endowed with opposite qualities." Thus, these different figurations of the divine pass from an initial *ambivalence* to a *cleavage*:
God and the devil would be two faces of the Father—or, more precisely, the
devil would be his true face, dissimulated behind the mask of God. Indeed,
in their representation of Satan, "religions bear ineffaceable marks of the fact
that the primitive primal father was a being of unlimited evil—a being less
like God than the Devil."[31] This affirmation is tantamount to justifying the
assassination of the tyrant by his sons: Like archaic mythologies and sacrificial
religions, Freud here adopts the point of view of the persecutors, legitimizing
murder and blaming the victim for every imaginable wrongdoing.[32] Having
discovered the role of projection in psychic life, why would he refuse to admit
that the *Urvater* is only a monster in the sons' phantasms, who project their

hatred onto him? That this primordial figure is an *object of projection* — which gains its ambivalence by concentrating the hatred and the love that men transfer onto him?

And more, is it quite evident that the devil should only be a Father-substitute? If Freud shows such great interest in Haizmann's case, it is because the latter provides a confirmation of his thesis: Suffering from depression after his father's death, the painter made a pact with Satan, handing over his life by "becoming his own child." There remains, in Haizmann's portraits of him, something Freud deems "unusual" and "a striking contradiction of [his] hypothesis": Satan is endowed not only with a penis but also numerous breasts. He sees in this only a pathological trait pertaining to Haizmann's neurosis. According to him, it would be impossible "that *the* Devil [. . .] the Adversary of God, should be represented otherwise than as a male, and, indeed, as a super-male, with horns, tail and a big penis-snake."[33] Here Freud missed the mark: Representations wherein the devil has both breasts and a penis are, on the contrary, frequently found in the medieval West.[34] How should we interpret Freud's error? Why would he discard every clue that would cast doubt on the paternal signification of the devil? Why does he not take into consideration the more archaic traits, the claws that lacerate, the gaping mouth that devours the wretched? Can psychoanalysis, by assigning this figure to either of the familial figures, by oedipalizing it, really help us in understanding who Satan is? Is he the Father, the Son rebelling against the Father, the Mother (a phallic and castrating mother of whose figuration could be found in the Witch), or even a composite figure, the "combined parent" of which Melanie Klein speaks? Perhaps we are dealing with an anonymous X, evading all these determinations. A method to reveal the true nature of this X — neither Father, nor Son, nor Mother, nor a figure to be assigned to any of the poles of the Oedipal triangle — must be found. Who is this X, both the target of the most ambivalent projections and the subject of a lethal *jouissance*, of this *jouissance* of hatred that "we never know how to give up?" To elucidate the enigma, we must proceed from the mythical figure of the devil to the fantasy that underlies it (Freud stopped at this point by making Satan a substitute for the Father); then sharpen the analysis by moving from the psychic fantasy to the primal phantasy where fantasies and myths find their ultimate source at the level of the ego's immanence. This change in levels requires changing methods: If fantasy implies a relationship with others and belongs to the realm of psychoanalysis, phantasy brings into play the relationship of the ego to the remainder and calls for egoanalysis.

How to uncover the elementary processes in which these phantasies take root? Spee had paved the way for an answer by observing that persecutors pro-

ject onto their victims their envy and hatred, without realizing that, in so doing, they were attributing their own affects to their victims. And we have found
yet the same process in accusations of profanation and infanticide prompted
by the new doctrine of the Eucharist. Each time, phantasies and affects concentrate on a projection object that they constitute as a malevolent Other, and
the persecution apparatuses orient them on certain men and women who are
themselves designated as *henchmen* of this Other. The more the persecutors
discharge their lethal affects by projecting them outward, the more they perceive themselves as "pure" and "good." The more they transfer their hatred on
the Other, the more the latter appears as a threat that, in return, legitimizes
their murderous violence. This confirms Engels's intuition; to exercise terror,
one must feel terrorized — and it is also true that the most ferocious persecutions were the acts of men who themselves felt persecuted by the ones they
tracked and killed. The Gospels evince this link between hatred and "lie" —
that is, the countertruth of the primordial projection — in affirming that Satan
is a "murderer from the beginning" and that he is, too, the "father of lies." It
becomes difficult to undo this deadly knot because it would imply that the
truth should overrun projections and phantasies; that the persecutors are able
to renounce the hatred's *jouissance* instead of displacing it onto substitutive
formations; that they could recognize the true origin of their affects and cease
to project them onto an Other. Whereas the apparatuses' might consists in retaining them in their illusion, to provide them with perpetually new enemies
on whom they can discharge their hatred.

Each time, the hateful projection polarizes on a certain figure of the Other
that becomes the vector of persecution, and it is persecution schemata that
render these figurations possible. What conditions are required to make a
schema operational? In the *Critique of Pure Reason*, the imagination's schematism that grounds all objective knowledge presupposes a preliminary orientation toward what Kant designates as a "non-empirical object," "a transcendental object = X." This X is an *ob-ject* in the literal sense: It is the opposite,
what stands "against" (*dawider*), the ob-jection horizon that grounds the constitution of the objects of our experience. The same goes for the schematization of affects operated by persecution schemata. The figure of an Other = X
is here required in order to capture affects of anxiety, envy, and hatred and
to mobilize them against a target that is not a real enemy, but an Absolute
Enemy, a transcendental principle of evil. This is what the three monotheistic religions have labelled as *the devil*. Recall the etymological meaning of
this word; *satan* in Hebrew and *diabolos* in Greek both signify the one who
opposes (in a literal sense: "the one who throws himself across"). In the most
ancient books of the Hebraic Bible, "satan" is not yet personified; the word

simply denotes an obstacle. Thus, it is said of the Lord's angel who blocks the road to the prophet Balaam that he stands before him "as satan."[35] What we call the devil is before all else this ob-jection act, the primordial Opponent that grants hatred its object. We had asked ourselves how hatred could at once be indifferent to its objects — that are ever merely opportunities for it to appear in the world — and yet indissociable from them. This paradox is illuminated if we distinguish the empirical objects that it finds as targets and the transcendental object-of-hatred, a diabolical arch-object that it gives itself to allow its manifestation. The beings we hate are never the primordial Object of our hatred but only its henchmen or the *figurants* of the remainder. The same distinction also applies to the objects of our anxiety, of our disgust, of our love.

How can this projection pole of hatred be more precisely characterized? If hatred is the matrix of wicked passions and the most radical evil, at stake here then is the age-old question of the origin of evil. Contrary to the Gnostics, who believed in the existence of a malevolent power exterior to man, Augustine situated its cause within each of us. Now is the moment to recognize that these two antinomic positions both say the truth but from a different perspective. It is true that the X-element at the origin of hatred is found within us, at the level of the ego's immanence and not in a transcendent entity. Also true is the fact that this X-element cannot be fully identified with the ego; it compels me *as if* from outside and the Other, as if both immanent and transcendent to the ego. This "transcendence in immanence" is what *in me* is *not yet* myself, the remainder of the ego-flesh. The very word *satan* or *dia-bolos* indicates what the "devil" is in truth: He is the remainder of my flesh, the ob-jection point that resists within me, what stands against me from within my own flesh and appears at first as absolutely foreign. Herein is found the hotbed of fundamental phantasms where from our fantasies and myths emanate, within this primordial illusion where the ego does not recognize the remainder as a part of its flesh; so that it expels it outward, constitutes it as this Other = X that becomes the projection pole of its affects. This does not mean that the devil and God himself would be *nothing but* projections of the remainder. Under the epochē, such a statement is without meaning: Since we henceforth forbid claims or denials of an existence thesis, we cannot affirm that the divine *does not exist* outside our projections and phantasms. The divine remains an enigma and the project for a phenomenology of the divine, and the obscure Ground it conceals stays open as a task for egoanalysis.

In searching for what hides behind the devil's mask, we are once again faced with the remainder . . . Does it here not play the same role as the "father" in Freud or Girard's "scapegoat" by explaining all things and their opposites, the king and the sacrificed victim, the devil and God? This bears repeating; egoanalysis's concepts are not tasked with providing an explanation for what occurs on a worldly plane. They expound elementary phenomena that take place in the immanence of the ego-flesh, and although these can foreshadow some historical phenomena, they are never their "cause." It may be that Satan is only a disfiguration of the remainder, but the disfigured remainder can manifest itself in a number of other ways, and egoanalysis cannot replace the historical genealogy that attempts to describe its different modes of apparition. I had to invent the concept of remainder to overcome the difficulties with which phenomenology is confronted when it asks the question of the conditions of fleshly self-affection (the chiasma that takes form when "my right hand touches my left hand touching an object"). This implies, following Husserl, acknowledging the privilege of tactile experience: It is in this field that the most originary phenomena that operate in the genesis of the own body and the *alter ego* are constituted. Yet witch hunts provided us with a number of significant examples of the roles of the body, of corporeal phantasms, and of the touch in the persecutors' beliefs. If we are dealing with a hereditary contagion, it is the primordial contact between the mother and her child that provokes the malevolent contamination; and if it is a free surrender to the demon, she is sanctioned by an inscription directly made on the body, a stigma most often insensitive to touch. Most of the *maleficia* are equally transmitted by corporeal contact ("I touch you in order to kill you"). Moreover, the effects of this contact are ambivalent: It is by touching them that the thaumaturge king miraculously cures some of the diseased and the exorcism rituals recur to the "sacred finger" of the priest, meant to deliver the possessed of the demon that haunts her.[36] The intervention of the exorcist and torturer consists in transferring this dread from flesh to speech, from the body's silent convulsions to the scream where it can enunciate and name itself. Impelling witches and the possessed to reveal the name of their demons indeed allows them to summon the latter in order to conjure him, and this naming is often indissociable to a bodily localization. The stupefying lists established by exorcists — where to the name of each demon and his place in the infernal hierarchy corresponds a "place of residence" in the body of the possessed — attest to this: "*Lion d'Enfer*, of the Archangels, lodged under the navel; *Astaroth*, of the Angels, lodged beneath the armpit; *Coal of Impurity*, of the Angels, lodged beneath the left hip," etc., without omitting "*Jabel*, of the Archangels, who comes and goes in all parts of the body."[37]

If where the Evil One takes residence in the anatomy of the witch seems more difficult to situate, it is because her body belongs entirely to him, that she *takes shape* (*fait corps*) with the devil. Far from being exclusive to witches and the possessed, this intrusion of the devil in the body concerns everyone.

All have the *devil in their body* (*le diable au corps*) and can become targets for apparatuses destined to wrest the devil away. This is Luther's opinion: Satan "sticks to man more tightly than his cloth or shirt, more tightly even than his own skin."[38] As such the devil is not only the Opponent, the-one-who-faces; he is the one who opposes *from within*, an intimate foreigner that seems to percolate through my flesh, closer still, more indissociable from myself than my skin. What is inversely presented in the phantasm as a penetration of the external element, in truth arises from the innermost layers of the ego-flesh; it is the disfigured remainder, where the ego projects its anxiety, its disgust, and its hatred. During the chiasma's crises, the remainder's disfiguration is accompanied by a disembodiment of the own body, which explains why the devil is represented through the form of a monstrous body, an Anti-Body wherein archaic phantasms of disintegration, intrusion, and devouring are condensed. And maybe this frightening figure plays the role of a protective screen, an ultimate defense in the face of an unbearable threat, a Black Hole where all things are swallowed without return . . .

In 1587, Walpurga Hausmann, a midwife from the Augsburg region, was accused of being a witch. She confessed, probably under torture, to most of the crimes that were traditionally leveled against them: She claimed to have caused the death of more than forty newborns (and sometimes to have devoured their cadavers after having roasted them . . .), and maledicted a number of other humans, nine cows, and a horse; she claimed to have provoked hailstorms to destroy harvests, renounced the Christian faith, participated in a Sabbath, fornicated with a demon named Federlin, profaned holy bread, blasphemed the Virgin Mary, whom her demon had incited her to call a "dirty wench." According to her, it was her lewdness that had brought her to worship the devil. Some thirty years earlier, she had let herself be seduced by a neighboring peasant and had invited him to spend the night at her home. Right after having sexual intercourse with him, she had noticed while touching one of his hands, to her horror, that it did not resemble a human hand: "it was as if it were made of wood." He disappeared as soon as she had invoked the name of Jesus. Although she was convinced that he was a demon, she had once again welcomed him into her home the next night and had delivered herself to him "body and soul." During all those years, she claimed, she had not ceased fornicating with Federlin, including in her cell after her arrest. She was to die at the stake.[39] Hers was not an isolated case: A similar misadventure would occur to Ellen Driver in 1645, accused of witchcraft in Suffolk. She had discovered on the night of her nuptials, at the contact of the frozen sex and limbs of her husband, that he "was the devil," which had not stopped her from living with him for more than twenty years and bearing his children . . .[40]

We know that the devil, a figure of the almost-same, cannot imitate the human form without an uncanny particularity betraying him sooner or later. In Walpurga's story, this does not meet the eye but the touch, as was the case for most of the diabolical stigmata or the glacial and painful contact of Satan's sex. Oddly, this contact that she first found frightening did not seem to deter her from delivering herself anew, again and again, to her demonic lover—as if what had provoked horror could equally prompt her desire. At stake is not a pathological perversion, but a sign of the affective ambivalence that the remainder arouses. In oscillating between phases of disfiguration and transfiguration, it provokes in turn attraction and repulsion, hatred and love. Heaving in this oscillation, these feelings present themselves as reversible affects, capable of changing into their opposites; and these affective dualities can at times associate and fusion. A single object could thus provoke intense yet opposite feelings at the same time, as had Walpurga's lover with his flesh-less hand. As for the demonic marks, the stigma presents itself here as a "dead part"; but Walpurga believed that it was *on the body of an other* that she had discovered it. This comes as no surprise if it is through transferring my flesh on the body of the other that I constitute him as an embodied ego, an *alter ego* similar to my own. When this transfer is interrupted, the other's body loses its fleshly dimension and can be apprehended as a dead body, an organ deprived of flesh. We project onto this other body the part of ourselves that we do not bear recognizing in ourselves, to the extent that we believe that it is this other who arouses these feelings of horror or hatred — or desire — when in fact these affects are rooted in our own flesh. Walpurga naively enacted this projection, without having realized that, in so doing, she was repeating what her perse-cutors had done and adhered to the same phantasm of those who would send her to her death. This same projection is at play in the search for a demonic mark, since it is always on the body of an other that the prickers and judges strove to uncover the untouchable part of our touch.

The projection that finds its target in an external other merely replays an originary projection where the ego rivets its affects on the remainder by trans-forming it into a first object of love and hatred. It is a remainder already dis-figured or transfigured by this immanent projection that will be transferred to a transcendent plane — and first on another being — to constitute the various figures of a desired or rejected, loved or hated other. In fact, the remainder is *originarily neutral*: neither a "good" nor an "evil" object, neither an angel nor a devil. It is only when it is disfigured by the crisis of chiasm that this First Stranger appears as a threat, an intruder that penetrates within me to destroy me, a dead thing lodged within my flesh; and what is disfigured can yet be transfigured into an object of desire and love. This primordial ambivalence, these incessant oscillations between love and hatred, can no longer be attributed to two opposing principles (as Freud's life and death drives); they stem from a unique originary phenomenon that *appears* to disjoin into a force of love and life and a force of hatred and death. What happens when this cleavage that dominated our affective life is translated into theological terms? It appears then as an eternal antagonism between a good and a bad Principle, a "race of light" and a "race of darkness." By aggravating the cleavage of the X-object and interpreting it as an eternal war between rival principles, the Manichean position forbids acknowledging the original unicity of this X: It fails to understand that these two principles that seemingly oppose one another are two aspects of a unique remainder. The monotheistic religions are closer to the truth when they affirm that the devil is one of God's Sons, a quasi-divine creature who became, at the moment of his Fall, a nefarious entity. They still only failed to understand that "Satan" is initially an Other = X, a Neutral, that is, also an innocent victim — not of God, but of primordial hatred and the phantasms projected on him and his so-called henchmen.

Must we conclude that the devil exists? If by that we mean the existence of being in the world, this affirmation pertains to an act of faith on which philosophy does not have to take a stand. We have simply discovered that "Satan" is one of the modes of the remainder, one of the names of this Other = X, that renders possible the schematization of our affects of hatred, to wit, a quasi-transcendental required by the persecution schemata. Disfigured by hatred, "Satan" is at work where these affects manifest themselves with the greatest intensity and, notably, in persecution apparatuses. I will not say, then, with Baudelaire, that the devil's most beautiful ruse is to persuade us that he does not exist. On the contrary, the devil's worst ruse is to persuade us *that he exists*, and that there are "diabolical" beings among men who need to be exterminated.

7

Worse Than Death

Do not kill the Jews, for God does not desire that they should all be killed and totally annihilated, but that they should be kept alive, like Cain the fratricide, to greater reproach and torment, a life worse than death.

PETER THE VENERABLE, LETTER TO LOUIS VII

[S]ince Auschwitz, fearing death means fearing worse than death.

THEODOR ADORNO, NEGATIVE DIALECTIC

At the end of this research on the witch hunt, we understand better how a persecution apparatus could send so many victims to their deaths; which schemes allowed it to constitute a target group as a "capital enemy" of sovereign power; which procedures of exception it implemented; and what is the kernel of historical truth of the "witches' conspiracy"—the panic that the popular rebellions aroused in the dominant classes. We have detected the phantasms of disembodiment that these revolts have reactivated, with the affects of anguish and hatred that they awaken. A number of points, however, remain obscure. We still do not know how the passage from exclusion to persecution, from a policy of confinement or banishment to a policy of extermination, can take place. Is it the same apparatus that changes while pursuing an identical project (as the example of the Nazi terror apparatus, when it leads from the ghetto to the gas chamber, would have us believe)? Or does this passage imply, on the contrary, a mutation of the apparatuses and the schemas that underpin them? We know that the schemes of exclusion and those of persecution mobilize different affects that give them a particular tonality. The fundamental affect that animates exclusion schemes is disgust, an affect that aims above all to keep its object at a distance. This is in contrast to hatred, which strives to annihilate its object and invests its murderous load in the apparatus of persecution. How does this mutation of affects occur?

To address these issues, the witch hunt is no longer a relevant example: No prior phase of confinement or expulsion preceded persecution. However, this persecution does not arise ex nihilo: We have seen that it was preceded by the "rise to majesty" of the devil, who became a counterfigure to sovereignty, and by the assimilation of witchcraft to heresy, that is to say, to a crime of exception. It is these historical mutations and campaigns of incitement to hatred that, without immediately triggering the persecution, made it possible. The accusations against the so-called witches did not suddenly appear at the beginning of the fifteenth century. They belong to a tradition of hatred that was formed long before by attacking other targets: The same accusations of poisoning, desecration, infanticide, and conspiracy had already been directed in previous centuries against Jews, heretics, and lepers. If we want to understand how these schemes came about, we must look further back than the witch hunt. If we broaden our field of investigation, we may discover target groups that, unlike the "witches," were not immediately victims of bloody persecution; they began by being excluded[1] — stigmatized and discriminated against by a specific apparatus — before becoming the target of extermination apparatuses. This is precisely the case of the lepers in the Middle Ages. Subjects of rigorous measures of marking and isolation, recluse in large numbers in leprosaria, they represent a major figure of the Excluded; and their exclusion will leave an imprint that will persist long after the disease has disappeared. In the first pages of his *Madness and Civilization*, Foucault evokes these "cursed cities" at the gates of the cities, left deserted at the end of the Middle Ages by the ebb of leprosy, which echoed mumbled cries for a "new incarnation of evil," for "renewed magics of purification and exclusion." In this sense, "the experience of madness is in rigorous continuity with that of leprosy"; and its "imaginary reactivation" will resurface each time that other categories — syphilitics, then the insane — become in their turn victims of internment measures.

By operating a historical variation (the case of the lepers), my aim is to test the validity of the method and the concepts implemented in the analysis of the witch hunt. Why not leave it at that? I hope to have shown that the persecution of witches is not an "archaic" phenomenon, that it participates in the process of secularization and in the genesis of the modern state. Nevertheless, it belongs to an already distant past that may seem outdated. If it is true that the tradition of hatred is interrupted only to resurface in other forms, it is appropriate to analyze this resurgence, the reactivation of these schemes in the conditions of a modern and fully secularized society: to carry out a new historical variation, no longer upstream, but downstream of the witch hunt; to identify how an apparatus of persecution was (re)constituted at the heart of a founding event of our modernity, the French Revolution. The example of the Revolutionary Terror concerns us for yet another reason. We have discovered that the persecution of witches can be interpreted as the backlash of popular revolts, the reprisals that the dominant classes exercised against the rebels and their lineage. We know, however, that the rebellion of the multitudes can also give way to hatred. The logic of hatred implies, in fact, a reciprocal contamination where dominants and dominated, masters and rebels, commune in the same deadly passion. We must try to understand how the passions of the multitudes and the patterns that capture them can lead them, in the conditions of a victorious revolution, to actively adhere to a policy of terror. Perhaps in this way we will be able to better understand the disasters of the twentieth century and to sketch out the perspective of a politics of emancipation that would be able to escape from the grip of hatred.

In Béroul's *Roman de Tristan*, King Mark is about to deliver his unfaithful wife to the flames: "Now, a hundred deformed lepers, their flesh gnawed and bleached, running on their crutches to the clatter of their rattles, crowded before the pyre and enjoyed the spectacle. Yvain, the most hideous of the sick, shouted to the king in a high-pitched voice: 'Sire, you want to throw your wife into this fire; it is good justice, but too brief [. . .] when this flame falls, her sentence will be over. Do you want me to teach you worse punishment, so that she lives, but with great dishonor and always wishing death? King, do you want it?' The king answered: 'Yes, life for her, but with great dishonor and *worse than death*. He who teaches me such a torment, I will love him better' — 'Sire, I will tell you briefly my thought. See, I have a hundred companions there. Give us Yseut and let her be common to us! Evil activates our desires. Give her to your lepers. Never a lady will have had worse end.'"[2]

In this text, which dates from the end of the twelfth century, we find all the features that defined the figure of the leper in the Middle Ages: the ugliness of faces and bodies deformed by the disease, cruelty, and lechery. The theologian Guillaume d'Auvergne described them as *"abjecti"*: beings who should be *rejected* because of their "abject" nature due to illness. In the Southwest, they were called *degiets* or "waste" (*déchets*). In accordance with the holding regulations — solemnly confirmed by the Third Lateran Council in 1179 — they were forbidden to enter churches, mills, taverns, and markets; to eat and drink in the company of other people and, of course, to have sexual relations with them; to wash their hands in fountains and rivers; to leave their homes with their shoes off, so as not to contaminate the ground; to answer those who question them if they are downwind, so as not to infect them with their breath; to pass through narrow paths, so as not to risk brushing against pedestrians . . . When a man or woman was afflicted with leprosy, he or she was officially cut off from the community. Henceforth deprived of all their property, of all their rights, they were to be banished for life in a "maladrerie" or to wander from town to town with other lepers, obliged to identify themselves with distinctive marks: a "leper's robe," a "sign of infamy" sewn on their garments (as was the case for Jews, perjurers, heretics), a rattle destined to warn others of their presence.

Of course, wherever it appeared, this disease aroused reactions of fear and rejection. But the Christian Middle Ages exacerbated them: At no other time did the segregation of lepers reach such intensity (around 1250, there were nearly twenty thousand leprosaria in Europe, including two thousand in France), and no other society set out to exterminate them en masse. For a long time, it was believed that this disease, almost totally unknown in Europe during the High Middle Ages, had come from the East in the wake of the Crusades; that the epidemic had reached its peak in the twelfth and thirteenth centuries before ebbing and disappearing. However, some historians question the extent and reality of this epidemic. Indeed, what the Middle Ages referred to as "leprosy" is only remotely related to what modern medicine calls this disease transmitted by Hansen's bacillus. It was considered a hereditary disease ("leprous mother, leprous son") and an extremely contagious disease, transmitted by simple contact or even at a distance: According to a popular adage, "whoever does not want to become a leper, should never greet a leper on an empty stomach, nor piss on an empty stomach against the wall where the leper has pissed that day." Yet Hansen's disease, which is only weakly contagious, is neither sexually transmissible nor hereditary. It seems that the inmates of the leprosarium were not always lepers in the clinical sense of the term: There were also patients with various skin diseases, vagrants, beggars, fugitive serfs, without forgetting the simulators who pretended to be lepers in order to find a refuge . . . According to Mary Douglas, the fear of a fictitious contagion would have been only a pretext to intern poor peasants and marginal people en masse. She points out that only a very small number of skeletons dating from this period show the characteristic bone lesions of Hansen's disease, so she does not hesitate to qualify the medieval leprosy epidemic as an "imaginary disease."[3] Let us rather say that it is the distorted representation of a real disease, that the threat of leprosy was amplified through imagination by becoming the target of a new exclusion apparatus that targeted all physical or social marginalities. From then on, this disease appeared as a formidable scourge,

carried by an immense multitude, just like the "sect of witches" in the following centuries. The exclusion of lepers was thus part of an apparatus that, by
identifying them, constituted the subjects over whom it exercised its power. It
is this apparatus that created the figure of the Leper by designating him both
as a highly contagious patient and as a cruel, devious, and lustful sinner.

In fact, in the Middle Ages, leprosy was understood not only as a disease
but as the visible stigma of a hidden stain. It pertains foremost to the domain
of the Sin, of sexual, moral, and religious transgression. And when Augustine
and other theologians denounced heresy as a "spiritual leprosy" or affirmed
that "lepers are heretics," these were not mere metaphors: In the order of evil,
the monstrous sin of heresy was one with the major calamity of leprosy. In
truth, the medieval leper is not only a sinner. During the solemn ceremony
that sanctioned his exclusion, he had to kneel at the bottom of a tomb or in
the church, covered with a shroud. The priest recited the prayer of the dead
for him, then thrice threw a handful of earth from the cemetery on his head,
pronouncing the ritual formula "die to the world to be reborn to God." All the
features of the ritual that excluded him from the world of men thus designated
him as a living dead; or as a being condemned — as had been queen Yseut
in Béroul's poem — to lead an existence "worse than death." He is thus part
of a long line of undead and evil revenants that goes from the Lamia of Antiquity to the vampires and zombies; and we have seen that the upside-down
world of the carnival and the Sabbath can be interpreted as a representation of
the world of the dead. The very name given to the lepers — *ladres* — attests to
their status as undead: It comes from the proper name Lazarus, which in the
Gospels is that of a beggar covered with ulcers, but also that of the Lazarus of
Bethany, whom Jesus had resurrected, even though he already had the smell
of a corpse.[4] In the composite figure of "Saint Lazarus," the state of the living
dead, extreme poverty, and a serious skin disease are thus concentrated.

More than just the fear of contagion, it is this undecidable confusion of
the living and the dead that made the lepers of the Middle Ages beings that
aroused disgust and horror. They were figures of the disfigured remainder,
of this foreign and hostile Thing, both living and dead, that emerges at the
heart of our flesh. No doubt because the symptoms of leprosy, in which the
body of the sufferer seems to be rotting while he is still alive, lend themselves
particularly well to this, as though they gave a visible image to the phantasm
of disincorporation that haunts all bodies. A hardened sinner and heretic, a
spectral survivor doomed to a life worse than death, the leper is nonetheless
sick, and this is what differentiates him from the other medieval figures of the
Outcast. His case is not only a matter for the priests or the judges; it is also
a matter for the doctors. Though they were unable to cure him, they were

able to diagnose the first symptoms of the disease, notably the characteristic insensitivity of the limbs. We know that, in order to detect it, they sometimes pierced the hands or feet of a presumed leper with an awl, a practice that may have been the origin of the search for the diabolic mark. The Leper is similar to the more recent figure of the Evil Witch in another significant way. Leprosy was considered a hereditary disease, transmitted by the primordial contact between mother and child, which led to the discrimination against the children of lepers, to the designation of cursed lines of lepers, bearers of "impure blood," in the same way that "races of witches" were sent to their deaths. The medicalization of the witch, which will transform her into a Hysteric, or that of the Insane, who will become the *Aliéné*, the "mentally ill" — is undoubtedly already announced in this equivocal figure of the Leper, object of a religious and moral condemnation, but also of a medical knowledge.

Although distinguished by these specific features, the proscription of the Leper was part of a broader movement that was then developing in Europe. During the previous centuries, neither Jews, nor prostitutes, nor homosexuals had been systematically discriminated against. From the twelfth and thirteenth centuries onward, Jews began to be confined to reserved quarters, forbidden most professions, and required to wear the *rouelle*, while the first accusations of murdering children and desecrating hosts emerged. During the same period, prostitutes were forced to stay in brothels (*bordeaux*) and to wear a distinctive sign; and a new category of outcasts appeared, that of "sodomites," whom the Third Lateran Council condemned to be locked up in a monastery if they were priests or excommunicated if they were secular. As the historian R. Moore points out, we are not dealing with the aggravation of older tendencies, but with a decisive turning point where "western Europe became a persecuting society."[5] More precisely, we would say that the Christian West became a *society of exclusion*, where new apparatuses of power created figures of the Excluded dedicated to an ever more rigorous segregation. It is only at a later stage that these measures of exclusion gave way to persecutions, in the strict sense that I give to this term: Homosexuals were no longer relegated or excommunicated, but sent to the stake; the time of the ghettos was succeeded by that of the pogroms and the auto-da-fés; and the lepers of France, instead of being simply put aside, were exterminated. How did this transformation take place?

A more precise analysis of the initial exclusion phase provides some insights. Historians stress the "ambiguous attitude" of medieval society toward lepers: "it seems to hate them and admire them at the same time," it "keeps them at a distance, but it fixes this distance close enough to have them within its reach," by decreeing that leprosy clinics must be located "within a stone's throw of the city."⁶ One would be mistaken to make them distant ancestors of the inmates of the *maisons de force,* asylums or camps. In the twelfth century, there was no Great Confinement of lepers, because their seclusion was voluntary, at least in the early days, and their existence differed profoundly from that of the madmen of the classical age, chained like wild beasts in the lodges of Bicêtre. They were regarded neither as monsters to be tamed nor criminals to be punished, nor as sick people to be cared for, but as "poor in Christ," "martyrs of Christ." In the regulations that the bishop of London issued for the leper colony of Illeford, it is stipulated that those who are confined there must live "in a spirit of prayer and devotion"; that they "must not miss any mass, unless they are prevented from doing so by a serious bodily infirmity [. . .] Each leper is to say the Our Father and the Hail Mary thirteen times every morning, and seven times at the first, third and sixth hours, as well as at Vespers and at Compline [. . .] On the day when one of the friars dies, each friar is to say an additional fifty prayers for the repose of the soul of the dead and of the faithful."⁷ It is not only their daily schedule, punctuated by times of prayer and meditation, that is regulated in this way but also their way of life: It is forbidden to fight, to get drunk, to play chess, cards or dice, to have the slightest sexual intercourse . . . To the usual measures of isolation inspired by the fear of contagion are associated here very different procedures, intended to ensure the salvation of souls. Seclusion in the leper colony was thus similar to initiation into religion: Through the rigorous observance of the Rule, periodic fasts, and special liturgical celebrations, it outlined an itinerary of conversion in which one had to *die in the world in order to be reborn to God* by imitating the example of the resurrected Lazarus. During a century in which the Church invented a middle ground between the eternal pains of hell and the delights of paradise, a place of temporary punishment where sinners were purified of their faults through suffering, the trials of the leper are part of this "logic of Purgatory."⁸ This is why contemporary authors speak of it as an *ordo leprosorum* similar to the monastic orders, and these leper fraternities were often led by a Master who was himself a leper. In order to enable the leprosy-afflicted Crusaders to continue to fight the infidels, the authorities of the kingdom of Jerusalem had even founded the Order of the Knights of Saint Lazarus, which went to war alongside the Knights Templar and other orders of soldier-monks.

The status of leprosy in the Middle Ages thus appears to be more complex, more ambivalent than is usually thought. What must this strange disease be for those affected to be both sinners and elected, glorified as "martyrs of Christ" and at the same time considered as "waste" to be rejected? What makes the leper a martyr, that is to say, a witness of Christ, is the intensity of his suffering: He is given to experience in his flesh the Passion of the crucified God, and his agony must allow him to expiate his sins here below. Preachers and theologians present leprosy as both a punishment and a grace granted by God: Addressing the lepers of Beauvais, Pope Celestine III greeted them as "those whom God's hand has touched and whom he has led on the probationary path of salvation." An evil sent by God, leprosy is also an evil that testifies to the divinity of Jesus Christ. To the Baptist who asks him if he is indeed "the one who is coming," Jesus answers, "The blind receive sight, the lame walk, those who have leprosy are cleansed."[9] By touching them with his hand to heal them, he attests that he is the Son of God. As one Church Father states, "He wanted the leprosy that usually stains the hand that touches it to disappear at the simple touch of his divine hand."[10] This miracle is based on the reversibility of the touch, that is to say, of the remainder: on the possibility of reversing its meaning by passing from the impure and contagious contact of the leper to this divine touch that heals and saves. According to medieval theology, the ambivalence that characterizes the leper thus finds its source in the ambivalence of God himself, God of wrath, whose hand strikes men with leprosy, and God of love, who delivers them from it. Indeed, this divine ambiguity is even more radical, for Jesus is not only the one who heals leprosy; he himself can be designated as a leper. In translating Isaiah's prophecy about the "suffering servant" — in which Christian apologists have taken it to mean a prefiguration of Christ — Jerome interpolates a passage that equates this messianic figure with a leper: "he bore our pains and carried our diseases, and we regarded him as leprous (quasi *leprosum*), smitten by God and humiliated."[11] Leprosy deserves to be called the *divine affliction*, in all the meanings of this expression: that which God sends to men and that which he himself suffers. Constantly revisited and commented upon by preachers, this theme will deeply mark the perception of this disease throughout the Middle Ages. In the Southwest of France, people did not hesitate to call the wounds of lepers "*christailles*." Can we measure the scandalous audacity of this comparison between the most ignoble of men and the Son of God? The abjection of the *degiet* is therefore not opposed to the holiness of the "martyr of Christ"; it is its necessary condition. For it is possible to catch a glimpse of the face of the Savior in the disfigured face of each sufferer. The legend of Saint Julian the Hospitaller brings to life this miracle. Having become a hermit in order to atone for his crimes, Julian hears a voice calling him on a stormy night. It was a repulsive-looking leper, whom he took home and offered his bed: "'Take off your clothes, so that I can have the warmth of your body!' Julian undressed; then, naked as the day he was born, settled back on the bed; and he felt against his thigh the Leper's skin, colder than a snake and rough as a file [. . .] 'Oh! I am going to die!

Come closer, warm me! Not just with your hands! No, with your whole body!'
Julian lay full length on top of him, mouth to mouth, chest to chest. Then
the Leper embraced him; and his eyes suddenly shone as bright as stars; his
hair streamed out like the rays of the sun; the breath from his nostrils was as
sweet as roses [. . .] The roof flew off, the firmament unfolded and Julian rose
up into the blue of space, face to face with Our Lord Jesus, who bore him off
to heaven."[12]

It is his ambivalent status that, even as it excludes the Leper, protects him,
for there can be no question of persecuting him who is a witness to Christ,
or even Christ himself. His ambivalence is thus rooted in his relationship to
divine sovereignty, of which he is both the victim and the image. A strange relationship is established between the abjection of leprosy and the most sacred
of things; and this intrigue is replayed on a different level by placing the Leper
in relation to the other figure of sovereignty, that of the king. After all, leprosy
is not only God's affliction: Since ancient times, it has also been called the
royal affliction, an expression that refers as much to the disease that kings manage to cure as to the disease that befalls them. It was seen as an allusion to the
Jewish and Christian legends about the divine punishment that struck the bad
kings, from the pharaoh of the Exodus to Vespasian and Herod. This figure of
the Leper King crossed the ages, arousing equivocal feelings of fascination and
rejection. Like that of the *quasi leprosus* Christ, it combines the two opposite
attributes of this heterogeneous element that I call the remainder: the most
extreme impurity and the sacred sovereignty. This ambivalence manifested
itself in a concrete way when Baldwin IV, who had suffered from this disease
since childhood, ascended the throne of the kingdom of Jerusalem in 1174.
Although the pope considered that the stain of leprosy forbade him to reign,
his subjects remained stubbornly faithful to him and venerated him as a saint,
as if his sufferings erased his stain and gave him a Christ-like dimension.[13]
Although he had become blind and, according to the chroniclers, the flesh
of his limbs was falling apart, he retained his throne until his death and was
buried on the hill of Golgotha. Leprosy was most often referred to as the "royal
affliction" for another reason: because it had the distinguished privilege of
being cured by the touch of kings. Elevated to a mystical dignity by the anoint-
ing of the coronation, celebrated as "images of God," "imitators of Christ,"
the kings of France and England had to prove it by repeating the miracle
attributed to the Savior. By purifying and healing a body affected by the worst
defilement, they showed that they were able, thanks to their royal dignity, to
cure the diseases of the social body. The first mention of their thaumaturgical
powers dates from the beginning of the eleventh century. The author of the
Vie de Robert le Pieux reports that this king approached lepers and "with his

own mouth, kissed their hands [. . .] When he touched the wounds of the sick with his most pious hand and marked them with the sign of the Holy Cross, he delivered them from all the pain of their affliction."[14] He would pass on this wonderful power to his successors. Yet, in medieval France, leprosy would soon lose this privilege. A century later, when a chronicler evoked the miraculous touch of King Louis VI, it was no longer a question of curing lepers but of patients suffering from *écrouelles*, that is, tubercular ganglions. This disease would become for centuries the "King's affliction." François I is said to have touched more than 1,300 scrofula patients in a single year, and this old ritual was to continue until the coronation of Charles X in 1824. Historians see this as a sign of a change in the status of leprosy, which had become an incurable and cursed disease, too full of sin to be cured by the august hand of a king.[15]

This is not to say that kings and clerics renounced the society of lepers. On the contrary, the practice of kissing the leper was to spread as a mark of devotion. The holy king Louis IX was particularly attached to it: He regularly visited a leprous monk at the Royaumont Abbey, "horrible to the eye," kissed his hands, and wiped the pus from his ulcers. However, unlike his ancestors, the pious monarch did not imagine that he could cure him of his disease. By lowering himself in this way, he simply demonstrated his Christian charity and humility, and it was his own glory that was enhanced. The intimate, highly ambivalent link that once joined the fate of the leper to that of the king is now undone. No divine grace can be seen under the horror of leprosy: A new perception of the disease has been established that considers only its abject character. This change in attitude was accompanied by an increase in exclusionary practices. More and more often, municipal authorities forbade lepers to enter cities, and expulsion measures were taken in Marseille, Bologna, Paris, and London. In 1250, the Church formally forbade them to take monastic vows, which brought about the definitive end of the *ordo leprosorum* and the hope of spiritual healing that drove it. Henceforth, the coercive function of the leprosaria outweighed their redemptive dimension. At the same time, literary representations of lepers changed, placing more and more emphasis on their evil nature. Thus, the *Roman de Jaufré* depicts a "giant leper" who abducts young girls to rape them. The demonization of lepers is underway: The physician Guy de Chauliac speaks of their pointed demon ears and their "fixed and horrible gaze in the manner of the Satanic Beast." Little by little, the ambivalent meaning of this disease will disappear entirely, as if the perverse cruelty of Béroul's lepers had erased the paradoxical sanctity of Baldwin IV and the "martyrs of Christ." Their mere existence was soon to be apprehended as a threat that had to be annihilated. We begin to see what motivates the passage from exclusion to persecution: It is the rupture of the initial ambivalence that transforms an ambiguous figure, both impure and sacred, into an abject entity, a monster unworthy of living.

Not only lepers were concerned by this state of affairs. It seems as if, during the thirteenth century, the exclusion apparatus had extended its hold by imposing the same infamous stigma on other targets. For some time now, Jews had been assimilated to lepers. Analogous measures of segregation were applied to both communities, and in many areas both lepers and Jews were forbidden to touch food in the markets to avoid defiling it.[16] In Paris, in 1213, the papal legate decreed that prostitutes should also be treated "like lepers," excommunicated and confined to their homes. Although it had been widely tolerated in the previous centuries, including among priests, male homosexuality was also the object of increased hostility. Pope Gregory IX — by ordering the Inquisition to extirpate it by all means — assimilated it to the "fetidity of leprosy," and, from then on, the "sin of Sodom" led to the stake. Thus, very different categories will tend progressively to merge: Heretics and sodomites, Jews and lepers, and later "witches" and "sorcerers," all will be designated indifferently as centers of contagion and defilement, debauched individuals practicing sexual promiscuity and incest, child murderers and Satan worshippers. Let us pause for a moment to consider this identification of the Jew and the leper. In ancient times, authors hostile to Jews had claimed that Moses and the Hebrews were in fact lepers driven out of Egypt.[17] Forgotten for more than a thousand years, the old accusation resurfaced in the fourteenth century in a different form, when the Jews were suspected of being the accomplices of the lepers, conspiring with them to infect the Christians. From the beginning of Christianity, however, an intense ambivalence characterized the Church's relationship with the Jews, who were considered both as "Christ's murderers" and as witnesses to his Passion, absolutely necessary to the logic of salvation. At the time when they were the object of growing discrimination and the first bloody persecutions, Bernard of Clairvaux could still warn their persecutors by declaring that "touching a Jew is as if touching Jesus himself [. . .] for they are the flesh and bones of Christ." When this ambivalence is undone, the Jew becomes a major figure of the maleficent Enemy. Nevertheless, unlike the Leper or the Witch, the initial ambivalence is never totally unraveled, at least as long as the Christian vision of the Jew prevails. It would only disappear from the nineteenth century onward, when religious anti-Judaism was secularized in the form of "scientific" racism: from then on, no longer would any kinship with Christ protect the Jews, and nothing would prevent the persecution apparatus from becoming radicalized into a Final Solution. In the case of the Witch, the break in ambivalence took place much more quickly. Since the dawn of time, a distinction had been made, as in other societies, between "white" and "black" magic, often practiced by the same person. This distinction began to fade from the fourteenth century onward, when any practice of magic was considered a heresy, and we know that, at the height of the witch hunt, it was argued that the good witch was "worse than the wicked." The Benandante who flies off into the night to fight "for the good" will soon be identified with the diabolical wizard; and the same will be true of the archaic character of the wolf-warrior, who will give way to the purely malefic figure of the werewolf. This process was already prefigured by the "demonization" of the devil and, even earlier, by his dissociation from God and his transformation into an absolutely evil principle. It was necessary for an ambivalent divine figure to split into two distinct and hostile entities for the antagonism of the devil and the good God to be born. This rift has affected the entire symbolic field of Western civilization, leading to a series of other rifts: When Good is opposed to Evil in such a clear-cut manner, it becomes impossible to preserve for long the ambiguity of the Leper, the Jew, the Sorcerer, or, on the opposite pole, that of the King.

Affecting these different figures is what Caillois defined as "the essential movement of the dialectic of the sacred. Any force which embodies it tends to dissociate: its first ambiguity is resolved in antagonistic and complementary elements to which one relates respectively the feelings of respect and aversion — feelings of desire and fervor that are inspired by its fundamentally equivocal nature."[18] My insistence on this initial ambivalence lies in the fact that it allows us to better understand the movement that leads from exclusion to persecution. By refusing to admit the ambivalence of the archaic sacred, Agamben fails to account for this passage. He indeed establishes a rigid demarcation between the sovereign and the *homo sacer* where he sees two antagonistic, but *nonambivalent figures*, which would refer to the fundamental opposition between *bios* and *zoē*, between the "qualified" political life and a "naked life" exposed to death — and he does not understand that the *homo sacer* is above all an *untouchable*, whose contact risks defiling the community and who must for this reason be expelled or slaughtered like a beast.[19] As we have seen, the relationship between the leper and the king or the Christ who is almost a leper is more equivocal. It is only when their ambivalent meaning is unraveled that the Leper, the Jew, or the Witch will carry the maximum defilement and appear as monsters to be eliminated. In reality, none of these cursed figures is ever originally present: They are all constituted at the end of a complex process in which they lose their sacred dimension to become objects of horror. It is time to put an end to Agamben's dichotomies, to recognize that *homo sacer* is always also a *sacred man* and, conversely, that the sacredness of the sovereign necessarily includes a more or less hidden "cursed aspect." In certain historical conditions, these ambiguous figures come to split between a pole of pure sovereignty and a pole of abjection. But this cleavage of ambivalence preserves its affective charge, the contradictory feelings of veneration and disgust, of hatred and love, that are initially attached to the sacred. Far from desacralizing sovereignty, it only distributes differently its affective dimension and the phantasms that it elicits.

Is this rift inevitable? Is it enough to trigger persecution? For it to unleash such murderous affects, it must have coincided with another dynamic: with the feeling of a growing undifferentiation, of a disappearance of the limits that allowed one to distinguish the same and the other, the pure and the impure, the own and the foreign. A crisis of the limit that is part of the process of disincorporation affecting collective bodies. It manifests itself particularly on the sexual plane, in the panic fear of forbidden relations, of a penetration of the foreigner in the own body, which would defile it irremediably. If the Fourth Lateran Council had imposed on Jews the wearing of a distinctive sign, it was to fight against the "confusion" that prevented them from being recognized and thus favored sexual relations between Jews and Christians. In the following century, the same obsession was to be found in the decree of Edward III, who banished lepers from the city of London. He noted that "many persons afflicted with the disease of leprosy reside publicly among the other citizens and healthy persons, staying continually with them and not hesitating to communicate with them. And that some [of these lepers] endeavour to contaminate other persons by transmitting to them this abominable disease [. . .] both by the contagion carried on their infested breath and by carnal relations with women [. . .] to the great peril of the inhabitants of this city."[20] In both cases, the Great Body defends itself by striving to reincorporate itself: to re-mark a boundary that is faltering, to draw a demarcation between its inside and its outside, its healthy parts and its sick members. This amounts to aggravating the measures of exclusion, either by imposing a stigma on the dangerous element, or by expelling it from the borders of the city or the kingdom. Any exclusionary apparatus is an attempt to resist this dynamic of disincorporation. When such a strategy fails, when reclusion in the leper colony or the ghetto can no longer ward off the anguish of undifferentiation, then exclusionary measures give way to persecution and extermination.

And yet for this to happen, the ambivalence must have become unbearable; the contradictory aspects of the initial Figure must have dissociated into two antagonistic poles — a split that constitutes the irreducible opposition between a "race of light" and a "race of darkness," between a celestial or earthly Sovereign and his Enemy. With this rift, the anguish caused by ambivalence is mitigated: Henceforth, veneration and love are addressed to an absolutely good object, disgust and hatred to a fundamentally evil one; and the more the monstrous aspects of the Enemy are reinforced, the more the sublime character of the divine or royal Sovereign increases. It is also for this reason that a sovereignty in crisis, when it tries to (re-)found itself, has recourse to the designation of a *capital enemy*. This mutation manifests itself on the level of the affects by a radical transformation of the relation of the self to its objects. The "object" in question is not necessarily another man in the world: It is first of all an immanent object-X, of this remainder that is our "first object," the First Stranger in each one of us, with the ambivalent feelings of attraction and repulsion that it arouses. Ambivalence that is at the origin of the opposite meanings of these names that designate the domain of the sacred: the Greek *hagios*, the Latin *sacer*, which mean at the same time pure and impure, sacred and soiled. Now, these opposite affects both imply a gesture of retreat that consists in putting at a distance an object of disgust or veneration. In both cases, the movement that accompanies the affect — its carnal *movement* — makes it possible to keep the distance by drawing an impassable limit between the self and the object, a border that protects them from one another by making impossible any contact. These two opposite affects are oriented in the same way toward their object, which makes possible their coexistence in the same ambivalent relation to it. It is this limit that is crossed when disgust gives way to hatred. For the movement of hatred differs from the repulsion of disgust: On the contrary, it turns toward its object to try to destroy it. The mutation of affects that accompanies the passage from exclusion to persecution thus implies the transgression of this limit that protected the object. However, the affect most opposed to hatred paradoxically accomplishes the same gesture as it does: The movement of love also consists in crossing the border, in moving toward the object that awakens desire, in letting oneself be attracted by it. Insofar as their movements are identical, love and hate can very well substitute for one another or coexist in an ambivalent relation to the same object. Freud privileged this affective ambivalence because he saw in it one of the major indices of the "dualism of the drives" — those of life and death, to which he grants an essential role in his later writings. However, if the orientation of hatred and that of love are similar, their *goal* is completely opposite: whereas love rushes toward its object to unite with it, hatred moves toward its own in order to annihilate it. From this point of view, these two affects are antagonistic. The emergence of hatred thus marks a decisive turning point: It is then that the primitive ambivalence is totally undone, that the target of the affect splits into an object of love and a "bad object" both dreaded and hated. How does hatred emerge by substituting itself for disgust, fear, or even love? Like any fundamental affect, hate is without reason, and nothing can explain its apparition. At least it is possible to describe the schemes that accompany it, intensify it, and insert it into power apparatuses by allowing it to break out onto the world.

We begin to understand that persecutory hatred is not an originary affect; that its appearance supposes a complex process, the cleavage of an initial ambivalence, a profound transformation of the schemes and the apparatuses, and that it is preceded by an intense campaign of incitement to hatred. How did the lepers who were once considered "witnesses of Christ" come to be massacred? In 1321, the consuls of Carcassonne sent a letter to the king of France in which — while denouncing the sexual crimes and the desecration of hosts allegedly perpetrated by the Jews — they announced that the lepers were seeking to spread their disease "with the help of poisons, pestiferous potions and spells." The rumor spread quickly: Everywhere, lepers were arrested, tortured until they "confessed" their crimes, and then sent to the stake. What is new and surprising is not only the extent of the persecution — in some regions, three-quarters of the inhabitants of the leprosaria were massacred — but the charges against them. According to the chroniclers, they "confessed" under torture that they had abjured the Christian faith, profaned the sacraments, and "conspired to kill all healthy Christians, noble or not noble, *and to have dominion over the whole world.*"[21] According to the account of the inquisitor Bernard Gui, they had already divided up the kingdoms, lordships, and bishoprics that they wanted to seize. Alerted, King Philip V decided to have all the lepers in France arrested for "crimes of lèse-majesté" and to confiscate their property. Those who confessed to their crimes were to be burned at the stake; the others were to be locked up in leprosaria until their death and a strict separation of the sexes was to prevent them from reproducing. It was no longer a question of keeping them out but, rather, of annihilating them to the last man, and what justified this Final Solution was a persecution scheme that we know well, the conspiracy scheme. This was, unless I am mistaken, the first time in history that a hated minority group was suspected of conspiring to achieve world domination. This new accusation could easily be extended to other targets. A different version of the conspiracy would soon spread: The lepers were merely instruments in the hands of the Jews, who had bribed them to poison the Christians. When questioned, the arrested Jews would "confess" that they were obeying an order from the king of Granada who wanted to destroy Christianity. The Leper, the Jew, the Muslim: an infernal triad that condensed the main figures of the Absolute Enemy. The furious crowds that were massacring the lepers would immediately turn against the Jews (160 Jews burned at the same stake in Chinon . . .), before the king decided to expel the Jews from France.

The persecution had thus achieved its objectives: The Jews had been murdered or banished, the lepers exterminated or condemned to a much more rigorous reclusion than before. Moreover, the lazar houses were rapidly emptying all over Europe. Was this the consequence of a general decline of the epidemic? Or was it the result of the new perception of leprosy, which had become so abject that all marginalized people could no longer be considered as lepers? Soon, the cursed cities would be deserted and ready to welcome other outcasts. The patterns that underpinned persecution had not disappeared, however. During the terrible plague of 1348–49, it was no longer the lepers but only the Jews who were again accused of having caused the epidemic by poisoning the wells. The same accusations of poisoning and conspiracy were later made against the so-called witches. This sheds light on the genesis of the witch hunt: The persecution apparatus that had attacked heretics in the thirteenth century, and then lepers and Jews in the following century, had found itself without an object. In order to be able to continue, it had to look for a new target at all costs and, in a sense, invent one. How did these persecution schemes take shape during the hunt for lepers? The accusation of poisoning rivers and wells to spread their disease obviously stems from the fear of contagion. For lepers were considered untouchables whose contact could contaminate food, air, and water. It is always tempting to "explain" a natural phenomenon such as an epidemic by a malicious action, for example, by claiming that the water was poisoned. The same accusation resurfaced in the 1832 cholera epidemic in Paris; and it was repeated in Tokyo in 1923, where the rumor was that Korean immigrants and communists were incriminated. Those who nowadays claim that the AIDS virus was deliberately created and spread by the CIA are reactivating the same scheme in a slightly different form.

The accusation of "conspiracy" directed against the lepers is more difficult to understand. If it is a crime of lèse majesté, it is because it implies a relation to *majestas*, to sovereign power — to the real sovereignty of the king and to the imaginary sovereignty of this "world empire" that the lepers would have dreamed of conquering. It is this representation of power that is projected in an inverted manner in the counterfigure of the Conspiracy, an imaginary replica of the State's arcane. The Leper appears here as the Anti-King, just as the Jew is a representative of the Antichrist and the Devil, an Anti-God. But how could these rejected cripples be associated with sovereign power? It should be remembered that an ambivalent relationship had once existed between the Leper and the King, and it may not have disappeared entirely by the fourteenth century. By attacking the lepers, their persecutors would have attacked the royal authority in a roundabout way. It would have been a rebellion against an unpopular king, suspected of protecting the Jews, a king who was judged incapable of saving the kingdom by curing it of the "spiritual leprosy" that was corroding it. By massacring the lepers and the Jews, their persecutors would have reappropriated in their way the power to cure the evil that Philip V no longer managed to exert effectively.[22] By accusing the lepers of wanting to become the masters of the world, the rumor attested in any case that leprosy had not ceased to be considered confusedly as the *kings' affliction*.

In order for persecution to occur, two quite distinct schemes had to merge. This is an astonishing conjunction, because their meanings are very different: Whereas the scheme of contagion implies an involuntary propagation of evil, that of the conspiracy supposes, on the other hand, a deliberate will to harm. We can recognize here the two fundamental positions that determine in the West the relation to the demonic Enemy. If the conspiracy scheme can accommodate the Augustinian position that attributes sin to a free decision, the contagion scheme refers to the Gnostic conception of an evil nature, of an impure race whose defilement spreads spontaneously, by simple contact. It is the fusion of these two apparently incompatible conceptions that is accomplished during the persecution of the lepers, and then during the witch hunt: The persecution scheme is again presented as a *synthesis of the heterogeneous*. A difficulty remains, however. Unless they were marked by distinctive signs, nothing could differentiate heretics, Jews, or witches from other men. One could therefore imagine that they managed without difficulty to mix with "good Christians" in order to devise obscure machinations. Thus, the Spanish Inquisition was going to work hard for centuries to unmask the *Judíos occultos* and the witch-hunters to search the bodies of their victims for the hidden stigma of Satan. On the contrary, leprosy is characterized by symptoms that are impossible to conceal, and it is difficult to understand how lepers could be assimilated to a secret threat, a conspiracy . . . However, let us not forget that, under the name of "leprosy," the Middle Ages apprehended a multiform, proliferating disease, all the more disturbing because it remained invisible or difficult to detect. When the lepers of Languedoc tried to escape the massacre by taking refuge in Spain, the king of Aragon, anxious to protect his kingdom, ordered his officers to arrest and imprison all foreigners without exception, since, he declared, "it is difficult and even really impossible to recognize those who are lepers and to identify them."[23] The fear of nonidentification persists, even in the case of leprosy, and justifies all measures of marking, segregation, expulsion, and, finally, extermination.

Under these conditions, it was impossible to state with certainty that leprosy had really disappeared, and the anguish it had caused would persist long after the end of the epidemic, generating a new and strange haunting. During the fourteenth century, as the epidemic receded, people in several regions of

WORSE THAN DEATH

France and Spain began to report "white lepers," apparently healthy people who were believed to be suffering from an invisible leprosy (they were "lepers in the body," said the doctors), but still contagious and obviously hereditary. They were first called *crestiaas*, that is to say Christians, which attests to the mysterious link between this disease and Christ *quasi leprosus*. Later they were given other names, *agotes* in Navarre, *cagots* in the Southwest, *kakouz* or *caqueux* in Brittany, *colliberts* in Saintonge. They are referred to as "those of the upside-down world"; they are considered descendants of Arian or Cathar heretics, or of converted Jews. They are also said to be the sons of sorcerers or werewolves, and they spread the rumors that we have come to know. Their touch or even their look is enough to transmit the disease; their breath is nauseating and highly contagious; and, of course, they "greatly desire coitus." As they are believed to be afflicted with an invisible disease, they are accused of hiding the evil from which they suffer, of being dissimulators, and the name *"cagot"* becomes—already in Rabelais—a synonym of deceiver, of hypocrite. They were discriminated against everywhere, subjected to the same prohibitions as lepers in previous centuries, forced to wear a distinctive mark, and sometimes a veil over their mouths, locked up in *"cagoteries"* or forced to live in separate settlements, with an absolute ban on having sexual relations with non-*cagots*. In some cities, they were forbidden to walk barefoot, to sit anywhere, and to enter the city after sunrise, "under penalty of having two ounces of flesh cut off their backs." Condemned by the Church, fought against by the public authorities, this segregation would take centuries to disappear: *Agote* settlements still existed around 1960 in remote valleys of the Spanish Basque Country.[24] This is certainly a marginal phenomenon, but it attests to the astonishing persistence of the apparatus that was once intended to exclude lepers. The passage from exclusion to persecution that began at the beginning of the fourteenth century was not inevitable. Or, more precisely, it was only a partial mutation that left some elements of the old configuration. This was characterized by the ambivalence of the Excluded, and we find it in an attenuated form in the case of the *cagots*, who were considered to be healers gifted with supernatural powers. Evoking the *cagots*, *caqueux*, and other *colliberts*, Michelet was indignant about the fate of "these cursed races who seem to be the Pariahs of the West"; and it is true that, in the whole history of Europe, no category of outcasts has resembled to such an extent the untouchables of India or the Burakumin of Japan. It is necessary to investigate why this phenomenon, which plays a fundamental role in other civilizations, has remained confined to the margins of Western society.

Leprosy's history confirms that the appearance of persecution apparatuses implies a mutation of affects and schemes; that it attests to a failure of the old logics of branding, internment, and expulsion, which are no longer sufficient to *contain* a heterogeneous element, to circumscribe it by keeping it at bay. However, it is difficult to pinpoint the exact moment of the caesura. If the transition from their exclusion to their persecution begins suddenly in 1321, it erupts in a region that had been the scene, a few months earlier, of another persecution. I have already mentioned the Shepherds' Crusade, an uprising of poor peasants revolted against the lords, which, on arriving in the Southwest, changed its objective and attacked Jewish communities. But the violence of the Shepherds was not limited to the Jews: They had also looted and burned leper houses because, according to one chronicler, they accused the lepers of wanting to poison the springs and wells.[25] Thus, the lepers' hunt is less an inaugural event than the repetition and extension of an earlier persecution that was primarily aimed at another target. Moreover, the Jews had already been victims of the same accusation: The rumor, almost always followed by pogroms, is documented as early as 1163 in Bohemia, then in Germany throughout the thirteenth century, before reaching France in 1309.[26] By becoming in turn the target of this accusation, the lepers appeared as substitutes for the Jews, before the latter became, during the Great Plague, substitutes for the lepers. In the following centuries, the "sorcerers' conspiracy" will replace that of the Jews and the lepers, until the modern era revives the old myth of the Jewish Conspiracy. These substitutions seem to follow one another endlessly.

If we take into account the persistence of these schemes, do we still have the right to say that, between the eleventh and thirteenth centuries, Europe *became* a society of exclusion and/or persecution? Perhaps massacres only echo other massacres. Perhaps the new strategies of power simply change the target by ordering earlier configurations differently. Historians are right to recall that in previous centuries, neither Jews, nor lepers, nor homosexuals were discriminated against and persecuted. Heretics and "witches" were not yet burned, the reality of the Sabbath was not yet accepted, and questioning to extract confessions was not practiced. It would be a mistake, however, to idealize the early Middle Ages, as if this period had not also known its cursed figures, its humiliated and its excluded. The main forms of discrimination at that time were against certain professions considered "illicit" or shameful. As in India and in many other cultures, ancient taboos concerning human excrement, blood, and corpses disqualified barbers, launderers and dyers, butchers, surgeons, executioners, and gravediggers. To this list of "vile professions," the Church had added usurers and merchants, prostitutes and their procurers, tavern-keepers and cooks, as well as jugglers "who incite lascivious or obscene dances." For it had long since forgotten the Good News that had announced that nothing and no one is impure by himself . . .

However, this picture began to change from the eleventh century onward, when a growing number of professions were rehabilitated. Soon, no
profession would be an obstacle to salvation, and the Franciscan Berthold of
Regensburg could proclaim that all "states" belonged without distinction to
"Christ's family" — with the exception of jugglers, vagabonds, and Jews, who
belonged to the "devil's family."[27] It is not the birth (or the end) of a society of
exclusion that we are witnessing, but only the displacement of old hauntings,
the redeployment of old apparatuses. And this recasting allows for the linger-
ing of certain figures of the Excluded. It must be acknowledged: No golden
age precedes the time of the ghettos and leper colonies. No welcoming era
for the foreigner precedes the stakes, the asylums, and the camps of modern
times. Each time, more peaceful phases of apparent integration are followed
by phases of exclusion and persecution. Archaic schemes that seemed to have
fallen into oblivion are suddenly reactivated, inserted into new apparatuses,
and begin to sow death again. No doubt it is futile to seek at all costs a decisive
break, a first beginning in the time of the world, when we are ceaselessly sent
back from one event to an earlier one. If the assimilation of Jews to lepers goes
back to Antiquity, that of witches to vampires or certain "shamanic" elements
of the myth of the Sabbath probably come from prehistory . . . Let us leave to
historians the task of restoring this genesis over the long term, and let us look
elsewhere for the phantasms and schemas that allow disgust and hatred to
barge into history. Our primordial phantasms are formed on the plane of immanence of the ego, in its originary relation to the remainder of its flesh. It is
necessary that certain schemes intervene so that they can appear on the plane
of the world, transformed into psychic phantasms putting in play our relation
to others, crystallized in figures, registered in beliefs and myths. In order to understand the phenomena of exclusion and persecution, it is these beliefs that
should be analyzed, as so many figurations of our fundamental phantasms.

How does one become a leper? This question was answered in different
ways in medieval society. Some authors claim that the leper is the child of
incest: He thus atones for the major transgression committed by his parents.
The same "explanation" is found elsewhere, for example, among the Azande
of Central Africa. One of the Fathers of the Church gave a different answer:
According to Jerome, "every month, the heavy and apathetic bodies of women
are afflicted with an outpouring of foul blood. At which time, if the man mates
with the woman, it is said that the children contract the vices of the seed, so
that they are born lepers and that this poisonous pus degenerates the bodies by
making them deformed."[28] Bishop Caesarius of Arles specified that children
conceived during the menstrual period could either be affected by leprosy
or possessed by the devil. This is a significant link between leprosy and the

demonic, both of which are purported to be the result of hereditary contamination through the mother's blood. Here again, this belief is found in other cultures: In the Marquesas Islands, it was believed that the simple contact with a menstruating woman was enough to cause leprosy. Unlike other bodily secretions that are highly valued, such as virile sperm and maternal milk, or on the contrary arouse disgust, blood concentrates all the ambivalence of the heterogeneous element. It is at the same time glorious, like the blood of the warrior who died in battle, even sacred — the Precious Blood of Christ — but also extremely impure, like the blood of menstruation, a major source of defilement in most cultures. To human blood applies what a legend said about the Gorgon's blood: One drop is a source of vigor and keeps away diseases, while another drop kills.

It is, therefore, possible to trade blood for blood. It was believed that leprosy, caused by the contact with menstruation, could be cured by the purest blood, by bathing in that of a young child or a virgin. This theme is frequently encountered in medieval literature: The hero of the *Roman de Jaufré* confronts an evil leper who murders children in order to bathe in their blood, and the hero of the *Geste d'Ami et Amile* does not hesitate to sacrifice his own sons so that their blood can cure another knight . . .[29] This belief takes on a different meaning when associated with the ancient figure of the leper king. It already appears in Jewish tradition, which accuses the pharaoh of this deed, and Christian authors explain in this way the massacre of the children of Bethlehem by King Herod. According to the *Golden Legend*, the emperor Constantine, also infected with leprosy, had recourse to this remedy and had three thousand children slaughtered, before converting and being saved from his illness by the water of baptism. Beyond their edifying intention, such tales can be understood as calls to revolt against a bad king, whose policy "bleeds out" the body of the kingdom. We have seen that the Ligueurs accused Henri III of sacrificing children to the devil, but a slightly different accusation had already been aimed at his brother François II a few years earlier. As the young king was in poor health, a rumor spread among the Reformed: It was said that he had children of Protestant families kidnapped to bathe in their blood. Shortly after his death, Protestant rioters broke his tomb and threw his heart into the fire . . . An ancestral belief could thus resurface in modern times and once again mobilize the passions of the multitudes. It will reappear on the eve of the French Revolution, with a more marked reference to the leper king.

Around the figure of the Leper, fantasies of incest and infanticide are thus concentrated, underpinned by schemes of contamination and purification by blood. However, the same crimes were also attributed to the Jews. They were suspected of practicing incest: When the Golden Legend tells the story of Judas, the eponymous figure of the perfidious Jew, the author assures us that, like Oedipus, he had killed his father and married his mother.[30] They were also accused of kidnapping young Christian children to bleed them to death. Other rumors mention a Jewish doctor who advised Saint Louis (or, according to other versions, Louis XI or Richard the Lionhearted) to drink children's blood to cure the leprosy that the king had contracted during the Crusade. Yet the pious monarch refused with horror and was content with a potion made from turtle blood. There is, between these different accusations, a common point: the obsession with blood, that of Christ which springs from the profaned host, that of the children whose murderers want to seize in order to accomplish a cruel rite. Why is the vampire-Jew so bloodthirsty? In the Middle Ages it was claimed that since they had spilled the sacred blood of Christ, the Jews had been condemned by God to suffer from hemorrhoids, a permanent flow of blood comparable to that of women's menstruation, and that they tried to cure themselves by drinking the blood of Christian children. This myth of "Jewish menses" made it possible to feminize the Jews by burdening them with all the impurity of menstruation, and their "rotten blood" was often equated with that of the other damned, the lepers. At the end of the eighteenth century, an author favorable to the Jews still mentioned rumors that they were "very prone to diseases involving corruption of the blood mass, such as leprosy in the past and scurvy today, scrofula, and blood flow."[31]

At times these accusations of poisoning, desecration, and infanticide are condensed into a single fantasy. The Jews of Zaragoza were accused in 1250 of having crucified little Dominguito del Val. They were said to have intended, after tearing out his heart and mixing it with a consecrated host, to throw this mixture into a river in order to poison the Christians. All of them were burned alive. Thus the infamous acts of which they are accused are first of all crimes of blood. They draw more or less directly on the double nature of this substance, the sacred blood of Christ, which allows the profaners to be confounded; the blood of menstruation, which transmits evil; the blood of martyred children, which stains the rivers or cures leprosy . . . The phantasmatic meaning of blood is also manifested in another way. It was thought that its occult properties were communicated from one generation to the next. When the Spaniards kept the descendants of converted Jews out of important positions, it was, as we have seen, in the name of the *limpieza del sangre*, the purity of blood of the Old Christians. And when the "infected blood" of the Jews is defined as an ineffaceable "macula," this extends to other bodily secretions, so that semen or even the milk of a wet nurse is just as capable of transmitting the "Judaic defilement." Forever doomed to impurity and evil, the life to which Jews are condemned is comparable to that of lepers. As Peter the Venerable, abbot of Cluny, wrote to King Louis VII, their life of opprobrium and torment is "a life worse than death."[32]

But what about the third cursed figure, the Witch? Constituted later, when the persecution apparatus was looking for a new target, she faithfully reproduces the main features of the Jew and the Leper. As Bodin writes, "there has never been a perfect Sorcerer and enchanter who was not begotten of a father and daughter, or of a mother and son."[33] Born of incest, the Witch is also thirsty for the blood of children, which she comes to suck at night in their cradle or which she feasts on after having sacrificed them to Satan. The *Malleus* mentions one of them who was said to have murdered forty-one children in order to "breathe in their blood."[34] The figure of the child-killing witch-vampire can be found in all human societies, probably because it is rooted in a powerful fantasy, an imago of the evil Mother. From the Stryges and Lamies of Greco-Roman antiquity to the Lilith of Jewish tradition, not forgetting the ghouls of Arabian folklore, demonologists have had only to draw on these popular legends to integrate them into the myth of the Sabbath. It was not only an area insensitive to pain that the prickers looked for on the body of the accused, but also a point where the penetration of the needle would not cause any bleeding. The reason why not bleeding is so suspicious is that demons are presented as vampires who drink the blood of their worshippers. Thus, an English "witch," Elisabeth Sawyer, declared to her judges that she had a kind of nipple near her rectum that allowed the devil to continuously suck her blood.[35] In 1618, in Saverne, the judges who had the accused Johann Fehsmann pricked and whipped deduced from the absence of any bleeding that Satan had drained his body of all its blood and that he was therefore a sorcerer: He was beheaded at the age of sixteen. It is possible that the presence of the devil is manifested by a flow of blood, but it is the impure blood of menstruation. The accused Maria Panzona told the inquisitors of Udine that during the Sabbath, witches entrusted their menses to the devil, who returned them as poison.[36] Similarly, the mother of a possessed young woman, Nicole Obry, assured the doctors who examined her that her daughter's possession had begun just after her first period: Her belly had swollen and Satan had told her that she was pregnant with his child . . . Conversely, the purity of saints and mystics is manifested by a total absence of menstruation, but it can very well be accompanied by abundant bleeding from their stigmata, as though "a saint's career presupposed a detour or sublimation of the impure blood of fecundity into a sacrificial blood which is purified by spilling itself for Christ."[37]

We meet again the enigmatic ambivalence of blood, demonic and sacred substance, which poisons and saves. How to interpret it? How can we account for the universal taboo that makes menstrual blood a source of defilement and sometimes also a magical remedy? It is in ourselves that the egoanalysis discovers the most originary ambivalence, in the relation that is tied between our ego and the remainder of our flesh, a remainder at the same time disfigured and transfigured, object of disgust and desire, of hate and love. When our primordial flesh becomes a body in the world, this process of embodiment expels the remainder from the body, so much so that this rejected element will be identified in our phantasms with the excretions of the human body, with the fluids and humors that it secretes. Excrement, saliva, sperm, milk, blood: so many fragments detached from the body, so many corporal figurations of the remainder. Laden with all its ambivalence, they will be inscribed in networks of symbolic oppositions (between cold and hot, wet and dry, shadow and light, left and right, feminine and masculine, etc.) that will give them, differently in each culture, their malefic or beneficial value.[38] Only blood preserves to a certain extent the initial ambivalence. Yet it, too, ends up being dissociated between the pure blood of the warrior or of the god and the foul blood of the female menses. Privilege of the blood — and of the virile sperm — which ratifies, in all the known societies, the Man's domination of the Woman. In certain conditions and at certain times, it is not only the menstruating woman but the Woman as such who comes to represent the remainder under its disfigured and abject form. No one has put it better than Odon, abbot of Cluny in the tenth century: "if people could see what is underneath the skin [. . .] they would find the sight of woman abhorrent. Her charm consists of slime and blood, of wetness and gall. If anyone considers what is hidden in the nostrils and in the throat and in the belly, he will always think of filth. And if we cannot bring ourselves to touch slime and filth with our fingertips, how can we bring ourselves to embrace the dirt bag itself?"[39]

This confirms our hypothesis on the feminization of the Sabbath. If a persecution that initially targeted men and women indifferently became almost totally focused on "witches" alone, it is because the dominant system of symbolic oppositions concentrated on women all the evil charge of the disfigured remainder. Victim of the curse of menses, the Witch became this infanticidal vampire, object of the most terrifying fantasies. We also understand how Satan could be associated with menstrual blood or excrements; so much so that a theologian could declare that "when the devil penetrates a living body to possess a man or a woman, he always lodges himself in the fecal matter of the intestine."[40] For he is the *dia-bolos*, he-who-is-opposed, that is, a privileged figure of the remainder, this object-X onto which our disgust and our hatred are projected, and that our body constantly strives to expel. An enigma remains, however: How is it that these evil figures — the Leper, the Jew, the Witch — are always associated with incest? Is there a connection between the transgression of this fundamental prohibition and the other crimes attributed to them, in which blood plays a major role each time? It is commonly admitted by anthropologists that the prohibition of incest ensures a positive function. By obliging human groups to practice exogamous marriages, it leads them to contract alliances with foreign or rival groups, and thus institutes a system of reciprocal exchanges between the different groups. It seems, however, that this theory does not succeed in elucidating the negative meaning of this prohibition, the horror that incest always and everywhere arouses. Durkheim once gave a more convincing interpretation. According to him, these feelings of rejection find their source in the "contact prohibition" that relates to menstrual blood. Since it is taboo, a source of defilement, it also makes contact with the women of the clan taboo by associating any sexual intercourse with them with the violent repulsion that menses inspire. However, this law would be valid only for the members of the same clan because they — in the primitive societies — consider themselves "as forming only one flesh, only one 'meat,' only one blood." This forces them to forbid incest in order to intermarry with women foreign to the clan.[41] An enlightening hypothesis that must nevertheless be rectified on one point: It is not only in societies with "weak individuation," but in any community that people tend to feel more or less intensely as members of a collective Body. Whether they are "primitive" or "civilized," all human societies are affected by the same processes of embodiment-disembodiment, by the same schemes, the same hauntings, and each of them responds in its own way by specific strategies of integration, exclusion, or persecution.

The anthropological theories that attempt to explain the prohibition of incest also run into another difficulty. If it is a universal prohibition, having a founding scope in all cultures, how is it that several of them incite on the contrary to transgress it? And especially in the case of chiefs, kings, and priests: Incestuous marriage with a sister or close relative was the rule among the pharaohs of Egypt, the kings and magi of Persia, the Inca rulers of Peru, and the chiefs of Hawaii. Forms of "ritual incest" can even be found in the investiture ceremonies of some African kings. The anthropologist Laura Makarius has confronted this question by taking Durkheim's hypothesis as a guideline. She concludes, as he did, that "the violation of the incest taboo is only a particular case of the blood taboo."[42] It is the transgression of this double taboo that is at the basis of sacred royalty and explains its ambivalent character. She describes, for example, the solemn ceremony that is supposed to give the Swazi king the power to fertilize the earth with his blood. After committing incest with his sister, the king becomes the target of "songs of hatred" ("O king, cursed be thy fate! / O king, they reject thee! / O king, they hate thee!"); then he dies and symbolically resurrects, celebrated again by his people as a sacred ruler.[43] She

214   WORSE THAN DEATH

also evokes the coronation of the king of the Mossi of Burkina-Faso, where he is greeted by this song: "You are an excrement, / You are a heap of garbage, / You come to kill us, / You come to save us." She relates this rite to the mythical origin of the dynasty, from a leper who, according to legend, had incestuous relations with his sister.[44] Likewise, the king of the Bushong of Kasai, whose lineage is also descended from an incestuous founding hero, must commit incest on the eve of his coronation; he is then offered a basket of rats and must designate himself to his people as a defiled being, a "scum," a "waste," at the moment he accedes to supreme power. This ambivalent attitude toward incest and the incestuous king finds its source in the ambivalence of blood, notably that of menses. By ritually violating the prohibition of incest, by putting to death his predecessor or one of his relatives, and sometimes by practicing ritual anthropophagy, the new king appropriates the sacred power of blood, and his transgressive sovereignty is thus similar to that of divine tricksters, magical clowns, and shamans. Laura Makarius notes that in many cultures, one can only be a powerful sorcerer by being born of incest or by violating this taboo oneself, sometimes by killing one's parents or children and eating their flesh or drinking their blood . . . In fact, among the Kaguru of Tanzania, the same word designates incest and witchcraft. The same applies to the divine king, who is often presented in Africa as an incestuous and cannibalistic sorcerer-king, a "being-of-transgression," a "sacred monster."[45] Thus, among the Rukuba of Nigeria, whoever becomes chief must eat the flesh of a young sacrificed child; as a result of this transgression, he acquires a "mystical power likely to infect those who would drink or eat from the same container as him."[46]

Undoubtedly we discover here the kernel of truth of these accusations of incest, cannibalism, ritual murder of children that have sent to death so many innocent people. As in the case of the nocturnal flights and the metamorphoses into animals, we are dealing with the sedimented remnants of very ancient rituals and ancestral beliefs: with transgression schemes that have ended up losing their constitutive ambiguity to become only monstrous. The *truth* of a belief is at stake, not its effective *reality*: We will probably never know whether, among the distant ancestors of the Western peoples, shamans and chiefs really practiced such rites. The kernel of hidden meaning of the violation of the prohibitions persists nonetheless throughout millennia by conserving its affective load, through cleaving processes, projection, disfiguration-transfiguration that have made it unrecognizable. When the ambivalent meaning of the transgression is dissociated in two antagonistic poles, only the king or the god still preserve their sacred dimension, while its impure and threatening aspects are concentrated on the devil, the Witch, the Leper. Thus, sovereign power erases the traces of its transgressive origin by transferring the ancient curse onto the different figures of the Enemy. A rift and a transfer make possible the transfiguration that will make the sovereign a sublime and divine being. The process ends when these schemes are entirely secularized — without nevertheless being desacralized — and transposed onto the political plane, where all trace of their initial ambivalence seems to have disappeared. Benveniste reminds us: If the Latin *sacer* qualifies, like the Greek *hagios*, the "ambiguous character" of what is "consecrated to the gods and charged with an ineffaceable defilement, august and cursed, worthy of veneration and arousing horror," on the other hand the term *sanctus* is the purely positive attribute of what is invested with divine favor and "can be venerated without ambivalence."[47] The passage from the *sacred* to the *saint* — the sanctification of the remainder — does not constitute in any way an ethical progress: It attests to the cleavage of the primitive *sacer* for which is substituted the irreducible opposition of the Holy and the Cursed. Even when the figure of the king has retained its ambivalence, it sometimes implies the existence of an opposite pole where all the horror of the founding transgression is concentrated. While the Great King of the Mossi is a sacred waste, coming from an incestuous lineage, incest is considered such a monstrous crime that there are lines of pariahs in their kingdom who are considered "incestuous" and who are supposed to transmit their defilement through heredity or by simple contact. When they die, they are not buried so as not to infect the earth, but their corpse is tied to a tree until it rots. In other regions of the Mossi kingdom, women who have never menstruated are rejected in these cursed lines, as though they had accumulated the evil power of menstrual blood due to the lack of menstrual flow . . .[48]

So what confers on menses blood such an ambivalence? Must we see in it a particular form of bloodshed, that is to say a metaphor of violence, in its function at the same time malefic and beneficial, destructive and pacifying? It would then become impossible to understand that other bodily secretions, such as saliva, sweat, and even sometimes urine and excrement — which have no direct relation to violence — can possess the same ambiguity. This is because it is precisely waste (*déchets*), dejections of the body, that give a sensitive image of that elusive phenomenon, always rejected and excluded, the remainder of the ego-flesh. How can the universal prohibition of incest and the exclusion of the remainder be related? The desire, the disgust, or the hatred that can be inspired in us toward another body (or a part of this body) find their origin in the affects that we feel toward our own body. Or, more precisely, toward the remainder that has been excluded from it. The intersubjective transfer that constitutes the communities repeats indeed the primordial chiasm where, in each of us, each pole of the ego-flesh unites to the other poles, incarnates them, and lets itself be incarnated in return by them. What, however, prevents them from merging, from identifying themselves entirely to each other? Nothing other than the remainder that interposes itself in the core of the chiasm and leads each pole of flesh to apprehend the other pole as a foreign thing. If the remainder no longer ensured this function of distance, each fleshly pole could merge without remainder with all the others, and the ego-flesh would implode, collapsing on itself until it disappears completely. I call this devastating implosion, this absolute undifferentiation, *aphanisis*, namely, "non-appearance," the total disappearance and without return.[49] Perhaps it never really occurs, even in the most serious psychoses, but it persists nonetheless as an originary phantasm that is schematized in different ways in our existence. It is this haunting of *aphanisis*, of a mortal fusion of the same and the other, that is translated on the psychic level by the fantasy of an incestuous enjoyment — no doubt because incest implies a fusional undifferentiation, a suppression of the difference between generations. The devil as a figure of an incestuous and sadistic Father (and/or Mother), the *coitus diabolicus* as a painful and sterile penetration would then be metaphors of this forbidden *jouissance*. And one could see in the gaping maw of hell where the damned are swallowed up an attempt to figure the unfigurable abyss of *aphanisis*. If, in all human societies, the violation of the prohibition of incest provokes anguish and horror, it is because it awakens the original anguish of *aphanisis*. And if it is indeed the resistance of the remainder that, on our plane of immanence, poses an obstacle to the *aphanisis*, one can conceive that one of its principal bodily representatives — the blood of the menses — can pose an obstacle to the *jouissance* of incest. Disgust and horror ensure here a protective function, that of a defense, of an ultimate barrier before the Black Hole of *aphanisis*. Thus the ambivalence of the incestuous and bloodthirsty sorcerer-king is rooted in the primordial ambivalence of the remainder that he transmits to his transfigured figures, to those divine and human sovereigns, those beneficent and fearsome beings who inspire in men a boundless veneration and a sacred terror. To unveil the violence of this transgression on which their power is based; to show that their sacred character is not original, but derives from a transfiguration process whose reverse side is the disfiguration of a fallen and abject remainder; to bring to light the strategies that allow them to divert this load of abjection onto innocent victims. It is in this way that egoanalysis will contribute to the deconstruction of sovereignty, to the desacralization of politics.

8

A Stranger among Us

The sole work and deed of universal freedom is therefore *death*, a death too which has no inner significance or filling [. . .] the coldest and meanest of all deaths, with no more significance than cutting off a head of cabbage or swallowing a mouthful of water [. . .] *Being suspected*, therefore, takes the place, or has the significance and effect of *being guilty* [. . .] the *terror* of death is the vision of this negative nature of itself.

HEGEL, PHENOMENOLOGY OF SPIRIT

Our enemies within are conspiring against us with the support of our foreign enemies. Their conspiracy has infiltrated all levels of society, all cogs of the State. Hidden under different masks, they only await the right moment to annihilate us. They are strangers among us, a race of incorrigible rebels whom we must put to death to the last man. They are not even men but ferocious animals, monsters, a cancer, a gangrenous limb that must be amputated. It is not a question of judging them but of exterminating them, of forcing them to return to the nothingness from which they should never have emerged.

We know these statements well: They have accompanied the long history of persecutions for centuries. I have merely collected them here from the writings of several protagonists of the French Revolution. This process may be considered questionable: What good are fragments of quotations taken out of their context? And besides, one might say, this simple exercise proves nothing. The political use of the metaphors of amputation and purge goes back at least to Plato, and, in all periods of crisis, one has given in to these rhetorical outbursts . . . This is precisely what I would like to show: that such statements attest to the reappearance of old schemes and that they will be followed by the same effects as during the persecutions of centuries past. When, in the spring of 1794, Barère declares in the name of the Committee of Public Safety that the enemies of the Revolution "resemble those poisonous plants that swarm as soon as the farmer forgets to extirpate them entirely," and he calls for "resuming this task with the utmost ardor," we are not simply dealing with a gardening metaphor, but with the imminent heralding of the Great Terror. Here, to say is to put to death.

After having discovered an antecedent of the witch hunt in the extermination of lepers, my aim is to analyze the constitution of another persecution apparatus at the time of the Terror of 1793–94. The purpose here is not to propose an overall interpretation of the Revolutionary Terror, but only to approach it from a certain angle, to consider it as an *apparatus* that mobilizes certain *affects* of the multitudes by means of prevalent *schemes*. The analogies we can observe do not mean in any way that these different apparatuses would be identical or that the oldest would be the distant origin of the most recent. And yet, from one event to another, the same affects crystallize; the same schemes are reactivated, revealing a hidden kinship. What conceals it is, first of all, the reverence that the revolutionary epic continues to arouse in France. The Revolution is the founding event from which France continues to draw its primary historical references, the legitimacy of its institutions, and even the very particular style of its political fervor. Drawing a comparison with the persecution of "witches" would be tantamount to blasphemy and would immediately classify the author of the comparison among the fiercest reactionaries . . . This parallel appears scandalous for yet another reason, because of the many misunderstandings about the witch hunt. However, if one refrains from casting it back into the darkness of the Middle Ages, if one stops considering it only as a religious persecution and highlights its political dimension, as I have tried to do in this book, it becomes possible to bring it closer to the phases of terror of modern revolutions. This "anachronistic" comparison can help us understand what is at stake in the event of the Revolution.

Provided, however, that we do not underestimate the differences. Contrary to the witch hunt, the violence exercised by the Revolution did not emanate from the ruling classes, but from the multitudes, even if, carried out through a series of popular uprisings, it was relayed by apparatuses of power. In its instituting aim, it is not reactive, but founding, and who could deny that the foundation of a new society goes through some violence? Advocating an ideal of universal equality and freedom, the French Revolution is a project of emancipation, of what I have called the Western utopia. Another striking difference is that, however expeditious and implacable they were, the revolutionary tribunals never resorted to the techniques of unveiling employed during the witch hunt. The "preliminary question" having been abolished in 1780, the accused appeared without having been broken by torture (on this point, the Jacobin Terror also differs from the Stalinist Terror). But these differences between the witch hunt and the Terror are only perceptible against the background of an essential proximity: In both cases, we are dealing with persecution apparatuses that construct a figure of the absolute Enemy, that have recourse to the conspiracy scheme for this purpose, and that tend to become radicalized, to get carried away in a phase of terror in which anyone can be accused. And although it is true that the Revolution is inscribed in a project of emancipation, it is also true that the logic of hatred diverts it from its first ends, leading it to betray its project by precipitating it in the bloody impasse of the Terror. Two centuries later, the relationship between the Revolution and the Terror still remains an enigma. This is already how the most lucid of contemporaries perceived it, those who, like Kant and Hegel, felt enthusiasm for the "magnificent sunrise" of 1789, and wondered about this moment when the course of the Revolution seemed to be reversed, when the advent of freedom unleashed the "coldest death." This is not an academic question that can be left to historians alone. The French Revolution served as a model for subsequent revolutionary attempts, from the Paris Commune to the Russian Revolution. And, those who still justify the Jacobin Terror today also justify the far more murderous terrors to which the names of Stalin or Mao are attached. Would any revolt against injustice, any policy of emancipation be condemned, as soon as it takes the form of a revolution, to go through one form or another of terror? Is it possible to carry out a criticism of the Jacobin Terror *in the name of the Revolution*? Or to recognize the founding scope of the revolutionary event, its capacity to initiate a new beginning, while dissociating it from its "terrorist" phase? After the disaster in which the revolutions of the twentieth century have sunk, these questions are still our questions.

By viewing the Revolutionary Terror in the long haul, we can at least avoid making a silk purse out of a sow's ear and confusing the irruption of the new with the repetition of the old. When they define the Terror as the "fatal legacy of the Old Regime" or when they denounce the "Jacobin Inquisition," Michelet and Quinet recognize, in spite of the historical rupture, resurgences of the past. As Quinet wrote, in the Terror "two epochs coexist, monstrously united; the sentimental logic of Rousseau takes for its instrument the axe of the Saint-Bartholomew." Many historians, unfortunately, lack this lucidity. Although he criticizes the illusion of a radical break with the Old Regime, Furet succumbs in turn to this illusion: He believes he discerns what is new in the revolutionary phenomenon in the emergence of the idea of conspir-

acy, which he defines as an "imaginary representation of power" characteristic of modern democracy.[1] We have seen that it is not. We are dealing with
a motif of theological-political origin—the conspiracy of rebellious angels
against God—that has been secularized to constitute a figure of evil sovereignty. Nothing less "modern" than the myth of the conspiracy: It is not the
reverse side of popular sovereignty, but that of the sacred monarchy, of which
it possesses all the imaginary predicates, the sovereign power, the ubiquity,
the dissimulation. What are the ghosts that haunt the French Revolution and
hide its true meaning? Are they the Brutus and Gracchus, the heroic figures of
Roman antiquity, as Marx believed? Or does it reproduce the fanaticism of the
medieval Inquisition and the despotic power of the absolute monarchy? And
is it a creative repetition, where there is a break with the past and historical
invention, or is it a mortifying repetition that crushes the present under the
burden of the past?

For a long time, it was claimed that the proclamation of the Terror was due
to the pressure of circumstances. The Jacobins, seeing the Revolution threatened by foreign armies and counterrevolutionaries, resorted to the Terror in
order to save the Republic. But this pious legend does not withstand analysis.
Here again, Quinet sensed it: "the great Terror showed itself almost everywhere after the victories." It manifested itself with the greatest intensity in the
spring of 1794, when the hostile forces had been defeated everywhere; and it
raged most violently in the defeated Vendée. Even if the proclamation of the
Terror could initially be part of a deliberate strategy, that of the Jacobin leaders
who used it to gain power and eliminate their opponents, this strategic and
limited violence was quickly overtaken, outflanked by a process in which the
persecution apparatuses ran amok, in which the Terror intensified and spread
without limits. If the "theory of circumstances" proves to be inconsistent, the
same is true of those that sharply oppose 1789 to 1793, a liberal and peaceful
Revolution to another terrorist and bloody Revolution. There is indeed a "terror of before the Terror" that has accompanied it like its dark underside since
the beginning of the Revolution.[2] The will to thwart the "conspiracies" of the
counterrevolution, to punish the "enemies of the people" in an implacable
way was present since the first riots. It was already expressed in the clamors
of Marat, and it was this desire that presided over the carnage of September
1792. These calls for exceptional measures are the object of a broad consensus
among the elites and the people, among the most moderate as well as the most
radical, with the images of amputation and eradication accompanying them.
It was the moderate Sieyès who, as early as 1789, designated the privileged
caste as a parasitic "excrescence" that should be extirpated from the body of
the Nation. The privileged, he adds, are men "whose very existence is a con-

tinual hostility against the great body of the people"[3] (Saint-Just will not speak differently about the counterrevolutionaries). It was another moderate, the Girondin Isnard, who called in 1791 for "bloodshed," because "it is necessary to cut off the gangrenous part to save the rest of the body." But their violence remained purely verbal. When Sieyès asked to send the aristocrats "back to the forests of Franconia," there was no law, no court that would have allowed them to be banished or executed for the simple crime of being born noble. In a few more years, though, a terror apparatus — surveillance committees and revolutionary tribunals — legitimized by exceptional laws would be put in place that would give these schemes their murderous force.

The Terror is precisely that moment when, by inserting itself into an apparatus, these schemes can be articulated to the affects of multitudes and materialize into a policy of persecution. A synthesis of the heterogeneous, a random conjunction of different elements that were not fatally destined to meet. If the Terror was from the start a *possible* outcome of the revolutionary process, it does not follow that it is a *necessary* phase of it and that this bundle of schemes and phantasms had necessarily to be knotted into a persecution apparatus. Quinet was incensed against those who legitimized the Terror under the pretext that it was inevitable, thus making the actors of the Revolution "automatons of fatality." It is this same understanding that Hannah Arendt rejects.[4] For her, the Terror is not the necessary accomplishment of the Revolution. Rather, it is the sign of its failure, of the impotence of the French revolutionaries to ensure the foundation of liberty, to institute a stable political order that would guarantee freedom, as the American Revolution had done. The French let themselves be diverted from their goal under the pressure of the social question. By giving in to the passion of pity, to their Rousseauist compassion toward the miserable masses, they abandoned their project of the republican foundation, thus precipitating the Revolution into the Terror. We may question the relationship that Arendt establishes between the "politics of pity" and the Terror, which leads her to completely dissociate the aim of equality and the foundation of a Republic. As she opposes the dignity of the political action to the inferior sphere of the social, dominated by the obscure necessity of work and life, she could not recognize the political scope of the social question. She failed to understand that the Revolutionary Terror is inseparable from a political concern about the forms of democracy, where the foundation problem is at stake in a more radical way than in the American Revolution. At least she avoided making the Terror an inevitable moment of any revolution, as many historians do, either to justify the Terror in the name of the Revolution (if they are of the neo-Jacobin school), or to condemn the Revolution because of the Terror (if they are of the liberal school).

In stressing the role of pity, Arendt has opened a fruitful avenue. She correctly saw that it was not so much the principles that the Revolution claimed to uphold as the affects that animated it that led it astray into the Terror. But is it mainly a feeling of pity that guides Jacobins and Sans-Culottes? The popular riots were provoked by *fear*, by this Great Fear that crossed the countryside in 1789, by the fear of an "aristocratic conspiracy" that fanned the rage of the people of Paris or, later, by that of foreign armies. This gives reason to Engels: Terror is indeed the work of men themselves terrorized. However, while the Revolution becomes more radical, another feeling is awakened: *revenge*, the will to avenge the "martyrs of Liberty." The wave of indignation and anger raised by the assassination of Marat was not unrelated to the decision to proclaim the Terror. The guillotine was nicknamed the People's Avenger (Vengeresse du Peuple), a festival of vengeance was instituted, and when the Vendée was reconquered, it was renamed Département-Vengé . . . A historian recently attempted to account for the Jacobin Terror and the Soviet Terror of 1918–21 by focusing his analysis on the "spiral of vengeance," the spiral of the Furies that are unleashed during revolutionary crises.[5] When the exasperation of antagonisms and the collapse of the judicial system provoke the "return of vengeance," it manifests itself under its most archaic forms, in acts of barbarism and lynchings. And this feeling easily turns to hatred, to the desire to eliminate *by any means necessary* those upon whom one wants to take revenge. Like hatred, revenge is a reciprocal feeling, that is to say, contagious: During times of crisis and civil war, when each side is bent on avenging the victims of the other side's avengers, it tends to grow without limits. By favoring the conversion of the affects of revolt into affects of hatred, the pivotal-affect that is revenge allows a *desire for terror* to be born and to be reinforced within the multitudes. The establishment of a State Terror would then be an attempt of the new regime to ensure for itself the monopoly on legitimate violence by putting an end to the infernal spiral of popular vengeances. "Let us be terrible to spare the people from being terrible!" exclaims Danton to demand the creation of a Revolutionary Tribunal that could "supplement the supreme court of the people's vengeance" and avoid new massacres. The fury of the Erinyes would not be appeased for all that: This exceptional apparatus paved the way for the Terror, and the tribunal that he himself had created to "find an antidote to vengeance" would soon send Danton to the guillotine.

To understand how affects can be invested in representations and practices and how subjects animated by these affects can adhere to power apparatuses, I turned to a theory of historical schematism. Schemes are intermediate representations that allow one to articulate heterogeneous instances, to unite the affect to the Idea, the individual to the apparatus. They are indeed schemas and not concepts. An entire tradition, since Burke and Hegel, has claimed to "explain" the Revolutionary Terror by incriminating the harmful influence of the Enlightenment and the *Social Contract* or the abstract concept of absolute freedom; just as we persist in our days in looking for the "causes" of Stalinist totalitarianism in the thought of Marx or those of jihadist terrorism in the Quran. Again, let us emphasize that a power apparatus is capable of reappropriating any doctrine in order to legitimize its action. What mobilizes these apparatuses is never a theory or a discourse. It is schemes and the affects they manage to capture by giving them a target. To be sure, several converging factors prevented the Revolutionary Tribunal from fulfilling the pacifying function that Danton had assigned to it. However, it would be wrong to neglect the role played by the conspiracy scheme, which, by constantly rekindling fear, the desire for vengeance and hatred, facilitated the transformation of a judicial apparatus of exception into an apparatus of persecution and terror. If we were to take into account—which would require lengthy analyses—all the schemes of emancipation, transgression, exclusion, and persecution that intertwine, reinforce each other, enter into conflict or cancel each other out by integrating themselves into antagonistic or allied apparatuses, we would succeed in shedding new light on certain aspects of the revolutionary process.

These schemes that reappear during the Revolution and influence its course do, in fact, come from a distant past, as if history were only repeating itself and no break had taken place. However, they operate within very different apparatuses. Although it takes its name from the former Dominican convent—once located on Saint-Jacques Street—where it was established, the Jacobin Society is not a simple avatar of the medieval Inquisition. In attempting to seize and retain State power through the Terror, in striving to control all public space and in systematically purifying their organization, Robespierre and his followers invented a new "political machine" (the expression is Michelet's) that bears a striking resemblance to the totalitarian parties of the twentieth century. The reactivation of these schemes is thus carried out in apparatuses quite different from those that had mobilized them formerly: There is at the same time continuity and discontinuity, repetition and caesura, "monstrous" coexistence of the old and the new. Whereas the apparatus is an unstable formation that is born and undone according to the power relations, the scheme is characterized on the contrary by its prevalence, which allows it to migrate from one apparatus to another while preserving its fundamental meaning. This is how the conspiracy scheme, so prominent in the discourse of Robespierre and Saint-Just, will be turned against them on 9 Thermidor by their enemies, who will denounce a "Jacobin conspiracy." Reversible and plastic like all historical schemes, it thus passes from the Jacobin power system to that of the Thermidorians, before being reappropriated by the counter-revolutionaries when they claim to "explain" the Revolution by a "Masonic conspiracy" or by the "Templars' revenge."[6]

Several features characterize a persecution apparatus. We have discovered (1) that it sets sovereign power in play — more precisely, that it has the vocation to defend a sovereign power in crisis; (2) that it constructs a figure of the absolute enemy; (3) that it "responds" to the resistance of a multitude; and (4) that it is inscribed in a politics of the body, engaging a certain image of the political Body. So many features that we find in the Revolutionary Terror. Of course, the context is not the same: It is no longer a question of protecting an established power by "diverting" popular passions onto other targets, but of refounding political sovereignty on entirely new bases. *The crisis of sovereignty* that began then will be more profound than during the seditions and civil wars of the past centuries. Through the successive crises that punctuated it from 1789 to 1799, the experience of the French Revolution laid bare the precariousness of modern sovereign power, its divided and unstable character, and it engaged a very different relationship between the apparatuses of power and the multitudes. The first act of the Revolution was consummated in June 1789, when the delegates of the Estates General set themselves up as a National Constituent Assembly, considered the "one and indivisible" representation of the Nation. For the first time since Antiquity, a purely secular legitimacy replaced the religious basis of sovereignty. A new configuration is presented, where political sovereignty is no longer embodied in the body of the monarch, but in a representative institution, destined to be periodically renewed by popular balloting. So much so that the place of power presents itself henceforth, as Lefort observed, as an "empty place," while its legitimacy and its ends become the stake of an unceasing questioning. It was Sieyès who would establish the topography of this new political field: He describes it as an immense sphere of which the law is the center and where "all citizens, without exception, are at the same distance on the circumference and occupy only equal places; all depend equally on the law."[7] One should nevertheless avoid overestimating this initial rupture. When Sieyès also declares that "the people can speak, can act only by their representatives," that it *"forms body only there"* (*ne fait corps que là*), he recognizes that, for the new ruling elites, the "sovereignty of the people" of which they speak is only an inconsistent fiction; that this first phase of the Revolution operated only a *transfer of sovereignty* of the king to the Assembly. Simple transfer of power that leaves intact the fundamental structures of the State domination, the alienating identification of the masses to a figure of the One-Body, their exclusion of any participation to the political life. The former "royal dispossession" was simply replaced by a "parliamentary dispossession."[8]

Yet the die was not cast: The Revolution liberated a new force, that of the multitudes, incensed against all forms of domination; and they were not long in organizing themselves, arming themselves, creating sections, popular societies. So many counterapparatuses where a new public space of freedom and action was outlined, the outline of a *democracy of multitudes*. It is as if the crisis of the political Body had liberated the flesh of the community, this an-archic flesh, broken up into innumerable poles and that resists any incorporation in a hierarchical Body. By making the voice of the voiceless heard, by claiming the "share of the shareless," these counterapparatuses will interrupt, on several occasions, the State and parliamentary capture of the Revolution. The "*journées*" impelled by the Parisian Sans-Culottes played an essential role in the radicalization of the revolutionary process. Thus, in 1792, they provoked the abolition of the monarchy and the proclamation of the Republic; then, the following year, the defeat of the Girondins and the conquest of power by the Jacobins; before forcing the Convention to "declare the Terror to be on the agenda." Within this movement, radical tendencies appear, like the one animated by the "Enraged" Roux and Varlet. They attacked the "new merchant aristocracy" and demanded measures to make "the excessive inequality of fortunes disappear." But they do not limit themselves to the social question: They attack the "legislative tyranny," the representative principle that dissociates its representatives from the people, and they ask that the Convention be dissolved, replaced by delegates mandated by the assemblies of the sections and revocable at any time. By fighting against the inequality of wealth and the political and social hierarchies, the Enraged revive the most radical tradition of the oppressed, that of the Taborites of Bohemia, the German Anabaptists, the Diggers of the English Revolution.[9]

Hannah Arendt attaches great importance to popular societies, the "elementary republics" where she detects the beginnings of a politics based on the multiplicity of power centers. This leads her to emphasize the conflict between the Parisian popular societies and the Committee of Public Safety in the spring of 1794. She sees there a foreshadowing of the conflict that was going to oppose in the twentieth century the exponents of the unique Party and the autonomous revolutionary organs — soviets of the Russian Revolution, Workers' Councils of the Hungarian insurrection of 1956 — where she identifies the ultimate heirs of the "lost treasure" of the modern revolutions.[10] She no doubt idealizes the Sans-Culottes. If some of their currents are more and more strongly opposed to the authoritarian centralization of the Jacobins, the emancipation schemes that orient their action are inextricably intertwined with persecution schemes, calls to intensify repression, to send more and more "suspects" to the guillotine, calls that are tirelessly relayed in Marat's journal, then in Hébert's. It is impossible to understand anything about the Revolutionary Terror without taking into account the ambivalence of the multitudes, the intensity of the desire for revenge, and the hatred that can engulf them. What makes it possible to harness their revolt by a terror apparatus is the designation by this apparatus of an enemy, a real or imaginary target that concentrates anguish and hatred on it. The main function of persecution schemes consists in figuring this enemy, in giving an identity and a name to this anonymous haunting. From the beginning of the Revolution, the "aristocratic conspiracy" plays this role, and it will continue to play it, even when the real aristocrats have been deprived of their privileges and their power, imprisoned or guillotined, and forced to submit or to emigrate. The conspiracy scheme makes it possible to designate an enemy all the more formidable as he remains invisible and to strip him of his humanity, by presenting him as a monster or as an abject remainder, a waste. At the height of the Great Terror, the Committee of Public Safety approved a report asking to "purge the prisons in an instant and clear the ground of this filth, this waste of humanity."[11] This figure, at the same time threatening and abject, will be identified successively with all the adversaries with which the Jacobins are confronted. How is such a representation formed? How does it take on the evil traits that once characterized Jews, lepers, and "witches"? A number of figure-schemes act as a hinge, allowing these new targets to be assimilated to those of past persecutions: the figures of the queen-witch, the vampire-king, and the pig-king. In order to understand how they were constituted, it is necessary to analyze the imaginary power of the Ancien Régime and its way of representing the Sovereign Body.

In his *Discours des États de France* (1588), Guy Coquille declares that "the King is the head and the people of the three orders are the limbs; and all together are the political and mystical Body whose bond and union is undivided and inseparable. And no part of it can suffer harm unless the rest feels it and suffers pain."[12] Such is the French version of the doctrine of the *Corpus mysticum Reipublicae*, transposing on the political level the theological conception of the Church as a mystical Body whose head is Christ. This supposes a doubling of the body of the king, whose visible body — a body of flesh exposed to sin and death — is distinguished from his invisible mystical Body, while remaining indissociable from it. From this theological-political scheme flow the fundamental characteristics of royal power: its *unicity* ("it is impossible," declared Bodin, "for the Republic, which has only one body, to have several heads"; its *perpetuity* ("the King never dies"); and its *infallibility* ("the King cannot do wrong"), which legitimizes his power to make law ("so wills the King, so wills the Law"). Contrary to its English version, the French conception of the Body politic concentrates all powers in the person of the monarch: The "absolutist" aspects of the Jacobin conception of sovereignty find their source here. In its various versions, however, the doctrine of the two bodies maintains a gap, a secret breach that risks leading to its ruin. In spite of the repeated affirmation of their union, the distinction of two bodies of dissimilar nature indeed allows for the possibility of their dissociation. When their link is distended, it becomes possible to invoke the authority of the Mystical Body against the one who personifies it, as witnessed by the slogan of the insurgent Puritans against Charles I: "Fight the *king* to defend the *King*." It is the same dissociation that will be accomplished at the beginning of the French Revolution. Nevertheless, we must recognize that the doctrine of the two bodies offers a remarkable solution to the fundamental aporia of the political body. Even if they are constituted by transposing certain features of the individual bodies, the collective "bodies" are never anything but quasi-bodies, forever deprived of flesh consistency, of the originary presence of my flesh to myself that provides my body with its foundation. Deprived of flesh, the Great Body always faces the threat that it may decompose, may disembody itself. This is why each collective Body has had to invent rites of reembodiment to resist this threat. The rite of the Eucharist thus allows the Body of the Church to become One again, each time the faithful take communion by absorbing the flesh of the sacrificed god. From the thirteenth century onward, the same function of reembodiment will be ensured on the political level by what Michelet calls the "mystery of the monarchic incarnation,"[13] where the mystical Body of the State gives itself to be seen and touched in the visible body of the monarch. Among the rites of this "royal religion," the coronation ceremony and the scrofula's touching are important. We remember that, since the Middle Ages, the kings of France and England were supposed to cure leprosy miraculously. Then those tubercular ganglia were called scrofula: By healing the wounds of an infected body by their touch, they attest that they are able to ward off the diseases and divisions of the political body.

What happens when a king seems unable to ensure the unity and prosperity of the State? Closely tied to the Body of the realm, his own body can present itself as a symbolic expression of disunity and ruin. According to some medieval authors, the king is not only the head but also the heart of the Great Body; he derives his dynastic legitimacy from what they call his "perpetual blood." When the meaning of this figure is inverted, the bad king appears instead as a vampire who sucks the blood of the kingdom and drains it. This figure-scheme — associated with those of the Leper, the Jew, the Witch — is so deeply rooted in the imagination of monarchical power that it reappears centuries later. We know that, at the time of the Wars of Religion, it was claimed that François II had children murdered to bathe in their blood. The same accusation resurfaced in Paris in 1750. While the police arrested beggars and young vagabonds, the rumor spread that they were kidnapping children because the king was suffering from leprosy and needed their blood to heal himself. A violent riot broke out, which was brutally suppressed. The rumor reached Louis XV, who was angry at the "wicked people who say that I am a Herod."[14] A similar rumor provoked another riot in Lyon in 1768: This time it was claimed that a "one-armed prince" was kidnapping children in order to cut off their arms and have them grafted . . . Michelet spoke passionately about the affair of the "child kidnappings" in Paris and the revolt that it had provoked. He sees there the premises of the Revolution ("The fear was great at the Court [. . .] It seemed as though the Bastille had already been taken"), the first sign of a divorce between the monarchy and the people. These years, he writes, are the "crisis of the century," the moment when "the king, this god, this idol, becomes an object of horror. The dogma of the royal incarnation perishes without return."[15]

No doubt Michelet overstates the importance of the event, but he underlines a fundamental phenomenon, the strange reversibility characterizing the relation of the king to his people. He had understood that the monarchic incarnation is precarious; that the love of the subjects can quickly change to disgust and hatred, when the glorious body of the monarch metamorphoses in their eyes in an *abject body*, that of a leper greedy for blood, of a ferocious or ignoble beast. This reversibility characterizes the heterogeneous element, the ambivalent remainder of the Great Body with which the body of the king is identified. What differentiates the Christian monarchies of the West from African royalty (or from the Indian caste system) is the breakdown of this ambivalence, which allows the Bushong king to present himself at his coronation as a "scum," an incestuous pariah, and at the same time as the sacred leader of his people. Such a ritual allows feelings of revulsion and hostility toward royal power to be expressed in the open and serves to defuse them. The Western apparatus of sovereignty, on the other hand, is intended to sacralize the monarch, or rather to "sanctify" him by depriving him of all ambivalence, to transfigure him irreversibly. And yet, by seeking to protect him, it exposes him to a catastrophic reversal, a passage from transfiguration to disfiguration. In times of crisis, this is accomplished in Western societies outside any ritual, in an uncontrollable and devastating way, by reactivating the most archaic figurations of the remainder. The successor of Louis XV would soon experience this.

When the new king ascended the throne, it was as if the transfiguration process had begun again, and the first phase of the Revolution spared the person of Louis XVI, who still retained the respect and love of the French. On the other hand, for several years, virulent attacks were aimed at Queen Marie-Antoinette, "the Austrian," doubly hated as a foreigner and as a woman. These attacks reached an unprecedented level of violence from 1789 onward. In the pamphlets that targeted her, the queen was caricatured as a wild beast (the queen-wolf), repulsive (the queen-tarantula), or monstrous (the queen-harp) and accused of the worst crimes. Indeed, she was charged with having murdered her eldest son by poisoning him and seeking to kill the king in the same way; with being a debauched and lesbian "Messalina"; with committing incest with her brother, with one of the king's brothers, and even with her own son.[16] This last accusation will be raised again during her trial by Hébert, who denounces her "criminal *jouissance*." The obsession with blood, the haunting of the vampire-king that had set the people of Paris against a king forty years earlier, was transferred to the queen. The public prosecutor Fouquier-Tinville referred to her as the "leech of the French," and the *Journal des hommes libres* hailed her execution by stating that she had "sworn to bathe in the blood of the French." Bestialization, overflowing and transgressive sexuality, incest, poisoning, vampirism: We recognize all the traits that the inquisitors and judges used to attribute to "witches." The only thing missing from the picture is devil worship and the desecration of the sacraments, for the persecution schemes are now secularized and have lost the trace of their religious origin. The day had come when the "enemies of the people" could be demonized without any belief in the devil or in the Good Lord. In spite of the Enlightenment and the disenchantment of the world, we see the figure of the queen-witch, Circe the poisoner or Medea the infanticide, the focus of a devouring *jouissance*, onto which is projected the horror and hatred from which the king is still spared. As always, the plasticity of the persecution scheme allows the apparatus to orient itself on another target while avoiding a frontal attack on the sovereign power. But this *diversion* would not protect Louis XVI for long.

The 1791 Constitution had stripped the king of his sacred dignity to make him the head of the executive, the State's "first civil servant." With the transfer of his sovereignty to the Assembly, the latter is now identified with the Body of the Nation, which leads to a desacralization of the royal body: Dissociated from its *Corpus mysticum*, it retains only its profane dimension. In the early days of the Revolution, representations of Louis XVI bear witness to this desacralization. Prints show him, for example, digging with a pickaxe on the Champ-de-Mars during the preparations for the Federation Day or walking around Paris wearing a tricolor cockade. He appears as a citizen among others, deprived of the stylization and the distance that characterized his traditional figurations. This all changed in June 1791, after the flight to Varennes, perceived by public opinion as a betrayal. In a few weeks, several hundred caricatures appeared in which the king was presented as a hypocrite (the two-faced king-Janus), a voracious Gargantua (it is "the ogre Capet" getting ready to devour France), and, most often, as a pig (one of them curiously specifies that it is a "leper pig") or a hybrid monster: half-man, half-pig. We are too familiar today with caricatures of politicians to fully appreciate these attacks on a figure revered for centuries as the image of God. The edifying imagery of the citizen-king gives way here to another mode of figuration where he appears as a body alien to the nation and to humanity. It is a monstrous body by its deformity, its bestiality; a carnivalesque body at the same time grotesque and threatening, whose caricature privileges the "low" functions (swallowing, vomit, defecation . . .). An excremental body-waste, as suggested by a print where he crawls in the mire of the "royal sewer" while he is defecated on. A fragmented body, where the unity of the *Corpus mysticum* is broken down: another print depicts him as a raving lunatic breaking a mirror, the fragments of which reflect his shattered face, so that, according to the legend, "each of the pieces multiplies his madness."[17] These representations show the body of the king as a heterogeneous and dangerous element that threatens the unity of the nation and must be eliminated. This would be accomplished in January 1793, at the end of the trial where the Convention condemned the pig-king to death. The caricatures and pamphlets of the Holy League, which presented Henri III as a beast, a sorcerer, or a demon, had guided the hand of his assassin; those of the revolutionaries were to send his distant successor to the guillotine. In both instances, we are dealing with the radical disfigurement of the royal body that makes it pass from sacred sovereignty to the most extreme abjection. Such a phenomenon occurs in times of crisis, when the fascinated identification of the subjects that alienated them from the One-Body is interrupted. No revolution, no major political transformation, is possible without this *disidentification*, but must this always pass through a disfiguration, through the designation of an "inhuman monster," of an Absolute Enemy to be annihilated?

If we want to attempt an answer, we must turn to that central episode of the Revolution, the trial of the king. During the debates that preceded it at the Convention, a conflict pitted two opposing conceptions of the Republic against each other. The Girondins, and in particular Condorcet, demanded that the crimes imputed to Louis XVI be "judged and punished like crimes of the same kind committed by another individual." They took a stand for an *inclusive foundation* where the Republic implied the equality of all citizens and their belonging to the same national community. By considering the king as a citizen equal to all the others, they plead for the "symbolic disenchantment" of the State, for the "renunciation to the magic authority and to the political servitude."[18] They show that they have recognized the *desacralization of politics*: For them, the king has definitively ceased to embody the Body of the Nation. The position of the Jacobins is quite different. "There is no trial to be had here," Robespierre declared. "Louis is not an accused. You are not judges."[19] It is not a question, he adds, of condemning him for his past crimes, but only of "throwing him back into nothingness." Indeed, he and Saint-Just demanded the execution of the "tyrant" without trial. There could be no question of legal forms and equality before the law precisely because a king is not a citizen. As Saint-Just insisted, he was always "the enemy of the French people," a "foreign enemy," a "stranger among us."[20] Contrary to the Girondins, their conception of the Republic implies an *exclusive foundation*, which means that a man or a group of men are severed from the Nation. He thus considers "Louis Capet" as an exception, an outlaw, a heterogeneous element within the social body. However, it is the same position that the king occupied under the monarchy of divine right, that of a being apart, of an *exlex* not falling under the common laws. Except that the meaning of this exception was reversed entirely: The dethroned king went from the Chief to the waste, from the glorious part to the cursed part of the Great Body. The Jacobins did not break with the sacralization of sovereign power. They continue to be secretly fascinated by "this species of *filthy and sacred* animals that we still call kings."[21]

It would therefore be wrong to credit them with the most decisive break. It is the opposing position, that of Condorcet, that breaks radically with the monarchical figure of the Body, whereas Robespierre and Saint-Just only perpetuate it in an inverted form. Quinet understood that, in spite of their apparent audacity, their pathos of absolute novelty, they had remained prisoners of the monarchic conception of absolute sovereignty. If the Girondins "rejected everything inherited from the old France," the Jacobins "bent to the old tradition. They used the political system of old France to destroy it, thereby incurring the risk of re-creating it": "the more one returned to the old forms, the more one believed this was innovation."[22] The status of the sovereign Body is indeed the stake of the conflict. For the Girondins, the fact of judging the ex-king as a simple citizen attests that his "two bodies" have been irreversibly dissociated and that the transfer of sovereignty has already been completely accomplished. For the Jacobins, this transfer remains imperfect or impossible as long as the king remains alive, and only regicide will make the foundation of a Republic possible. It may be, as Michelet argued, that the "mystery of the monarchic incarnation" transposes the mystery of the Eucharist onto the political plane.[23] The conflict that divides the Convention then takes a theological dimension where, as in the thirteenth century, the question of the status of the *Corpus mysticum* plays a fundamental role. The Girondins admitted only a symbolic presence of the Mystical Body of the State in the person of the king, so that a simple juridical act could cancel it by removing him from office. On the other hand, just as Catholic theologians maintain that the body of Christ is really present in the host, the Jacobins believe in the *real presence* of the Great Body in that of the king, in a union of the two bodies so intimate that it survives the fall of the monarch, who continues, even on the scaffold, to embody France. That is why, Saint-Just declares again, "this man must reign or die."

The conflict that opposed the two parties involved two very different approaches to the execution of the king. Opposed to this execution for political or humanitarian reasons, Condorcet and his friends can nevertheless easily consider it as the conclusion of a legitimate legal procedure. For the Jacobins, it takes the meaning of a sacred ceremony where the living incarnation of the *Corpus mysticum* must be annihilated. It is ultimately the entire political body that must die with its mystical head in order to be reborn, to *regenerate* itself: "It is necessary at last," proclaims a Jacobin deputy, "that everything that breathes die and be reborn at the moment when the head of the tyrant falls. It is to your care that the generation of a great people is entrusted. Yes, it is through you that the French people must take on a new being."[24] From the regeneration of the people by the regicide, they were about to move to its regeneration by the Terror. Their vision of the regicide as a "religious feast" (the formula is Marat's) seems widely shared by the Sans-Culottes and a part of the people of Paris. The public execution, with its solemn and bloody dimension, awakens indeed an ancient haunting. From the king's last words to the behavior of the crowd, everything betrays the ambivalent obsession with blood, that of the Precious Blood of Christ as well as that of the royal vampire. Louis was perhaps no longer certain that he embodied France, but he conceived himself more than ever as an *image of Christ* and was about, he said, to "to drain the cup of sorrow to the dregs." "I die innocent," he cried on the scaffold, "and I pray that the blood you are about to shed will never fall on France and that it will appease the anger of God." As soon as the executioner held up his severed head, spectators rushed to dip their handkerchiefs or spikes in his blood. According to the more or less romanticized account of a newspaper of the time, "a citizen climbed onto the guillotine and, plunging his whole arm into Capet's blood, he took clots in his hand and sprinkled them three times on the crowd of assistants who were crowding around the foot of the scaffold to receive a drop on their foreheads. 'Brothers,' the citizen said as he sprinkled his blood, 'we were threatened that Louis Capet's blood would fall on our heads. May it fall. Louis Capet washed his hands so many times in ours! Republicans, the blood of kings carries luck.'"[25] In a way, this man and those around him continue to identify the king with the figure of Christ ("may his blood fall on our heads!"). At the same time, they obscurely continue to believe in the legend of the vampire-kings: by sprinkling themselves with royal blood, they take revenge on both Louis XV and Herod. Indeed, they appropriate this figure-scheme of the hated monarchy to become the vampires of the Republic. The execution of the king thus condenses contradictory meanings. Legal punishment of a head of State condemned for high treason, it ratifies the desacralization of politics and thus makes possible another relationship to sovereign power, which would no longer involve a fascinated identification. A staging of a founding sacrifice or a republican black mass, it is experienced at the same time as an archaic rite, as if the foundation of the Republic were to replay in reverse the mystery of the monarchic incarnation through the "perpetual blood" of kings. This confirms that the knot of the theological and the political has not been untied. Through the ritual of the capital execution, the ambivalent sacralization of the sovereignty is perpetuated: Even if it becomes negative and hateful, the identification with the sovereign does not cease, and it leaves open the possibility of a new transfiguration, of a loving reidentification to an Emperor or a Guide. It is for this reason that Michelet condemns the regicide: "Royalty [. . .] had just resurrected by the force of pity and the virtue of blood [. . .] Louis XVI, by perishing, gave strength to the monarchic religion [. . .] It was in great need of a saint, of a martyr. This worn-out institution was revived by two legends: Louis XVI's sanctity and Napoleon's glory."[26]

What is the historical significance of regicide? Should we identify in it, as Kant seems to suggest, a "suicide of the State," an "abyss that swallows everything without return"?[27] Is this the birth of the Jacobin Terror? Or even that of the "nihilistic revolutions of the 20th century," as Camus affirms? The trial of Louis XVI had nothing to do with the expeditious practices of the future Revolutionary Tribunal or any other justice of exception. Not only had the ex-king not been forced to "confess his crimes," but he had the possibility of defending himself and even had competent and faithful lawyers: so many rights that were not granted to the victims of persecution. From this point of view, the trial of the king is the antithesis of the Terror. However, this was only possible because the Convention finally embraced the theses of the Girondins. If it had adopted those of the Jacobins, no trial would have taken place. On this occasion, Robespierre and Saint-Just expressed their conception of the Enemy of the People publicly, and the name of "Louis Capet" was only the first in a long list of enemies to be put down. The traits they attributed to the king — his foreignness, extimacy, and duplicity — would soon be conferred on the "suspects" and "counterrevolutionaries" they would send to the guillotine.

From this point of view, the trial of Louis XVI is indeed the matrix of the Terror. Kant is not wrong to see in it a juridical fiction in which the decision to eliminate an enemy is hidden behind the appearance of a legal procedure, as will be the case during the trials of Hébert and Danton, or the Moscow trials.

If Saint-Just opposes the trial of the former king, it is because he considers him a "foreign enemy." He nevertheless designates him as a stranger among us, as if he recognizes that the deposed monarch remains intimately linked to those who reject him and kill him. It is precisely his "extimate" position — that of the remainder of the Great Body — that makes him an *enemy from within* and makes him so dangerous. This character will be attributed thereafter to all the suspects, denounced as a threat of external origin (the "conspiracy of the foreigner") that penetrates "in the guts of the Republic." For the Jacobins, the king is guilty simply by the fact of having reigned, for royalty is an "eternal crime." His acts or qualities do not count: He is and remains a monster whatever he may do. This is why Saint-Just insists on his "falseness," his "appearance of goodness" masking his "hidden malignity": There is such a gap between the reality of his actions and his evil nature that the Enemy can only be a dissimulator, a hypocrite. The passion to unmask the Jacobins, their doggedness against hypocrisy, has sometimes been explained by invoking their "despotic moralism," their virtuous will to discover, behind the visible appearance of actions, their secret moral intention.[28] It seems to me that such an attitude has first of all, a political, or rather theological-political, meaning. Indeed, it comes from their representation of the sovereign Body: The *duplicity* that they attribute to Louis XVI is rooted in the figuration of the *double body* of the Sovereign with which they did not break. Just as classical doctrine distinguished from the person of the king his mystical Body that "cannot do wrong," they denounce his hidden principle, behind his concrete acts, which *can only* do wrong. The same scheme is maintained through an inversion of meaning, a disfigurement that transforms the Mystical Body into a diabolic Anti-Body. It is the same duplicity that the Jacobins will find in all the successive figures of the Enemy, thus reviving an essential motif of past persecutions. Associated with the schemes of conspiracy and the stranger from within, this scheme will be particularly effective when it will be a question of indicting the "ultra-revolutionaries," then Danton and his supporters. Exagérés or Indulgents, the two seemingly opposed parties would, in fact, belong to the same conspiracy and pretend to fight each other to better deceive the patriots. "All the conspiracies are united," says Saint-Just in his *Report on the Factions of the Stranger*: "it is the stranger who stirs up these factions, who makes them tear each other apart [. . .] to deceive the observant eye of popular justice." And Robespierre escalates: "some skilful leaders make the machine move and remain silent, hidden backstage [. . .] but they are always the same actors with a different mask [. . .] two kinds of factions directed by the stranger party."²⁹ Prosecutor Vichinsky spoke similarly when he accused in 1936 the so-called "bloc of Trotskyites and rightists" of being a "nest of spies" and "agents of imperialism."

The witch hunt has shown us what happens when a persecution apparatus attacks a *hidden enemy* under the cloak of the Good, like the devil under the mask of God. Since there is no longer any way to distinguish friend from foe, the persecution runs amok, and its target expands indefinitely. All women are witches; the whole city of Arras is Waldensian; anyone can be accused and condemned. As chance would have it, it was in this same town of Arras, where one of the most ferocious persecutions of "witches" that France had ever known had taken place, that the man who was to preside over the Terror would be born three centuries later . . . For the witch-hunters, the witches concealed their submission to Satan under the guise of piety; for Robespierre and his followers, the enemies of the Republic hid behind the mask of republican virtue. According to this view, every citizen is virtually a suspect, and every suspect is already guilty. In the first months of the Republic, however, it was a matter of fighting real enemies (the royalists of the Vendée and the Chouans, the federalist insurrections, the foreign armies). This way of determining the enemy changed when the Terror was put "on the agenda" in September 1793. In the wake of this, the Convention adopted a law on suspects, and, a few days later, Saint-Just declared to the Committee of Public Safety that it was necessary to "punish not only the traitors, but even the indifferent [. . .] whoever is passive in the Republic and does nothing for it," because "all that is outside the sovereign is an enemy."³⁰ Soon, it will be not only the indifferent, but also the most intransigent revolutionaries, Enragés and Hébertistes, who will be accused of being "foreign agents" and sent to the scaffold. The Committee of Public Safety now attacked the radical tendencies of the revolutionary movement by trying to subdue the Sans-Culotte sections and by having their leaders arrested and executed. By changing its target, the Jacobin Terror changed its meaning, or rather it revealed its true face, that of an apparatus of persecution that, like the witch hunt in the past, responded to the uprising of a multitude in order to defend the sovereignty of the State.

Throughout this process, the real enemy has given way to an absolute enemy, omnipresent, elusive, who constantly reappears under new masks. The logic of political action is replaced with that of war, of a war without mercy and without end. Robespierre can indeed assert that "the Terror is nothing other than justice [. . .] [I]t is less a particular principle than a consequence of the general principle of democracy."³¹ This is to recognize that it has ceased to be an exceptional measure, necessarily temporary, limited violence put in the service of a policy, to become the very essence of the regime. The consequences of this turn of events were felt in the spring of 1794: While the number of arrests and executions increased rapidly, a new law on suspects was adopted in June, depriving the accused of their last legal guarantees. As in the days of the witch hunt, it authorized indictment on the basis of a simple denunciation, abolished the assistance of a lawyer, and made it optional to hear witnesses. Set in place "to punish the enemies of the people," the new Revolutionary Tribunal rendered judgments without appeal and pronounced only one punishment: death. The way was clear for an unlimited terror, which only the fall of Robespierre would avoid. Who were these suspects, most of whom ended up on the scaffold? Archives tell us the reasons for their indictment. Among them were declared opponents, but also the parents or relatives of other suspects: the mother of a refractory priest, the wife of an Englishman ("incorrigible race which will never love the Revolution"); indifferents ("never liked the Revolution since he did nothing for it"); paupers ("without estate, without confession, consequently suspect"); as well as those libertines whom Saint-Just hates so much ("he liked his pleasure and that's all"); and, more generally, the possible authors of a future crime ("his arrest must be based, if not on the evil he did, at least on the one he could do").[32]

If we were to consider only this aspect of persecution, we would undoubtedly miss a fundamental dimension of the Terror. Although the relatives of the suspects were themselves suspects, although the aristocrats were "naturally" suspects, the crimes of which the Suspect or the Enemy of the People were accused remained voluntary crimes, those of a man who had freely devoted himself to evil. Of course, confessions extracted by torture do not belong to the Jacobin apparatus of Terror, nor do the "bursting torments" of the Old Regime justice, to which the guillotine — a "machinery of quick and discreet deaths" (Foucault) — is now preferred. The Terror nevertheless retained the judicial form of the trial and that of public execution that had once characterized the persecution of heretics and witches. It has not totally given up the old theatrical ritual where the sovereign exhibition of death is staged. This distinguishes it from the terrors to come, where mass murder will be carried out in secret. If there is a judgment, it is because there is a fault: It is the free act of a faulty conscience that must be punished, and not an evil nature that must be annihilated. This persecution apparatus therefore belongs to the position that I have called Augustinian and not to the Manichean position. At least this is the case of the hunt for suspects that was unleashed in 1793–94. Another dimension of Jacobin ideology is manifested when it is a question of the "foreign enemy," in particular the English and the inexpiable struggle to be waged against them. As Barère proclaims, "it is a people foreign to Europe, stranger to humanity: it is necessary that they disappear." "It is necessary," he adds, "that the young republicans draw the hatred of the name 'English' with the milk of the nurses [. . .] This tradition of hatred must become national."[33]

This conception of the enemy as a monster to be annihilated would be concretely implemented in the Vendée. The policy of the Convention was in line with the logic of war as long as it was a matter of military repression of an armed insurrection. This all changed after the defeat of the insurgents, crushed at Savenay in December 1793: Although there was no longer any danger to the Republic, this strategic and limited violence gave way to unlimited violence. Between January and May 1794, the "infernal columns" of General Turreau roamed the region massacring the population, including women and children, without sparing the Vendeans who had supported the Republic. "I know that there may be some patriots in this country," one of Turreau's deputies declared to his troops, "it's all the same, we must sacrifice everything." A soldier of the republican army would bear witness to the carnage by evoking "the old men immolated in front of their children, the women, the girls raped on the chest of their fathers, their husbands mercilessly sacrificed, the children massacred, thrown into the furnaces, carried at the end of the bayonets, the fire, the fire devouring everything."[34] Here, the persecution apparatus has become an extermination apparatus. Historians are still debating to what extent and at what level this carnage was decided and planned. In any case, it was preceded by an intense campaign of incitement to hatred in which the Jacobin leaders explicitly equated all the Vendeans with an enemy "race." In October 1793, Barère argued against all evidence that "the entire population of the revolted country is in armed rebellion" and called for "exterminating this rebellious race." In a letter sent to the Committee of Public Safety, the representative in mission Carrier — who distinguished himself in Nantes by organizing "republican baptisms," that is, collective drownings of suspects — proclaimed that it was necessary to put to death in the Vendée "all the individuals of both sexes who will be found there, indiscriminately,' because it was a 'spawn'" from which "it is absolutely necessary to purge the ground." While commanding the infernal columns, Turreau was closely supervised by two other representatives on mission, Hentz and Francastel, and they wrote to the Committee that "the race of men who live in the Vendée is bad" and that it was therefore necessary to "depopulate" this region in order to "repopulate it with republicans."[35] Turreau himself explicitly declares that "it is necessary to exterminate all the men who have taken up arms, and to strike with them their fathers, their wives, their sisters and their children. The Vendée must be a great national cemetery."[36] Of course, he would later say that he had only obeyed orders: "As for my instructions, I drew them from several decrees of the Convention, various rulings of the Committees of government and those of the Representatives on mission in the West."[37] His deeds in the Vendée earned him the right to have his name inscribed on the Arc de Triomphe among those of the heroes of the Homeland . . . Although it was regularly informed of the situation by the reports of its emissaries, the Committee of Public Safety allowed these atrocities to continue until Turreau's recall to Paris in May. The civil war and the campaign of extermination that followed it caused the "Département-Vengé" to lose nearly a quarter of its population in a few months, half in some cantons.

In a way, this persecution apparatus is not different from those that at the same time hit suspects throughout France: The massacres of the Vendée are also the work of the Great Terror. They differ, however, in one crucial respect. The real enemy was also replaced by an absolute enemy, but it was no longer as a suspect that he was defined. It is by his belonging to an "evil race" that he must be annihilated. Can we define, "anachronistically," the results of the policy applied in the Vendée in 1794 as genocide? To be sure, the Vendeans do not constitute a *genos*, an ethnically homogeneous group, but they were designated and treated as such by the exterminators. To characterize this policy, a contemporary writer coined the term "populicide." This term, which qualifies, independently of any ethnic criterion, as the "system of general extermination" of a population, could be appropriate to designate the policy of terror in the Vendée. The person who coined it was not a royalist pamphleteer, but an uncompromising revolutionary who would pay with his life for his allegiance to the ideals of equality and emancipation, the author of the *Manifesto of the Plebeians*, one of the fathers of modern communism, Babeuf. He was convinced that Carrier and Turreau, carried away by the "dazzling delirium of an unlimited domination," were in fact, only a "subordinate spring," an "exterminating cog" that received its impulse from "the center of the political machine."[38] What outraged him the most was that an entire population was attacked indiscriminately, as if he had noticed that the Terror had now changed its meaning; that it had ceased to target insurgents and political opponents to attack all the members of a cursed "race." With this "system of depopulation," "rebels and faithful, everything is fit for destruction [. . .] 'I am a patriot, and I will prove it to you,' said a poor honest Vendean. Too bad, replied a tricolor brigandine [. . .] 'You live in a cursed land, you will die.'"[39] Babeuf's indignation was not heard: Even now, it is very difficult in France to acknowledge this dimension of the Terror in the Vendée. It remains an unthought of our national memory, a *crypt* of the Republic, and its concealment still prevents us from understanding how, in the revolutionary process, persecutory hatred was unleashed in its most extreme form.

This conversion of an apparatus of political terror into an apparatus of extermination should come as no surprise. We know from the analysis of the witch hunt that the persecution schemes that guide these apparatuses are inspired by both the Augustinian and the Manichean positions. This leads them to represent the Enemy as containing both a guilty freedom, but also as an evil nature, a contagious, hereditary evil, which destines to death races of darkness. When persecution escalates, the two modes of apparatus — judicial and exterminating — and the two styles of terror — political and "racial" — are brought closer to each other, until they merge. This fusion already characterized the witch hunt, when it was directed against "races of smoke." We find it again at the zenith of the Terror, and it will reappear during the Stalinist purges, when the families of the "enemies of the people" will be deported and murdered. However, if the judicial terror fits easily into the Jacobin power apparatus, the same cannot be said of the exterminating terror. Nothing in the heritage of the Enlightenment and the ideals of the French Revolution justifies the project of annihilating a wicked "spawn," different by nature from other men. Here, the persecution scheme that orients the apparatus is at odds with the Idea of the Republic. In this kind of conflict, it is always the scheme that prevails over the Idea: for it draws its strength from elementary affects and phantasms that are rooted in the very depths of our flesh.

By attempting to refound sovereign power on a State Terror and by completing the secularization of the Enemy, the Jacobins accomplished Bodin's program. The results were remarkable: Their hunt for suspects and counter-revolutionaries was more deadly in a few months than three centuries of witch hunts throughout Europe.[40] Indeed, they gave the persecution apparatus the resources of a modern centralized state that the inquisitors and judges of past centuries lacked. The twentieth century would do even better. In reality, it is not only the persecution policy of the *Demon-Mania* that they have reactivated, but also the schemes and phantasms that underlie it. The proclamation of the Terror was indeed accompanied by a significant transformation of the Jacobins' discourse, where bodily metaphors became more and more insistent. They surfaced in the prose of Barère, who described the Vendée as "a canker that devours the heart of the Republic"; they blossomed in the work of one of their main leaders, Billaud-Varenne. Entrusted with the task of justifying the concentration of power in the hands of the Committee of Public Safety, he addressed the Convention in these terms: "It is time to give back to the body politic a robust health at the expense of the gangrenous limbs," because "the limbs want to act without the direction of the head" and sink the body into chaos.[41] A fragmented body, struggling against itself, where everything that escapes the authority of the Center "becomes exuberant, par-

asitic, without unity"; where the head must withdraw from the body and fight
"on all sides" the "dangerous coalition" of its limbs. Onto this head without
body, or that is attacking its own body, is superimposed the opposite image of
a body without a head, of the deformed body of the defeated monarchy that
continues to threaten the Republic: "We have decreed the Republic and we
are still organized in monarchy. The head of the monster is cut down, but the
trunk still survives with its defective forms." It seems as if we are witnessing
the conflict of two mystical Bodies, where the Body of the Republic is battling
with an Anti-Body. It becomes clear that, for the Jacobins, the Revolution
has accomplished only a partial, unfinished transfer of sovereignty, where the
Corpus mysticum survives the abolition of the monarchy and even the death of
the king. The opposition between the head of the State and the Body politic
has yet another meaning. These "gangrenous limbs," these "diseased organs,"
are also the most radical of the Sans-Culottes, who begin to challenge the
"tyranny" of the Jacobins and demand that all power be given to the sections
and the popular societies. When all is said and done, the rebellious body that
needs to be tamed is that of the people, whom Billaud-Varenne considers to
be an amorphous and unstable mass. This leads him to praise the Chief, the
only one capable of gathering the popular "herd": "With a leader, the people
are capable of the greatest efforts; if they lose him, they are nothing more than
a herd, that a nothing frightens and scatters in an instant."[42] This surprising
admission reveals the secret spirit of the Jacobins' politics: Behind the cult
of the Sovereign People, a bottomless contempt for the real people, to whom
they deny any consistency of their own, any capacity to unite and to act by
themselves. By instituting the Terror, they give themselves the means to put
an end to the democracy of the multitudes, and it is an incorporation scheme
that authorizes them to crush it.

In reasserting the unity of the sovereign principle — "the body politic, like
the human body, becomes a monster if it has several heads" — and the hierarchy of its organs — "you are," he wrote to the supervisory committees, "like the
hands of the body politic of which the Convention is the head and of which
we are the eyes" — Billaud-Varenne was following a tradition that goes back
to the Greeks. Nevertheless, he was to inflect it on a decisive point, since this
One-Body appears to him to be in conflict with another body that penetrates
and ravages it from within. If he takes up the classical doctrine of the *Corpus mysticum*, he nevertheless deviates from it on this point: In the Ancien
Régime, the perpetuity of sovereign power was guaranteed by the hereditary
succession of monarchs. For Billaud-Varenne, the immortal body of the Republic can only perpetuate itself through the Terror, by constantly regenerat-
ing itself through the amputation of the "gangrene" that eats away at it: "the

only plan that can ensure the indestructible duration of the Republic is the one that attacks, at the same time, the waywardness of the mind and the heart; it is the political gangrene that must be extirpated down to the smallest ramifications."[43] He goes so far as to compare the Terror to the magician Medea, "who, in order to give youth back to the old Aeson, needs to dismember his worn-out body before throwing it back into the melt."[44] What must give to the Republic its "indestructible" character is thus its capacity to designate and to annihilate the Enemy, the always reiterated destruction of the heterogeneous elements that "similar to the heads of the hydra are reborn unceasingly from their trunk." Thus, the Enemy constantly reappears, gangrene spreads, and it becomes impossible to circumscribe it, to distinguish the sick member from the healthy parts: The remainder comes to be confused with the whole body. Amputations, butcherings, dismemberments . . . The image of the body that runs through these texts is that of a body beset by disfigured figurations of the remainder that it strives to expel relentlessly, of a body incapable of dissociating itself from the Anti-Body that invades it in order to destroy it. We can easily see that those who are obsessed by such phantasms call for terror, for a persecutory violence that would finally deliver them from the "monsters" that haunt them. When they call for the extirpation of the gangrene that eats away at the Great Body, it is the remainder of their flesh that they wish to annihilate. Any extermination is always also a self-destruction.

These are not (or not only) pathological obsessions, but patterns of incorporation that structure a vision of the world and mobilize affects in the service of a policy of persecution. These are the schemes that, by being inscribed into apparatuses, are expressed concretely in 1793–94 by the extreme centralization of power and the intensification of the Terror. We have seen that the extermination of "witches" was, in Bodin's view, part of a politics of the body, of the representation of a collective Body, the Body of the Sovereign, from which it was important to cut off the sick members "by applying cauteries and hot irons." The reappearance of these motifs in the Jacobin discourse attests to the persistence of these embodiment schemes. It is the expression of a new politics of the body, of a politics aiming at reconstituting a sovereign Body, at refounding and consolidating it through the Terror. Lefort, seeking to locate the historical conditions of the "democratic invention" and those of the totalitarianisms of the twentieth century, placed great emphasis on the representations of the body that they convey. The modern democracy is characterized, according to him, by a dynamic of disembodiment of the social, initiated by the major act of the French Revolution, the regicide: "when the body of the king is destroyed, when the head of the political body falls [. . .] by the same token the corporality of the social dissolves." The power ceases to be embod-

ied, to be identified with a body, to appear henceforth as an "empty place" that
no one can occupy in a natural and permanent way. Its disembodiment entails
that of the civil society, its "release out of a State until then consubstantial to
the body of the king," and that of the individuals who cease to identify themselves as members of the Great Body.[45] The Stalinist and Nazi totalitarianisms
can then be understood as attempts to *rebuild the body*, "from democracy and
against it," to reinvest the empty place of power and to reembody the social by
absorbing it in the One-Body of the Party and its Guide.

The time has come to question Lefort's analysis. If it is true that democratic
revolutions engage a process of disembodiment, why do the old schemes of
the Body politic immediately reappear in the discourse and the imagination
of the Jacobins? With the Revolution and the regicide, are we witnessing the
advent of a disembodied society, finally delivered from the ancient spell that
subjugated people to the body of the sovereign? It is, rather, necessary to admit that the revolutionary process implies a *transfer of corporality* where the
"regenerated" Body of the Republic takes the place of the old *Corpus mysticum*. If there is a disembodiment of the political Body, it remains partial and
is accompanied by an inverse movement of *reembodiment* that takes a par-
oxysmal form during the Terror. This double movement of disembodiment-
reembodiment is neither a passing phase nor a simple survival of the Ancien
Régime. It continues to cross our State democracies, where democratic disembodiment remains unfinished and precarious, and reembodiment tendencies
have manifested themselves throughout the twentieth century in authoritarian and persecutory forms. And there is every reason to believe that they will
continue to do so on the occasion of the crisis of sovereignty that is affecting
Nation-States today. Only a democracy of the multitudes—the one that was
outlined during the revolutions, which they have bequeathed to us as their
"lost treasure"—would succeed in radically disembodying human communities. At least if these multitudes manage to tear themselves away from the fascination of the One-Body and the apparatuses of power that sacralize it, if they
avoid letting themselves be reembodied in a system of political sovereignty,
as they have always done in the past. How can we stop sacralizing sovereign
power? How can we stop identifying with the Chief, at the head of a Great
Body, oscillating between love and hate toward him? The French Revolution
gives us elements of an answer: As the trial of the king shows, a dispute opposes those who try to desacralize politics, to remove it from these ambivalent
identifications that alienate the multitudes from a sovereign figure, and those
who remain captive of such identifications. This first attempt to desacralize
sovereign power also belongs to the heritage of the Revolution.

Is it right to maintain, as Lefort does, that the disembodiment of the political body begins with the French Revolution? If we take the historical processes back to the elementary phenomena that are their immanent condition, it appears that this double movement of disembodiment and reembodiment finds its origin in the life of singular bodies. It is there that these phenomena of disfiguration and transfiguration, of exclusion and rejection of the remainder that are translated in various ways in the historical communities, begin. In other words, the tendency to disembody is not only a Western and modern phenomenon but runs through all collective bodies as an ever-present possibility. The Church and the monarchical State have tried to resist it with rites of reembodiment and doctrines such as those of the Real Presence or the Two Bodies of the King. When these rituals and schemes no longer serve their purpose, exclusion and persecution apparatuses take over by stigmatizing or expelling, or even exterminating, the heterogeneous elements of the Great Body. The revolutions of modern times do not therefore innovate as much as one might think: They accentuate a dynamic of disembodiment-reembodiment that has been going on for centuries in the West, with its phases of integration and pacification followed by phases of exclusion and terror. They nevertheless mark a historical break. Since the English Revolution, the rebellion of the multitudes has found spaces of action where it can deploy itself, create counterapparatuses, try to concretize its schemes of emancipation, the utopia of an "upside-down world," of a community disembodied from the Great Body, disidentified from all the figures of the Sovereign, delivered from injustice, from inequality, from voluntary servitude. But we now know that, after having broken the chains of their former servitude, these multitudes must confront other adversaries, the new power apparatuses stemming from the revolution and sometimes from their own ranks. Apparatuses that try to divert them from their emancipation project, to harness their affects of anger, revolt, hope, to make them turn to hatred, to subject them to a politics of terror.

More radically than the English and American Revolutions, the French Revolution experienced the political foundation, its ambiguous and conflicting relation to the social question, the limits of representative democracy, the resources and the aporias of the democracy of the multitudes. This experience has taught us that the embodiment schemes that structure the political Body survive the regime change and that they can always resurface by favoring the reconstitution of persecution apparatuses. No one understood this better than Quinet. He understood that the Jacobin Terror is a legacy of the Ancien Régime; that this legacy of absolute monarchy is invested in a pervasive image of the body; that regicide brings it back in a spectral form, that of a *phantom limb*: "What happens to a man whose limb has been amputated happened to the French; he still feels it with every movement. France felt in all things the royalty long after it had been cut off. From then on [. . .] the political soul of the Ancien Régime seemed to live again in them" and "they were getting ready to exterminate each other to reach this phantom of reborn royalty that one felt in the depths of souls."[46] What Billaud-Varenne apprehended as a *real* threat — the intrusion of the old monarchical Body in the regenerated Body of the Republic — Quinet envisages it as a *phantasm*: the afterlife of an old embodiment scheme in a society worked by disembodiment. But a phantasm can produce real effects if it is invested in a power apparatus. Such is the case of the Jacobin terror, of all the terror apparatuses of our time: So many spectral survivals, afterlives of a Great Body that hinder the process of democratic disembodiment, tend to resacralize and reembody the political through the persecution of a remainder.

To this striking intuition of Quinet there is nothing to add. Except that this reembodiment by the Terror is not the fatal outcome of a democratic revolution; that it is possible, as the struggle of Condorcet and the Girondins testifies, to admit the desacralization of politics without immediately seeking to reconstitute a new sovereign Body; to invent new forms of political thought and action without giving in to the phantasm of unmasking a hidden enemy. The Republic must be grounded not on Terror but on the authority of the law and the equality of citizens. The Girondins, however, lost interest in the social question. They turned away from the popular societies and the Sans-Culottes sections and let them ally themselves with the Jacobins, without realizing that the spaces of freedom they had opened also participated in the foundation of a Republic. Even though they ultimately had a common enemy — the "political machine" of the Jacobins — the Girondins' fight against authoritarian centralization and the resacralization of power failed to join that of the Enragés and the radical Sans-Culottes. This failed encounter between the proponents of a desacralized politics and the democracy of the multitudes, this conjunction that has never yet taken place, this improbable alliance of Condorcet and Babeuf, remains the stake of all emancipation politics, its "lost treasure" and its horizon of hope.

Conclusion

The Truth Will Set You Free

Come; the destroyed prison abolishes Gehenna! [. . .] / The archangel
rises and the devil falls; / And I blot out the sinister night, and nothing
remains of it; / Satan is dead; be reborn, O heavenly Lucifer!

It is with these verses that Victor Hugo's *The End of Satan* closes, a long
unfinished poem in which he wanted to embrace the whole history of Creation, from the Fall of the Devil, the Flood, and the death of Christ to the
French Revolution. When Lucifer is thrown into hell by the wrath of God,
"a feather escaped from the wing of the archangel" rests on the edge of the
abyss. It will give birth to the Angel Liberty, who, at the time of the storming
of the Bastille, will descend to the depths of hell in order to liberate the devil
from the hatred that consumes him and to bring him God's forgiveness . . .
An epic fresco that intends to celebrate the advent of a new era where, guided
by France, humanity would finally be freed from evil. The poet recovers here
the old doctrine of the *apocatastasis*, of the final reconciliation of Satan with
God, condemned by the Church in the sixth century. By associating, in his
inimitable style, the Passion of Christ and the storming of the Bastille, Hugo
shows that he had seen the deep continuity of what I have called the Western utopia. From the Good News announcing that there is "neither Jew nor
Greek" and that "nothing is in itself impure," to the Declaration of Human
Rights, it is the same emancipatory project, the same aim of a universal community that crosses the entire history of the West. No doubt it has become
difficult for us to share Hugo's enthusiasm and his faith in Progress. Hegel had
already sensed it while meditating on the Terror, and the bloody history of the
twentieth century confirmed it: This universal emancipation project does not

only come up against external obstacles. Indeed, it is its own dynamics that leads it to betray its Idea, to realize itself "as the opposite of itself," through a series of catastrophic reversals. The creation of the Inquisition by the medieval Church, followed by the extermination of lepers and the witch hunt, is one of those moments in which the Christian message is inverted into its opposite. In the same way that the Terror marks a point of inversion of the revolutionary project of modern times. If the West, throughout its history, oscillates between phases of inclusion and exclusion, of pacifying reconciliation and persecuting violence, it is because its project is grounded, as we have said, on a denial of the remainder: on the illusion of a radical catharsis, of an irreversible trans-figuration that would manage to absorb it completely, in that morning light where the "sinister night" dissipates forever, where *none of it remains*.

By refusing to recognize the persistence of a remainder and its ambivalence, by dissociating in an increasingly clear-cut manner its abject and sublime figures — by transforming the archangel Lucifer into Satan — the dominant theologico-political configuration in the West has favored the demonization of victims, the designation of absolute enemies condemned to extermination. We do not see this as a sinister fate that characterizes only Western society. The succession of phases of integration, exclusion, and persecution that punctuate our history is one manifestation among others of elementary phenomena that appear in different forms in all human societies. It is always a question of the same phenomena of projection, ambivalence, and division, of the same phantasms, of the same corporal figurations of the remainder; because they are rooted in our primordial flesh, in its incessant oscillations between incorporation and disincorporation, disfiguration and transfiguration. It is so with all the affects that these fluctuations generate, anguish, love, disgust, and also hatred; these affects more powerful than the Ideas, which arise without reason, "flourish because they flourish." In each of these affects, our immanent life affects itself, and hatred is no exception. Although no "cause" in the world permits explanation, its emergence obeys certain rules, is based on a logic that I have tried to render. Like the other affects, it manifests itself in history through the intermediary of schemes that give it concrete targets, harness it in apparatuses where it invests its destructive charge. Thus, we don't only have to fight Ideas, or even to resist affects: We have to deal with sedimented and yet mobile schemes, at the same time prevalent and plastic, which persist through the centuries. The reminiscence of the persecution schemes founds a tradition of hatred, a tradition of persecutors, capable of being transmitted from one epoch to another by propagating the same accusations and by provoking each time new massacres. When they seize these schemes, the persecution apparatuses manage to mobilize the indignation, the anger, the desire of vengeance of the multitudes to change them into hatred. This allows them to divert their revolt from a real enemy to a demonized Absolute Enemy. By provoking in its victims the desire to take revenge in their turn, hatred becomes contagious and endlessly grows. The French Revolution has shown us that these schemes and apparatuses can be grafted onto a project of emancipation, turning it against itself, dragging it into a mortifying escalation where it ends up betraying itself and losing itself. If the name of Satan can designate the mysterious focus of primordial hatred, we would be tempted to agree with the Council of Constantinople, which, in rejecting the doctrine of apocatastasis, recognized that this hatred could never be entirely eradicated.

It may be futile to claim to draw "lessons" from history, a history punctuated by unpredictable events that thwart all calculations and escape all grasp. At least this investigation will have allowed us to identify certain features of the phenomena of persecution and to better define the field of possibilities. We now know that resistance is possible; that it is more originary than the power apparatuses that only ever resist it; and the simple fact that there is resistance is enough to foil them. Of course, the end of the witch hunt was only a temporary truce that allowed the apparatuses to reconfigure themselves by changing their style and targets: In the long run, exclusions and persecutions have never ceased. And yet, the courage of these thinkers, jurists, priests, and physicians who risked their lives to denounce the persecution, the courage of the anonymous victims who refused to confess their "crimes" under torture and to accuse their loved ones, all this cumulative resistance finally disarmed the executioners and extinguished the flame of the stake. Desperate as their resistance may seem, it is a testament to the fact that there are men and woman who are capable of overcoming submission and fear, of breaking free from the grip of the apparatuses, and sometimes of speaking out and bearing witness. The stories of Junius, Spee, and Bukharin have shown us the power of such a word; for they testified for all those stifled voices whose testimony no one could gather. By bearing witness to the truth, they have revealed the lie of the apparatuses, that countertruth that strives to annihilate everything that could refute it.

We have also learned from our investigation that the passage from exclusion to persecution is not inevitable. The history of the lepers of the Middle Ages has shown us that the phenomena of persecution *are not originary*. An explosion of hatred, however murderous, is not enough to trigger persecution: For this to happen, this affect has to be harnessed by a specific apparatus that integrates it into a strategy of power. The formation of such an apparatus presupposes a random conjunction of heterogeneous factors. The phases of persecution are almost always preceded by phases of exclusion, stigmatization, expulsion, or confinement. It is the failure of this strategy of exclusion, incapable of resisting the contagion of the remainder, that leads to the appearance of persecution apparatuses. When no exclusion phase precedes them, as in the case of the witch hunt, these apparatuses take over from previous persecution apparatuses by simply displacing their target. If it is true that hatred is not present from the outset, this also means — and Arendt knew this — that not every political foundation necessarily calls for terror.

Since the passage to persecution brings about a mutation of affects and apparatuses, it must be possible to act on them in order to interrupt this mutation. This is what Danton had tried without success, by creating the Revolutionary Tribunal in the hope of appeasing the people's vengeance. What Bernard of Clairvaux had succeeded in doing at the time of the Crusades, by facing up to the persecutors and declaring that the Jews are "the flesh and bones of Jesus Christ." Indeed, if it is particularly difficult to deconstruct schemes that have been sedimented for centuries, it is possible, on the other hand, to act on the affects that they harness and the mechanisms in which they are inscribed. Like Bernard, it is also possible to mobilize the resources of faith or those of political action to prevent these mechanisms from inciting hatred. The disasters of the twentieth century were the occasion to invent counterapparatuses, to implement procedures of reconciliation and forgiveness, a work of mourning, of memory, and of education intended to counter the return of hate. Notwithstanding those who denigrate the rule of law and value the state of exception, among these safeguards, the use of the law is one of the most effective. The institution of a tribunal is required, as Aeschylus already knew, to appease the vengeful rage of the Erinyes. And if it was a new judicial procedure that led to the creation of the Inquisition and the rise of the witch hunt, if the latter was conducted most often by judges, it was also magistrates who prevented it from spreading in France: By opposing Bodin's attempt to massively repress the "capital enemy"; by overturning the death sentences that were aimed at so-called witches; and, finally, by inciting Louis XIV to decriminalize witchcraft. Nevertheless, it must be recognized that the authority of the law and the rule of law often seem powerless in the face of the desire for terror that finds its source in the passions of the multitudes. Perhaps it is impossible to defuse it without acting against all forms of injustice that give hatred an opportunity to manifest itself. This fight for a more just society remains insufficient, however, as long as it does not question the very principle of sovereign power. It is not sovereignty as such, as we have seen, but its crisis that favors the designation of an absolute enemy and its extermination through terror. The fact remains that the principle of sovereignty implies a more or less intense cleavage between the transfigured figure of the Leader and the disfigured figure of his Enemy. It is a deconstruction of sovereignty that it is a question of undertaking, a "perhaps unending" task that requires accomplishing at the same time the disidentification of the subjects alienated to the sovereign figures, their disincorporation of the Great Body and this de-sacralization of the political that we have seen beginning during the Revolution. Only a *disenchanted* politics would be able to neutralize the ambivalent affects that the exercise of sovereign power elicits. This "normalization" of politics, this neutralization of passions and antagonisms, however, comes at a very heavy price. If they are not combined with the struggle against injustice, they risk awakening the rage of the excluded, which can be harnessed by apparatuses of terror. This is the challenge that modern democracy is facing today.

Why are the dynamics of disembodiment and desacralization shaping contemporary societies unable to prevent the resurgence of hatred, the reactivation of old persecution schemes (such as the conspiracy scheme), the reappearance of terror apparatuses exemplified by the totalitarian movements of the twentieth century or by Islamic terrorism today? Nothing in the world seems capable of averting the return of hatred, because it does not find its source on this level: The events of the world are never for it more than "occasional causes," pretexts that allow it to be unleashed. To understand persecution phenomena, we must not only have recourse to a historical genealogy: It is to this end that I appeal to egoanalysis. What does it teach us about hatred? First of all, that this primordial affect *is not originary*, that it comes from the disfiguration of the remainder, just as desire and love come from its transfiguration. The principle of evil is not itself an evil: Neither object of hate nor object of love, it is a neutral element, an intimate stranger that protects me from the abyss of *aphanisis*. It should therefore be possible to reconnect, beyond projections and disfigurations, with the initial neutrality of the remainder. But how can this be achieved, as long as the cycle of disfigurations and transfigurations continues? If, as Freud affirms, "we don't know how to renounce anything," at the very least would it be possible to "exchange one thing for another"; to *sublimate hatred*, to turn it against itself by giving it another goal than aggression and destruction? We may doubt it: Because what could be true for a "death-drive," an undifferentiated aggressiveness aiming at no particular object, is not true for hatred, which is indissociable from its object-of-hate, from this irreducible object-X, this *dia-bolos* that is the remainder. The possibility of a sublimation of hatred, of its transmigration beyond flesh and bodies, beyond the phantasm, on an incorporeal surface where it becomes a verb and a symbol, this possibility still remains enigmatic.

If hatred is not the expression of a death-drive, it is because such a drive does not exist: All our affects, all our drives, are our life's self-affectations. But life, by affecting itself, can also blind itself to itself, turn against itself and strive to destroy itself. At the root of hatred, we discover an illusion where our living ego does not recognize a part of itself as its own flesh, dissociates itself from it and rejects it outward. This excluded element becomes the target of our affective projections, the diabolical or sublime X-object that awakens our hatred or our love. It is in this sense that hatred is not originary: It is not rooted in an evil nature or a destructive drive but is based on a self-blindness in which the remainder disfigures itself. It is very difficult to tear oneself away from an illusion that transits us in the depths of ourselves, but nothing forbids us to foresee it. What delivers us from the illusion is called *truth*. Since hatred is based on a primordial illusion, only the truth can cure us of it. This is the meaning of the words: "Then you will know the truth / and the truth will set you free."[1] As the context shows, the Nazarene is speaking to men who hate him and want to kill him. It is at this point that he speaks of Satan, "murderer from the very start," "because there is no truth in him," "a liar and the father of lies." He thus reveals that hatred finds its source in a countertruth, and the freedom of which he speaks is one with this truth that delivers from hatred. At least if it is coupled with the demand for justice: Without justice, truth is powerless; but without truth, the revolt against injustice is blind and risks being sidetracked into vengeance and hatred.

To overcome hatred, truth is needed. The truth of the remainder must be revealed to me so that I can recognize it as the flesh of my flesh, my doomed part, my obscure Background, at once different from me and identical to me. Performative truth that does not let itself be locked up in any doctrine or any statement, because it is not distinguished from its self-revelation. This truth that delivers, I proposed in *The Ego and the Flesh* to name it the *instasis*. I thus designate a possible reconciliation of the self and the remainder, where the ego would finally recognize it as a part of its flesh, where it could identify itself with it without denying it or merging with it. This possibility, each time singular, is offered to each of us as a horizon of hope. If it can happen in the individual existence, would it be impossible on the level of the collective existence? Even if the latter remains deprived of any anchorage in a flesh chiasm, even if the flesh of the community is only an unstable and precarious quasi-flesh, woven of phantasms and exposed to the disaster, what can be written "in fine print" in each existence must also be able to be written "in large print" in human history. Nothing forbids us to hope that hell — the eternal return of hatred — can be overcome. But this messianic promise must be inscribed in history as the utopia of a community, and it must be a reparation, a resurrection: the time of a *yizkor*, of a reminder of the names, of all the names of the defeated, of the victims. Only in this way will it be possible, as Walter Benjamin wrote, to "free the future from everything that today disfigures it."

Afterword to J. Rogozinski's *The Logic of Hatred*

Carlo Ginzburg

Among the many books devoted to the subject of witch-hunting, *The Logic of Hatred* stands out for its originality. Its author, Jacob Rogozinski, is a philosopher: His in-depth examination of the evidence involves a dialogue, not devoid of polemical elements, with historians who have dealt with these issues. I consider it a privilege to be able to continue such a stimulating discussion.

1. "Is there a radical caesura between the witch hunts and the genocides of our times?" Rogozinski asks himself in presenting his research. The negative answer to this rhetorical question is reiterated in the double, painful list of names ("In Memoriam"/"Yitzor") that closes the book. In fact, the alleged continuity with the Shoah, despite the repeated references that punctuate the narrative, is not addressed, unlike that with the Terror. And in this regard Rogozinski once again asks, "Would we, in affirming this, succumb to the cardinal sin denounced by historians, that is, anachronism?" And he answers: "A history of persecutions can only be *anachronistic*, as understood by Rancière: It takes temporal flow 'against the grain,' subtracting an event from 'its' time to reveal unexpected connections between one phenomenon and another. From this angle, witch hunts aren't only an occurrence from a foregone era. From this forgotten persecution to the ones of the twentieth century, the same horror persists; similar accusations are repeated and produce the same effects."

The repeated appearance of the term "anachronism" throughout the book shows that we are confronted with a crucial point. A clarification is necessary.

The positive role of anachronism in historical research, advocated by Jacques Rancière and other French scholars before and after him, is unacceptable, because it ignores the distinction between the anachronism of questions and the anachronism of answers. The former, as I have argued by developing a series of enlightening reflections by Marc Bloch, are, at the beginning of research, inevitable; but research allows, through a reformulation of the initial questions, to rework answers that are as nonanachronistic as possible, and that rescue the point of view of the actors.[1] In Rogozinski's research on witch hunts, the reformulation of the initial questions arising from the "genocides of our times" does not occur. The continuity between present and past is taken for granted and is not questioned. Rogozinski might object that the "anachronistic" perspective "reveals unexpected connections between one phenomenon and another." But this decontextualization seems incompatible with the strategy to which Rogozinski subscribes: that of microhistory, which uses the "estrangement" that "helps delegitimize the version of the victors by varying perspectives, by adopting 'the savage's, the peasant's, the child's, the animal's point of view.'"[2] Rogozinski focuses more on the attitudes of the persecutors than on those of the witches (an entirely legitimate choice). But to what extent is his attempt to "delegitimize the version of the victors" compatible with "anachronistic" decontextualization?

This question clarifies the implications of Rogozinski's interpretative strategy. Faced with the tension between "anachronistic" decontextualization and microhistory based on contextual analysis, Rogozinski has chosen a tool consistent with his training as a philosopher: an "anachronistic" analysis, that is, "egoanalysis."

2. In Rogozinski's narrative, the trajectory that led to the witch hunts opens with the accusations, spread in France in 1321, of a plot organized, depending on the version, (a) by lepers, (b) by lepers inspired by Jews, or (c) by lepers and Jews inspired by the kings of Granada. Regarding these accusations as the beginning of the historical trajectory leading to the witchcraft trials: Rogozinski, taking up this periodization, has developed it in a very different direction. To understand how the persecution of witches was possible, he observes, "To understand the possibility of such a reversal, it is not enough to consider the collective life, that of the species or of the 'populations': It is necessary first to examine the immanent life, the most singular life, that of the living ego. It is on this level that hatred is born; that the ego, to protect itself from the intimate foreigner who seems to threaten it, can turn against itself and desire death, its own as well as that of the foreigner in it; before directing its hatred on other men in the world. In other words, a historical genealogy of the apparatuses of power must be founded on an egoanalysis." The intricate connection between *The Logic of Hatred* and the book that preceded it, *The Ego and the Flesh: An Introduction to Egoanalysis* (2010), is very close. The point at which it first manifested itself is indicated in a section of *The Logic of Hatred* that underlines a convergence with the research on witchcraft processes I con-

ducted in the past. In *Ecstasies: Deciphering the Witches' Sabbath*, I traced the term "typological convergeance between "symbolic structures independent of the interplay of historical influences" and "primordial experiences of bodily character," a theme that is close to what is at the center of *The Ego and the Flesh*. More specifically, I spoke of the "autorepresentation" of the body, remarking, "we can consider that this one operates as a scheme, as a intermediary link of a formal character."[3] In *The Ego and the Flesh*, the Kantian term "scheme" is practically absent. It recurs instead, with great prominence, in *The Logic of Hatred*. After talking about "*scheme's work*," "scheme's *prevalence* [*prégnance*]," Rogozinski writes: "If we want to describe the logic of hatred, we must bracket our worldly existence to recapture our ego's immanent life, below any relation with others [. . .] This is where the original schemes of incorporation and disincorporation crystallize; where they take on these affects to transpose them on the plane of community and history. The analysis of this originally schematism — which is one of the tasks of the egoanalysis — allows us to answer some fundamental questions with which phenomenology has been confronted."

3. Rogozinski regarded my remark on "schemes" generating "potentially universal symbolic configurations" as a fruitful hypothesis that allowed me to overcome tensions "between microhistory and long duration, between the singularity of the experience and its universality," clarifying "several features of the myth of the Sabbath." Rogozinski reinterpreted the witchcraft trials through the idea of "originary schematism," which he regarded as one of the objectives of "egoanalysis." This partial convergence invites me to return to the "singularity of experience," a topic I have discussed in the past, criticizing the undue extension of the notion of "collective mentality." Today I would reformulate that theme on the basis of some reflections I have had on the notion of the individual.

4. I propose to define the individual as the point of intersection of a (vast, though not unlimited) series of sets. For example, I am a member of the animal species *homo sapiens*; of its masculine moiety; of the set constituted by retired professors born in Turin — and so on, modifying and specifying, until we arrive at a set, based on fingerprints, that has only one component (myself). In some contexts, the individual can be identified with his fingerprints, but for the historian, the singularity of the individual is constituted by the relationship between all these sets — generic, less generic, and so on, including the set with a single component.

All this may seem obvious: Today the notion of "one and multiple identity" is often discussed, as in the case of Edgar Morin's recent autobiography.[4] But an in-depth analysis of their relationship may have unexpected consequences.

It must be emphasized that the definition of the individual I have suggested is a far cry from the variants of "egocides" discussed, and rejected, by Rogozinski. But it is equally distant from the attempt formulated by Rogozinski to "recapture our ego's immanent life, below any relation with others": All the sets I have evoked, with the exception of that constituted by fingerprints, are characterized by some form of sharing.

The perspective explored by Rogozinski in his *The Ego and the Flesh* is situated on an ontological level. The one proposed here, which addresses the "singularity" of the individual on an epistemological level, can help the historian to connect an individual to a variety of contexts, documented or hypothetical. (I made such an experiment in the book *The Cheese and the Worms*). It is a tool that facilitates comparison.

5. *The Logic of Hatred* is a book that deals with a hotly debated topic in an original way. A proper examination of this originality would have required an expertise that I lack. I preferred to take advantage, on the one hand, of Rogozinski's emphasis on the divergence between his own perspective and that of historians, and on the other, of the stretch of road we have traveled together, to continue a discussion that will be developed, I hope, by his readers.

A Response to Carlo Ginzburg

Jacob Rogozinski

The dialogue between historians and philosophers is quite rare today, and Carlo Ginzburg shows great generosity in commenting on some aspects of my book, notably on the epistemological and methodological ones. These are difficult questions that would require long discussions.

He observes that, in this book, I assert a continuity between mass persecution such as the witch hunt and contemporary genocides, but without demonstrating it. This is certainly a shortcoming of this book, but to remedy it, it would have been necessary to address the Shoah, the Armenian and Rwandan genocides, Stalinist-type terrors, etc., which cannot be done superficially. Hence, this investigation has been limited to the witch hunt and the Terror. That said, it seems obvious that, despite the singular character of each of these persecutions, some similarities can be identified, particularly in the accusations aimed at the targets of these terror apparatuses.

As Ginzburg's work has taught us, the denunciation of a "conspiracy" aimed at destroying the social order and conquering the *imperium mundi* appeared as early as 1320 in France, targeting lepers and then Jews. We know that it resurfaced in the following centuries, first targeting the so-called witches, then, from the eighteenth century onward, the Freemasons, associated a little later with the Jews. It culminated in the twentieth century with the *Protocols of the Elders of Zion*, which Hitler, it is claimed, had learned by heart. As for the accusation of poisoning, which was aimed at the Jews and led the medieval Church to forbid Christians to be treated by Jewish doctors, is it surprising to see it reappear in the USSR in the 1950s, when the so-called "Doctors' Plot" was denounced? Similar accusations have resurfaced quite recently, during the COVID-19 pandemic, often attacking personalities of Jewish origin such as George Soros or Agnès

Buzyn, the former French minister of health, and sometimes reactivating the old accusation of infanticide intended to draw the blood of murdered children . . .[1]

Are we only dealing with "superficial analogies"—to borrow an expression from Marc Bloch—that should be dispelled? It is, rather, possible to consider them as examples of what Ginzburg himself designates as "typological connections" between phenomena belonging to very different times and contexts. Identifying such connections does not prevent us from "recontextualizing" these phenomena by analyzing the specific differences between these situations, differences that exist even when the words used are identical. That is why I have been careful to distinguish between the meaning of the term "race" at the time of the witch hunt and the meaning it would take on in Nazi ideology. It is also for this reason that I have evoked the difference between the witch trials, where torture and confession had a decisive function; those of the revolutionary tribunals of 1793–94, where they no longer played any role; and the Stalinist trials, where they once again resurface, which led Bukharin to denounce their "medieval" character.

It could be that recent historical and anthropological works have put too much emphasis on discontinuity, on the gaps between epochs and cultures: It is time to rehabilitate the search for continuities registered in the *longue durée*. From this perspective, it seems possible to refer to the notion of "anachrony" put forward by Jacques Rancière and other French thinkers, but it does not play an important role in this book. Indeed, Ginzburg is right to warn against an abusive use of this notion that could lead to a relativistic skepticism. I did not seek to discover anachronistic similarities, but to identify what he calls "schemes," "potentially universal symbolic configurations," rooted "in primordial experiences of a bodily character."

I have chosen to designate these configurations, which span the different eras, as *schemes*, and Ginzburg is right to observe that this notion of Kantian origin did not appear in my previous books.[2] If I use it now, it is partly thanks to him, to a book like *Ecstasies: Deciphering the Witches' Sabbath* (and also to my earlier work on Kant). However, my approach differs from his on one important point: In order to describe the most originary schemes, I have recourse to phenomenology, to this approach that I call egoanalysis. It implies a reduction, a bracketing of the world and of any relation with others; but it is, as Husserl often reminds us, a methodological abstraction, a kind of thought experiment. I readily acknowledge that our concrete existence in the world is always "characterized by some form of sharing" with others. Nevertheless, I think that, by putting our worldly existence in suspension, the phenomenological reduction gives access to a fundamental dimension of our experience, to the affects that characterize it and to the schemes that structure it.

Is such an "achronic" approach necessarily ahistorical, as he seems to judge? I do not believe so. It is in order to avoid rigidifying these schemes by turning them into immutable archetypes that I distinguish between an originary schematism and a historical schematism. I consider indeed that, "for the apparition of their historical imaginings, these original schemata are intertwined with historical ones that are modified from one epoch to the other and do not take the same forms within different human cultures." Thus, the anguish of contamination, of contagion through bodily contact, brings into play an originary scheme, probably universal, but it is translated in various ways in each epoch and in different human cultures, as the works of historians and anthropologists show.[3] And it may be in certain cases that this scheme of contagion is associated with the historical scheme of conspiracy, which generates the accusations of poisoning of which the lepers, the Jews, and the witches were victims. I have shown in my book that these three categories aroused the same anguish, the same disgust provoked by the fear of contamination through bodily contact. This is why Jews were forbidden to touch food in the markets and why some judges in witch trials tried to avoid any physical contact with the accused during interrogations . . . To avoid an excessively speculative approach (the professional failing of philosophers!), I have chosen to analyze concretely these historical schemes, their genesis and their implementation during the witch hunt by calling upon the works of historians, those of Ginzburg, of Robert Muchembled, Wolfgang Behringer, Brian Levack, and many others.

Is his assertion that the book is "focusing more on the attitudes of the persecutors than on those of the witches," which would prevent me from practicing "*estrangement*," the change of perspective that allows one to "delegitimize the version of the victors," correct? As we know, the victims of the witch hunt, unlike those of the Shoah and other genocides of the twentieth century, were for the most part illiterate and could not leave any testimony of their persecution — with the remarkable exception of the letter of Junius, the burgomaster of Würzburg, which I quoted. I have tried to make these "stifled voices" heard, to bring to light their protests (such as that of Aldegonde de Rue or Jeanne Bachy) and their different strategies of resistance to persecution and torture, as they appear in the minutes of the trials. I would have liked to echo more of these voices. I wholeheartedly hope that the future work of historians inspired by Ginzburg's research will make it possible to "resurrect" a greater number of victims.

Continuing Our Dialogue

Dear Jacob Rogozinski,

Thank you for your reply. You are right: The dialogue between philosophers and historians is quite rare, and I regard as a privilege and an honor the possibility that you have given me to engage in a dialogue with you.

Two small remarks. The word "achronic" has for me no negative nuance. The morphological approach that I used in my book on the witches' sabbath was, following the path opened by Goethe, outside of space and time. That said, the problem for a historian is to create a connection between an achronic perspective (in your case, the one related to phenomenology) and the historical perspective, related to time and space. On this point, in my opinion, it will be necessary to reflect further.

You have no doubt "delegitimized the version of the persecutors," but from an *etic* perspective (which I share, of course). The "estrangement" would have involved, in my opinion, something else: a thorough analysis of the trials to grasp the *emic* perspective of the alleged witches or wizards, through the (very rare) discrepancies between their answers and the expectations of the judges. Your choice was different and (as I pointed out) completely legitimate. No criticism.

Once again, many thanks!
Carlo Ginzburg

Dear Carlo Ginzburg,

Thank you very much for your great generosity!

You are right: The question of the articulation between originary (or "morphological") schemes and historical schemes is a decisive issue and a difficult question. Thus, a universal anxiety such as the fear of defilement, of contagion through bodily contact takes, as you know, very different forms according to times and cultures, and each time we ask how it crystallized in a particular form (the poisoning of wells by lepers and Jews, the bite of the vampire, the permanent impurity imputed to the Indian Pariahs, etc.). This "contextualization" is the task of anthropologists and historians, much more than that of philosophers . . . This is also the case with the "emic" analysis of the witch hunt that you evoke: That would indeed be based on a detailed analysis of the trial archives, and, not being a historian, I did not have any access to them (except in very rare cases, such as the report of the interrogations of Gauffridi and Jeanne Bachy that I have analyzed in the book).

With all my gratitude and friendship,
Jacob Rogozinski

In Memoriam

LICHTENAUER, Peter, burned in Molsheim in 1630 at the age of eleven
PARMENTIER, Chrétienne, burned in Lorraine in 1624
PERCHEVAL, Reine, burned at Bazuel in 1599
ROLANDE DU VERNOIS, burned in the Jura in 1600
SAWYER, Elizabeth, hanged in London in 1621
SEMLER, Ursula, hanged at Bergheim in 1683
TANNOYE, Jean, burned in Arras in 1460

Yizkor

in memory of:

Yankel-Fayvel Rogozinski, my grandfather
Salome Rogozinska, my father's wife
Helena Rogozinska, my father's daughter
Helena and Guta Lewand, my aunts,
Sara and Rosa Kuttner, my cousins
Krzysztyna and Lew, their children
Bronislaw Lando, my mother's husband

murdered by the Nazis

in memory of all mine,
of all victims of persecutory hatred.

Notes

Introduction: A Forgotten Massacre

1. On the trial of Aldegonde de Rue, I quote documents published by Robert Muchembled in *La Sorcière au village* (Paris: Gallimard-Juilliard, 1979). For the witch hunt in the region of Bazuel, see also, from the same author, *Sorcières, justice et société aux XVIe–XVIIIe siècles* (Paris: Imago, 1987), 134–65. Unless otherwise indicated, the translations of quoted material are those of this work's translator, Sephr Razavi.

2. Baruch Spinoza, *Ethics*, in *The Collected Works of Spinoza*, trans. Edwin Curley (Princeton, NJ: Princeton University Press, 1985), III–P24, Scholium, 507 (translation modified).

3. Cited by Norman Cohn, *Warrant for Genocide: The Myth of the Jewish World Conspiracy and the Protocols of the Elders of Zion* (London: Serif, 2005), 198. We also know that Himmler was interested in witch hunts and had accumulated an important amount of documentation on the subject.

4. "An anachronism, is the word, the event, a significant sequence taken out of 'their' time, and thus provided with the capacity to define novel temporal levers, assuring the jump or the connection from a temporal line to another." (Une anachronie, c'est un mot, un événement, une séquence signifiante sortis de "leur" temps, doués du même coup de la capacité de définir des aiguillages temporels inédits, d'assurer le saut ou la connexion d'une ligne de temporalité à une autre). See "Le concept d'anachronisme et la vérité de l'histoire," *L'Inactuel*, no. 6 (1996): 35–69 (my translation).

5. See Fernand Braudel's preface to *The Mediterranean and the Mediterranean World in the Age of Philip II* (Oakland: University of California Press, 1996).

6. Jules Michelet, *La sorcière* (Paris: Garnier-Flammarion, 1966), 163.

7. See the numbered toll of the executions provided by Wolfgang Behringer in

"Allemagne, 'mère de tant de sorcières,'" in *Magie et sorcellerie en Europe* (Paris: Armand Colin, 1994), 59–98, or that of Guy Bechtel, *La sorcière et l'Occident* (Paris: Plon, 1997), 658–67.

8. Wolfgang Behringer, "Weather, Hunger, and Fear," in *The Witchcraft Reader*, ed. D. Oldridge (London: Routledge, 2002), 82.

9. Robert Muchembled, *La sorcière au village* (Paris: Gallimard, 1979), 23. According to one of his discipline peers, "the movement that had wished to kill witches is also that which would later birth the thought of Montesquieu, Voltaire, and Kant. The death of witches was one of the crises that birthed the modern world" (Bechtel, *La sorcière et l'Occident*, 900). Poor Montesquieu, Voltaire, and Kant . . .

10. Carlo Ginzburg, *Ecstasies: Deciphering the Witches' Sabbath* (London: Hutchinson Radius 1990), 95.

11. As much as possible because nothing could be as difficult: By designating here my research as an "inquiry," I would already be talking like the inquisitors . . .

12. Maurice Merleau-Ponty, *Signs*, trans. Richard McCleary (Evanston, IL: Northwestern University Press, 1964), 20.

13. John's Gospel (15:25), taking up Psalm 35.

14. See Primo Levi, *If This Is a Man*, trans. Stuart Woolf (New York: Orion, 1959), 24. "Driven by thirst, I eyed a fine icicle outside the window, within hand's reach. I opened the window and broke off the icicle but at once a large, heavy guard prowling outside brutally snatched it away from me. '*Warum?*' I asked him in my poor German. '*Hier ist kein warum*' [Here there is no why], he replied, pushing me inside with a shove."

15. We can find this text in a collection of Michelet's theoretical writings published by Claude Lefort under the title of *La cité des vivants et des morts* (Paris: Belin, 2002), 416–17. I would like to highlight here the significant debt my work owes to Lefort and his now classic analyses of the image of the political body, of its democratic "disembodiment" and its totalitarian "re-embodiment."

16. Ils ont brûlé les livres, brûlé les hommes, rebrûlé les os calcinés, jeté la cendre [. . .], point de noms, point de signes [. . .] Est-ce avec ces tristes restes que je puis refaire cette histoire? (ibid., 197, "De la religion du Moyen Âge," introduction to *Histoire de la Révolution française*).

17. La vie a sur elle-même une action de personnel enfantement qui, de matériaux préexistants, nous crée des choses absolument nouvelles [. . .]. Ainsi va la vie historique, ainsi va chaque peuple, se faisant, s'engendrant [. . .]. La France a fait la France, et l'élément fatal de race m'y semble secondaire. Elle est fille de sa liberté (ibid., 398–39, preface to *Histoire de France* [1869]).

18. Jules Michelet, *Satanism and Witchcraft: A Study in Medieval Superstition*, trans. Alfred Richard Allinson (New York: Kensington, 1992), 74–77.

19. On this question, see my introduction to egoanalysis in the third part of *The Ego and the Flesh: An Introduction to Egoanalysis* (Redwood City, CA: Stanford University Press, 2010).

20. Maurice Merleau-Ponty, *Le visible et l'invisible* (Paris: Gallimard, 1964),

307–8, trans. Alphonso Lingis as *The Visible and the Invisible: Followed by Working Notes* (Evanston, IL: Northwestern University Press, 1968), 254–55.

21. Edmund Husserl, *Ideas Pertaining to a Pure Phenomenology and to a Phenomenological Philosophy, Second Book: Studies in the Phenomenology of Constitution*, trans. Richard Rojcewicz and André Schuwer (Dordrecht: Kluwer Academic, 1989), §41, p. 167, Hua IV, 159. On the touching-touched experience and the "double constitution" of the flesh, see §36–39.

22. Sigmund Freud, "Instincts and Their Vicissitudes," in *The Standard Edition of the Complete Psychological Works of Sigmund Freud*, vol. 14 (London: Hogarth, 1957), 136. See also his 1925 "Negation" in volume 19 of *Standard Edition*, 235–39.

23. The phenomena that I am describing here can seem analogous to such self-destructive defense mechanisms of the organism that biologists define as *autoimmunity*. It is not at this level — that of organic bodies — where egoanalysis takes place, but on the plane of ego-flesh where biological processes such as autoimmunity find their immanent meaning.

24. Rogozinski, *The Ego and the Flesh*, 268.

1. "All Women Are Witches"

1. Mary Douglas, "Witchcraft and Leprosy: Two Strategies for Rejection," in *Risk and Blame* (London: Routledge, 1994), 83–101.

2. See his letter to Marx of September 4, 1870, in *Marx-Engels Werke* (Berlin: Dietz Verlag, 1961), 33:53.

3. *Demonology* (1597), III-6, quoted in B. Levack, *The Witchcraft Sourcebook* (London: Routledge, 2004), 141.

4. See J. Roehrig, *L'holocauste des sorcières d'Alsace* (Strasbourg: Éditions de la Nuée bleue, 2011), 223.

5. On this question, see the first part of my *The Ego and the Flesh: An Introduction to Egoanalysis* (Redwood City, CA: Stanford University Press, 2010).

6. As argued by G. Agamben in *"What Is an Apparatus?" and Other Essays* (Stanford, CA: Stanford University Press 2006). Deleuze insists, on the other hand, on the "fissures" and the "lines of flight" that traverse the apparatus, destabilize them, and lead them to recompose themselves; see his contribution to the collection *Michel Foucault philosophe* (Paris: Seuil, 1988), 185–93.

7. See "The Schematism" in *Critique of Pure Reason*. As I have shown in *Le don de la Loi* (Paris: Presses Universitaires de France, 1999), the possibility of a *practical schematism* is at the heart of Kantian ethics.

8. On this passage from disgust to hatred, see my *The Ego and the Flesh*. In this book, I did not address the question of the schematization of primordial affects as the analysis was at the immanent level of the ego-flesh, without insight into the unraveling of affects on the plane of world and history.

9. This is why historians define the myth of Sabbath as an "accumulative concept" (Levack) and a "cultural formation of compromise" (Ginzburg).

10. H. Fründ, "Chronique de Lucerne" (ca. 1430), quoted in *L'imaginaire du sabbat* (Cahiers lausannois d'histoire médiévale, 1999), 43.

11. On the cognitive and practical functions of the consipiracy myth, see P. A. Taguieff's work, notably *La foire aux illumines* (Paris: Mille et une nuits, 2005) and *L'imaginaire du complot mondial* (Paris: Mille et une nuits, 2006).

12. On this point, see N. Cohn's investigation *Europe's Inner Demons* (Sussex, UK: University of Sussex Press, 1975).

13. See C. Zika's study "Les parties du corps, Saturne et le cannibalisme: Repésentations sicuelles des assemblées de sorcières au XVIième siècle," in N. Jacques-Chaquin and M. Préaud, *Le sabbat des sorcières en Europe* (Paris: J. Million, 1993), 389–418.

14. This engraving can be found in R. Decker's *Hexen* (Darmstadt: Primus Verlag, 2004), 42.

15. C. Ginzburg retells Chiara's story in his study "Witchcraft and Popular Piety: Notes on a Modenese Trial of 1519," in *Myths, Emblems, Clues* (London: Hutchinson Radius, 1990).

16. See Ginzburg's classic study *The Night Battles: Witchcraft and Agrarian Cults in the Sixteenth and Seventeenth Centuries* (London: Routledge, 2015).

17. He has detailed the results of his investigations in *Ecstasies: Deciphering the Witches' Sabbath* (London: Hutchinson Radius, 1990).

18. See the first part of Ginzburg's *Ecstasies*.

19. On this concept, see my *The Ego and the Flesh*, 255.

20. See Arendt, *The Origins of Totalitarianism* (San Diego, CA: Harvest, 1973), 93–95.

21. See his *Histoire de la folie à l'âge classique* (Paris: Gallimard, 1972), 31, 218, 449.

22. Edmund Husserl, *Origin of Geometry* (Lincoln: University of Nebraska Press, 1989).

23. "Tradition of hatred" is the expression used by one of the members of the Committee of Public Safety (Comité de salut public) in 1794 when calling for directing this hatred toward the enemies of the Republic. I will come back to this in the last part of this book.

24. Ginzburg, *Ecstasies*, 233–34, 265. On the relation between typological connections and historical connections, see also 29–38, and the preface to *Myths, Emblems, Clues*.

25. Sigmund Freud, "Creative Writers and Day-Dreaming," in *Criticism: The Major Statements*, ed. Charles Kaplan (New York: St. Martin's, 1991), 422.

26. See *La France trompée par les magiciens et démonolâtres* (1803), quoted in E. Kreis, *Les puissances de l'ombre* (Paris: CNRS Éditions, 2012), 47–48.

27. I follow here the analyses of G. Klaniczay in "The Decline of Witches and the Rise of Vampires," in *The Witchcraft Reader*, ed. D. Oldridge (London: Routledge, 2002), 387–98. On the Hungarian, Dalmatian, and Caucasian equivalents of the Benandanti, see Ginzburg, *Ecstasies*, 149–95.

28. On this point, see Barbara Ehrenreich and Deirdre English's *Witches*,

Midwives, and Nurses (New York: Feminist Press at the City University of New York, 2010).

29. On Wier's position, see Foucault's remarks in "Religious Deviations and Medical Knowledge," in *Religion and Culture*, ed. Jeremy R. Carrette (New York: Routledge, 1999); and T. Maus de Rolley's study "La part du diable: Jean Wier et la fabrique de l'illusion diabolique," *Tracés*, no. 8 (2005): 29–46.

30. Quoted in Michel de Certeau, *The Possession at Loudun* (Chicago: Chicago University Press, 2000), 135.

31. From P. de L'Estoile's *journal*, quoted in R. Mandrou, *Magistrats et sorciers en France au XVIIe siècle* (Paris: Plon, 1968), 166.

32. Quoted in Ginzburg, *The Night Battles*, 126.

33. He systematizes his observations in his treaty *Des maladies mentales*, vol. 1 (Brussels: Tircher, 1838), 238–58.

34. On the figure of the "criminal monster," see Foucault's seminar on the *Abnormal (1974–1975)* (London: Picador, 2004); and Julie Mazaleigue-Labaste's important work *Les déséquilibres de l'amour* (Paris: Ithaque, 2014).

35. Jean Bodin, *On the Demon-Mania of Witches* (Toronto: Victoria University Press, 1995).

36. *Malleus maleficarum* (Grenoble: Jérôme Millon, 2005), 174.

37. Ibid., 185.

38. Letters to Fliess no. 56 and 57, in *La naissance de la psychanalyse* (Paris: Presses Universitaires de France, 1973), 166–68.

39. On these rituals of truth in nineteenth-century psychiatry, see Foucault's analysis in *Psychiatric Power: Lectures at the Collège de France, 1973–1974* (London: Palgrave Macmillan 2006).

2. A Death Mark

1. Michel Foucault, *Psychiatric Power: Lectures at the Collège de France, 1973–74*, trans. Graham Burchell (New York: Palgrave Macmillan, 2006), 105–6.

2. Michelet details the story in his *Satanism and Witchcraft*. Of his experience, Fontaine produced a small volume that would prove seminal, *Des marques des sorciers et de la réelle possession que le diable prend sur le corps des hommes* (Lyon: Larjot, 1611).

3. J. d'Autun, *L'incrédulité savante* (1671), quoted in Michel de Certeau, *The Possession at Loudun* (Chicago: University of Chicago Press, 2000), 167.

4. G. Bouchet, *Le Livre des Sérées* (1598), quoted in F. Michel, *Histoire des races maudites de la France et de l'Espagne* (1847), 256–57 (emphasis mine). "Ladre" is an ancient term for lepers.

5. Pierre de l'Ancre, *De l'inconstance des mauvais anges et démons* (1613; Paris: Aubier, 1982), 179.

6. Madeleine's deposition can be read in R. Mandrou, *Possession et sorcellerie au XVII° siècle* (1979; Paris: Hachette, 2008), 21–31.

7. On this primitive version of the diabolic stigma, see M. Ostorero, "Les marques du diable sur le corps des sorcières (XIV°–XV° siècle)," in *Micrologus*, vol. 13 (2005), 359–88.

8. Nicolas Remy and Montague Summers, *Demonolatry*, trans. E. A. Ashwin (Whitefish, MT: Kessinger, 2010), 9.

9. On this, I refer to the classic study of Marc Bloch, *Les rois thaumaturges* (1924; Paris: Gallimard, 1983). On the relationship between these sacred marks and the satanic mark, see F. Delpech, "La 'marque' des sorcières: Logique(s) de la stigmatisation diabolique," in N. Jacques-Chaquin and M. Préaud, *Le sabbat des sorciers en Europe* (Paris: J. Million 1993), 347–68.

10. B. Gui, "Manuel de l'inquisiteur" (1320), *Belles Lettres* 1 (1964): 54–56. It seems that the yellow *rouelle* imposed on the Jews is also a representation of a host, an emblem of the Christian faith they rejected.

11. Quoted by R. Moore in *The Formation of a Persecuting Society* (Hoboken, NJ: Wiley and Blackwell, 2006); see also D. Sansy, "Marquer la différence: L'imposition de la rouelle aux XIII° et XIV° siècles," *Médiévales* 41 (2001): 15–36.

12. See B. Geremek, *Les marginaux parisiens aux XIV° et XV° siècles* (1976; Paris: Flammarion, 2009), 283.

13. Fontaine, *Des marques des sorciers*, 6, 16–19.

14. See J. Bodin, *De la démonomanie des sorciers* (1580; Paris: Gutenberg Reprint, 1979), 214; and N. Boguet, *Discours exécrable des sorciers* (1602; Paris: le Sycomore, 1980), 120.

15. Jean-Martin Charcot, *Leçons du mardi à la Salpêtrière, vol. 1* (1887–88; Paris: Bibliothèque des Introuvables, 2006), 108.

3. Confessing the Truth

1. *Translator's note:* The *quaestio* is a seventeenth-century criminal procedure's interrogation technique during which the victim was made to answer questions under the threat of torture; "the torture consists in driving a series of increasingly large wedges between the boards within which the legs are enclosed and the legs, until the bones break" (Michel de Certeau, *The Possession at Loudun*, trans. Michael B. Smith [Chicago: University of Chicago Press, 2000], 173).

2. This transcript is cited *in extenso* in G. Bechtel, *Sorcellerie et possession: L'affaire Gaufridy* (Paris: Éditions Culture-Arts-Loisirs, 1972).

3. Heinrich Kramer, *Le marteau des sorcières* (Grenoble: Jérôme Millon, 2005), 460.

4. See Foucault's "La vérité et les formes juridiques" (1974), in *Dits et écrits*, vol. 1 (Paris: Gallimard, 2001). He was going to deepen his analysis in his 1981 course, in *Mal faire, dire vrai* (Louvain-la-Neuve, Belgium: Presses Universitaires de Louvain, 2012).

5. See Y. Thomas, "L'aveu, de la parole au corps," in *L'aveu*, ed. R. Dulong (Paris: PUF, 2001), 17–36.

6. See B. Johansen, "Vérité et torture: Jus commune et droit musulman entre le X° et le XIII° siècle, in F. Héritier, *De la violence* (Paris: Odile Jacob, 1996).

7. A good synthesis of this subject can be found in C. Jallamion's study "Entre ruse du droit et impératif humanitaire: La politique de la torture judiciaire du XII° au XVIII° siècle," *Archives de politique criminelle*, no. 25 (2003): 9–35.

8. Foucault, *Mal faire, dire vrai*, 204.

9. *La Démonolâtrie* (1595; Nancy: Presses Universitaires de Nancy, 1998), 304.

10. Cited by Delcambre, "Psychologie des inculpés lorrains de sorcellerie," *Revue historique de droit français* (1954): 386.

11. Thomasius, *Über die Folter*, pt. II, §9 (1705; Vienna: Böhlaus Verlag, 1960), 181–82.

12. To his interlocuter who asked him, "what convinces the victim herself to admit guilt" during the witch hunts or Stalin's trials, Girard answered: "The mimetic pressure! The witches are the doubles of their judges, they share their belief in their own guilt" (*Quand ces choses commenceront* [Arléa, 1994], 67).

13. Here, I follow closely the description of the trial given by R. Muchembled in *Les derniers bûchers, un village de Flandre et ses sorcières sous Louis XIV* (Paris: Éditions Ramsay, 1981), 68–71.

14. See Claude Lefort, *Écrire — l'épreuve du politique* (Paris: Calmann-Lévy, 1992).

15. Michel Foucault, *La volonté de savoir* (Paris: Gallimard, 1976), 78–80. In English, 58 (translation modified), 1978.

16. *Paroles des Pères du désert*, cited by G. Jeanmart, *Généalogie de la docilité*, (Paris: Vrin, 2007), 147. On the "self-mortification" implied by this rule, this "total ingress of all existence, all actions, by the will of another," see Foucault, *Mal faire, dire vrai*, 136–37.

17. See J. Delumeau, *Le péché et la peur* (Paris: Fayard, 1983). On the evolution of sacramental formulae, see P. M. Gy, "Les définitions de la confession après le IV° concile de Latran," in *L'aveu — Antiquité et Moyen Âge* (Rome: EFR, 1986), 283–96.

18. See Boguet's *Discours exécrable des sorciers* (1602; Paris: le Sycomore, 1980), 151–54.

19. For an English translation, see Friedrich Spee, *Cautio Criminalis, or a Book on Witch Trials*, trans. Marcus Hellyer (Charlottesville: University of Virginia Press, 2003).

20. Junius's letter can be found in W. Behringer, *Hexen und Hexenprozesse* (Munich: Deutscher Taschenbuch, 1995), 305–10.

21. As declared by Trotsky in 1924. This belief was shared by all the "Old Bolsheviks," even those the Party would put to death as "traitors" and "enemies of the people."

22. Cf. Anna Larina Bukharina, *Boukharine ma passion* (Paris: Gallimard, 1990), 362.

23. See Hannah Arendt, "Vérité et politique," in *La crise de la culture* (1963; Paris: Gallimard, 1972).

4. The Capital Enemy

1. Quoted in Brian P. Levack, *The Witch-Hunt in Early Modern Europe*, 3rd ed. (Harlow, UK: Pearson, 2006), 85.

2. See the important study of J. Chiffoleau, "Dire l'indicible — remarques sur la catégorie *du nefandum* du XII° au XV° siècle," *Annales ESC* (March-April 1990): 289–324.

3. Quoted in G. Lizerand, *Le dossier de l'affaire des Templiers* (Paris: Belles-Lettres, 1964), 16–17.

4. See A. Renczes, *Wie löscht man eine Familie aus? Eine Analyse der Bamberger Hexenprozesse* (Bamberg: Germany: Centaurus, 1990). I am grateful to Natalia Tauber for drawing my attention to this work.

5. Jean Bodin, *De la démonomanie des sorciers* (1580; Paris: Gutenberg Reprint, 1979), 212; hereafter cited parenthetically in this chapter.

6. I follow here the excellent analysis of G. Mairet in *Le Dieu mortel* (Paris: Presses Universitaires de France, 1987).

7. Jean Bodin, *Les six livres de la République* (The Six Books of the Republic) (1576, 8 vols.; Paris: Fayard, 1986), vol. 1, 191. It was Carl Schmitt who best understood the significance of this thesis of Bodin's; see his *Political Theology*, trans. George Schwab (Boston: MIT Press, 1986), 8–9.

8. Bodin, *The Six Books of the Republic*, vol. 1, 180.

9. "If the covenant made with the subject at the suasion of him who is the capital enemy of his Prince is punished by death without any remission, how could the covenant made with Satan, the enemy of God, be excused?" (Bodin, *Demon-Mania*, 262). See the commentary of N. Jacques-Chaquin in *Jean Bodin, Nature, History, Law and Politics*, ed. Y. Zarka (Paris: Presses Universitaires de France 1996), 63–66.

10. *Discourse of the Damned Art of Witchcraft* (1608), quoted in Levack, *The Witch-Hunt in Early Modern Europe*, 67.

11. Quoted in Michel de Certeau, *The Possession at Loudun*, trans. Michael B. Smith (Chicago: University of Chicago Press, 2000), 27, 151.

12. See the pamphlets quoted by M. Yardeni in "Henri III sorcier," in R. Sauzet, *Henri III et son temps* (Paris: Vrin, 1992), 57–64; and by A. Duprat in *Les rois de papier* (Paris: Belin, 2002).

13. See the letter of Guy Patin quoted in R. Mandrou, *Magistrats et sorciers au XVII° siècle* (Paris: Plon, 1968), 337.

14. Carl Schmitt, *Glossarium* (1947–51; Berlin: Duncker & Humblot 1991), 19.

15. Stuart Clark, *Thinking with Demons* (Oxford: Oxford University Press, 1999), 618. This leads him to present Bodin's *Demon-Mania* as a "political manifesto in favor of absolutism."

16. On this question, it is necessary to read the masterly study of Ernst Kantorowicz, "Mystères de l'État," in *Mourir pour la patrie* (Paris: Presses Universitaires de France, 1984), 75–103.

17. On this "gift of ubiquity," see Kantorowicz's *Les deux corps du roi* (Paris: Gallimard, 1989), 19, 446–47.

18. See H. Rauschning, *Hitler m'a dit*, quoted in C. Ginzburg, *À distance* (Paris: Gallimard, 2001), 201.

19. Carl Schmitt, *The Theory of the Partisan*, trans. A. C. Goodson (East Lansing: Michigan State University Press, 2004), 61; see also *Ex captivitate salus*, a profound meditation written in 1946 where this motif appears for the first time.

20. Schmitt, *The Theory of the Partisan*, 78n52. One may wonder whether Schmitt is not trying to exonerate Nazism by implicitly accusing the victors of 1945 of "demonizing" it.

21. See Schmitt, *Political Theology*, 16–35.

22. Quoted in F. Mercier, *La Vauderie d'Arras* (Rennes: Presses Universitaires de Rennes, 2006), 284.

23. *Against Felix the Manichean* (398), II-8, in *Œuvres de Saint Augustin*, vol. 17 (Paris: Desclée de Brouwer, 1961), 721.

24. On this "ethical vision of evil" and on its later abandonment by Augustine in favor of a "quasi-gnostic" position, one can read the enlightening pages of P. Ricoeur in *Le conflit des interprétations* (Paris: Seuil, 1969), 265–310.

25. As Peter states in the Acts of the Apostles, 10:28, "Nothing is unclean in itself," as Paul also states in the Epistle to the Romans, 14:14.

26. W. Perkins, in B. Levack, *The Witchcraft Sourcebook* (London: Routledge, 2004), 96–97.

27. Quoted in R. Mandrou, *Possession et sorcellerie au XVII° siècle* (1979; Paris: Hachette, 2008), 29.

28. Friedrich Spee, *Cautio Criminalis, or a Book on Witch Trials*, trans. Marcus Hellyer (Charlottesville: University of Virginia Press, 2003), 281.

29. This engraving is reproduced and commented by A. Duprat in *Les rois de papier* (Paris: Belin, 2002), 56.

30. Saint-Just, "Rapport sur les factions de l'étranger" (March 1794), in *Œuvres choisies* (Paris: Gallimard, 1968), 213–16.

31. It is, of course, the young Augustine, the one of the *Treatise on Free Will* and the anti-Manichean writings.

32. Quoted by Certeau, *The Possession at Loudun*, 100. The Scottish judge Mackenzie also mentions a defendant who "asked earnestly if one could be a witch without knowing it" (see Levack, *The Witchcraft Sourcebook*, 159).

33. N. Boguet, *Discours exécrable des sorciers* (1602; Paris: le Sycomore, 1980), 188.

34. Quoted in C. Arnould, *Histoire de la sorcellerie* (Paris: Tallandier, 2009), 334.

35. On the "child-sorcerers" of Bouchain, see R. Muchembled, "L'autre côté du miroir: Mythes sataniques et réalités culturelles aux XVI° et XVII° siècles," *Annales ESC* 2 (1985): 291.

36. *La Démonolâtrie* (1595; Nancy: Presses Universitaires de Nancy, 1998), 185–86 (emphasis mine).

37. Melchior Pelaes de Meres (1575), quoted in H. Méchoulan, *Le sang de*

l'autre ou l'honneur de Dieu (Paris: Fayard, 1979), 126–27; see also the study by
Y. H. Yerushalmi, "De la *limpieza del sangre* espagnole au nazisme: Continuités et
ruptures," *Esprit* (March-April 1993): 5–35.

38. See, in particular, *La nouvelle science du politique* by E. Voegelin (Paris:
Seuil, 2000). On the thesis of the "Gnostic recurrence" and the debates to which it
gave rise, consult the study of J. C. Monod, *La querelle de la sécularisation* (Paris:
Vrin, 2002).

39. See his seminar on *Anormaux* (Paris: EHESS-Gallimard-Seuil, 1999),
298–300.

40. "I am a god born of gods," declares a Manichean profession of faith. That is
why the Pure ones stay among the other men "like gold fallen in the mud."

41. See the texts quoted by Z. Sternhell in *La droite révolutionnaire — 1885–1914*
(Paris: Gallimard, 1997), 202–14.

42. On the assimilation of the Jew to the pig in the Middle Ages, see F. Raphaël,
"La représentation des Juifs dans l'art médiéval en Alsace," *Revue des sciences
sociales*, no. 1 (1972): 26–42. On "the structural identity between the symbolic
representation of the witch and that of the Jew," see, by the same author, "Juifs et
sorciers dans l'Alsace médiévale," *Revue des sciences sociales*. no. 3 (1974): 69–106.

43. On this case, see Mandrou, *Possession et sorcellerie au XVII° siècle*, 33–109.

44. *The Hammer of Witches*, trans. Christopher S. Mackay (Cambridge:
Cambridge Press, 2009), 318.

45. A. du Laurens, *Des maladies mélancoliques* (1597), quoted in J. Baltrusaitis,
"Physiognomonie animale," *Aberrations* (Paris: Flammarion, 1995), 32.

46. Aristotle, *Politiques* V-9, 1309 b.

47. A. Brossat, *Le corps de l'ennemi* (Paris: La Fabrique, 1998), 103.

48. L. F. Céline, *Les beaux draps* (1941), quoted in J. Kristeva, *Pouvoirs de
l'horreur* (Paris: Seuil, 1980), 218.

49. See F. Mercier, *"Membra diaboli,"* *Cahiers de recherches médiévales et
humanistes*, no. 13 (2006).

50. On these questions, let me refer again to the analyses elucidated in the last
part of *The Ego and the Flesh*.

51. C. Lefort, "L'image du corps et le totalitarisme," in *L'invention démocratique*
(Paris: Fayard, 1981), 175.

52. Thomas Aquinas, *De regimine principum* (1256), I-1, *Du gouvernement royal*
(Candillac: Éditons Saint Rémi, 1923), 29–30.

53. Bodin, *The Six Books of the Republic*, vol. 1, 41.

54. Just as the physician is right to purge or amputate us, "provided it is for the
good of our body," so the true politician has the right to "purge the city for its benefit
by putting some people to death or else by exiling them" (*Statesman*, 293cd).

55. Bodin, *The Six Books of the Republic*, vol. 4, 139–40 (emphasis mine).

56. "The leader or the leading idea might also, so to speak, be negative; hatred
against a particular person or institution might operate in just the same unifying way,
and might call up the same kind of emotional ties as positive attachment" (Sigmund

Freud, *Group Psychology and the Analysis of the Ego*, trans. James Strachey [London: Hogarth, 1949], 53).

57. Georges Bataille, "La valeur d'usage de D.A.F. de Sade," in *Œuvres complètes*, vol. 2 (Paris: Gallimard, 1970), 59.

58. Georges Bataille, "La royauté de l'Europe classique," in *Œuvres complètes*, vol. 2, 224.

59. Edmund Husserl, *Cartesian Meditations* (1930; Paris: Vrin, 2000), §44, p. 97 (translation modified).

60. Ibid., §60, p. 139.

61. Étienne de La Boétie, *Discours de la servitude volontaire* (1548; Paris: Payot 1978), 115.

62. See their "Address to the King" and the other texts quoted in Y. M. Bercé, *Croquants et nu-pieds* (Paris: Gallimard, 1991), 45–55.

63. According to Gauffreteau, *Journal*, quoted in Y. M. Bercé, in *L'image du monde renversé et ses représentations littéraires*, ed. J. Lafond and A. Redondo (Paris: Vrin, 1979), 10.

5. The World Upside Down: Contribution to a Phenomenology of Multitudes

1. See Bodin, *De la démonomanie des sorciers* (1580; Paris: Gutenberg Reprint, 1979), 135–36; and Pierre de l'Ancre, *De l'inconstance des mauvais anges et démons* (1613; Paris: Aubier, 1982), 194, 313.

2. See S. Clark's fundamental study, *Thinking with Demons* (Oxford: Oxford University Press, 1999), where this theme is explored through all its implications.

3. See R. Mandrou (who cites G. Naudé's testimony), *Introduction à la France moderne* (Paris: Albin Michel, 1961), 188–89.

4. "In the present day, evil Christians imitate these corrupt practices, although in terms of debauchery they have transferred these acts to Carnival [. . .] [S] orceresses too now practice their acts of sorcery around the beginning of the year (for instance, the feast of St. Andrew and the festivities of Christmas) in order to please the demons" (*The Hammer of Witches*, trans. Christopher S. Mackey [Cambridge: Cambridge University Press, 2009], 318–19).

5. Quoted in Y. M. Bercé, *Fête et révolte* (Paris: Hachette, 1976), 208.

6. See J. C. Schmitt's study "Le masque, le diable, les morts," in *Le corps, les rites, les rêves, le temps* (Paris: Gallimard, 2001), 211–37.

7. See Le Roy Ladurie, *Les paysans du Languedoc* (Paris: S.E.V.P.E.N., 1966), 411–14.

8. This is the central motif of Christopher Hill's work on the English Revolution, *The World Turned Upside Down* (New York: Penguin, 1972).

9. Quoted in J. Delumeau, *Le péché et la peur* (Paris: Fayard, 1983), 149. In sixteenth- to seventeenth-century Japan, a period of political unrest and peasant revolts was also referred to as the "upside-down world."

10. J. Taincture, *Invectives contre la secte de vauderie* (1460), quoted in F. Mercier,

La Vauderie d'Arras (Rennes: Presses Universitaires de Rennes 2006), 119. The "villains" referred to are obviously the villagers, the peasants.

11. Quoted in Y. M. Bercé, *L'image du monde renversé et ses représentations littéraires,* ed. J. Lafond and A. Redondo (Paris: Vrin, 1979), 9.

12. On these "archer-sorcerers," see *The Hammer of Witches,* trans. Mackey, 332–33.

13. "[I]t was no accident that the witch-hunting of the late 1640s should follow the millenarian expectations of the early 1640s [. . .] after the Apocalypse-seeker, the Witch-finder" (W. M. Lamont, *Godly Rule: Politics and Religion* [London: Macmillan, 1969], 98–100).

14. It is the hypothesis proposed by J. Heers in *Fêtes des fous et carnavals* (Paris: Fayard, 1983).

15. See his marvelous *Rabelais and His World* (Boston: MIT Press, 1971).

16. On all this, see Bercé, *Fête et révolte;* and E. Le Roy Ladurie, *Le Carnaval de Romans* (Paris: Gallimard, 1979).

17. Quoted in Bercé, *L'image du monde renversé et ses représentations littéraires,* 13.

18. Bakhtin, *Rabelais and His World,* 35.

19. Ibid., 266.

20. The concept of multitude has been rediscovered by contemporary political philosophy; see Antonio Negri's work and *A Grammar of the Multitude* by P. Virno.

21. By amending Foucault's line, I am staying in tune with Deleuze's lesson and that of Françoise Proust's *De la resistance* (Paris: Cerf, 1997).

22. See N. Cohn, *The Pursuit of the Millenium* (Oxford: Oxford University Press 1970), 199–204.

23. *De Cive* (1642), VI-1 (note). On this fundamental between "people" and "multitude," see also XII-8 and *Leviathan,* II-17.

24. "The worst hypocrites, animated by the same rage, persecuted everywhere men of singular probity [. . .] by enflaming the anger of the ferocious multitude against them" (*Theologico-Political Treatise* [1670], chap. 18).

25. On the determination of politics as a "community founded on a wrong" and the process of resubjectivation, see Jacques Rancière's great contribution, notably in *Dissensus* (1995).

26. Spinoza, *Political Treatise* (1677), III-9 and IV-6. Cicero's definition of anger is found in *Tusculanes,* IV-9.

27. See, on indignation, definition 20 of book III of *Ethics;* on anger, Scholia III-40.

28. It is not a coincidence that Hobbes makes *rage* a fundamental affect of multitude; see B. Manchev's analysis "The Rage: The Affect of the Political," in *Über Wut* (Frankfurt: Revolver Verlag, 2011).

29. *Ethics* IV-45, Corollary I.

30. I follow here D. Nirenberg's analysis in *Communities of Violence: Persecution of the Minorities in the Middle-Age* (Princeton, NJ: Princeton University Press, 1998).

31. Introduction to *Histoire de la Renaissance* (1855), in *La cité des vivants et des morts* (Paris: Belin, 2002), 321.

6. Behind the Devil's Mask

1. Hannah Arendt, *The Origins of Totalitarianism* (San Diego, CA: Harvest, 1973), 445.

2. Friedrich Spee, *Cautio Criminalis, or a Book on Witch Trials*, trans. Marcus Hellyer (Charlottesville: University of Virginia Press, 2003), 154.

3. See Michel de Certeau, *The Possession at Loudun*, trans. Michael B. Smith (Chicago: University of Chicago Press, 2000), 98 (translation modified).

4. Michel Foucault, *Abnormal: Lectures at the Collège de France 1974–1975*, trans. Graham Burchell; ed. Valerio Marchetti and Antonella Salomoni (London: Verso, 2003), 212 (translation modified p. 197 in French).

5. On the birth of the "Jewish face" stereotype during the thirteenth century, see Sara Lipton, *Dark Mirror* (New York: Metropolitan Books, 2014), 169–200. On its progressive demonization, see Joshua Trachtenberg, *The Devil and the Jews* (1943; Philadelphia: Jewish Publication Society, 1983).

6. See Second Epistle to the Corinthians, 11, 13.

7. "I am YHWH, and there is no other, I form the light and create darkness, I bring prosperity and create disaster; I, YHWH, do all these things" (Isaiah 45:6–7).

8. F. W. J. Schelling, *Philosophical Investigations into the Essence of Human Freedom*, trans. Jeff Love and Johannes Schmidt (Albany: State University of New York Press, 2006), 27 (SW 356f).

9. See Jérôme Baschet's study "Satan ou la majesté maléfique dans les miniatures de la fin du Moyen Âge," in N. Nabert, *Le mal et le diable* (Paris: Beauchesne, 1996), 187–220. On the evolution of Satan from the Middle Ages to modern times, see Robert Muchembled, *A History of the Devil: From the Middle Ages to the Present* (Cambridge, UK: Polity, 2003).

10. Spee, *Caution Criminalis*, 214. Jules Michelet would call the *Malleus maleficarum* a "treatise on God's impotence."

11. Paul Ricœur, *The Conflict of Interpretations: Essays in Hermeneutics*, trans. Don Ihde (London: Athlone, 1989), 271.

12. *The Hammer of Witches*, trans. Christopher S. Mackay (Cambridge: Cambridge University Press, 2009), 317.

13. Ibid., 572–73.

14. Ibid., 294.

15. Georges Bataille, *Death and Sensuality: A Study of Eroticism and the Taboo*, trans. Mary Dalwood (New York: Walker, 1962), 121.

16. Martin Luther, *A Commentary on St. Paul's Epistle to the* Galatians, trans. Edwin Sandys (Cambridge: James Clarke, 1978), 189.

17. See G. Mackenzie, in B. Levack, *The Witchcraft Sourcebook* (London: Routledge, 2004), 159.

18. See Gilles Deleuze's magistral analysis of the simulacrum in "Plato and the Simulacrum," in *The Logic of Sense*, trans. Mark Lester (London: Athlone, 1990), 253–66.

19. This engraving is reproduced in E. Castelli, *Le démoniaque dans l'art* (Paris: Vrin, 1958), 54). We might remember the horns that pierced through the monk's hood of the "Great Hypocrite" Henri III . . .

20. Sigmund Freud, "A Seventeenth-Century Demonological Neurosis," in *The Standard Edition of the Complete Psychological Work of Sigmund Freud*, vol. 19, ed. James Strachey and Anna Freud (London: Hogarth, 1961), 85.

21. Ibid., 89.

22. On the identification of the impure — or the "wicked sacred" — with the hybrid, the mixture, the unclassifiable of the symbolic system, see Mary Douglas, *Purity and Danger* (London: Routledge, 1966).

23. This also applies a fortiori to female demons: According to Rémy, the succubi's vaginas are "like a cavity filled with cold water."

24. Ephesians 6:12.

25. On this question, see Henri de Lubac, *Corpus Mysticum* (Paris: Aubier-Montaigne, 1944).

26. On profanation as a "negative proof" of the Eucharist, see J. L. Schefer, *L'hostie profanée* (Paris: POL, 2007). On the persistence of these anti-Jewish accusations in contemporary Poland, see Joanna Tokarska-Bakir, *Légende du sang* (2008; Paris: Albin Michel, 2015).

27. See Hyam Maccoby's analysis of this in *The Sacred Executioner* (London: Thames and Hudson, 1982), 159–62.

28. His "confession" can be read in Rita Vollmer's *Hexenwahn: Ängste der Neuzeit* (Wolfratshausen, Germany: Ehlers Verlag, 2002), 72–81; and Antoinette's in Giuseppina Battisti, *La civiltà delle streghe* (Lerici, 1964), 75.

29. Cited by Robin Briggs, "Le sabbat des sorcières en Lorraine," in *Le sabbat des sorciers en Europe*, ed. Nicole Jacques-Chaquin and Maxime Préaud (Grenoble: Jérôme Millon, 1993), 172.

30. Cited by Emmanuel Kreis, *Les puissances de l'ombre* (Paris: CNRS Éditions, 2012), 193n.

31. Freud, "A Seventeenth-Century Demonological Neurosis," 86.

32. René Girard, *Violence and the Sacred*, trans. Patrick Gregory (Baltimore, MD: Johns Hopkins University Press, 1977), 92–118. Girard rightfully criticizes this same tendency in Freud.

33. Freud, "A Seventeenth-Century Demonological Neurosis," 90. For Freud's understanding of Satan, its ambiguities and limits, see Louise de Urtubey, *Freud et le diable* (Paris: Presses Universitaires de France, 1983).

34. We find one such illustration in the fifteenth trump of the Tarot de Marseille. Jurgis Baltrušaitis provides more examples in his *Fantastic in the Middle Ages* (Woodbridge, UK: Boydell, 1999).

35. Numbers 22:23–25.

36. "After several exorcisms during which said sister remained peaceable, said exorcist took her and, putting the sacred finger in her mouth commanded [the demon] Béhérit to manifest himself and rise to the upper parts. Said sister

immediately fell into a very violent convulsion" (quoted by Certeau, *The Possession at Loudun*, 143).

37. On this "Diabolic Atlas," see Certeau, *The Possession at Loudun*, 90–93.

38. Cited by Robert Muchembled, *Une histoire du diable* (Paris: Seuil, 2000), 151.

39. Walter Stephens tells Walpurga's story in the introduction to his *Demon Lovers: Witchcraft, Sex and the Crisis of Belief* (Chicago: Chicago University Press, 2002).

40. Darren Oldridge, *The Witchcraft Reader* (London: Routledge, 2002), 324.

7. Worse Than Death

1. This is a recurring theme in Foucault's *Histoire de la folie à l'âge classique* (Paris: Gallimard, 1972); see, for example, 15–16, 31n, 218, 449.

2. Béroul, *Le Roman de Tristan* (1170; Paris: Firmin Didot, 1903), 38–39 (emphasis mine).

3. Mary Douglas, *Risk and Blame* (London: Routledge 1994), 84, 96–97.

4. Gospel of John (11:1–44). During the Middle Ages, this character was often confused with "poor Lazarus," the beggar of the Gospel of Luke (16:19–31).

5. Moore defends this thesis in his remarkable study *The Formation of a Persecuting Society: Authority and Deviance in Western Europe 950–1250*, 2nd ed. (Malden, MA: Blackwell 2007), ix.

6. Jacques Le Goff, *La civilisation de l'Occident médiéval* (Grenoble: Arthaud, 1964), 388.

7. Cited in S. N. Brody, *The Disease of the Soul — Leprosy in Medieval Literature* (Ithaca, NY: Cornell University Press, 1974), 77–78.

8. I rely here on the rich analysis of F. O. Touati, "Les léproseries aux XII° et XIII° siècles, lieux de conversion?," in Bériou and Touati, *Voluntate dei leprosus* (Spoleto: Centro Italiano di Studi sull'alto Medioevo, 1991), 3–32.

9. Matthew 11:5.

10. Ambrose of Milan, quoted by G. Pichon, "Essai sur la lèpre du haut Moyen Âge," *Le Moyen Âge* 90 (1984): 351. The episode of the healing of the lepers is recounted in the Gospel of Matthew (8:1–4) and the Gospel of Luke (17:12–19). These texts can be compared with the passage in Exodus 4:5–7 on Moses's leprous hand.

11. Isaiah (53:4). On the theme of Christ *quasi-leprosus* in medieval theology, see G. Pichon, "La lèpre et le péché," *Nouvelle revue de psychanalyse*, no. 38 (1988): 147–57.

12. Gustave Flaubert, *Three Tales*, trans. A. J. Krailsheimer (Oxford: Oxford University Press, 1999), 69–70.

13. See M. G. Pegg's analysis "Le corps et l'autorité: La lèpre de Baudoin IV," *Annales ESC* (1990–92): 265–87.

14. Helgaud de Fleury (around 1033), quoted by Marc Bloch, *Les rois thaumaturges* (Paris: Gallimard, 1983), 36–37.

15. This is the interpretation proposed by J. Le Goff in "Le mal royal au Moyen Âge: Du roi malade au roi guérisseur," *Mediaevistik*, no. 1 (1988): 101–9.

16. M. Kriegel, "Un trait de psychologie sociale au bas Moyen Âge: Le Juif comme Intouchable," *Annales ESC*, no. (1976): 326–31.

17. On this accusation, see J. Assmann's important contribution, *Moïse l'Égyptien* (Paris: Aubier, 1997), 59–80.

18. Roger Caillois, *Man and the Sacred*, trans. Meyer Barash (Glencoe, IL: Free Press, 1959), 37 (translation largely modified to render the original meaning).

19. In Rome, Caillois reminds us, the word *sacer* designates "that which cannot be touched without being soiled or without defiling" (*Man and the Sacred*, 35, 48).

20. Cited in Brody, *The Disease of the Soul*, 96–97.

21. Quoted by Ginzburg in *Ecstasies: Deciphering the Witches' Sabbath* (London: Hutchinson Radius, 1990), 33 (translation modified; emphasis mine).

22. This is the appealing hypothesis proposed by D. Nirenberg in *Violence et minorités au Moyen Âge*: "in 1321, it is the people and not the king who 'heal' the kingdom by attacking the lepers. Probably because the people saw the king himself as a source of corruption rather than of healing" (72–78). Original English in *Communities of Violence: Persecution of the Minorities in the Middle-Age* [Princeton, NJ: Princeton University Press, 1998).

23. Quoted in Nirenberg, *Violence et minorités au Moyen Âge*, 117.

24. The most important study devoted to the *cagots* remains that of F. Michel, *Histoire des races maudites de la France et de l'Espagne* (1847); see also, more recently, P. Antolini, *Au-delà de la rivière — les cagots, histoire d'une exclusion* (Paris: Nathan, 1989).

25. See the texts quoted by F. Bériac, "La persécution des lépreux dans la France méridionale en 1321," *Le Moyen Âge* 93 (1987): 203–21.

26. See J. Trachtenberg, *The Devil and the Jews*, 101, 238.

27. On all this, see J. Le Goff, "Métiers licites et métiers illicites dans l'Occident médiéval," in *Pour un autre Moyen Âge* (Paris: Gallimard, 1977), 91–107, as well as *La civilisation de l'Occident médiéval*, 387–89.

28. Commentary on the book of Ezekiel (fourth century), quoted by J. L. Flandrin, *Un temps pour embrasser* (Paris: Seuil, 1983), 74.

29. See P. Rémy, "La lèpre, thème littéraire au Moyen Âge," *Le Moyen Âge* 47 (1946): 195–242.

30. On the context of this legend, see A. Boureau, "L'inceste de Judas et la naissance de l'antisémitisme," in *L'événement sans fin* (Paris: Belles-Lettres, 1993), 209–30.

31. H. Grégoire, *Essai sur la régénération physique, morale et politique des Juifs* (1788) (Paris: Éditions du Boucher, 2002), 40.

32. Letter 130 (1146), quoted in D. Nirenberg, *Anti-Judaism* (New York: Norton, 2013), 202.

33. Bodin, *De la démonomanie des sorciers* (1580; Paris: Gutenberg Reprint, 1979), 219.

34. *The Hammer of Witches*, trans. Christopher S. Mackay (Cambridge: Cambridge University Press, 2009), 368. Some Benandanti also admit to being "bloodsuckers."

35. *The Trial and Confession of Elisabeth Sawyer* (1621), in B. Levack, *The Witchcraft Sourcebook* (London: Routledge, 2004), 195.

36. Carlo Ginzburg, *The Night Battles*, trans. John Tedeschi and Anne Tedeschi (London: Routledge, 2011), 100.

37. J. P. Albert, *Le sang et le ciel* (Paris: Aubier, 1997), 102.

38. On this question, one can consult the works of F. Héritier, in particular, *Masculin / Féminin — la pensée de la différence* (Paris: Odile Jacob, 1996).

39. Quoted by Johan Huizinga, *The Autumn of the Middle Ages*, trans. Rodney J. Payton and Ulrich Mammitzsch (Chicago: University of Chicago Press, 1996), 3.

40. Césaire de Heisterbach, *Dialogue sur les miracles* (1250), quoted by G. Bechtel, *La sorcière et l'Occident*, 142. As an inquisitor wrote, "the Church has its sacraments, witches have their excrements."

41. E. Durkheim, *La prohibition de l'inceste et ses origines* (1897; Paris: Payot, 2008), 80–109.

42. See Makarius's *Le sacré et la transgression des interdits* (Paris: Payot, 1974). It is regrettable that the importance of her work has not been sufficiently recognized.

43. Laura Makarius, "Une interprétation de l'*Incwala* swazi: Étude du symbolisme dans la pensée et les rites d'un peuple africain," *Annales* 28, no. 6 (1973): 1403–22.

44. Makarius, *Le sacré et la transgression des interdits*, 147–49.

45. I take these expressions from another anthropologist who studied royal incest in Africa (see L. de Heusch, *Écrits sur la royauté sacrée* [Brussels: Éditions de l'Université de Bruxelles, 1987]).

46. Ibid., 266–68. On the relationship between royal power and witchcraft in African cultures, the aversion that female witches inspire, and the rites involving cannibalism and infanticide, see also A. Adler, *Roi sorcier, mère sorcière* (Paris: Le Félin, 2006).

47. E. Benveniste, *Vocabulaire des institutions indo-européennes*, vol. 2 (Paris: Minuit, 1969), 188–90.

48. Héritier, *Masculin / Féminin — la pensée de la différence*, 84, 125–26. On the transmission of defilement among "those-who-are-suspended-from-the-trees"; see also M. Izard, "Transgression, Transversality, Wandering," in Izard and P. Smith, *La fonction symbolique* (Paris: Gallimard 1979), 289–306.

49. Jacob Rogozinski, *The Ego and the Flesh: A History of Egoanalysis* (Redwood City, CA: Stanford University Press, 2010), 144–45, 243–44 (on the relationship between *aphanisis* and the incest fantasm).

8. A Stranger among Us

1. See his *Penser la Révolution française* (Paris: Gallimard, 1978), 78–81.

2. On this point, read the remarkable study by P. Gueniffey, *La politique de la Terreur* (Paris: Fayard, 2000).

3. See *Qu'est-ce que le Tiers Etat?* et *Essai sur les privilèges* (1788–89) (Paris: Presses Universitaires de France, 1982), 4, 90–93.

4. See Arendt's *On Revolution* (New York: Penguin, 1963).

5. See the stimulating book by Arno J. Mayer, *The Furies: Violence and Terror in the French and Russian Revolutions* (Princeton, NJ: Princeton University Press, 2000); and the rather similar analysis by Sophie Wahnich in *La liberté ou la mort* (Paris: La Fabrique, 2003).

6. As early as 1795, a certain Cadet de Gassicourt accused the Freemasons and the Jacobins of being, in fact, clandestine "Templars" seeking to take revenge on the descendants of Philip the Fair "by exterminating all the kings" (see *Le Tombeau de Jacques Molai* [sic] *ou le secret des conspirateurs*, quoted in E. Kreis, *Les puissances de l'ombre* [Paris: CNRS Éditions, 2012]), 36–38). Between 1797 and 1799, the *Mémoires pour servir à l'histoire du jacobinisme* of the abbé Barruel appeared, where the myth of the "Masonic plot" appeared.

7. *Qu'est-ce que le Tiers Etat?*, 88.

8. I borrow this formulation from M. Gauchet; see *La Révolution des droits de l'homme* (Paris: Gallimard, 1989), 19–28.

9. Some of their writings can be found in P. Kessel, *Les gauchistes de 89* (Paris: 10/18, 1969).

10. See the last part of Arendt's *On Revolution.*

11. Quoted by P. Gueniffey, *La politique de la Terreur*, 290.

12. Quoted by A. de Baecque, *Le corps de l'histoire* (Paris: Calmann-Lévy, 1993), 114–15.

13. Jules Michelet, *Histoire de la Révolution française (1847–1853)*, vol. 2 (Paris: Robert Laffont, 1979), 193. On the relationship between the doctrine of the "two bodies of the king" and the principle of the sovereign exception, see the analyses of E. Santner in *The Royal Remains* (Chicago: University of Chicago Press, 2011), chap. 2.

14. The episode was analyzed in detail by A. Farge and J. Revel in *Logiques de la foule* (Paris: Hachette, 1988). See also the similar incidents evoked in J. Nicolas, *La rébellion française* (Paris: Gallimard, 2008), 536–48.

15. The introduction of *Histoire de la Révolution française* (1847), in Claude Lefort, *La cité des vivants et des morts* (Paris: Belin, 2002), 213–14.

16. Some examples of this nauseating literature can be found in Chantal Thomas, *The Wicked Queen*, trans. Julie Rose (Princeton, NJ: Princeton University Press, 2001); and in Lynn Hunt, *Family Romance of the French Revolution* (Oakland: University of California Press 1992).

17. These engravings are reproduced by A. de Baecque in *La caricature révolutionnaire* (Paris: Presses du CNRS, 1988); and by A. Duprat in *Le roi décapité* (Paris: Cerf, 1992), and *Les rois de papier* (Paris: Belin, 2002).

18. I quote here the remarkable work of M. Walzer, *Régicide et révolution* (Paris: Payot, 1989), 154–55.

19. Speech of December 3, 1792, in Walzer, *Régicide et révolution*, 219–22.

20. Speech of November 13, 1792, in Walzer, *Régicide et révolution*, 208–10.

21. Robespierre, Speech of July 26, 1794 (emphasis mine).

22. E. Quinet, *La Révolution*, vol. 1 (Paris: Belin 2009), 479–80.

23. "Kings have a special religion; they are devout to royalty. Their person is a host, their palace is the holy of holies" (Michelet, *Histoire de la Révolution française*, vol. 1, 467).

24. Fayau's speech, quoted by J. Jaurès, *Histoire socialiste de la Révolution française (1901–1904)*, vol. 5 (Paris: Editions Sociales, 1986), 133.

25. "Mort de Louis XVI, dernier roi de France," *Les Révolutions de Paris*, no. 185 (January 1793), quoted by J. P. Roux, *Le sang: Mythes, symboles et réalités* (Paris: Fayard, 1988), 28.

26. Michelet, *Histoire de la Révolution française*, vol. 2, 235, 262.

27. Immanuel Kant, "The Doctrine of Right," in *The Metaphysics of Morals*, trans. Mary Gregor (Cambridge: Cambridge University Press, 1991), 132. I once tried to explain myself with this difficult text — see "Un crime inexpiable," *Rue Descartes*, no. 4 (1992): 99–120

28. This is Kant's position but also that of Arendt.

29. Speech of January 8, 1794, quoted in L. Jaume, *Le discours jacobin et la démocratie* (Paris: Fayard, 1989), 135.

30. Report of October 10, 1793, in *Œuvres choisies* (Paris: Gallimard, 1968).

31. Speech of February 10, 1794, quoted in L. Jaume, *Le discours jacobin et la démocratie*, 112.

32. Quoted in A. Bouland, "Le suspect parisien en l'An II," *Annales historiques de la Révolution française*, no. 280 (1990): 187–97.

33. Speech of March 26, 1794 (emphasis mine), quoted in S. Wahnich, "Anglais: Des ennemis extraordinaires," in *Dictionnaire des usages socio-politiques (1770–1815)* (Paris: Klincksieck, 1987), 56.

34. Quoted in Jean-Clément Martin, *La guerre de Vendée* (Paris: Seuil, 2014), 246.

35. See the texts cited notably by Gueniffey, *La politique de la Terreur*, 255–67; and by Martin, *La guerre de Vendée*, 227–44.

36. Letter to Hentz, quoted by J. Crétineau-Joly, *Histoire de la Vendée militaire*, vol. 2 (Paris: Librairie Gosselin, 1840), 107.

37. L. M. Turreau, *Mémoires pour servir à l'histoire de la guerre de Vendée* (1795; Paris: Éditions Pays et Terroirs, 2007), 197.

38. G. Babeuf, *La guerre de la Vendée et le système de dépopulation* (1795; Paris: Cerf, 2008), 108, 124.

39. Ibid., 128.

40. Taking into account the massacres of the Vendée, "the overall toll of the Terror would be between a minimum of 200,000 and a maximum of 300,000 deaths" (Gueniffey, *La politique de la Terreur*, 235): between three and four times more than that of the witch hunt.

41. Speech of November 18, 1793, quoted in de Baecque, *Le corps de l'histoire*, 376–80.

42. *Principes régénérateurs du système social (1795)* (Paris: Publications de la Sorbonne, 1992), 81.

43. Ibid.

44. Ibid., 116.

45. See "L'image du corps et le totalitarisme," in *L'invention démocratique* (Paris: Fayard, 1981), 172. He deepens his analysis of the French Revolution in "La Terreur révolutionnaire," in *Essais sur le politique* (Paris: Seuil, 1986), 75–109.

46. Quinet, *La Révolution*, vol. 1, 458.

Conclusion: The Truth Will Set You Free

1. Gospel of John, 8:32.

Afterword to J. Rogozinski's *The Logic of Hatred*

1. C. Ginzburg, "Anacronismi. Appunti su un equivoco," in *Ad placitum: Pour Irène Rosier-Catach*, ed. L. Cesalli, F. Goubier, A. Grondeux, A. Robert, and L. Valente, vol. 1 (Rome: Aracne, 2021), 323–27; C. Ginzburg, "Nos mots et les leurs: Une refléxion sur le métier de l'historien, aujourd'hui," *Incidence* 16 (spring 2022): 277–97.

2. See C. Ginzburg, "L'estrangement," in *À distance: Neuf essais sur le point de vue en histoire*, trans. P.-A, Fabre (Paris: Éditions Gallimard, 2001), 15–36, 187–91.

3. C. Ginzburg, *Ecstasies: Deciphering the Witches' Sabbath* (London: Hutchinson Radius 1990), 160.

4. E. Morin, *Leçons d'un siècle de vie* (Paris: Éditions Denoël, 2022), 9–28.

A Response to Carlo Ginzburg

1. I touch on this question in a recent text titled "Croire au Grand Complot" (Believing in the Great Conspiracy), *Lignes*, no. 69 (2022).

2. See *The Ego and the Flesh: An Introduction to Egoanalysis* (Stanford, CA: Stanford University Press, 2010).

3. Among the anthropologists, I am thinking of Mary Douglas and Françoise Héritier.

Jacob Rogozinski is Professor of Philosophy Emeritus at the University of Strasbourg. He is the author of *The Ego and the Flesh: An Introduction to Egoanalysis*.

Sepehr Razavi is a graduate student in philosophy at the University of Edinburgh.

Carlo Ginzburg is Professor Emeritus of History at UCLA. His books include *The Cheese and the Worms* and, most recently, *The Soul of Brutes*.

Printed in the USA
CPSIA information can be obtained
at www.ICGtesting.com
JSHW021533190224
57666JS00004B/76